Hydrology

C. O. WISLER

Professor Emeritus of
Hydraulic Engineering

University of Michigan

E. F. BRATER

Professor of Hydraulic
Engineering

University of Michigan

SECOND

EDITION

HYDROLOGY

New York · JOHN WILEY & SONS, Inc.

London · CHAPMAN & HALL, Limited

To the memory of

DR. ROBERT E. HORTON

whose untiring efforts throughout more than a quarter of a century contributed immeasurably toward the development of the science of hydrology, this book is respectfully dedicated.

Preface

After ten years of classroom experience with this book, we have discovered numerous opportunities to improve it by condensing certain parts, expanding others, and adding a considerable amount of new material.

We recognized that the first edition provided inadequate coverage of the hydrologic problems found in semiarid regions and areas where snow melt plays a vital part in establishing the stream-flow characteristics. Therefore, we added two new chapters—"Semiarid Regions" by F. G. Christian and W. J. Parsons, Jr., of the Sacramento, California office of the U. S. Army Engineers, and "Snow" by W. T. Wilson of the U. S. Weather Bureau. We wish to express our very sincere appreciation to these men for their contributions.

We have made many other changes, of which unquestionably the most important is the introduction of a new procedure for applying the unit hydrograph principle to determine the maximum flood that may be anticipated on any given stream with any stated rare frequency. We believe that in due time this method will entirely supplant the direct application of probability methods to stream-flow records, a system which has often proved to be misleading.

C. O. WISLER

E. F. BRATER

July 1, 1959
Ann Arbor, Michigan

Preface
to the First Edition

Hydrology is one of the newest of the natural sciences. As a result of intensive researches, new theories have been advanced during the past twenty years that have almost completely revolutionized our previous concepts of the subject and have accordingly changed many of our techniques. Although scores of articles in current literature have recorded these new developments, no single volume has appeared during all this time that has served to correlate them and bind them together into a cohesive unit. Therefore, nearly ten years ago, Dr. Robert E. Horton and the authors undertook this task. First as a result of World War II and then because of the untimely death of Dr. Horton, the preparation of the manuscript was delayed. Another factor contributing to its delay was the rapid accumulation of new data and new concepts that have caused the science to be in a state of flux. In fact, before the final chapter was finished some of the earlier ones had to be rewritten.

When Professor H. W. King first offered a course in hydrology at the University of Michigan in 1912 it was more or less an experiment. No textbook and but few references were then available. As a matter of fact, at that time hydrology was not generally recognized as a science. Nevertheless, the need for knowledge in this field was so apparent that the course was a success from the beginning and has been continued ever since. Because of the ever-increasing demands made upon our water resources, this subject becomes of greater and greater importance in the fields of civil engineering, forestry, agriculture, and allied sciences. Indeed, no important hydraulic structure and no utilization of our water resources can be properly planned without a thorough knowledge of this subject. Surely the time is not far distant when every college and university will include in its curriculum a course in hydrology.

Because of the evolution through which this science has passed since the earlier books on the subject were published, the authors have had practically no guideposts to follow. Perhaps not everyone will agree with the order of presentation that has been followed herein. Although it is hoped that the book will be valuable to all who are interested in hydrology, it is primarily intended to fill the need for a textbook for college and university use. It is therefore expected that many of its readers will not have had previous contact with this subject. Inasmuch as the central theme is stream flow, its fluctuations and the causes thereof, it was considered desirable first to acquaint the student with the characteristics and peculiarities of the hydrograph and with the nature and diversity of the problems connected therewith. It is believed that after he has been presented with this general preview of what is in store for him he will better appreciate the need for a knowledge of precipitation, evaporation, infiltration, and related subjects which might otherwise be of but little interest to him.

The authors are deeply indebted to Mr. John G. Ferris for his splendid cooperation in writing the chapter on ground water. They also wish to express their gratitude to W. W. Horner, S. W. Jens, Professor M. L. Albertson, Dr. C. R. Hursh, LeRoy K. Sherman, Walter T. Wilson, and Don M. Corbett for the assistance that was so generously given.

C. O. WISLER
E. F. BRATER

April 4, 1949
Ann Arbor, Mich.

Contents

1

Introduction

Water constitutes one of our most valuable natural resources. Without it no form of life is possible. It not only supplies both the animal and vegetable kingdoms with daily sustenance but also provides highways of transportation, is a source of power, and serves many other useful purposes. At times, however, through the medium of storms and floods, this normally helpful servant becomes temporarily transformed into a most destructive agent, laying waste valuable property, taking a heavy toll of life, and eroding and carrying to the sea millions of tons of rich and fertile soil.

As the population of the earth increases, the demands upon this vital resource are becoming ever more severe. Already there are areas where water is being used at a rate which is near the maximum available supply. As urban centers develop in our river valleys, the destructive effects of floods grow more and more devastating. It is, therefore, becoming increasingly important that we strive to gain a better understanding of the occurrence and behavior of the waters of the earth.

Hydrology Defined

Hydrology is the science that deals with the processes governing the depletion and replenishment of the water resources of the land areas of the earth. It is concerned with the transportation of water through the air, over the ground surface, and through the strata of the earth. It is the science that treats of the various phases of the hydrologic cycle. A knowledge of hydrology is of basic importance in practically all problems that involve the use and supply of water for any purpose whatsoever. Therefore, hydrology is of value not only in the field of engineering but also in forestry, agriculture, and other branches of natural science.

Following are some typical questions that the hydrologist is called upon to answer.

Is the flow of this stream sufficient to meet the needs of (a) a city or industry seeking a water supply, (b) an irrigation project, (c) a proposed power development, (d) navigation, (e) recreation?

Would a storage reservoir be required in connection with any of the proposed uses, and if so, what should be its capacity?

In the design of a flood-protection system, a bridge, a culvert or a spillway for a dam, what is the maximum flood that may be expected to occur with any specified frequency?

What would be the effect of draining an upland area or a swampy region upon the flow of the stream from that watershed?

How would certain changes in land use, or the removal of forests, affect the ground-water level or the stream flow from such an area?

These are only a few of the many problems that the hydrologist is called upon to solve. They have been presented here primarily as illustrations of the scope of the science of hydrology.

The Hydrologic Cycle

In one form or another, water occurs practically everywhere, varying in quantity from an almost unlimited supply in the oceans to nearly none in desert regions. It occurs in the atmosphere as water vapor, clouds, and precipitation. On the earth's surface it is found principally in streams, in lakes, and in the oceans. Beneath the ground surface it occurs under various classifications, as will be explained later.

Although at any instant by far the largest portion of the total water supply is stored in the oceans, a constant circulation is taking place. Evaporation from the ocean's surface is continuous. Although much of the moisture so evaporated condenses and falls directly on the ocean, a considerable portion is carried by the winds over the land areas where it is precipitated as rain, hail, sleet, or snow or condenses as dew or frost on the surfaces of vegetation and other objects. Nearly all the moisture in the form of dew and frost either is evaporated directly or is consumed by vegetation and then transpired through the vegetal pores. That which falls as precipitation, however, has a much more varied experience. Some is re-evaporated before it reaches the earth. Another part is intercepted by vegetation, buildings, and other objects, and part of this is re-evaporated directly. Another portion runs off from the ground surface into the streams and is returned to the sea. Still another portion percolates into the ground. For this portion there are numerous outlets: part of it is held by capillarity at or near the surface and is evaporated therefrom; another part is used by vegetation and returned to the air through the process of transpiration; still another portion joins the ground water and slowly finds its way to the streams, appearing after days, months, and sometimes much longer periods as ground-water flow; and finally, an amount that is usually insignificant but in a few drainage basins is of considerable importance,

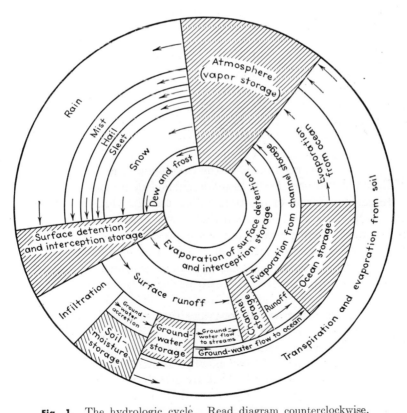

Fig. 1. The hydrologic cycle. Read diagram counterclockwise.

percolates to great depths and appears after long intervals, often at far distant points, as springs, artesian wells, and geysers.

Of the water that reaches the streams comprising the headwaters of the large drainage systems only a portion flows directly to the sea. The remainder is evaporated from the surface of streams and lakes through which the streams flow, is used and transpired by vegetation growing along their margins, or seeps into the ground along the water courses where the ground-water table is lower than the surface of the streams. This last portion may later return to the same channel at points downstream; it may through underground channels find an outlet in distant springs, other river channels, lakes, or the sea; it may be reached and utilized by deep-rooted vegetation; or, finally, it may join the more or less permanent ground waters, appearing perhaps years later as springs and geysers.

This sequence of events, which is represented graphically in Fig. 1, is called the *hydrologic cycle*. It provides the groundwork upon which the science of hydrology is constructed.

History of Hydrology

Hydrology is a relatively new branch of the natural sciences. Although in ancient ruins unmistakable evidence has been unearthed that advanced knowledge in many of the sciences was held by man thousands of years ago, it appears that no such evidence of an early knowledge of the principles of hydrology has ever been found. In fact, one need not go back many years to find a time when there was practically no literature on the subject. It is believed that greater advancement has been made in the development of this science during the present century than was made during all previous history.

As an illustration of the tremendous changes that have occurred in this science, one need but recall that it was only a few years ago when runoff was generally considered and expressed as a percentage of rainfall. We now know that runoff is that which is left from the total rainfall after evaporation, transpiration, and various other factors have taken their toll; in other words, stream flow may be better expressed as rainfall minus losses, not rainfall times a percentage factor. In a similar manner, it was not long ago that engineering literature was replete with discussions of the use of statistical and probability methods for determining maximum flood flows that could be anticipated with any given frequency. It can now be shown conclusively that such methods often produce results that are grossly misleading when applied to short-term discharge records for determining the maximum flood that may be expected to occur with a frequency of, say, once in a thousand years. Therefore these and many other of the earlier concepts have been replaced by better and sounder theories.

Two milestones mark this progress. The first, the concept of the unit hydrograph, stands as a monument to LeRoy K. Sherman. The second, the theory of infiltration capacity, is one of the many contributions of Robert E. Horton. These, along with the work of W. W. Horner, Merrill Bernard, and a great many others, have so changed our knowledge of this subject that we may refer to the present century and, in fact, even to the period since 1930 as representing the dawn of the science of hydrology. Other advances are unquestionably in the making, but sufficient progress has already been made so that the student may rest assured that this science now provides him with a most useful tool for determining the answer to almost any problem that he may encounter in this field.

Practical Value of Hydrology

To the beginning student of hydrology, the natural question that first arises is: Why are we concerned with knowing all the complicated relationships between precipitation and runoff? Inasmuch as it is easier to measure the runoff from a drainage basin than to determine the average precipitation on that basin, since the latter requires measurement at a number of places, why not measure the runoff in the first place and be done with it? Why bother about the precipitation?

The difficulty of course lies in the fact that a river is not like a tract of land which, once surveyed, forever retains these same dimensional characteristics. Instead, the quantity of water flowing in any given stream varies from day to day and from year to year. It is never absolutely constant even for a day. Frequently the magnitude of these changes is slight, but occasionally it is very large. For some streams the maximum flow is many thousand times the minimum, but for others this ratio is relatively small. Likewise for any stream the maximum flow for any one year will bear a certain ratio to the minimum flow, but for any other year that ratio will be entirely different. Furthermore, for any given stream the maximum, minimum, and average flows for any short period, for example five years, may be and often are radically different from those for any other, similar period.

Therefore, in order to determine the regimen of a stream over a long period of time, as must be done in the solution of a wide variety of engineering problems, it is necessary either to have discharge records covering such a long period or to have other data and a knowledge of the relationship between the known data and the stream flow, so that the flow may be determined with a satisfactory degree of accuracy. Rainfall and general climatic conditions affect our daily lives more directly than does stream flow. This statement is true at least for the average layman, even though it may be questioned by the engineer. As a result, records of rainfall, temperature, humidity, barometric pressure, and the like were initiated long before stream-flow records were even considered. Furthermore, rainfall and general climatic records require but little skill and training on the part of the observer, whereas reliable stream-flow records demand the services of an observer trained in this field.

Consequently, rainfall and climatic records are available for almost any drainage basin in the entire United States, oftentimes covering periods of fifty years and sometimes a hundred years or more. On the other hand, stream-flow records are comparatively few and far between. On only a few streams are there good, reliable records that are continuous for a period of fifty years or more. Many records are brief or intermittent and usually missing for the period for which they are most urgently needed. Sometimes good records are available on the main stream, whereas the problem at hand calls for a knowledge of the yield of a tributary far removed from the site of the available records, or vice versa. Often a close examination will reveal the fact that some of the existing records were obtained by methods or under circumstances that subject their accuracy and reliability to serious question.

Practically never does the engineer have the experience of finding available all the necessary stream-flow records at the proper site on the stream in question. Nearly always it is necessary either to use the records obtained at a more or less distant point or to extend the records to cover a longer period. In any case, the selection of the proper procedure is dependent upon a thorough understanding of the principles of hydrology.

Increasing Importance of Hydrology

In the early stages of the development of our country, the water resources did not possess the same importance that they now have, nor do they now play the prominent role that they seem destined to assume in the future. In the early days those resources were entirely adequate to meet all the needs that existed. They could be had merely for the asking. Water resources, seldom developed to the limit of their possibilities, were often utilized only to the extent of meeting the existing requirement. As a result, but little concern was felt regarding the need for data and knowledge of the ultimate capacities of our rivers and underground sources to meet the many demands to which they now are and in the future will be subjected.

With the advance of civilization and a steadily increasing population, rivalry and competition for the use and control of our water resources have developed and are becoming more and more intense. In the pioneer days that use was restricted to logging, fishing, navigation, and small commercial power plants where the power was used in saw mills, flour mills, and small factories. Seldom was any attempt made to utilize all the power that was available at any site. How different is the picture today! Now, nearly all water-power plants are hydroelectric and are installed right up to the limit of economic feasibility—in fact, many contain installations that are well beyond that limit. Storage reservoirs are in demand whereby the flood waters may be conserved and utilized during periods of low flow. For the benefit and protection of wildlife, however, the recreational interests insist that those reservoirs be maintained as nearly as possible at a constant level, a point which is at variance with power, flood control, and navigation interests.

An increasing number of municipalities and industries are obtaining their water supplies from rivers. Their need for a supply that is as free as possible from contamination is in direct conflict with the interests of other cities and industries, located upstream, that wish to discharge their sewage and industrial wastes into that same river. Where the rainfall during the growing season is insufficient to meet the needs of vegetation, the withdrawal of water from the streams for irrigation purposes is in conflict with almost all other needs.

A careful examination of the manner in which each different utilization of our water resources affects the availability of those same waters for other purposes reveals the fact that each different use may be in conflict with most of the others. Although it is true that occasionally two uses may be found that on the surface appear to operate in harmony, more often than not that harmony will be found to be more apparent than real. As an illustration, the storage of flood waters in reservoirs to supplement the low flows for power development, irrigation, water supply, or other purposes appears to be in perfect accord with flood prevention. Upon second thought, however, we realize that storage for any of the former purposes demands that the reservoir be kept filled as much of the time as possible so that the water will be available when needed, whereas for flood prevention the reservoir should be emptied as quickly as practicable so that its capacity for storage will be available when the next flood arrives.

Furthermore, the competition for our water resources is certain to become more and more keen in the years to come. This increase will occur not only among the various types of uses that now exist but among the new uses that will develop. For instance, the fact is now well established that farm irrigation is profitable not only in the western part of the United States, to which area this practice was long confined, but also in the Midwest and even in certain sections of the East. When this idea becomes fully realized, a new impetus will be given to the demands for water in those areas.

Likewise the field of air conditioning is only in its infancy at the present time. This practice is almost certain to undergo a tremendous growth. Inasmuch as some of the methods of air conditioning require large amounts of water, usually obtained from underground supplies, serious problems are almost certain to be created. With the advent of other unforeseen developments of similar nature and with a steadily increasing congestion of population, the competition for our water resources is certain to increase as time goes on.

In the adjustment of these conflicts and for the proper solution of the many problems arising in connection with them, complete data on our water resources and a full understanding of the principles of hydrology become a vital necessity.

Need for New Laws

To meet the new conditions and the ever-expanding demands, new laws will have to be enacted. Although literally deluged with a superfluity of legislation governing most of our daily activities, by way of strange contrast we are left almost entirely in the dark on the important question of our rights in connection with our natural water resources. At least that is the situation in most of the states. For example, in Michigan there are only a few legislative enactments relating to matters such as fish ladders in dams and the right of the public to fish in waters in which fish have been planted at public expense, a law restricting the pollution of streams, and a few others. All other matters are governed by judicial decree, and these decisions are frequently conflicting. In general, they find root in the old common law of England and are based upon priority of use, a doctrine which under present conditions is woefully inadequate. On such an important point as the extent and limitations of the right of the public and the riparian owner on any stream, one will search in vain for a clean-cut definition either by legislative act or by court decree. Those acts and decrees frequently contain references to "navigable" and "nonnavigable" waters, to "the water's edge," to "the low-water mark" and "the high-water mark," etc., but specific definitions of these terms are glaringly absent.

A few states, principally in the West, have good up-to-date laws regulating the use of our water resources, but in most states a complete new water code is urgently needed. In the preparation of that code, the hydrologist should take an important part, for only he fully understands the proper solution of the many intricate problems that are arising and will continue to arise with increasing frequency in connection with the use and control of our natural water resources.

Basic Data

The most serious obstacle that always confronts the engineer in his study of problems dealing with stream flow is invariably the lack of data. These data include the following:

1. Stream-flow records.
2. Precipitation records.
3. Topographic maps.
4. Ground-water data.
5. Evaporation and transpiration data.
6. Data on the quality of the available supply.

It may be observed that these data can be divided into two general classifications. The first class includes records of variable factors showing the variations in either quantity or quality of the supply from time to time. Stream-flow and precipitation records are of this type. The other class includes data of a more or less permanent character, such as for instance topographic maps of the drainage basin. To obtain the first kind requires a long period of time, and, other things being equal, the value of the records increases directly with the length of period covered. On the other hand, the value of the other class of data has no relation whatever to the length of time required for collection. It would be possible, for instance, to obtain the topography of an entire drainage basin in a month or even less with a sufficiently large staff, but not even an army of the most highly trained engineers could determine the regimen of a stream in so short a time.

Throughout the entire United States, the federal government maintains about 2900 stream-gaging stations. A number of other stations are maintained by private agencies, but the records obtained are not always available to the public. Large areas oftentimes covering important drainage basins can be found that are almost without any discharge records. On many others the records are so short and intermittent as to be of little value. It is conservative to say that few, if any, government expenditures are more urgently needed or yield greater dividends than money for stream-flow records.

The U. S. Weather Bureau is at present maintaining about 12,000 precipitation stations throughout the country. Some additional records are being obtained by the Forest Service, the Soil Conservation Service, and a few other agencies. Throughout the entire United States the average distance between adjacent precipitation stations is between 20 and 30 miles. Taking into consideration the large differences in rainfall that are often shown by the records of any individual storm at two stations less than 20 miles apart, it at once becomes apparent that, with the present number of precipitation stations in operation, it is impossible to determine to a satisfactory degree of accuracy the amount of precipitation that falls on any drainage basin during one of the more intense storms. For the more general storms of less intensity but covering large areas, the present records may provide a satisfactory basis for such determination, but unquestionably there are many intense storms covering relatively small areas that fall between stations and are unrecorded. This fact constitutes one of the serious obstacles in the path of those who attempt to determine the relationship between precipitation and runoff. Consequently a great many additional precipitation stations, judiciously located, are needed.

Furthermore, of the above total number of precipitation stations now being maintained by the Weather Bureau, only about 3500 have recording rain gages. For many hydrologic studies, continuous records showing the varying intensities of rainfall are essential. The number of recording stations should therefore be increased as rapidly as possible.

Topographic maps and also soil and geologic maps provide a most valuable aid in the study of problems relating to stream flow and ground-water supply. From them data may be obtained on the character of the terrain, rock outcrops, area of basin, length of stream channel, stream density, and a vast amount of other valuable information. The U. S. Geological Survey is engaged in making a topographic map of the entire United States. At present that work is only about half completed. The map is published in sections, each section being about 16½ inches by 20 inches and usually covering either 15 minutes or 30 minutes of latitude and the same amount of longitude, although either larger or smaller scales are sometimes used depending upon the importance and nature of the terrain covered. This work is carried on by the Survey in cooperation with the individual states. The progress in any state, therefore, depends upon the extent of the cooperation accorded. In about ten states, most of them in the eastern part of the country, the work is completed; in the remainder, varying degrees of progress have been made, and in many states the areas covered are so scattered that the available maps are of but little value in hydrologic studies.

Most of the data that have been collected on evaporation, transpiration, and ground water have resulted from investigations conducted by the U. S. Weather Bureau, the U. S. Geological Survey, the Bureau of Plant Industry, the Bureau of Soils, the Forest Service, the U. S. Corps of Engineers, and other government agencies. Valuable contributions have been made by various universities, scientific organizations, and private individuals. An enormous amount of further investigation and study is needed along these lines, however, before these data can be properly correlated and used in the solution of hydrologic problems.

The collection of these basic data is primarily a governmental function. No private individual or organization can be expected to finance and carry on the long, laborious, and expensive observations and experiments that are required for their collection. Especially is this true inasmuch as these data are used for the benefit of the general public. In view of the vast current government expenditures, it is unfortunate that the federal departments in charge of the important function of collecting these basic data continually find themselves seriously handicapped through lack of funds so that their work is either curtailed or completely stopped, thus greatly reducing the final value of the results.

Sources of Hydrologic Data

Many types of hydrologic data are collected and published by agencies of the federal government. Other data are collected by such organizations as the Tennessee Valley Authority, the Miami Conservancy District, and agencies of state governments. It is frequently possible to obtain valuable information from the engineering staffs of municipalities or power companies, from consulting engineering firms, and sometimes from amateur observers. More detailed information than that which is published may often be obtained from the organization that made the observations.

A complete description of information available from federal agencies is given in "Principal Federal Sources of Hydrologic Data," *Technical Paper* 10, Water Resources Committee of the National Resources Planning Board. Another useful general reference is "Inventory of Unpublished Hydrologic Data," *U. S. Geological Survey Water-Supply Paper* 837.

In the following list are given some of the more important sources of hydrologic data.

Precipitation

Climatological Data, U. S. Weather Bureau (hourly).

Hydrologic Bulletin, Daily and Hourly Precipitation, U. S. Weather Bureau and U. S. Corps of Engineers. (These bulletins may be found at regional offices located in Albany, N. Y.; Macon, Ga.; Chicago, Ill.; Cincinnati, Ohio; Kansas City, Mo.; Fort Worth, Tex.; Albuquerque, N. Mex.; Portland, Oreg.; and San Francisco, Calif.)

"Storm Rainfall of Eastern United States," *Tech. Reports*, Part V, Miami Conservancy District. (Intense storms.)

Storm Rainfall in the United States, U. S. Corps of Engineers. (Intense storms.)

"Rainfall Frequency-Intensity Data," *U. S. Department of Agriculture Misc. Pub.* 204.

Other sources of information on precipitation are the Tennessee Valley Authority, the U. S. Soil Conservation Service, and the U. S. Forest Service.

Stream Flow

U. S. Geological Survey Water-Supply Papers.

Stream-flow data are also obtained by the U. S. Corps of Engineers, the Tennessee Valley Authority, the U. S. Forest Service, and the U. S. Soil Conservation Service.

Evaporation from Water Surfaces; Temperature; Wind Velocity; Humidity

Climatological Data, U. S. Weather Bureau.

Information may also be obtained from the U. S. Bureau of Reclamation, the U. S. Soil Conservation Service, the U. S. Forest Service, and the Tennessee Valley Authority.

Ground Water

U. S. Geological Survey Water-Supply Papers.

Ground-water records are also obtained by many state agencies, the U. S. Corps of Engineers, the Tennessee Valley Authority, the U. S. Soil Conservation Service, and the U. S. Forest Service.

Opportunities for Research

Here is a field in which the opportunities for research are almost unlimited. There are so many factors that affect stream flow, precipitation, and their interrelationship, that to prepare a complete list of all the subjects that are in need of investigation would be a long and difficult task. However, the vast extent of the work that remains to be done in this field should deter no one from engaging in it. Although the main problem taken in its entirety is much too large for any one person to solve singlehanded, it naturally divides itself into a large number of smaller fields, any one of which provides abundant opportunity for research. Just as tiny raindrops slowly wear away the rock, so also will small contributions toward our general store of knowledge on these subsidiary questions eventually build up a chain of evidence that will solve the many current problems in the field of hydrology.

Hydrologic Failures

It is an unfortunate trait of human nature that all professions alike hesitate to advertise their failures. Notable successes are broadcast for all the world to hear, but failures are spoken of only in muffled tones. Professional pride and ethics are the principal reasons for this situation. It is nevertheless true that a full knowledge of the failures and their causes provides some of the most valuable information that can possibly serve to guide the engineer or other professional practitioner.

No attempt will be made here to present a list of the almost countless failures that have resulted from a faulty understanding of the principles of hydrology. The history of hydraulic structures is literally filled with examples of such failures. Beyond question a very large majority, perhaps over 90 per cent, of all failures of hydraulic structures are directly due to hydrologic reasons rather than to structural weaknesses. This may be due in part to the fact that the principles of structural design have been more completely formulated and have been better understood, but it is also due in part to the fact that a greater safety factor is used in structural work than will ever be permissible in hydrologic computations. In the former, a factor of 3 or 4 is not uncommon, whereas in the latter case the requirements of economic design do not permit such high factors of safety.

Examples of hydrologic failures include the failure of dams resulting from inadequate spillway capacity, causing overtopping and erosion of embankments; the economic failure of water-power developments, storage reservoirs, and water-supply systems resulting from an overestimate of the available supply; the failure of a sewerage or drainage system to function as planned due to the occurrence of more intense storms than were anticipated; the failure of highway and railway bridges and culverts resulting from inadequate waterway openings; and so on for every type of hydraulic structure. At this point, it should, however, be explained that structures are usually designed to accommodate the maximum flood ever expected, only if failure of the structure would result in great human suffering, loss of life, or tremendous property damage. In other cases, the problem is purely economic. The question is simply one of determining to what extent expenditures are justifiable from an economic viewpoint. In other words, it may oftentimes be true that the best-designed structure would have insufficient capacity for the very largest floods, whereas a structure having adequate capacity would be poorly designed from an economic point of view.

It is not uncommon to hear a learned judge, in rendering a decision in a case involving damages resulting from an unprecedented flood or other unusual natural phenomenon, refer to such occurrence as "an act of God." Such expressions are often misleading. It would be equally appropriate to refer in the same way to every rainfall or to every wind that blows. Every natural phenomenon springs from natural causes and occurs in exact obedience to definite natural laws. When those laws are once fully understood it will in all probability become possible to predict the occurrence of storms, floods, and all other natural phenomena far in advance and with a high degree of accuracy.

2

The Hydrograph

In order to obtain a full appreciation of the importance of such basic phases of hydrology as precipitation, evaporation, transpiration, infiltration, and soil moisture, any student of the subject should have as a prerequisite at least some knowledge of the factors that influence and determine the ever-varying rate at which water is supplied to our streams. Inasmuch as the hydrograph is the result of the runoff process and portrays the characteristics of the flow of a stream, it will be used to illustrate the subject matter of this chapter.

The hydrograph of a stream is a graphical representation of its fluctuations in flow arranged in chronological order. Discharge, usually expressed as cubic feet per second (cfs or sec ft) or as cubic feet per second per square mile (csm), is plotted vertically, and time is plotted horizontally.

Terms and Units

Although slightly different shades of meaning are sometimes given to these terms by various writers, throughout this book the terms *stream flow, runoff, discharge,* and *yield of drainage basin* are used almost synonymously. However, yield is usually considered in terms of total volume per year or as average flow for long periods of time, whereas these other terms ordinarily are applied to instantaneous rates or to average rates for shorter periods. Attention is here called to the fact that *runoff* is by no means the same as *surface runoff*. Runoff includes all the water flowing in the stream channel past any given section, whereas surface runoff includes only the water that reaches the stream channel without first percolating down to the water table. The units in which these quantities are expressed are always volume per unit of time. Many different units of volume and time are used, however. The following are the most common:

1. Cubic feet per second (cfs).
2. Cubic feet per second per square mile (csm).
3. Acre feet per day, month, or year.
4. Inches depth on drainage basin per day, month, or year.
5. Million gallons per day (mgd).

The first two of these terms are self-explanatory. An acre foot per day is the rate of flow of that stream which, if it discharges into a reservoir having an area of 1 acre, will fill it to a depth of 1 ft in 1 day. It is, therefore, a rate of 43,560 cu ft per day. Since there are 86,400 sec in a day, for most practical purposes it is sufficiently accurate to consider a cubic foot per second as being equivalent to 2 acre feet per day.

Rainfall is usually expressed as inches depth on the drainage basin. For comparison, it is convenient to express runoff in the same units. If we let T_d represent the number of days in the period during which Q is the average discharge in cubic feet per second, then $86,400T_dQ$ is the total runoff in cubic feet. Also if we let A represent the area in square miles from which Q is the runoff, then 5280^2A is the total area in square feet, and the depth in inches is

$$D_i = \frac{86,400T_dQ \times 12}{5280^2A}$$

In some branches of engineering the commonly used unit of discharge is a million gallons per day. For this conversion

$$\frac{\text{cfs} \times 7.48 \times 86,400}{1,000,000} = \text{mgd}$$

Hence,

$$1 \text{ mgd} = 1.547 \text{ cfs}$$

Sources of Runoff

The water flowing in a stream may have found its way into the stream channel from one or more of several different sources, namely:

1. Precipitation falling directly on the surface of the stream and its tributaries.
2. Surface runoff, that is, water that falls as precipitation on the

ground surface and finds its way into the stream channel without infiltrating into the soil and percolating down to the water table.

3. Ground-water flow or water that had its origin in precipitation but infiltrated into the soil, joined the ground water, and then, after days, weeks, or even much longer periods, found its way through the soil into the stream.

In the above classification, the second source should, for certain areas, be divided into (1) water that flows directly over the ground surface and (2) water that infiltrates and then percolates, usually through a thin layer of loosely textured surface soil, until it encounters a relatively impervious substratum, after which a part of it may continue its downward journey, whereas the remainder moves laterally toward the stream channel and never penetrates to the water table. This latter quantity will be called *subsurface storm flow*. It behaves more nearly like surface runoff than like ground-water flow because it reaches the stream so quickly that it is usually difficult to distinguish it from true surface runoff. On the other hand, ground-water flow is oftentimes long delayed before it reaches the stream. For this reason, subsurface storm flow will, throughout this book, be treated as though it were a part of surface runoff.

For streams draining most basins except those having a large percentage of lake area such as the St. Lawrence, the first of these sources, direct precipitation, provides a relatively small portion of the total flow. Even in such exceptional areas as above noted, the evaporation from those water surfaces may nearly or more than balance the precipitation on them. This factor will therefore be ignored in the present discussion.

Except for some glacier-fed streams or streams with a large amount of lake storage, surface runoff from drainage basins whose area does not exceed a few thousand square miles is intermittent, occurring only during or immediately following periods of precipitation or of the melting of accumulated snow and ice. It provides the vast bulk of the water that produces floods. Drainage basins that are so pervious as to permit little or no surface runoff are seldom if ever subject to disastrous floods.

The Runoff Process

When rain starts falling on a more or less pervious area, there is an initial period during which (1) the rainfall is intercepted by buildings, trees, shrubs, grasses, or other objects and thus prevented from reaching the ground; (2) it infiltrates into the ground; or (3) it finds its way to innumerable small and large depressions, filling them to their overflow level. The first of these quantities, I,[1] is termed *rainfall interception*. Although not usually of major importance, it is oftentimes the means of disposal of the greater portion of the lighter rains. The second quantity is called *infiltration, F*. The maximum rate at which a soil, when in a given condition, can absorb water is its *infiltration capacity, f*. The last quantity is termed *depression storage, S_d*. All this storage is either evaporated or used by vegetation, or it infiltrates into the soil—none of it appears as surface runoff. The difference between the *total rainfall, P*, and that which is intercepted is called *ground rainfall, P_g*.

If, after the depression storage is filled, the rain intensity exceeds the infiltration capacity of the soil, the difference is called *rainfall excess, p_e*, or *supply*. Hence $p_e = p - f$. This excess first accumulates on the ground as *surface detention, D*, and then flows overland toward the stream channels. This movement is called *overland flow*, and the water that thus reaches the stream channels is *surface runoff*. Surface runoff can occur only as a result of storms having a rainfall excess. All water contained at any instant within the permanent stream channels is called *channel storage, S_c*. Surface runoff is said to be occurring at the basin outlet throughout the entire period of passage of water that reached the stream channels through overland flow.

The rain that falls in the beginning of a storm before the depression storage is completely filled is called the *initial rain*, and that falling near the end at a rate less than infiltration capacity is called *residual rain*. The intervening period is the *net supply interval*. Infiltration occurring after the end of the net supply interval is called *residual infiltration*. It consists of residual rainfall plus that portion of the surface detention which is on the ground at the end of the net supply interval but later infiltrates. The total rainfall excess is equal to the total surface runoff plus the difference between the residual infiltration and the residual rainfall. However, because the latter quantity is usually small, the rainfall excess is often considered to be equal to the surface runoff.

Soil Moisture and Ground Water

Beneath the surface of most drainage basins whose overburden extends to any considerable depth is a *water table* below which the

---

[1] Throughout this discussion capital letters, with or without subscripts, are used to designate quantities, whereas lower-case letters symbolize rates. Both quantities and rates are usually expressed in terms of inches depth on the basin.

voids are completely filled with water. Only the water that is below the water table is called *ground water;* that which is above is called *soil moisture.* The region above the water table is divided into three zones: (1) capillary zone, (2) intermediate zone, and (3) soil zone. Extending above the water table a distance usually ranging from about 1 ft to 8 or 10 ft, depending principally upon texture, is a zone called the *capillary fringe* throughout which the moisture content is maintained practically constant by capillarity. Extending down from the ground surface is the *soil zone*, which is defined as being the depth of overburden that is penetrated by the roots of vegetation. Throughout this zone the moisture content varies tremendously, ranging from a partly saturated state during and immediately following periods of protracted rainfall to a minimum content after a long-continued drought.

The region between the capillary fringe and the soil zone is called the *intermediate zone.* Throughout this zone, except during the period of ground-water accretion from rainfall, the amount of water contained within any given space is nearly constant year in and year out. In some places the capillary fringe extends up into the soil zone, and where this occurs there is, of course, no intermediate zone.

Soon after a rain when all the gravity water has drained down to the water table, a certain amount of water is retained on the surfaces of the soil grains by molecular attraction. This is called *pellicular water.* The maximum depth of this water (if it were spread over the basin) that any soil can retain indefinitely against the action of gravity is called its *field capacity.* That portion of the pellicular water that is easily abstracted by the root action of vegetation is called *available moisture;* the remainder is *unavailable moisture* and by some writers has been termed *hygroscopic* water. The depth of water required to bring the soil moisture content up to field capacity is called the *field moisture deficiency.* During a rain any existing deficiency occurring at a given point must first be supplied before there can be any ground-water accretion. However, because of the varying amounts of soil moisture deficiency and the varying rates of replenishment at different points in a drainage basin, it is not at all uncommon for ground-water accretion to be occurring throughout certain portions of the basin although soil moisture deficiencies still exist in the remainder.

The water table normally slopes more or less gently toward its outlet which may be a stream, a lake, or the sea. The movement of ground water is usually extremely slow. Its velocity depends principally upon the gradient of the water table and the texture of the soil. Since that gradient is affected but little by ground-water accretion, the velocity itself varies only to a minor extent, and, as a result, the fluctuations in the ground-water contributions to stream flow are usually slow. Hence streams which drain pervious areas and which are dependent largely upon ground water for their supply are relatively steady in their yield. The Manistee River near Grayling, Michigan (see Fig. 5), is a good example of a stream of this type.

Ground-Water Depletion Curves

When there is no surface runoff from rainfall or melting snow, the stream flow is derived entirely from ground water. This results in a steady lowering of the water table and a constantly diminishing stream flow until a rain occurs of sufficient magnitude to produce either surface runoff or ground-water accretion. If the ground-water level were at its maximum height at the end of a period of surface runoff and no further precipitation should occur until stream flow ceased entirely, the resulting hydrograph during this period would represent a *ground-water depletion curve*. In a region of moderate or high precipitation, rarely if ever is there a rainless period of sufficient duration to permit the continuous development of a complete depletion curve. However, such a curve can usually be constructed from a number of segments of hydrographs each connecting successive periods of surface runoff. In Fig. 2 is shown a depletion curve for Iowa River at Iowa City as derived by Horton.[2]

The hydrograph of the Lualaba River (Fig. 3) in the Belgian Congo presents a striking example of a ground-water depletion curve. This is a tropical stream with extensive ground-water storage, almost no surface storage, and marked seasonal rainfall with light or no rainfall in the months of May to September inclusive. During this period there is a uniform depletion or recession curve, representing outflow from ground-water storage, whereas during the remainder of the year the rainfall is relatively heavy and surface runoff predominates. In Fig. 4 are shown depletion curves of Lualaba River for the years 1921 to 1926 inclusive. These are plotted so as to coincide when the flow is 3500 cfs. It will be noted that from then on until the fall rains set in several months later, the curves are remarkably similar.

The shape of the ground-water depletion curve is influenced by the rate of transpiration, soil evaporation and evaporation from the contributing water areas. Diurnal variations may be observed during

[2] Robert E. Horton, *Surface Runoff Phenomena,* Edwards Brothers, Inc., Ann Arbor, Michigan, 1935, p. 43.

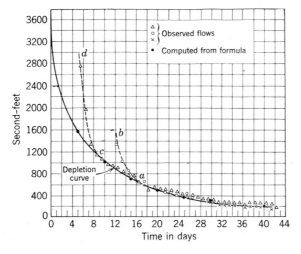

Fig. 2.

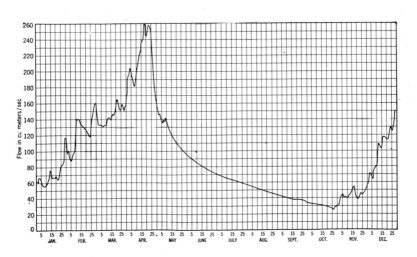

Fig. 3.

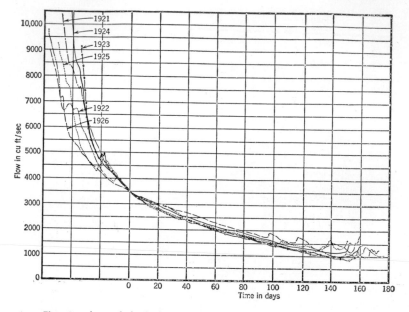

Fig. 4. Annual depletion curves for Lualaba River at N'Zilo.

warm summer days as illustrated by Fig. 83. It has also been observed that at the end of the growing season, after a killing frost, the ground-water depletion curve will continue for some time at a constant rate due to the cessation of the transpiration draft. In some instances the hydrograph may even rise slightly, under such conditions.

Variability of Stream Flow

In Fig. 5 are shown hydrographs of two streams draining basins of nearly the same size, both in central Michigan, less than a hundred miles apart, and for the same two consecutive years. Graphs A_1 and A_2 are for the Salt River near North Bradley which has a drainage area of 138 square miles. Graphs B_1 and B_2 are for the Manistee River near Grayling with a drainage basin of 159 square miles.

In Table 1 are listed some of the characteristics of flow that are illustrated by these four hydrographs for two years, chosen at random.

This example clearly illustrates the tremendous differences that often exist between the various characteristics of two streams draining areas of nearly the same size and located only a short distance apart; it also shows the great variations in flow that may occur from day to day and from year to year on the same stream. For instance, the

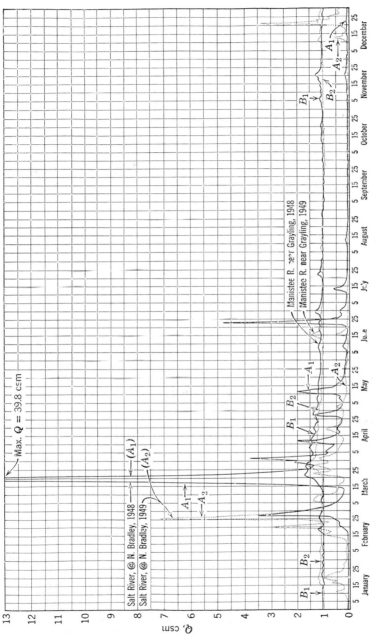

Fig. 5.

TABLE 1

	Salt River		Manistee River	
	1948	1949	1948	1949
Max. 24-hr average, CSM	39.8	7.3	1.77	1.63
Min. 24-hr average, CSM	0.033	0.025	0.94	0.94
Mean for the year, CSM	0.605	0.312	1.12	1.08
Ratio, max. to min.	1206.	292.	1.88	1.73
Ratio, max. ('48) to max. ('49)	5.50		1.09	
Ratio, min. ('48) to min. ('49)	1.32		1.00	
Ratio, mean ('48) to mean ('49)	1.94		1.04	

maximum flow of the Salt River in 1948 was over 1200 times as great as the minimum, whereas, for the Manistee River this ratio was less than two. Also, the variation in the several characteristics for these two consecutive years ranged from 32 per cent to 450 per cent for the Salt River, whereas the corresponding variations for the Manistee River were only zero to 9 per cent.

Countless other examples could be cited that would show the great differences in the flow characteristics of different streams and in the flow of any stream from time to time, some of which would be even more striking than those above. Furthermore the regimen of a stream varies greatly from point to point along its length, depending on the inflow from the intervening area, so that records of flow obtained at one point may have but little value in determining the regimen at some other point.

Because of the variability of stream flow, a minimum of about twenty years of discharge records may be considered necessary to determine the general nature of the regimen of a stream at any point. Seldom are sufficient records available where needed. More commonly, stream flow must be estimated by relying upon a short period of records and a knowledge of the fundamental laws of hydrology. Even with 20 years of records available on a particular stream, unusually large discharges or very low flows can only be predicted by making use of the fundamental principles of hydrology. Despite the erratic behavior of the hydrographs shown in Fig. 5, every rise and recession shown thereon occurred in strict conformity with those principles. Many of the characteristics of these hydrographs could have been predicted with only a knowledge of the physical nature of their drainage basins. For instance, the flashy discharge of the Salt River, with its high spring floods and its low late summer flows in marked contrast to the unusually steady and high normal flow of the Manistee River could definitely have been known in advance.

Classification of Streams

All streams may be divided into three general classes, each having a characteristic type of runoff depending upon the physical character-istics and climatic conditions of the drainage basin, namely: (1) ephemeral, (2) intermittent, (3) perennial.

Ephemeral streams carry only surface runoff and hence flow only during and immediately after periods of precipitation or the melting of accumulated snow. They have no permanent or well-defined channels but follow slight depressions in the natural contour of the ground surface. The drainage basin is either impervious or the ground-water table is always below the bed of the ephemeral stream throughout its entire length; otherwise at times the flow would be sustained by ground water.

Intermittent streams, in general, flow during wet seasons and are dry during dry seasons. The ground-water table lies above the bed of the stream during the wet season but drops below the bed during dry seasons. Hence the flow is derived principally from surface runoff but during wet seasons receives a contribution from ground water. However, in the arid southwestern part of the United States there are many drainage basins, some having large areas, in which the stream channels are always above the water table and therefore carry only surface runoff. At times these basins are subjected to brief but intense rainfalls. Following such storms, gulches that are normally dry may carry raging torrents for brief periods, only to return to their dry state a few hours later. Another type of intermittent stream is sometimes found in northern latitudes where in the winter the flow is interrupted by the freezing of the ground water to some depth below the stream bed. This phenomenon usually occurs only in the smaller streams.

Perennial streams flow at all times. In such streams, even during the most severe droughts, the ground-water table never drops below the bed of the stream and therefore maintains a continuous supply.

It should be understood that the above classification applies only to a section or reach of a stream and ordinarily not to the entire drainage system. Perhaps only streams that have springs as their origin, or are fed by melting glaciers, are perennial throughout their entire length, and few if any of importance are intermittent in their lower reaches.

Stream Rises and Floods

Surface runoff invariably produces a stream rise but does not necessarily cause a flood, the difference being in magnitude only. It is
impossible to differentiate rigidly between these two phenomena or to
say that one particular stream rise is a flood and that another nearly
as great is not a flood. A flood is commonly defined as being an
unusually or abnormally high stage of the river. It is sometimes
further described as being a stage so high as to overflow the banks and
inundate the adjacent lands. Although it is true that the latter
condition usually accompanies floods, it is not an essential characteristic, for, if it were, streams flowing through deep ravines, gorges,
or canyons would never be subject to floods. However, streams are
commonly recognized as being in flood when their stage is unusually
high. Increases in flow of a lesser magnitude, such as normally occur
many times each year, are called stream rises.

Classification of Stream Rises

The effect that a storm has upon the subsequent stream flow depends
both upon the nature of the storm and upon the physical characteristics
of the drainage basin. The following classification of stream rises,
summarized in Fig. 6, is patterned after one originally presented by
Horton.[3]

Type 0 is so designated because nothing happens as far as the stream is
concerned. For this type the rain intensity is less than the infiltration
capacity. There is, therefore, no surface runoff. The total infiltration is less
than the field moisture deficiency and there is therefore no accretion to ground
water. The normal depletion curve continues its downward course uninter-
rupted. There is therefore no rise in the stream. These phenomena are
characteristic of light rains occurring during generally dry weather, particularly after long droughts when the soil has the maximum infiltration capacity
and large field moisture deficiency. Type 0 is, however, something more than
a gesture since soil moisture accretion takes place. Soil moisture accretion
effects are cumulative and the occurrence of conditions of Type 0 may hasten
the time when a real rise in the stream will occur. It should be noted that it
is impossible to have a pure Type 0 rain because of the rain which falls
directly on the surface of the stream. In some cases this may be sufficient in
magnitude to make a noticeable rise in the hydrograph.

Type 1. Again the rain intensity is less than the infiltration capacity and
no surface runoff occurs. The total infiltration (F) is greater than the field
moisture deficiency (FMD) and some ground-water accretion takes place,
accompanied either by an increase in ground-water flow or a slowing down of
the ground-water depletion rate. Included in this type of stream rise is the
precipitation falling directly on the stream. On some drainage basins there

[3] *Ibid.*, pp. 46 and 47.

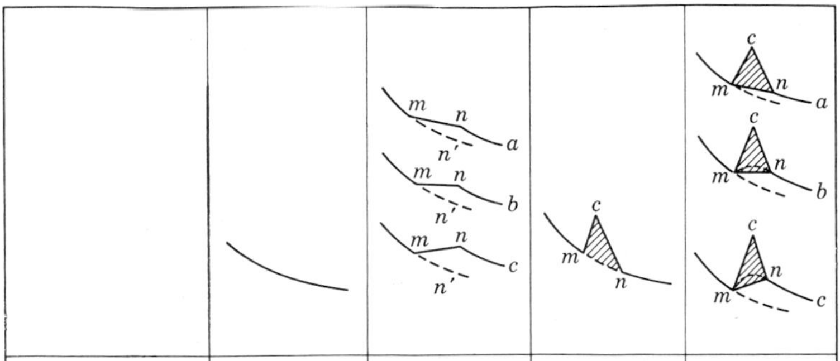

Type	0	1	2	3
Rain intensity (p)	$<f$	$<f$	$>f$	$>f$
Field-moisture deficiency (FMD)	$>P$	$<P$	$>F$	$<F$
Surface runoff (Q_s)	None	None	$Q_s = P_e$	$Q_s = P_e$
Ground-water accretion	None	$P-\text{FMD}$	None	$F-\text{FMD}$
Flow increase	None	Ground-water flow only	Surface runoff only	Surface and ground-water runoff

Fig. 6. Classification of stream rises. (Surface runoff is cross-sectioned.) After Horton.

may also be some subsurface storm flow (see page 17) included in the hydrograph. Type 1 rises may be so small that they appear to be observational errors. They are typical effects of light rain in the spring and of somewhat heavier rain of low intensity in the summer and fall.

Three different cases occur under Type 1. In each case accretion to the water table takes place during the interval denoted by mn. Normal ground-water depletion interrupted at m is resumed at n, while n' shows the corresponding stage had there been no ground-water accretion. In case (a) the rate of accretion is less than the rate of normal ground-water depletion. The depletion therefore continues but at a reduced rate. In case (b) the accretion and depletion rates are equal and the ground-water flow rate remains constant for a time. In case (c) the rate of ground-water accretion exceeds the rate of normal depletion and there is a rise of the water table and an increase in the ground-water outflow rate.

Type 2. Here the rain intensity exceeds the infiltration capacity and surface runoff occurs, but the total infiltration is less than the initial field moisture deficiency, and there is no accretion to the ground-water and hence no change in ground-water flow. The normal depletion continues during the rise, and the ground-water regimen is resumed at n. The stream falls after the rise to a lower stage than pertained when the rise began. This is a growing season or midsummer type and commonly occurs when the field

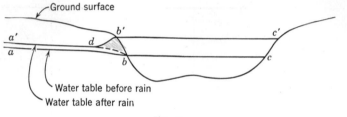

Fig. 7.

moisture deficiency is large enough so that the field moisture capacity is not fully restored by infiltration. Such rises are typical of the effect of short, intense showers of the thunderstorm type.

Type 3. Again the rain intensity exceeds the infiltration capacity and surface runoff (Q_s) occurs. In this type of rise, the total infiltration exceeds the field moisture deficiency and accretion to the water table takes place. The point n at which the rise ends is the point at which the recession side cn of the discharge graph coincides with the normal depletion curve.

There are three cases under Type 3 identical with those for Type 1 rises, each dependent on the rate of ground-water accretion. Normal depletion flow is resumed at the end of a rise of Type 3 at a higher stage than for a rise of Type 2, other things equal, but the stage at the end of the rise may or may not be higher than the initial stage. In cases (*a*) or (*b*), Type 3, the stage at which the normal depletion flow is resumed will not be higher than the initial stage; in case (*c*) it will be higher. Whether a given rise is of Type 2 or Type 3 can be determined by extending the normal depletion curve underneath the rise. If the recession side of the graph returns to this curve as extended, the rise is of Type 2. If the normal depletion curve at the end of the rise is at a higher level than the extended curve under the graph, the rise is of Type 3.

Having a hydrograph of a rise plotted on a suitable scale, together with the rain graph which produced it, it is possible by inspection to determine with considerable certainty to which of the above-described classes the rise belongs.

Hydrograph Analysis

The analysis of a hydrograph involves a separation of the various component contributions to stream flow with respect to their sources, which combined produce the total flow at the outlet of the drainage basin. As explained in the preceding paragraphs these sources consist of (1) precipitation received directly on the surfaces of the contributing waters, (2) surface runoff, (3) subsurface flow, and (4) strictly ground-water flow or, in other words, water draining into the stream from beneath the water table.

At this point let us consider the subsurface conditions during a period of rainfall and the subsequent stream rise. In Fig. 7 is shown a vertical cross section of a stream channel and the adjacent banks, together with a profile of the water table, *ab*, as it existed at the end

of a rainless period. Later, after a period of rainfall of sufficient duration and intensity to permit the infiltration to replenish the field
moisture deficiency and provide ground-water accretion and after a
period of surface runoff, this water table becomes $a'db'$. Had the
water surface in the stream remained at bc, the water table would
have become $a'db$. Except for the smallest stream rises, the rise in
the stage of the river occurs more quickly and is much greater in
magnitude than the corresponding rise of the water table. This is
evident when one considers the fact that, although an inch of infiltration can raise the water table only a few inches, an inch of surface
runoff can easily produce a stream rise of several feet. Consequently
as quickly as the water surface in the stream rises higher than the
adjacent water table, thus creating at any given elevation a greater
hydrostatic pressure in the stream than in the banks, ground-water
inflow into the stream channel ceases temporarily and the direction
of flow reverses, creating bank storage represented in Fig. 7 by $db'b$.
The volume of this bank storage continues to increase as long as the
water level in the stream is higher than the water table at d or until
after the stream has passed its peak stage. As soon as the stage starts
to fall, the direction of flow again reverses, and for a time, because of
the accumulated bank storage, the ground-water contribution to the
stream is considerably increased. As soon as the bank storage is
drained out, the ground-water flow again follows the normal depletion
curve.

The manner in which the ground-water contribution to the stream
fluctuates during this rise is, therefore, represented by the ordinates
to the dashed line adc, Fig. 8. The portion falling below the horizontal
axis represents outflow from the stream or bank storage. Inasmuch
as it is impractical to determine the actual amount of ground-water
flow occurring at any time during a stream rise and because it ordinarily represents but a small portion of the total runoff, the most

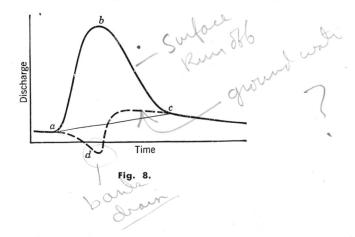

Fig. 8.

common method of separating ground-water flow from surface runoff is by drawing a straight line, such as ac, Fig. 8. The exact location of c usually cannot be determined, but this is not of great importance as long as one always follows a consistent procedure. It may, however, be taken as the point of greatest curvature near the lower end of the recession side of the hydrograph.[4] This point can usually be determined with the greatest assurance for a hydrograph of a single sharp stream rise resulting from a relatively short but intense rain. The location of c on such a graph may then be used as a guide for selecting a similar point on a more complex graph, by making the duration of surface runoff following the end of rainfall excess the same in all cases.

In cases where sufficient records are available, the ground-water depletion curve may be utilized as an aid in determining the point where surface runoff ends. This is done by plotting the ground-water depletion curve on transparent paper, using the same scale as that of the hydrograph being analyzed. This sheet is then placed over the hydrograph and shifted horizontally until the depletion curve coincides with the portion of the hydrograph which followed the end of surface runoff. The surface runoff portion of the hydrograph will then lie above the ground-water depletion curve and point c is the point where the curves join.

Another method which may assist in selecting a consistent location of c is to use as an index the ratio of discharge at any time to the discharge a short time, such as an hour, earlier. For many streams the value of this ratio will increase steadily along the recession side of the hydrograph until channel storage derived from surface runoff is depleted and will then become more nearly constant for the ground-water depletion curve.

    [4] C. R. Hursh and E. F. Brater, "Separating Storm-Hydrographs from Small Drainage-Areas into Surface—and Subsurface—Flow," *Trans. Am. Geophys. Union*, 1941, Part III, p. 863.

3

Factors Affecting Runoff

It is the purpose of this chapter to provide a general discussion of the effects of the various factors which determine the nature of the discharge of a river. However, some of these factors are of such importance that they are treated in much greater detail in subsequent chapters, and are introduced here only to make the picture complete.

The flow of any stream is determined by two entirely different sets of factors, the one depending upon the climate with special reference to the precipitation, and the other upon the physical characteristics of the drainage basin. The influence of the first group depends upon:

1. Type of precipitation.
2. Rainfall intensity.
3. Duration of rainfall.
4. Distribution of rainfall on basin.
5. Direction of storm movement.
6. Antecedent precipitation and soil moisture.
7. Other climatic conditions which affect evaporation and transpiration.

The effect of the second group is determined by the following characteristics of the drainage basin:

1. Land use.
2. Type of soil.

3. Area.
4. Shape.
5. Elevation.
6. Slope.
7. Orientation.
8. Type of drainage net.
9. Extent of indirect drainage.
10. Artificial drainage.

Anyone seeking a simple and convenient equation for determining the maximum flood flow, the minimum flow, or the average flow of a stream will see the difficulty of such a procedure when he realizes that any such equation has to be expressed in terms of all the above variables, and that almost any of the factors may affect the result by a hundred per cent or more. Furthermore, if the flow is expressed in terms of only one variable, the result may easily be in error by over a thousand per cent. From this it follows that a trustworthy appraisal of any of the several characteristics of stream flow must be based upon a careful consideration of the influence of all the foregoing factors and cannot possibly be determined by the use of a simple equation involving only one, or at best, two or three of those variables. Consideration will now be given to the manner in which these factors affect the runoff from any given drainage basin.

CLIMATIC FACTORS

Type of Precipitation

In considering the influence of precipitation upon the hydrograph, the type of precipitation is of great importance. For instance, if precipitation falls in the summer in the form of rain, its influence is felt almost immediately provided only that its intensity and magnitude are great enough to affect runoff. On the other hand, if the precipitation during a given period is entirely in the form of snow with no thawing temperatures, the hydrograph will, at the time, be unaffected except for the slight influence of the snowfall that is received directly on the surface of the stream.

In northern latitudes and in mountainous areas the effect that snowfall exerts upon stream flow is of such importance that it will be treated at some length in a later chapter.

Rain Intensity

The effect of rain intensity upon the resulting hydrograph has already been shown under the classification of stream rises (pages 26–28).

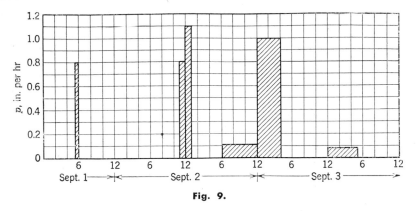

Fig. 9.

When the intensity is great enough to exceed the infiltration capacity, f, and produces surface runoff, the height of the stream rise increases rapidly with any further increase in the intensity. For instance, if the storm has been in progress long enough to permit the infiltration rate to become practically constant and, let us say, equal to 0.2 in. per hr, then if the rainfall rate, p, is 0.3 in. per hr, rainfall excess, p_e, will accumulate at the rate 0.1 in. per hr, whereas if p is 1.0 in. per hr, p_e will accumulate eight times as fast, or at a rate of 0.8 in. per hr. It follows therefore that, after infiltration capacity is exceeded, surface runoff will increase rapidly with an increase in rainfall intensity. However, the increase in stream flow is not at the same rate as the increase in rainfall excess because of the lag effect resulting from storage.

Figure 9 is a rain intensity diagram of a storm that occurred in the Thunder Bay River basin near Alpena, Michigan, September 1–3, 1937. If f_a is assumed to have been constant and equal to 0.2 in. per hr, the surface runoff would have been 5.0 in., which on that river would have produced a major flood. However, if the same total rainfall, 7.45 in., had fallen in the same time interval but at a uniform rate, there would have been no surface runoff and no flood would have occurred.

Duration of Rainfall

The effect of duration of rainfall will be more fully discussed in Chapter 8, where it will be shown that for each drainage basin there is a critical period such that, for all storms of that duration or less, regardless of intensity, the period of surface runoff will be practically the same, and that for rains of longer duration the period of surface runoff is increased.

Another effect of duration of rainfall is that the infiltration capacity decreases during a rain. As a consequence, rains of long duration may produce considerable surface runoff, even though the intensity is relatively mild. If rains continue over an extended period, the water table may reach the surface of the ground in low-lying areas, thus reducing the infiltration capacity to zero over such portions of the drainage basin and creating a serious flood hazard.

Distribution of Rainfall on Basin

In the foregoing discussion it has been tacitly assumed that the various rainfalls considered were uniformly distributed over the drainage basin with respect both to area and to time of occurrence. If the topography, soil, and other conditions are also uniform throughout the basin, then, for all storms in which the total volume of rainfall is the same, the minimum peak runoff will be produced by that rain that is uniformly distributed.

For drainage basins of appreciable size, large flood-producing storms are very seldom uniformly distributed. For small drainage basins high peak flows are the result of intense thunderstorms that cover only small areas. For large basins the highest peak flows are usually produced by general storms of less intensity but covering much larger areas. In neither case are they uniformly distributed.

Consider for instance the two storms shown in Fig. 10. The total average depth of rain on the basin during these two storms was nearly the same. The storm intensity patterns figured as inches depth per hour on the entire basin might be very similar. Yet the hydrographs of surface runoff resulting from these two storms would be radically different. In fact, little or no surface runoff might result from the storm shown in Fig. 10a, whereas a severe flood might have resulted from the storm shown in Fig. 10b. The reason for this difference is that in the first storm the rain was fairly uniformly distributed over the basin and perhaps nowhere did the intensity at any time exceed the infiltration capacity. In the second storm, the infiltration capacity was in all probability greatly exceeded, resulting in heavy surface runoff.

Because the runoff resulting from any rain depends to a considerable extent upon rainfall distribution, it is desirable to have a means of measuring this factor. This measurement is provided by the distribution coefficient, which for any storm is obtained by dividing the maximum rainfall at any point by the mean on the basin. Hence for any given total rainfall, all other conditions being the same, the greater the distribution coefficient the greater will be the peak runoff.

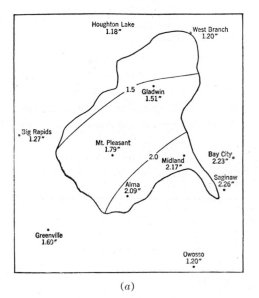

(a)

(b)

Fig. 10.

If, however, the storm centered in the lower part of the basin near the outlet, as in Fig. 10b, a higher peak runoff would result than from a storm having the same distribution coefficient but which centered in the headwaters.

Direction of Storm Movement

Rarely if ever does a rain begin or end simultaneously over an entire drainage basin, for usually the center of disturbance is in motion. The direction in which the storm travels across the basin with respect to the direction of flow of the drainage system has a decided influence upon the resulting peak flow and also upon the duration of surface runoff.

Consider for a moment the Skunk River basin above Augusta, Iowa (Fig. 11). A storm striking this basin from the west and traveling

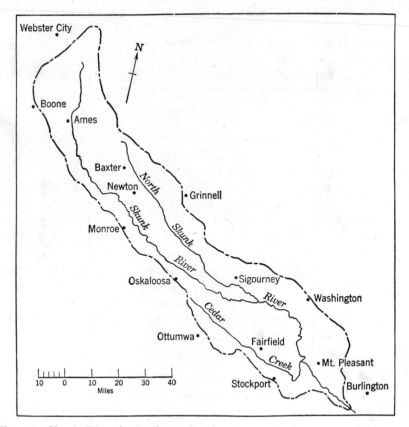

Fig. 11. Skunk River basin above Augusta, Iowa. Drainage area 4290 square miles. From *U. S. Geological Survey Water-Supply Paper* 772.

with a velocity of 20 miles per hour in the direction of flow would reach Augusta about 8 or 9 hr later. Surface runoff from the upper part of the basin would have reached the stream channels and would have flowed toward the outlet during that time interval before any surface runoff from the lower part of the basin reached the stream. When this water from the upper portion of the basin reached Augusta, a congestion would occur producing a higher peak and a shorter period of surface runoff than would otherwise occur. On the other hand, a storm from the southeast, striking Augusta first and traveling upstream, would have the opposite effect. In this case, surface runoff from the lower part of the basin would have been flowing past the gaging station at Augusta for 8 or 9 hr before any surface runoff from the upper portion of the basin reached the stream channel. This situation would result in a lower peak flow and a period of surface runoff longer by 16 or 18 hr than for a storm from the opposite direction.

A storm from the northeast or southwest that would cross this basin transversely would produce a stream rise whose height and period covered would be somewhere between the values resulting from the two cases described above.

Antecedent Precipitation and Soil Moisture

The amount of soil moisture in the surface layers of the soil has an important effect on the infiltration capacity (see page 105) and also on the determination of whether or not there will be ground-water accretion. When the soil moisture content is high, the infiltration capacity is low, and the drainage basin is susceptible to floods. Also, when the soil moisture content is raised to field capacity (see page 26), infiltrated water will reach the water table and increase the ground-water discharge. In the late summer or early fall evapotranspiration losses often reduce the soil moisture content to a small value. Even intense rains falling under such conditions rarely produce substantial stream rises, because most of the water enters the soil and is held there as soil moisture. However, a rain following shortly after a previous rain of considerable magnitude may produce a stream rise or even a disastrous flood.

Other Climatic Conditions

Inasmuch as precipitation is the source of all runoff, it is quite naturally the most important of all the climatic factors which affect and determine the magnitude of that runoff. It is not, however, the only one to be considered. Such factors as the temperature, annual precipitation, wind velocity, relative humidity, and average barometric pressure determine the climate of an area and also affect the runoff. Their influences, however, instead of being direct, combine to determine how much of the precipitation that falls on the basin shall be used and transpired by vegetation and how much shall be evaporated, the residual only being available for stream flow.

The effects exerted by these other factors will therefore be considered at some length in a later chapter dealing with water losses, which represent the difference between the amount of water that falls on a basin as rain and that which later appears in the stream as runoff.

PHYSIOGRAPHIC FACTORS

Land Use

Of all the many physiographic factors that affect the runoff of any area, one of the most important is land use, or land management. Suppose we consider for a moment an area of virgin forest, under which such a thick layer of mulch of leaves, twigs, and grass has accumulated, that even during the heaviest downpours no surface runoff would reach the streams, and no floods would result. Now suppose that this forest is removed, the land is cultivated, and all the mulch that previously protected the ground surface is gone. The ground becomes compacted, and, as a result, rains that previously soaked into the ground now run quickly over the surface to the stream channels and produce floods of magnitudes never before experienced.

It is thus apparent that the hydrograph of a stream is tremendously affected by the manner in which the area within the basin is utilized. So important is this factor that it will be treated in more detail in the chapter on infiltration.

Type of Soil

In any drainage basin the runoff characteristics are greatly influenced by the predominant type of soil because of the varying infiltration capacities of different soils, which in turn is the result of the size of the soil grains, their aggregation, shape, and the arrangement of the soil particles. Soils containing colloidal material shrink and swell with changes in moisture content, thus affecting the infiltration capacity.

Porosity, which is defined as the percentage of voids in any given volume of aggregate, affects both infiltration and storage capacity and varies greatly for different soils. Some rocks have a porosity of less than 1 per cent, whereas soils composed mainly of organic matter may run as high as 80 or 90 per cent. Porosity does not depend upon size of soil particles, but rather upon arrangement, sorting, shape, and degree of compaction. This subject will be considered more fully in the chapter on infiltration. (See pages 105 and 106.)

Area of Basin

Every drainage basin is surrounded by a *divide,* so called because it is a line of separation that divides the precipitation that falls on two adjoining basins and directs the ensuing runoff into one or the other river system.

It has already been shown that the total volume of water carried in the stream channels is made up of surface runoff and ground-water flow. Seldom are these two quantities drawn from the identically same areas. In other words, surrounding every drainage basin is a surface or *topographic* divide that demarks the area from which the surface runoff is derived. Determined usually by the geological structure, although sometimes influenced by the topography, there is an underground or *phreatic* divide that fixes the boundary of the area that contributes ground water to each stream system.

Where these two divides are not coincident, *watershed leakage* is said to occur and is equal to the ground-water flow from the area between them. This ground-water flow or watershed leakage always moves across the topographic divide. The area of the drainage basin is considered to be the area that contributes the surface runoff and is bounded by the topographic divide. The exact location of the phreatic divide is usually unknown.

Figure 12a shows how watershed leakage may be caused by geological formation. Because of the dip of the impervious stratum toward stream *A,* the ground-water flow from the area between *C* and *D* is diverted from stream *B* to stream *A.* In Fig. 12b is shown a cross section through the divide between two drainage basins which are similar topographically to those shown in Fig. 12a, but in which there is no impervious stratum such as was shown in the previous case. In Fig. 12b the diversion of ground-water flow is from stream *A* to stream *B.*

The location of the phreatic divide usually is not fixed and permanent but shifts with the changes in ground-water stage. The higher the stage of the ground water, the more nearly do the phreatic and topographic divides coincide. As the stage lowers, the two divides may become more and more widely separated.

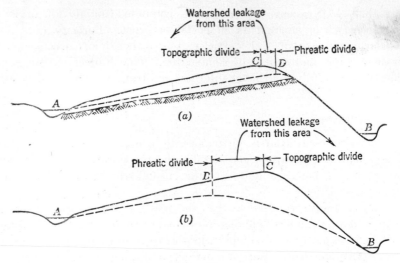

Fig. 12.

In general, if two adjacent streams flow more or less parallel, watershed leakage is likely to occur from the higher to the lower basin. It may also occur at the head of a basin where a stream on the opposite side of the divide heads at a lower level. Watershed leakage through artesian aquifers occurs under a variety of conditions. Inasmuch as the profile of the free water table generally follows roughly that of the ground surface, the surface and ground-water divides are likely to differ less for steep impervious areas than for flat areas with permeable soils. If information to the contrary is lacking, it is generally assumed that the two divides are coincident. This assumption, however, may be greatly in error, especially in small drainage basins in highly permeable deposits. Area of basin affects the magnitudes of floods, minimum flows, and average flows in different ways, and as a result, the effects on these several flow characteristics will be considered separately. Unless otherwise stated, the effects are on flow expressed in cubic feet per second per square mile, or inches depth on the drainage basin per unit of time.

Effect upon Flood Flow. If all other factors including the depth and intensity of rainfall remain constant in all instances, the total runoff expressed in inches depth on the drainage basin will be the same regardless of the size of basin. However, the base of the hydrograph of flood flow will broaden out as the area of basin increases; in other words, the larger the basin the longer it takes for the total flood flow to pass a given station. Inasmuch as under the previous assumptions the total runoff per square mile remains the same, it necessarily follows that the peak flow must decrease as the area of basin increases.

One other factor affects this relationship, however. It was assumed above that the depth of rainfall is the same in all instances. Actually for any locality the maximum intensity of rain that is likely to occur with any given frequency varies inversely with the area covered by the storm. Consequently, the larger the basin the less will be the intensity of the storm and therefore the lower will be the flood peak. This result can be accounted for by noting that surface runoff is equal to rainfall minus infiltration, neglecting other losses. As an illustration, suppose that the maximum flood on a certain small basin results from a 6-in. rain in 1 day. On a near-by large basin the maximum flood is produced by a 12-in. rain in 4 days. Now if the average infiltration capacity is the same in both cases and is equal to 2 in. per day, the net supply rate for the small basin is 4 in. per day as compared with 1 in. per day for the large basin. Hence, although the rainfall rate on the small basin was only twice that on the large basin, the supply rate was four times as great.

Although the previously mentioned factors tend to cause flood flows, expressed in cubic feet per second per square mile, to be more intense for small basins, this effect may easily be obscured by the effect of the other basin characteristics. As a result, maximum flood flows may differ greatly even for watersheds of the same size. To illustrate this point the basins and pertinent data shown in Table 1 were selected more or less at random from the records of the U. S. Geological Survey.

These streams were chosen primarily for the purpose of comparing the flood flows to be expected from drainage basins of approximately 10,000 square miles area located in various sections of the United States. This table shows the enormous variation in the maximum flood flows recorded on different drainage basins of approximately the same size. Longer records will undoubtedly show increased flood flows for all these streams, but probably their relative magnitude will not be materially changed. It will be observed that the actual maximum flood flow of the Little River at Cameron, Texas, was over fifty times as great as that of the Souris River at Minot, North Dakota, despite the fact that the basins have about the same area. Correspondingly large variations in flood flows can be found for other streams of any given size located in different sections of the United States.

On the other hand, if one would compute the average of the peak flood flows that have occurred on all the streams of each different size throughout the country and then plot average peak flow against size

TABLE 1

Basin	Station	Area, sq miles	Period, yr	Max. Q, cfs	Max. Q, cfs/sq mile
Souris River	Minot, N. Dak.	10,270	31	12,000	1.17
Deschutes River	Moody, Oreg.	10,500	39	43,600	4.27
Gila River	Coolidge Dam, Ariz.	12,890	30	130,000	10.1
Cumberland River	Carthage, Tenn.	10,700	21	186,000	17.4
Susquehanna River	Wilkes-Barre, Pa.	9,960	45	232,000	23.3
Potomac River	Point of Rocks, Md.	9,650	43	480,000	49.7
Little River	Cameron, Tex.	7,030	27	647,000	92.0

of basin, he would find a certain degree of correlation between these two quantities for the reasons explained (see Fig. ·101). So, although the magnitude of flood to be expected from any drainage basin, expressed in cubic feet per second per square mile, varies inversely with the size of basin as long as all the other characteristics remain the same, it is by no means a dominant factor, and as a result much greater variations in flood flow are to be expected among the different basins of any given size because of these other factors.

Effect upon Minimum Flow. After surface runoff ceases, the entire flow of the stream is drawn from ground-water storage. Consequently, as this storage is depleted more and more, the stream flow becomes less and less until either the stream goes dry or the supply is replenished by precipitation. These replenishing rains are often local, some covering an area of only a few square miles. Scores of such rains may fall on various portions of a large drainage basin during a given drought, although many of the small component basins may be left untouched. Because each of these local rains contributes to the discharge of the main stream, larger basins are likely to provide a more sustained flow than smaller ones.

Effect upon Average Flow. A study of a great many drainage basins throughout the United States reveals that the average unit yield seldom remains constant throughout the length of stream channel. The reasons for these changes are usually, however, attributable to surface conditions; in other words, the character of basin seldom if ever is the same throughout a large drainage system, and this factor exerts a dominant influence on the unit yield at various points on the stream. These variations are, therefore, not directly attributable to size but to other factors which will be discussed later.

Shape

The shape of a drainage basin mainly governs the rate at which water is supplied to the main stream as it proceeds along its course from the source to the mouth. This fact has an important bearing on the economic utility of the stream as well as its profile and channel dimensions.

The outlines of large drainage systems are, as a rule, fixed at least in part by major geologic structures, folds, and mountain ranges. Such structures commonly fix the position of the watershed line across the head of the more important drainage basins, whereas the lateral boundaries may be fixed either by geologic structures or by competitive erosion. For the smaller basins erosion is usually the dominant factor.

Although it is difficult to express satisfactorily by means of a numerical index the shape of a drainage basin as that characteristic affects the hydrology of the stream, several indices have been suggested which are of value. Gravelius[1] proposed the use of the term "form factor" to express the ratio of the average width to the axial length of basin. The axial length is measured from the outlet to the most remote point on the basin. The average width is obtained by dividing the area by the axial length. For basins with side outlets the width may exceed the axial length, giving a ratio greater than unity. The form factor gives some indication of the tendency toward floods, because a basin with a low form factor is less likely to have an intense rainfall simultaneously over its entire extent than an area of equal size with a larger form factor.

Another index of the form of a drainage basin as suggested by Gravelius[1] is the ratio of the perimeter of the watershed to the circumference of a circle whose area is equal to that of the drainage basin. This ratio may be termed the *compactness coefficient*.

Snyder[2] has found that shape, as it affects the runoff characteristics of a watershed, is related to the distance along the main stream from the outlet to a point adjacent to the geographical center of the basin.[3]

Elevation

The variation in elevation and also the mean elevation of a drainage basin are important factors in relation to temperature and to precipitation, particularly as to the fraction of the total amount which falls as snow. Not only does elevation, because of the resulting differences in temperature, have a profound effect upon water losses, which are all evaporative in nature, but it is also an important factor in determining the extent to which the available water supply in winter is

[1] Gravelius, *Flusskunde,* Berlin and Leipzig, 1914.

[2] Franklin F. Snyder, "Synthetic Unit-Graphs," *Trans. Am. Geophys. Union,* 1938, Part I, p. 447.

[3] See also p. 257 of this book.

impounded as frozen assets in the form of snow storage, ice in lakes and rivers, and soil moisture within the zone of frost penetration.

For large basins the mean elevation can be most easily determined by the intersection method. A topographic map of the basin is subdivided into squares of equal size by enough lines so that at least 100 intersections fall within the area. The mean elevation of the basin is then taken as the average of the elevation at all the intersections.

A more complete analysis of the elevation characteristics of a basin may be made by measuring on a suitable map the area lying between successive pairs of contours. The percentages of the total that each of these areas constitute are then computed, and the percentage of the total area lying above or below each different contour is obtained by summation, as shown for the San Pablo drainage basin, near Richmond, California, in Table 2.

TABLE 2

Limiting Contour Elevations 1	Area between Contours, acres 2	Per Cent of Total 3	Per Cent of Total over Given Lower Limit 4
170– 300	500	2.4	100.0
300– 400	1700	8.2	97.6
400– 500	1900	9.2	89.4
500– 600	2400	11.6	80.2
600– 700	3000	14.5	68.6
700– 800	2970	14.3	54.1
800– 900	2270	11.0	39.8
900–1000	2180	10.5	28.8
1000–1100	1500	7.2	18.3
1100–1200	640	3.1	11.1
1200–1300	610	3.0	8.0
1300–1400	410	2.0	5.0
1400–1800	620	3.0	3.0

If a is the area between any given pair of contours of which e is the mean elevation, the mean elevation of the basin is

$$E = \frac{\Sigma ae}{A} \tag{1}$$

in which A is the area of basin. Substituting the data contained in Table 2 in equation 1, we find that the mean elevation of the San Pablo basin is 758.

If the data contained in Table 2 are shown graphically, by plotting column 4 against the lower elevations in column 1 a typical hypsometric curve will be obtained (Fig. 13). This curve shows that 50 per cent of the drainage area lies above elevation 732, which is called the median elevation and is more representative of the effect of elevation in relation to hydrology than the mean elevation. As a usual thing the mean elevation is higher than the median, but the difference is generally unimportant.

Slope

The slope of a drainage basin has an important but rather complex relation to infiltration, surface runoff, soil moisture, and ground-water contribution to stream flow. It is one of the major factors controlling the time of overland flow and concentration of rainfall in stream channels and is of direct importance in relation to flood magnitude. Alvord[4] suggested a method of estimating slope based upon the area between different contours within the basin. Such a method, used by Horton,[5] is as described on page 46.

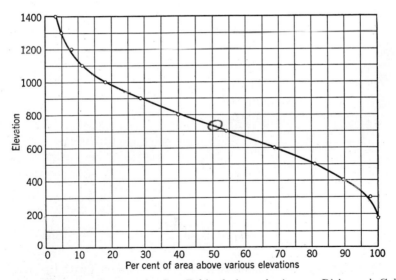

Fig. 13. Hypsometric curve for San Pablo drainage basin near Richmond, Calif.

[4] John W. Alvord and others, "Tables of Excessive Precipitations of Rain at Chicago, Ill.," from 1889 to 1897 inclusive, *J. Western Soc. Engrs.*, April 1899, p. 157.

[5] R. E. Horton, "Derivation of Runoff from Rainfall Data," Discussion, *Trans. A.S.C.E.*, 1914, vol. 77, 369–375.

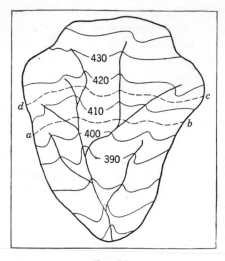

Fig. 14.

In Fig. 14 a drainage basin is shown that is crossed by a number of contours having equal differences in elevation. Lines ab and cd are drawn midway between contours 400 and 410 and between 410 and 420 respectively. Now let

a_1 = area of strip $abcd$.
w_1 = average width of strip $abcd$.
l_1 = length of contour 410.
s_1 = average slope of strip $abcd$.
S = average slope of basin.
D = contour interval.
A = area of basin.
L = total length of contours.

$$S = \frac{D \; L}{A}$$

Then

$$s_1 = \frac{D}{w_1} = \frac{Dl_1}{a_1}$$

and by weighting the slope of each strip in accordance with its area,

$$S = \frac{Dl_1}{a_1} \cdot \frac{a_1}{A} + \frac{Dl_2}{a_2} \cdot \frac{a_2}{A} \dots \frac{Dl_n}{a_n} \cdot \frac{a_n}{A} \tag{2}$$

From which

$$S = \frac{D}{A} (l_1 + l_2 + \dots l_n) = \frac{DL}{A} \tag{3}$$

In other words, the average slope of the basin is equal to the total length of contours multiplied by the contour interval and divided by the area of basin. The work involved in measuring the length of all contours on large and rugged basins is likely to be time consuming and tedious. Fortunately, however, satisfactory results can usually be obtained by measuring with an opisometer the length of contours at 20-ft or 40-ft intervals for small or flat areas and the length of contours at 100-ft to 500-ft intervals for large or steep areas.

Orientation

Although slope affects the rainfall-runoff relationship principally because of a speeding up of the velocity of overland flow, thereby shortening the period of infiltration and producing a greater concentration of surface runoff in the stream channels, a secondary influence resulting from the general direction of the resultant slope, or orientation of basin, must not be overlooked. This factor affects the transpiration and evaporation losses because of its influence on the amount of heat received from the sun. Also the direction of the resultant slope to the north or the south affects the time of melting of accumulated snows. If the general slope is to the south, each successive snowfall may soon melt and either infiltrate into the ground or produce surface runoff. On the other hand, if the slope is to the north, these snows may accumulate throughout the winter and remain on the ground until late spring when they may be removed by a heavy rain, thus producing a high flood peak and a low minimum flow. The effect of the orientation of the basin with respect to the direction of storm movement was discussed on page 36; also the effect of the orientation of a hilly or mountainous watershed with respect to the direction of the prevailing winds is discussed on page 65.

The Drainage Net

Another important characteristic of any drainage basin is the pattern or the arrangement of the natural stream channels which through past ages has been developed by nature within the area. The reasons for this importance are twofold. In the first place, the efficiency of the drainage system and therefore the characteristics of the resulting hydrograph are dependent upon this factor. For instance, if the basin is well drained the length of overland flow is short, the surface runoff concentrates quickly, the flood peaks are high, and in all probability the minimum flow is correspondingly low. In other words, the more efficient the drainage the more flashy is the stream flow, and vice versa.

Perhaps of equal if not greater importance, however, is the indication that this factor gives to the hydrologist of the nature of the soil and surface conditions existing in the drainage basin, for there can be no question but that the character and extent of nature's carving of stream channels through erosive processes is definitely related to and restricted by the type of materials from which these channels are carved. It is entirely conceivable that, when this subject has been fully explored, analyzed, and understood, it may be found that an ordinary map of the drainage system provides a reliable index of the permeability of the basin and will give some indication of the yield.

The characteristics of the drainage net may be fairly well described by (1) order of streams, (2) length of tributaries, (3) stream density, and (4) drainage density and length of overland flow.

Order of Streams. Every large stream has its important tributaries, each of which has its own tributaries, and so on until at last the ultimate branches or finger tips of the drainage net are reached which have no branches. As a rule, the larger the stream the greater is the number of branchings or bifurcations. It is convenient to classify streams according to the number of bifurcations of the tributaries. The most common procedure is to designate all nonbranching tributaries, regardless of whether they enter the main stream or its branches, as of the first order. Streams which receive only nonbranching tributaries are of the second order. Streams of the third order are formed by the junction of two streams of the second order, and so on. In accordance with this system, the order number of the main stream indicates at once the extent of bifurcation of its tributaries and, as a rule, is a direct indication of the size and extent of the drainage net. Streams of the same order have the same system of bifurcation, regardless of whether they enter the main stream, enter another tributary, or flow directly into the sea.

For almost every stream there are some undivided feeders that flow directly into the main stream or into the larger tributaries. The relative numbers of divided and undivided tributaries afford an indication of the character of the drainage. For example, in watersheds in the Middle West that are covered with a heavy blanket of permeable deposit, there are, as a rule, relatively few minor tributaries, whereas, for streams draining steeper slopes, such as those tributary to the Finger Lakes in central New York, there are usually comparatively few major or branching tributaries.

To determine correctly the order of a stream and make a complete analysis of the drainage net, it is necessary to have a map of the basin showing all tributaries. This map should include both perennial and intermittent tributaries, but it cannot well include ephemeral rain gullies that have not developed definite stream channels. On this map each different stream and tributary should be numbered according to its order. Figure 15 is a map of the Thunder Bay River drainage net which has been so numbered. This map shows that the Thunder Bay River is a stream of the fourth order and that it has two tributaries of the third order, eight of the second, and thirty-three of the first. Aerial photographs provide an excellent aid not only for determining the order of streams but also for other hydrologic purposes. For example, karst topography and swamps oftentimes can be recognized in aerial photographs.

The number of tributary streams of a given order per square mile of drainage basin is a function of the order of the tributaries. For this purpose, it is convenient to use the *reverse order,* in which the main stream is given the order of *one,* tributaries of the next lower order have the reverse order of *two,* and so on. If each order of tributaries had a given number of branches of the next higher order and no others, the number of tributaries of a given order would decrease in a geometrical progression as the reverse order decreases in an arithmetical progression. Actually this does not occur. If it did, a fifth-order stream would receive, let us say, two fourth-order streams and no others; each of these fourth-order streams would receive two third-order streams and no others; and so on. As a matter of fact, the fifth-order stream may receive directly from first-, second-, and third-order streams, in addition to the two fourth-order streams. However, the

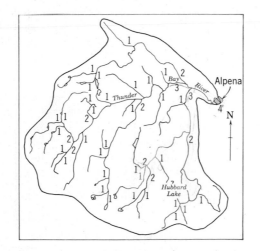

Fig. 15.

geometrical ratio is usually well sustained in actual experience, as is illustrated in Fig. 16, which shows for eight different streams the number of tributaries of different orders, plotted semi-logarithmically. Horton found that the equation of the resulting graph is of the form

$$\log N = K O_R - C \tag{4}$$

in which N is the number of streams of reverse order, O_R, per 100 square miles of drainage basin; K is the slope of the graph with respect to the $\log N$ axis; and C is the negative value of $\log N$ when O_R is equal to zero. For Ganargua Creek in New York, the equation becomes

$$\log N = 0.406 O_R - 0.70$$

For the Saginaw River in Michigan, the equation is

$$\log N = 0.594 O_R - 2.37$$

Usually for a given stream the actual number of tributaries falls very close to a straight line. It is interesting to note in Fig. 16 that the graphs for most of the streams in New York are approximately parallel with each other; in other words, they have approximately the same values of K but different values of C. Those for the Michigan streams are also nearly parallel with each other but have steeper slopes

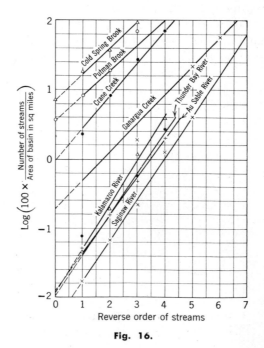

Fig. 16.

or higher values of K than those for the New York streams. Therefore, it appears that certain broad general characteristics of basin more or less common to any particular region determine the slope of these graphs or the value of K in equation 7. On the other hand, certain minor variations that are more or less common to all basins regardless of location seem to determine the value of C. As to what particular characteristics of basin affect the values of K and C, little is at present known. However, there can be but little question that there is a close relationship between these constants and certain drainage-basin characteristics, which in turn are closely related to stream flow. Here in all probability lies a fertile field for reseach. No one can predict the extent of the possibilities of correlating these factors and determining thereby the stream-flow characteristics based entirely upon the type of drainage net.

Length of Tributaries. The length of tributaries is an indication of the steepness of the drainage basin as well as of the degree of drainage. Steep well-drained areas usually have numerous small tributaries, whereas in plains regions where the soils are deep and permeable only relatively long tributaries are, as a rule, maintained as perennial streams. In different basins it is better to compare the average length of tributaries of the same order, especially of the first order, than to compare the average length of all tributaries.

The lengths of tributaries increase as a function of their order. This statement is also approximately a geometrical law of progression. The relation does not hold closely for individual streams. Comparison has been made of the average lengths of tributaries of a number of streams of different orders in central New York and central Michigan. It was found that for any particular order the average length of the streams in Michigan is considerably greater than that of the New York streams. For instance, the average length of first-order streams in New York is less than a mile, whereas in Michigan it is over 6 miles; in New York second-order streams average about 2 miles in length, and in Michigan, 12 miles, and so on.

In measuring stream lengths by opisometer on topographic maps the course of the stream can, in general, be followed quite closely. The measured length of all except meandering streams and the length along the axis of the valley are, as a rule, nearly the same.

For meandering streams the length is sometimes measured along the valley axis, the measured length consisting of a series of linear segments joining at various angles. Sinuosities due to oxbows and the general tortuosity of the stream are neglected, and the resulting length may be materially less than the actual distance through which the water flows in its course down the valley. The relations between the air-line length and the meander length of a number of Midwestern streams is shown in Table 3. These stream valleys were fairly straight

TABLE 3

Stream	State	Length, meander miles	Length, air-line miles	Ratio of Measured Length to Air-Line Length	Average Fall	
					by Meander	by Air Line
Cottonwood R.	Kans.	120.0	62.0	1.94	1.89	3.66
Maria de Cygnes	Kans.	138.0	88.0	1.57	1.43	2.24
Salt Creek	Nebr.	78.0	36.0	2.17	1.78	3.86
Nemaha R.	Nebr.	42.4	24.9	1.70	3.07	5.22
Elkhorn R.	Nebr.	21.8	13.6	1.60	3.88	6.25
Deep Fork	Okla.	62.0	41.0	1.51	1.90	2.90
Des Moines R.	Iowa	68.0	37.0	1.84	1.54	2.84
Big Sioux R.	Iowa	36.6	17.0	2.15	1.37	2.94
Locust Cr.	Mo.	59.0	25.0	2.36	1.59	3.76
Saline Cr.	Mo.	38.0	18.5	2.04	1.47	3.00

throughout the lengths of most of the reaches, so that the air-line length represents approximately the length as measured along the axis of the stream valley. The last two columns of this table show the slopes of these streams computed by means of the air line and also the meander length of the streams.

Stream Density. The stream density or stream frequency of a drainage basin may be expressed by relating the number of streams to the area drained. If N_s is the number of streams in the basin and A is the total area, the stream density, D_s, may be expressed as

$$D_s = \frac{N_s}{A}$$

i.e., the number of streams per square mile. The inverse form, namely the area per stream, might also be used as a measure of stream density.

In determining the total number of streams, only the perennial and intermittent streams are included. The main stream, extending from its source to the mouth, is counted as one; there are then n_1

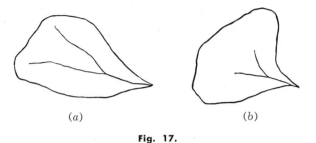

(a)   (b)

Fig. 17.

tributaries of the next lower order, each extending from its source to its junction with the main stream; n_2 tributaries of the next lower order, each extending from its source to its junction with a stream of the next higher order; and so on down to the first order of tributaries.

That the relationship between the number of streams and the area drained does not provide a true measure of drainage efficiency is shown in Fig. 17. In this figure (a) and (b) represent two basins of equal size, each having the same numbers of streams. However, it is quite evident that (a) is better drained than (b).

Drainage Density. Drainage density is expressed as the length of stream per unit of area. Let D_d represent the drainage density, L the total length of perennial and intermittent streams in the basin, and A the area; then

$$D_d = \frac{L}{A}$$

Drainage density varies inversely as the length of overland flow and therefore provides at least an indication of the drainage efficiency of the basin.

Indirect Drainage

Throughout the preceding discussion it has been assumed that all parts of the drainage basin are tributary through direct overland flow to some surface stream. In two important cases this condition may not exist, viz., in areas characterized by (1) karst topography and (2) a very pervious surface and flat slopes. In neither of these cases does any precipitation find its way through overland flow directly into the stream channels; instead it infiltrates into the soil and later finds its way through underground channels either into adjacent or far distant streams, lakes, or the sea.

Regions underlain by soluble rock formations, especially limestone, oftentimes have characteristic undulating surfaces with conical knolls and circular sinks. Such areas are said to have a *karst* topography. The runoff usually enters the ground through sinkholes and fissures and pursues its course to an outlet through a system of underground passages or solution channels. The resulting underground drainage net is often complex but is somewhat similar to a surface drainage net in its characteristics. The surface is pock-marked with depressions, some dry, some containing pools; streams flow into some and out of others.

Extensive karst regions are to be found in France and in other parts of continental Europe and in various localities in the United States, especially in the cave regions of Kentucky and Virginia. In the Helderberg region in eastern New York there are considerable areas where the fissured limestone is at the surface and the runoff enters directly into widened joint openings and solution channels. In northern Florida and in the basin of the north branch of the Thunder Bay River in Michigan, there are hundreds of sinkholes usually 20 ft to 80 ft deep and several hundred feet in diameter, caused by the dissolution of the underlying soft limestone and the subsequent collapse of the overlying thin, hard strata. Most of the runoff from these areas finds its way to these sinkholes and thence through underground channels to distant outlets.

In regions of low relief and high permeability, especially regions overlain with recent glacial deposits, numerous undrained depressions often occur. Most common among these are kettle holes, which are generally pockets left in the surface by the melting of stranded blocks of ice as the glaciers disappeared from the region. In such areas all rain passes directly into the soil, so that there is no surface runoff and no drainage net is developed.

In determining the runoff from basins containing karst topography, it is best to exclude all karst areas, for it is seldom that they contribute either runoff or ground-water flow to the stream to which they are immediately tributary. For instance, it is doubtful that the karst areas of the Thunder Bay basin make any appreciable contribution to the flow of the Thunder Bay River. However, probably these areas contribute equally with other adjacent areas to the flow of the St. Lawrence, for the underground channels very likely find an outlet in Lake Huron.

On the other hand, in estimating the yield of drainage basins containing highly permeable depression areas, these areas should usually be excluded only in making estimates of surface runoff but should be included in making studies of ground-water flow, for usually the water table beneath these areas drains directly into the adjacent streams.

Artificial Drainage

Lowlands such as swamps and marshes, if not inundated, at least have a water table at or near the ground surface. Such areas can be made available for pasture and agriculture by drainage, using either tile or open ditches. Likewise uplands, even though under cultivation, can often be improved by the same method by removing the surface waters more promptly after rains and by lowering the water table to an optimum level for crops. The manner in which drainage affects the flood peaks, low flows, and average yields of streams will now be considered briefly.

Open drains speed up the removal of surface runoff and therefore increase the flood flow from the immediate area drained. However, if this area is only a portion of, and lies in the lower part of the entire basin under consideration, its drainage may actually reduce the flood peaks at the basin outlet by getting rid of the waters from this lower area before the arrival of the waters from the upper tributaries. Conversely, if the drained area lies in the headwaters, the time of concentration will be reduced and the flood peaks will be increased. Also if the entire basin were drained, flood peaks would be increased although the increase might be less than if only the headwaters were drained.

Open drains reduce the length and period of overland flow and therefore the total amount of infiltration. As a result the water table is lowered, and the low water flow is reduced. Because of the reduced time of overland flow and also because of the increased depth to the water table, surface evaporation and transpiration losses are reduced, and therefore the total yield is usually increased.

In order for tile drains to operate effectively they must be placed below the water table. Inasmuch as infiltration capacity is determined at the ground surface, and usually by the condition of the top quarter inch of soil, tile drainage of uplands can have little or no effect upon surface runoff. However, tile drainage does have an effect on the hydrograph that is quite similar to that of subsurface storm flow. Consequently tile drains, although having little effect on flood peaks, usually reduce low water flow as a result of the more rapid draining of the ground water. They increase the total yield by lowering the water table and thereby reduce the water losses.

Because of the high consumption of water by the vegetation usually found in swamps and marshes, it is not unusual for the evaporation and transpiration losses from such areas to equal or exceed the total rainfall on them. Drainage, by lowering the water table, reduces soil evaporation and causes a change in the type of vegetation to one that uses less water. The usual effect of the drainage of swamps and marshes is therefore to increase flood flows, reduce low water flow, and increase the total runoff. However, the drainage of some lowlands containing soils that are more or less porous, by lowering the water table, creates a subsurface storage reservoir that may actually reduce flood peaks.

Although the effects of drainage appear to be as described previously, the magnitudes of these effects are difficult of exact determination. The reason for this difficulty is quite obvious. It would be necessary to have two rather long periods of records of precipitation that were identical, the one occurring before drainage and the other after. Unfortunately, precipitation patterns do not repeat in that manner. Nor is it possible to obtain positive proof of the effects of drainage upon runoff by comparing the results of individual storms, or of monthly, or of seasonal, or of annual totals, for the reason that so much depends upon the exact manner in which those totals were distributed, and upon the condition of the ground surface, the vegetation, and many other variables.

In 1928 Woodward and Nagler[6] made a study to determine the effect of agricultural drainage upon floods on the Des Moines and Iowa rivers. It was their conclusion that although more than a third of the area of each of these basins has been artifically drained, the effect upon flood flows has been negligible. However, it does not follow that such is always the case. In fact, it is believed that in most instances surface drainage increases flood peaks and total yield, and reduces low water flows, and that on small streams these effects may be quite marked.

[6] S. M. Woodward and F. A. Nagler, "The Effect of Agricultural Drainage upon Flood Runoff," *Trans. A.S.C.E.*, 1929, p. 821.

4

Precipitation

The term precipitation as used in hydrology includes all forms of water deposited on the earth's surface and derived from atmospheric vapor. The principal forms are mist, rain, hail, sleet, and snow. Unless otherwise specified, the terms precipitation and rainfall are often used indiscriminately to apply to any or all of the forms included in this group. Condensation on solids and water surfaces as dew and frost is sometimes considered a form of precipitation.

This chapter deals with the properties and behavior of atmospheric water vapor, the causes of precipitation, methods of measuring rainfall and snowfall, and the nature and variation of precipitation. Methods of analyzing precipitation data for solving hydrological problems are also described.

Water Vapor

Water vapor is one of the atmospheric gases. Within a moderate range of temperatures and pressures and for conditions not too close to the point of condensation, water vapor obeys the gas laws reasonably well. Atmospheric water vapor is chiefly derived by evaporation from oceans, lakes, and rivers, by evaporation from moist soil, and by transpiration from plants. A small amount of water vapor is added to the atmosphere by artificial means, such as by exhaust steam or residue from combustion engines. Evaporation from the oceans is the principal source of atmospheric moisture. Although there are differences of opinion, it is probable that 75 per cent of the precipitation in the United States is derived from oceanic evaporation. It is brought to the United States as part of a world-wide system of atmospheric circulation.[1]

Any given space can hold only a certain amount of water vapor in the presence of a solid or liquid surface. If more vapor is added, some will ordinarily be condensed on the surfaces. When there is a mixture of gases or vapors, as in the case of moist air, each component behaves physically as if it alone were present. The pressure exerted on the walls of a container by each component of such a mixture is called the *partial pressure*. The partial pressure exerted by the water vapor in saturated air at a given temperature is called the *saturation pressure* and is commonly expressed in inches of mercury. Values of saturation pressure for various temperatures are given in Table 4.

If, without change in barometric pressure, the air is cooled until it becomes saturated, the corresponding temperature is called the *dew point*. Any further cooling would result in the condensation of moisture on surfaces in contact with the air. If the dew point is greater than 32° F, condensation will be in the form of dew, whereas for temperatures less than 32°, frost will be formed.

The moisture content of air, expressed in weight per unit of volume, is called the *absolute humidity*. For any given temperature, the absolute humidity is related to the partial pressure of the water vapor. The difference between the partial pressure of the water vapor, at any temperature, and the saturation pressure for the same temperature is the *saturation deficit*. The *relative humidity* is the ratio between either (1) the amount of water vapor actually contained per unit volume and the amount that it could hold at the same temperature when saturated, or (2) the actual vapor pressure and the saturation vapor pressure at the same temperature. Inasmuch as these are ratios, they are dimensionless and are equal regardless of the units or methods used in their derivation.

Measurement of Humidity

Humidity may be measured by any one of four methods. The most direct method consists of extracting the water vapor from a certain volume of air and weighing it. This is done by passing the moist air

---

[1] Benjamin Holzman, "Use of Aerological Soundings in Determining the Sources of Moisture for Precipitation," *Trans. Am. Geophys. Union*, 1937, Part II, pp. 483–489.

TABLE 4

Saturation Vapor Pressure in Inches of Mercury

Temperature, °F	V_p	Temperature, °F	V_p	Temperature, °F	V_p	Temperature, °F	V_p
−30	0.007	10	0.063	50	0.363	90	1.423
−29	.007	11	.067	51	0.376	91	1.469
−28	.008	12	.070	52	0.390	92	1.515
−27	.008	13	.074	53	0.405	93	1.563
−26	.009	14	.077	54	0.420	94	1.612
−25	.010	15	.081	55	0.436	95	1.662
−24	.010	16	.085	56	0.452	96	1.714
−23	.011	17	.089	57	0.469	97	1.767
−22	.011	18	.094	58	0.486	98	1.822
−21	.012	19	.099	59	0.504	99	1.878
−20	.013	20	.103	60	0.522	100	1.936
−19	.013	21	.108	61	0.541	101	1.994
−18	.014	22	.114	62	0.560	102	2.055
−17	.015	23	.119	63	0.580	103	2.117
−16	.016	24	.125	64	0.601	104	2.181
−15	.017	25	.131	65	0.623	105	2.246
−14	.018	26	.137	66	0.645	106	2.314
−13	.019	27	.143	67	0.668	107	2.382
−12	.020	28	.150	68	0.691	108	2.453
−11	.021	29	.157	69	0.715	109	2.525
−10	.022	30	.165	70	0.740	110	2.599
− 9	.024	31	.172	71	0.766	111	2.676
− 8	.025	32	.180	72	0.792	112	2.754
− 7	.026	33	.188	73	0.819	113	2.833
− 6	.028	34	.195	74	0.847	114	2.915
− 5	.029	35	.203	75	0.876	115	2.999
− 4	.031	36	.212	76	0.906	116	3.085
− 3	.033	37	.220	77	0.936	117	3.173
− 2	.034	38	.229	78	0.968	118	3.264
− 1	.036	39	.238	79	1.000	119	3.356
0	.038	40	.248	80	1.033	120	3.451
1	.040	41	.258	81	1.068	121	3.548
2	.042	42	.268	82	1.103	122	3.647
3	.044	43	.278	83	1.139	123	3.749
4	.047	44	.289	84	1.176	124	3.853
5	.049	45	.300	85	1.215	125	3.960
6	.052	46	.312	86	1.254	126	4.069
7	.055	47	.324	87	1.295	127	4.181
8	.057	48	.336	88	1.336	128	4.295
9	.060	49	.349	89	1.379	129	4.412

through a granular desiccant, the increase in weight of the drying agent being the weight of moisture contained in the air. The development of techniques to adapt this method to field use has been reported by Thornthwaite and Holzman.[2]

The dew-point method of measuring humidity utilizes the fact that, when water vapor is saturated, a reduction in temperature will produce condensation. The dew-point apparatus usually consists of a polished cup containing a volatile liquid such as ether. The surface of the cup is cooled by forcing air through the liquid. The water vapor in contact with the cup is also cooled, and, when the dew point is reached, condensation may be observed on the cup. The corresponding temperature is noted from a thermometer immersed in the liquid. The dew point is taken as the average between the temperature at which the condensation appears during the cooling process and the temperature at which it disappears when the liquid is allowed to warm again. The vapor content of the air is then determined by referring to tables giving the unit weight of saturated water vapor for various temperatures.[3]

The simplest method of measuring humidity is by means of a sling psychrometer such as that shown in Fig. 18. This instrument consists of two thermometers mounted side by side, one of which has its bulb covered with muslin. Before use, the muslin is wetted so that evaporational cooling will lower the temperature of that thermometer. The difference in the readings of the two thermometers may be converted to relative or absolute humidity by means of calibration tables.[3] It is recommended that the psychrometer be "whirled rapidly for 15 or 20 seconds; stopped and quickly read, the wet bulb first. This reading is kept in mind, the psychrometer immediately whirled again and a second reading taken. This is repeated three or four times or more if necessary, until at least two successive readings of the wet bulb are found to agree very closely." Instead of whirling the psychrometer, the air may be blown over the thermometers. Such a procedure has been described by Rohwer.[4] During subfreezing temperatures the water in the muslin is likely to freeze, causing some difficulty in the use of this method. It is claimed, however, that the proper results

[2] Measurement of Evaporation from Land and Water Surfaces," *U. S. Dept. Agr. Tech. Bull.* 817, May 1942.

[3] C. F. Marvin, "Psychrometric Tables for Obtaining the Vapor Pressure, Relative Humidity and Temperature of the Dew Point," *U. S. Dept. Agr., Weather Bureau* 235, 1937.

[4] "Evaporation from Free Water Surfaces," *U. S. Dept. Agr. Tech. Bull.* 271, December 1931.

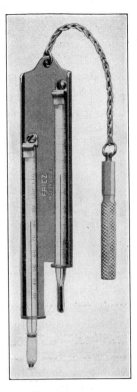

Fig. 18. Friez pocket sling psychrometer. Courtesy Bendix Aviation Corp.

may still be obtained by whirling the ice-covered bulb until its minimum temperature is reached.[5]

The fourth method of measuring atmospheric moisture content is by means of hygrometers. Hygroscopic fibers such as hair increase in length when the relative humidity increases and shrink when it decreases. By careful calibration a group of such fibers attached to an indicator arm may be made to register relative humidity. Such instruments lend themselves very readily to obtaining automatic continuous records of relative humidity. They must, however, be recalibrated frequently since they tend in time to deviate from their original calibration.

Variations in Humidity

The amount of water vapor present in the atmosphere varies constantly with respect both to place and to time. The major controlling

[5] C. F. Marvin, "Psychrometric Tables for Obtaining the Vapor Pressure, Relative Humidity and Temperature of the Dew Point," *U. S. Dept. Agr. Weather Bureau* 235, 1937.

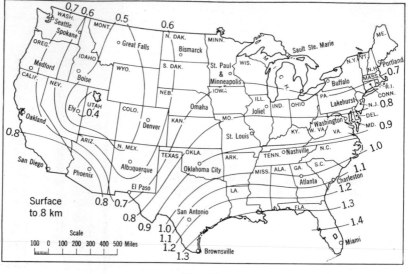

Fig. 19.

factors are temperature and source of supply. Because the oceans provide the principal supply, the greatest concentration occurs near the surface of the ocean in the tropics. Concentration decreases with altitude, with latitude, and with distance inland from the seashore. This fact is illustrated in Fig. 19,[6] which, for the United States, shows the average water content of the atmosphere from the surface to an elevation of 8 km.

Absolute humidity decreases rapidly with altitude. Approximately one half of the total moisture content of the atmosphere occurs within 1 mile of the earth's surface. Vapor is carried aloft by ascending air currents. The principal process by which such currents are produced is through convective action, and at the higher altitudes this action becomes feeble.

The variation of the water content of the atmosphere with elevation is illustrated by the values in Table 5.[6] These values show the water content of successive layers from the surface to an elevation of 8 km, at St. Paul and Minneapolis, Minnesota. The values in Table 5 also illustrate the variation of atmospheric moisture from month to month during a year. Data from this table, together with similar data for 28 other locations, were used to prepare the average annual curves shown in Fig. 19.

[6] U. S. Weather Bureau, "Mean Precipitable Water in the United States," *Tech. Paper* No. 10, 1949.

TABLE 5

Mean Precipitable Water (Inches)

St. Paul and Minneapolis, Minn.

Elev. 225 miles   Sept. 1939–July 1940   Jan. 1941–Dec. 1943

Layer (km)	J	F	M	A	M	J	J	A	S	O	N	D
Sfc–0.5	0.018	0.022	0.031	0.055	0.082	0.125	0.148	0.148	0.093	0.063	0.039	0.028
0.5–1	0.036	0.161	0.054	0.095	0.136	0.206	0.225	0.224	0.151	0.108	0.068	0.051
1–1.5	0.036	0.038	0.046	0.078	0.117	0.174	0.187	0.188	0.128	0.085	0.055	0.044
1.5–2	0.035	0.033	0.037	0.066	0.098	0.147	0.158	0.156	0.106	0.075	0.045	0.037
2–2.5	0.029	0.029	0.031	0.055	0.083	0.110	0.131	0.119	0.084	0.059	0.037	0.031
2.5–3	0.024	0.024	0.026	0.043	0.067	0.089	0.097	0.097	0.067	0.050	0.030	0.026
3–4	0.036	0.035	0.038	0.063	0.093	0.125	0.136	0.136	0.094	0.071	0.044	0.038
4–5	0.022	0.022	0.023	0.038	0.054	0.077	0.083	0.085	0.059	0.044	0.029	0.025
5–6	0.013	0.012	0.014	0.022	0.031	0.046	0.051	0.050	0.035	0.026	0.017	0.014
6–7	0.006	0.006	0.007	0.012	0.017	0.025	0.030	0.029	0.020	0.014	0.009	0.008
7–8	0.003	0.003	0.004	0.006	0.009	0.014	0.017	0.016	0.010	0.007	0.005	0.004
Sfc–8	0.258	0.385	0.311	0.533	0.787	1.138	1.263	1.248	0.847	0.602	0.378	0.306

W. H. Dines[7] gives the following data bearing on this subject.

1. Humidity records obtained from **250** registering balloons sent up over England and continental Europe show that the average moisture content of the atmosphere in winter, in terms of equivalent rainfall, varies between 0.25 in. and 0.80 in. with an average of about 0.40 in.; whereas in summer the mean is about 0.80 in. and ranges between 0.50 in. and 1.50 in. Therefore it appears that in summer the moisture content is just about twice as great as in winter.

2. The total depths of water contained in a column of saturated aqueous vapor at various temperatures are given in the following table. In this it is assumed that the maximum vapor pressure exists throughout and that the reduction in temperature is $10°$ F per kilometer of height, which is about the average normal rate prevailing in the lower strata.

Ground Temperature in ° F	Total Contents in in.
80	2.86
70	1.90
60	1.24
50	0.84
40	0.53
30	0.33
20	0.18

[7] *Symon's Meteorol. Mag.*, October 1918, pp. 95–97.

It should be kept clearly in mind that the previously stated figures represent, for the given ground temperatures and for the normal lapse rate, the total water content of the atmosphere when *saturated*. Alone, they provide no indication whatever of the amount of rainfall to be expected from such an air mass. As a matter of fact, there is no relationship between the amount of moisture in the air over any given area and the resulting precipitation. For instance, it is not uncommon for the atmosphere over the arid regions of the Southwest to contain a greater amount of moisture during any given period than is contained over an equal area in the North Central States; nevertheless there may be no precipitation in the first area and an abundance in the other. As an illustration, at El Paso, Texas, the average moisture content is nearly the same as at St. Paul, Minnesota (see Fig. 19). Yet at El Paso the mean annual precipitation is less than 8 in., whereas at St. Paul it is about 26 in. (see Fig. 25).

The foregoing tabulation, however, brings out the fact that the amount of rain that can fall at any given place is definitely limited, unless the supply is replenished from outside sources. For instance, with a ground temperature of 80° F, even though the air were completely saturated at the beginning and every drop of moisture in it were condensed and precipitated, the total resulting rainfall would be only 2.86 in. Actually, greater rains often occur at temperatures of 80° F or less. It thus appears that such rains must be supplied by inflowing winds from other areas.

Condensation

Condensation of atmospheric vapor results, in general, in the formation of clouds, but not all clouds produce precipitation. Close observation of small clouds on a hot day often reveals that they gradually grow smaller and smaller and finally disappear as a result of evaporation. It is, therefore, necessary to distinguish between the conditions that produce condensation and those that result in precipitation.

Condensation may result from any one or more of four principal causes, viz.:

1. Dynamic or adiabatic cooling.
2. Mixture of two air masses of different temperatures.
3. Contact cooling.
4. Radiational cooling.

Several other processes produce condensation but are of minor importance. Condensation resulting from mixing, contact, and radiational cooling occurs at such feeble rates that it seldom produces precipitation. Contact and radiational cooling cause the formation of dew, frost, and fog. The most important condensation process is adiabatic cooling, because it is the cause of nearly all precipitation.

Types of Precipitation

When unsaturated air at or near the earth's surface is carried to higher levels, either through convection or through other means, expansion will occur due to the reduction of pressure with altitude. Except near the earth's surface this expansion is adiabatic, meaning that no heat is added to the air from outside sources, and none is subtracted from it. However, its temperature is lowered because of the heat energy that is transformed into work in the process of expansion. This reduction in temperature is called *dynamic* or *adiabatic cooling*. It is the principal cause of condensation and is directly responsible for practically all rainfall.

Therefore it appears that a rising air column is a necessary antecedent to precipitation. It naturally follows that precipitation may be classified in accordance with the conditions that produce such a rising column, of which there are three:

1. Convectional.
2. Orographic.
3. Cyclonic.

Convectional precipitation is most common in the tropics but frequently occurs at many places in the United States during the summer. On a hot day the ground surface becomes heated unequally as does the air in contact with it. This causes the air to rise, expand, and cool dynamically, causing condensation and precipitation.

If because of a topographic barrier, moisture-laden air is forced to rise to higher levels, expansion, cooling, and precipitation follow. Where conditions are favorable for the production of this *orographic rainfall,* as it is called, the heaviest precipitation occurs. For instance, where the prevailing winds, heavily laden with moisture from the Pacific, strike the western slopes of the coast ranges in Washington and Oregon and are thereby forced to rise, the areas having the highest precipitation in the United States are to be found. Here is a region having a mean annual precipitation of over 100 in. Similar conditions are to be found at many other places such as the Philippines, the East Indies, and on the southern slope of the Himalayas near the head of the Bay of Bengal in India, where, at Cherrapunji, the average annual rainfall is nearly 500 in. Air may also be forced to rise when it passes from a water to a land area, without the aid of a mountain barrier. If in winter or at night, when the land is cooler than the water, moisture-laden air is carried over the land, two factors combine to produce precipitation: (1) the temperature of the air is lowered through contact with the cooler land and may be reduced below the dew point; (2) because of the greater roughness of the land surface, air turbulence and friction are increased, the velocity is retarded, and the depth of the air current is increased, forcing the upper air to rise and cool dynamically. Although relatively flat areas adjacent to large bodies of water oftentimes receive precipitation from these causes, these areas are not subject to such excessively high annual precipitation as noted above.

Especially throughout the central part of the United States the major portion of the precipitation is *cyclonic* in character. Cyclones are of two general classes, tropical and extratropical, so called depending upon whether they occur within or beyond the tropics. Inasmuch as all cyclones occurring in the United States are of the extratropical variety, this kind alone will be considered. When the word cyclone is used it will be understood to refer to the extratropical type. These cyclones are seldom destructive. A typical cyclone is a large whirling mass of air ranging from 500 miles to 1000 miles or more in diameter and normally having a velocity of about 30 miles per hour. At the center of this mass the barometric pressure is low; in the Northern Hemisphere the air approaches the center spirally in a counterclockwise direction with a vertical component. The central portion acts as a chimney through which the air rises, expands, cools dynamically, and produces condensation and usually precipitation.

In the United States, cyclones have certain fairly well-defined paths of travel. The most frequented path is that of those originating in northwestern United States and southwestern Canada which travel eastward along the Canadian border, dipping somewhat to the south as they approach the Great Lakes, and then passing out through the St. Lawrence valley. Some others having the same origin are deflected to the south in the general direction of the Gulf of Mexico. Numerous other paths are less frequently followed, but practically all are characterized by having a decidedly easterly component to their general direction. It usually requires about 4 days for one of these storm centers to cross the United States. The average speed of travel is about 30 miles per hour.

The approach of a cyclone is heralded by increasing cloudiness, rising temperature, a falling barometer, and shifting winds. If the path of the storm lies to the north of the observer, the wind usually sets in from the southeast and then shifts around to the south, the west, and finally the northwest. If the path is south of the observer, the wind at the beginning is from the northeast, then the north, the west, and finally from the southwest. Precipitation is usually confined to the southwest quadrant of the cyclonic area. With the passing of the storm center the temperature falls, the barometer rises, and the skies clear.

Cause of Cyclones

Numerous explanations of causes and conditions essential to the production of a cyclone have been advanced. The theory that has gained widest acceptance may be called the *air-mass concept*. Although it is not susceptible of definite proof and leaves unexplained certain features of cyclones, it appears to provide the most satisfactory and plausible explanation of these phenomena that has been proposed to date. For a clear understanding it is necessary first to review briefly the general atmospheric circulation.

At and near the thermal equator lies a belt perhaps 30° in width, throughout which, because of the more direct rays of the sun, the air near the earth's surface is heated, rises, expands, cools dynamically, and releases a portion of its moisture in convectional precipitation. It is important to keep in mind, however, that only that portion of the total moisture is precipitated that is in excess of its dew-point content after expansion. In other words, after this air has released its convective precipitation and has started its journey poleward, it is still relatively warm and is laden with moisture.

The lower atmosphere near the equator rotates about the earth's axis with nearly the same velocity as the earth's surface itself. Because of the diminishing diameter in the higher latitudes and, therefore, the lower linear velocity of rotation of the earth's surface, this air from the tropics flowing poleward has a greater easterly component of velocity than has the earth's surface, and hence to an observer on the ground it appears to be moving in a northeasterly direction. The northerly limits of such an air mass is called a *warm front*. In a similar manner, as the descending cold dry air in the polar regions spreads out and starts flowing toward the equator, it has an easterly velocity that is less than that of the earth's surface over which it flows, and, hence, to an observer it appears to be coming from the northeast. The southerly boundary of such an air mass is called a *cold front*. A warm front is, therefore, one in which warm air replaces colder air, whereas in a cold front the opposite occurs.

The surface separating the warm air mass and the cold air mass is called a frontal surface. In the Northern Hemisphere the frontal surface slopes upward toward the north, the air above the surface being warm, moist, and light, while that below is cold, dry, and heavy. For normal conditions in the middle latitudes, Petterssen[8] gives the slope of this surface as being approximately 1 in 100. In a cold front, the moving cold air is in contact with the earth so that the layers of air nearer the ground are retarded by friction and turbulence, causing a relatively steep frontal surface (Fig. 20a). Thus the warm moist air is forced to rise abruptly, producing intense rains over small areas. The lower strata of warm air in a warm front are also retarded, but in this instance the effect is to produce a flattened slope (Fig. 20b). As a result, the moist air rises relatively slowly, the rainfall being spread over a large area. Hence, cold fronts produce intense storms that cause greatest floods on small drainage basins, whereas warm fronts are accompanied by more widespread storms that are productive of the maximum floods on large drainage basins.

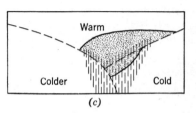

(a)

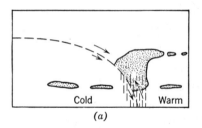

(b)

Fig. 20. After Petterssen. By permission from *Introduction to Meteorology,* by Sverre Petterssen, copyrighted 1941 by McGraw-Hill.

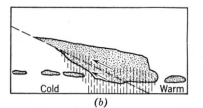

(c)

[8] S. Petterssen, *Introduction to Meteorology,* McGraw-Hill, second edition, 1958.

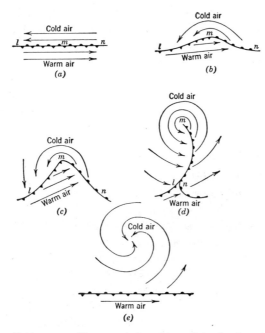

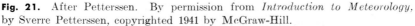

Fig. 21. After Petterssen. By permission from *Introduction to Meteorology*, by Sverre Petterssen, copyrighted 1941 by McGraw-Hill.

Assume now that two air masses approach each other in the Northern Hemisphere, one from the tropics and the other from the polar regions. By the time they meet between latitudes 30° and 60° they will be moving nearly in easterly and westerly directions respectively. In Fig. 21a let *lmn* represent the intersection with the ground of the frontal surface separating the two air masses. It is now seen that this surface is a surface of discontinuity not only with respect to temperature, density, and moisture content but also with respect to velocity. It is this last feature that explains the formation of cyclones. The shear stresses and turbulence occurring at the surface of discontinuity tend to cause waves as shown in Figs. 21b and 21c. The entire wave is moving to the right, *lm* being a cold front and *mn* a warm front. In its later stages the cold front gradually overtakes the warm front as shown in Fig. 21d, thus forcing upward the warm moist air that occupied the intervening space to form what is called an occluded front. A section through an occluded front is shown in Fig. 20c. When the wave has developed to the stage shown in Fig. 21d it is called a cyclone. Petterssen states that the time required for the cyclone to develop to the stage shown in Fig. 21c usually requires 12 to 24 hr, while the remaining stages require 2 to 3 days. In the final stages the cyclone is simply a large mass of whirling air (Fig. 21e) which gradually dissipates its energy by means of shear.

The preceding discussion was presented for the purpose of giving the reader an elementary knowledge of cyclones. For a more complete and detailed presentation of this subject the reader is referred to Petterssen,[9] from whom this discussion was largely taken, or to any other standard textbook on meteorology.

Thunderstorms

Ordinarily the most intense rainfalls that occur on small areas are the result of thunderstorms. This type of storm occurs in all parts of the earth, although its frequency decreases rapidly from the tropics, where there may be as many as 200 per yr, toward the polar regions, where the average occurrence is less than once a year. They are also more common over land and in mountainous regions than over water and in level country. In the United States, thunderstorms range in frequency from about 60 per yr in the Gulf States to about 15 to 20 per yr along the Canadian boundary, except on the Pacific Coast where they occur on an average of only about twice a year.

When a thunderstorm first develops, it usually covers but a small area, perhaps not more than 3 or 4 square miles. As it advances it spreads out so that the area covered is pear-shaped. The average life of a thunderstorm is about 6 hr, at the end of which time the frontal length is oftentimes between 50 and 100 miles with a depth about half as great. Their usual travel is from west to east and with an average velocity of about 30 miles per hour. They most frequently occur in the southern quadrants of a cyclonic low.

The most outstanding characteristic of a thunderstom is a strong vertical air current supporting a cumulus cloud with a cauliflower-shaped head. Within this characteristic feature is contained a clue to the cause of the thunder and lightning and the heavy downpour of rain that accompanies these storms. It has been experimentally determined that raindrops, regardless of size, cannot fall through air of normal density at velocities greater than about 18 miles per hour. Large drops, upon attaining this velocity, break up into smaller drops whose speeds cannot, because of friction, exceed this limiting value. It has also been demonstrated by Simpson[10] that the breaking up of raindrops is productive of electrical energy, some of the drops

[9] *Ibid.*

[10] G. C. Simpson, "Physics of the Air," *Mem. Indian Meteorol. Dept.*, Simla, India.

becoming negatively charged and some positively. Suppose that in the turbulent air of a cumulo-nimbus cloud, raindrops form and start to descend. Caught in a strong vertical updraft they are broken into smaller drops and carried back to higher levels where they again coalesce and start to descend, only to repeat their previous experience. Throughout this time the cloud's water content is being constantly increased by the condensation from the rising air current. However, this process cannot go on indefinitely. Eventually, unless other processes have developed in the meantime, the weight of the water being supported will retard the rising air current enough to permit the rain to descend. This descent is accompanied by thunder and lightning, usually, however, only after an abundant supply, sufficient to produce an intense downpour, has been stored up.

The Formation of Raindrops

It has been previously mentioned that condensation does not necessarily cause precipitation. Condensation forms fog or clouds which consist of small droplets of water having an average diameter according to Petterssen[11] of 40 microns. Raindrops, on the other hand, have diameters varying from 500 to 4000 microns. It follows that some process which will increase the size of the drops is necessary before precipitation will occur. Petterssen indicates that there are two principal methods by which precipitation is thought to occur. The more important one, known as Bergeron's theory, requires that particles of ice and droplets of water, cooled below freezing temperature, be mixed in a cloud. For subfreezing temperatures the saturation vapor pressure is lower at an ice surface than at a water surface. The air in the cloud will have a vapor pressure somewhere between these two saturation pressures. As a result the water droplets will evaporate and at the same time condensation will occur on the ice particles. Large droplets are thus built up which begin to fall. In falling they collide and combine with other droplets to further increase their size.

A second process of forming raindrops which does not require subfreezing temperatures consists of mixing warm and cold droplets together. Here again the vapor pressure of the air would be between the saturation vapor pressures of the warm and cold droplets. As a result, the warm droplets will evaporate, and at the same time condensation will occur on the cold drops. Showers produced by this method are usually quite light.

[11] S. Petterssen, *Introduction to Meteorology*, McGraw-Hill, second ed., 1958.

Measurement of Rainfall

In the United States daily measurements of rainfall are made at about 12,800 Weather Bureau stations. At about 3500 of these stations automatic continuous recorders provide records not only of the total daily precipitation but also of the intensity variations throughout the day. At the remainder, which are known as cooperative stations, observers read and record daily only the total precipitation for the preceding 24 hr.

Unfortunately observations are not made at a certain fixed hour. Most of the measurements are made in the late afternoon, usually about sundown, and are recorded as the precipitation for that day, although actually they represent the amount that fell during the preceding 24 hr. The records obtained at all automatic recording stations, and at a few others usually located at power plants, represent the precipitation occurring from midnight to midnight. An additional few observers make their readings in the mornings and record them as the precipitation falling on the preceding day. It is seen from the previous statements that at three adjacent stations, a 24-hr rain that may have fallen, let us say, on June 2, might be recorded at one station as having fallen on June 1 and 2, at another on June 2 and 3, and at a third on June 2 only.

Because of this situation, in determining the mean depth of rainfall on an area for each day of a storm, it is necessary to adjust the precipitation records obtained at some of the stations so that the daily values for all the stations will be for the same 24-hour period. For instance, assume that the following records are available from southeastern Michigan.

	Detroit*	Eloise	Monroe†	Ypsilanti	Ann Arbor
June 1	0.	0.	1.08	0.	0.
June 2	3.20	2.35	1.46	1.72	1.60
June 3	0.	0.47	0.	0.33	0.22
Totals	3.20	2.82	2.54	2.05	1.82

* Recording gage; records are from midnight to midnight.

† Readings are taken at 8 A.M. and recorded for the day preceding. All other readings are made at about sundown and are for the preceding 24 hr.

In this case, as usual, most of the records cover the period from sundown to sundown. It is, therefore, easiest to adjust the other records to cover the same period. If the Detroit continuous record were available, from it the total catch prior to sundown could be determined and this would be taken as the rainfall at Detroit for June 2 and the remainder would be considered as having fallen on June 3. If the continuous record at Detroit were not at hand, then Eloise is the nearest station, and its records would be used for prorating the total Detroit catch between June 2 and June 3, giving 2.67 in. for June 2 and 0.53 in. for June 3. To determine the Monroe rainfall for the same periods beginning and ending at sundown, the Eloise and Ypsilanti records are used because they are about equidistant from Monroe, and both are nearer than Detroit and Ann Arbor. On the average, 84 per cent of the rain that fell during this storm at Eloise and Ypsilanti fell before sundown on June 2, and 16 per cent fell after that time. Prorating the total Monroe catch on this same basis results in 2.12 in. for June 2 and 0.42 in. for June 3. Although of course values thus obtained will not be exactly correct, they will seldom be greatly in error.

Nonrecording Rain Gages. At the cooperative stations, standard U. S. Weather Bureau rain gages such as those shown in Fig. 22 are used. This gage consists of a can, B, 8 in. in diameter and 24 in. deep. Fitted over the top is a copper receiver, A, whose top rim is a knife edge. The bottom consists of a funnel that carries the water into the brass

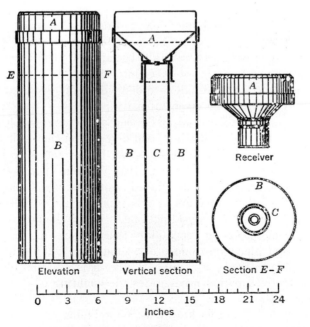

Elevation   Vertical section   Section E-F

Fig. 22.

measuring tube, C. A measuring stick 24 in. long by $\frac{3}{8}$ in. wide and about $\frac{1}{8}$ in. thick completes the equipment. The cross-sectional area of the measuring tube minus the cross-sectional area of the measuring stick is exactly one tenth of the area of the opening of the receiver; in other words, the measured depth of water in the tube is ten times the actual depth of rainfall. The tube filled with water and containing the measuring stick therefore represents 2 in. of rainfall. If the day's rainfall exceeds 2 in., the excess overflows into the 8-in. can. In such cases, when the observer makes his reading he first submerges the measuring stick, empties the measuring tube, and then pours this excess into the tube for measurement.

Recording Rain Gages. Although there are a number of different types of recording rain gages, only three have gained widespread use, (1) tipping bucket, (2) weighing, and (3) float.

For years the tipping-bucket gage has been commonly used. This gage consists of a bucket that is divided into two compartments so arranged that when the one is filled the bucket tips, empties, and brings the other into position. When it in turn is filled, it tips back to its original position, and so on. The bucket is electrically connected with a recorder so that, inasmuch as 0.01 in. of rain on the opening of the receiver fills a compartment, each tipping records 0.01 in. of rainfall.

There are two principal objections to this type of gage. In the first place, if the buckets are designed to tip at exactly the right instant for any given intensity of rainfall, because of inertia they will tip either too soon or too late for other intensities. As a result, both the intensity and the total rainfall recorded will be in error, except during the period when that one given intensity prevails. The total rainfall, as determined from the record at the end of the day, can be corrected by measuring the water that has been dumped by the buckets into the bottom of the gage. The intensities can be corrected by judiciously distributing the total error among the different periods when the intensity as recorded exceeded the intensity for which the gage was designed. The other objection to this type of gage is based upon the inconvenient form of the record obtained. When the intensity of rainfall is high, the bucket tips so rapidly that the jogs in the record tend to overlap and blend into one broad solid line, making it difficult if not impossible to read. Furthermore, the determination of the intensity for any given period necessitates the counting of the jogs in the record during that period.

Another type of recorder known as the weighing gage is widely used. In this instrument, illustrated in Fig. 23, the receiver rests on a weigh-

Fig. 23. Stevens snow-rain recorder. Courtesy Leupold and Stevens Instruments.

ing scale which actuates a pen that draws a graph in the form of a mass diagram of the rainfall. Such a record is shown in Fig. 24. Inasmuch as in this graph the abscissas represent time and the ordinates represent inches depth of rainfall, the slope of the graph with respect to the horizontal axis gives the intensity of the rainfall. It is, therefore, an easy matter to determine from the graph the average intensity of rainfall for any given period. As an illustration in Fig. 24 the total rainfall up to 2:25 P.M was 0.58 in.; at 2:35 P.M it was 1.09 in.; hence,

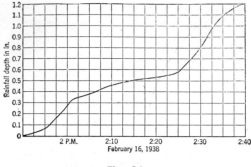

Fig. 24.

in this 10-min period a depth of 0.51 in. fell, and the average rate was therefore 3.06 in. per hr. This method of measuring both the intensity and the total rainfall is believed to give more accurate results than can be obtained by the tipping-bucket type of gage, and its use is becoming more general.

The float gage is quite similar to the weighing gage. The pen is actuated by a float on the water surface in the receiver in the same manner as for the water-stage recorders described in greater detail in Chapter 12. The record produced by this gage is also in the form of a mass diagram as illustrated by Fig. 24.

Use of Radar. Techniques have been developed[12] for using radar as an aid in the measurement of rainfall. Although some quantitative determinations can be made by means of radar, its principal value is in the determination of the areal extent, orientation, and movement of rain storms. This method is usually used to supplement data obtained from a network of rain gages.[13]

Measurement of Snowfall

The equivalent depth of water contained in any snowfall may be found by melting a sample obtained at a point where no drifting has occurred. The 8-in. rain-gage cylinder is inverted and used as a cookie cutter in obtaining the sample. A measured quantity of hot water is poured into the can, the snow is melted, and the mixture is measured in the brass tube. The difference between these measured quantities is the depth of water precipitated.

[12] *Proceedings, Conference on Water Resources,* Part III Radar-Weather, *Bull.* 41, Illinois State Water Survey, 1952.

[13] F. A. Hunt, R. G. Semonin, S. A. Changnon, Jr., and D. M. A. Jones, "Severe Rainstorms in Illinois," *Rept. of Investigation* No. 25, Illinois State Water Survey, 1958.

At cooperative U. S. Weather Bureau stations, the usual practice is to melt the catch obtained in the standard 8-in. cylinder with the receiver and measuring tube removed. Usually this method gives results that are too low because of the effect of the wind in deflecting snow over and around the gage. Several different types of shields have been devised for the purpose of eliminating this error.

Annual Precipitation

Figure 25 is a map showing the variation in the mean annual precipitation in the United States as prepared by the U. S. Weather Bureau. It may be seen that the highest precipitation occurs along the northern Pacific coast where values in excess of 100 in. are not unusual. Just east of the coastal mountain ranges there lies a belt of very low annual rainfall, varying from 5 to 10 in. From this region eastward through the Rocky Mountain area the precipitation is irregularly distributed, with small areas of relatively high rainfall but for the most part less than 20 in. East of the Rockies, beginning at about the 101st meridian, the annual precipitation increases in an easterly and southerly direction culminating in values ranging from 40 to 64 in. along the Gulf coast, and in some mountainous areas. Records obtained by the U. S. Forest Service show annual values as great as 80 in. at several places in the highest mountains. It is interesting that the 101st meridian, running from Texas to the Dakotas, corresponds approximately to the 20-in. rainfall line as well as to the western boundary of the corn belt.

Variations in Annual Rainfall

With rainfall records covering only a limited period at any station, it is of course impossible to determine the true long-term mean. If the period covered by the records is more than 30 yr, however, the average does not depart greatly from the true mean. Alexander Binnie[14] made a study of the periodic variation in rainfall, and his findings are shown in Fig. 26 in the form of a curve giving the average percentage of deviation from the true mean for records whose lengths are shown as abscissas. For instance, according to this figure any record 5 yr in length is likely to be nearly 15 per cent in error; a record 10 yr in length is probably within 8.2 per cent of the true mean; one 20 yr in length should be within 3.3 per cent of the correct value, and so on. Records 30 or 40 yr in length in all probability give the

[14] Alexander Binnie, "The Variation in Rainfall," *Proc. Inst. Civil Engrs.* (*London*), Vol. 109.

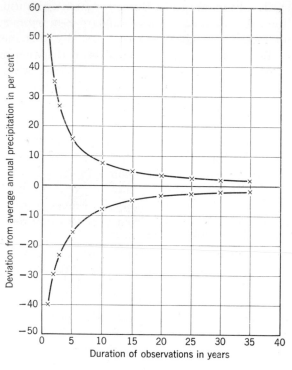

Fig. 26.

true long-term mean rainfall with an average error of about 2 per cent, which is ordinarily near enough for all practical purposes.

Binnie analyzed data from 26 stations having periods of observation of 50 to 59 yr, to obtain the values for the curves of Fig. 26 for durations of 5 to 35 yr. For the shorter durations (1 to 3 yr), the points on the curves are averages from 153 stations for periods varying from 33 to 97 yr. The rain gages were located in Europe, the United States, Canada, South America, Africa, India, Australia, and Asia. The values used in plotting the curves are averages for all the stations. Extreme differences from the average annual precipitation at individual stations were approximately 2.35 times as great as those shown. Binnie found no significant differences from the values presented in Fig. 26, either for different locations or for differences in average annual precipitation.

As explained in the preceding paragraphs, the total annual rainfall occurring at any station varies greatly from year to year. Furthermore these variations appear to be most irregular. The dotted line in Fig. 27a represents the fluctuations in the annual rainfall at Lansing, Michigan, over a 90-yr period. From this graph it is difficult to judge whether there is any tendency for the rainfall to increase and decrease in a cyclic manner. In only one 5-yr period (from 1880 to 1885) was the annual rainfall for every year appreciably above the average, and never were there 5 successive years below the average.

If, however, a curve is plotted representing progressive 5-yr means as shown by the solid line in Fig. 27a, a somewhat different picture is presented. In the construction of this curve the value of 29.83 in. for 1866 is the average of the total annual rainfalls for 1866 and for the two preceding and the two succeeding years. In a similar manner, the value of 30.78 in. for 1867 is the average for the 5 yr from 1865 to 1869 inclusive.

If one had only the records covering the period from 1870 to 1910 he might draw the conclusion that there is a 20-yr cycle in rainfall. The subsequent records, however, do not indicate such cyclic variation. For instance in 1922 and 1923, at the very time that, if there are regular cycles, a peak should be occurring, the graph shows that there is actually less than average rainfall. Furthermore the progressive 5-yr mean rainfall at Ann Arbor, Michigan, shown in Fig. 27, does not reveal any such 20-yr cycles. In this graph, peaks occur in 1882, 1892, 1904, and 1918, with intervening periods of 10, 12, and 14 yr. The 5-yr progressive mean at Ann Arbor for 1918 lacks only a fraction of an inch of being the highest on record, whereas at Lansing the corresponding value is about the average. If there are any regular cyclic variations in rainfall, it seems but reasonable that the forces and causes controlling them must be vast and far-reaching in extent. Most assuredly they cannot be local, or all rainfall records, at least in a given locality, would necessarily exhibit the same cyclic variations. The fact that the records at different stations located not far apart oftentimes show strikingly different characteristics seems to present strong evidence that the variations in annual rainfall are very largely governed by chance and not by any universal law.

In this connection attention might be called to the records obtained at Mt. Pleasant, Bay City, and adjacent cities in Michigan for 1911. At Mt. Pleasant the total recorded rainfall for this year was 16.31 in., the lowest in 40 yr of records. At Bay City, 45 miles from Mt. Pleasant, the corresponding rainfall was 46.67 in., the highest in 44 yr of records. At Midland, which is only 20 miles from Bay City, the total rainfall for 1911 was 17.05 in.; and at Alma, less than 20 miles from Mt. Pleasant, it was 35.31 in. These figures well illustrate the large differences that oftentimes occur in the amount of rainfall experienced

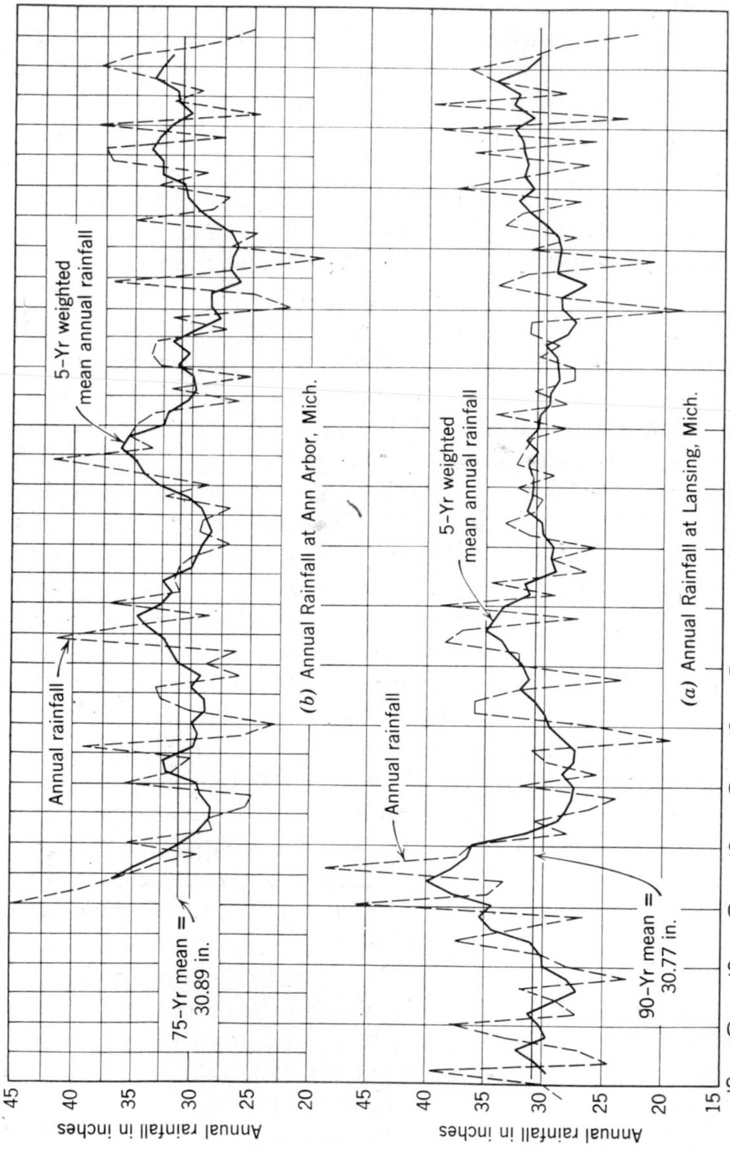

5-Yr weighted mean annual rainfall
Annual rainfall
75-Yr mean = 30.89 in.
(b) Annual Rainfall at Ann Arbor, Mich.
5-Yr weighted mean annual rainfall
Annual rainfall
90-Yr mean = 30.77 in.
(a) Annual Rainfall at Lansing, Mich.
Annual rainfall in inches
Annual rainfall in inches
45
40
35
30
25
20
15
1865
1870
1875
1880
1885
1890
1895
1900
1905
1910
1915
1920
1925
1930
1935
1940
1945
1950
1955

Fig. 27.

at different stations not far apart and in an area throughout which the rainfall characteristics do not vary greatly.

Mean Rainfall on Basin

Three methods are commonly used for computing the mean rainfall on an area, viz., (1) arithmetic mean, (2) Thiessen mean, and (3) isohyetal method. As will presently appear, the first two are purely mechanical processes requiring no special skill or judgment; on the other hand, the results obtained by the third method, which perhaps should be the most accurate, depend for their accuracy upon the good judgment of the person making the computations. These methods may be used for determining the mean depth of rainfall on an area either during a storm or for any longer period such as a month, year, or period of record.

Arithmetic Mean. As the name implies, this result is obtained by dividing the sum of the depths recorded at all the stations on the basin by the number of stations. If the stations are uniformly distributed over the basin and the rainfall varies in a regular manner, the results obtained by this method will not differ appreciably from those obtained by either of the other methods. On the other hand, if records are available at a relatively few irregularly spaced stations and there is a large variation in rainfall over the area, the arithmetic mean is likely to differ considerably from the more accurate results derived by either of the other methods.

Thiessen Mean.[15] In the application of this method, adjacent stations are joined by straight lines thus dividing the entire area into a series of triangles (Fig. 28). Perpendicular bisectors are erected on each of these lines, thereby forming a series of polygons, each containing one and only one rainfall station. The entire area within any polygon is nearer to the rainfall station contained therein than to any other, and it is therefore assumed that the rainfall recorded at that station should apply to that area. If P is the mean rainfall on the basin whose area is A, and $P_1, P_2 \cdots P_n$ represent rainfall records at the stations whose surrounding polygons have areas $A_1, A_2 \cdots A_n$, then

$$P = \frac{A_1P_1 + A_2P_2 + \cdots A_nP_n}{A} \tag{1}$$

or

$$P = \frac{A_1}{A} P_1 + \frac{A_2}{A} P_2 + \cdots \frac{A_n}{A} P_n \tag{2}$$

[15] A. H. Thiessen, "Precipitation Averages for Large Areas," *Monthly Weather Rev.,* July 1911, p. 1082.

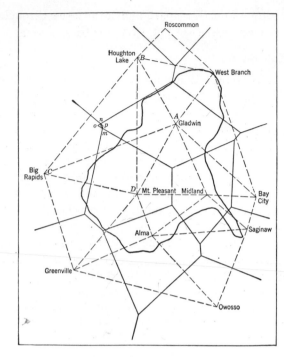

Fig. 28.

In constructing the triangles upon whose sides the perpendicular bisectors are erected, sometimes a question will arise as to which stations should form the vertices of a triangle. In Fig. 28, for instance, should the quadrilateral $ABCD$ be divided into triangles by the line AC or BD? Most frequently it is found that the correct line to be drawn is the shorter of the two diagonals, but this is not necessarily true, as in the present case. By drawing BD, which is shorter than AC, it is found that the polygons enclosing A and C overlap, forming a quadrilateral $onpm$, in which onm is nearer to C than to A and the area npm is nearer A than C. By drawing the diagonal AC, however, this difficulty is eliminated. Such cases can be determined only by trial.

Isohyetal Method. In Fig. 29, isohyets, or contours of equal rainfall, have been drawn. By planimetering the areas between adjacent isohyets, the mean rainfall on the basin can be found from equation 2, in which now $A_1, A_2 \cdots A_n$ are the areas between the successive isohyets and $P_1, P_2 \cdots P_n$ represent the mean rainfalls on the respective areas.

To obtain best results from this method, however, good judgment is required both in drawing the isohyets and in assigning the proper mean rainfall values to the areas between them. If the entire area is subject to the same rainfall no special judgment is necessary in drawing the isohyets, but if, for instance, the upper part of the basin were a high plateau the isohyets should perhaps be drawn as shown in Fig. 30. To provide a comparison of the results obtained by the above methods, the mean rainfall for June 1946, as determined (1) by the arithmetic mean of the stations within the basin is 2.78 in.; (2) by the Thiessen mean, 2.97 in.; and (3) by the isohyetal method, 3.08 in. If the isohyets were drawn as shown in Fig. 30, the mean would be 2.64 in.

An advantage possessed by both the isohyetal and Thiessen methods arises from the fact that stations located a short distance beyond the boundary of a drainage basin are used in determining the mean rainfall on the basin, but their influence diminishes as their distance from the boundary increases. This is as it should be. On the other hand, in the arithmetic-mean method every station has equal weight regardless of its location.

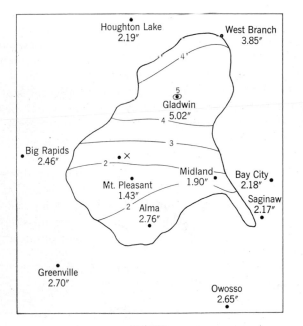

Fig. 29.

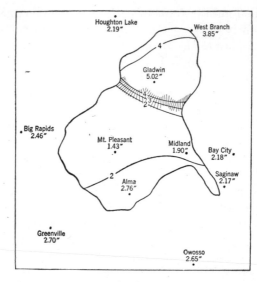

Fig. 30.

Supplementing Precipitation Records

It is often necessary to supplement certain incomplete rainfall records by estimating values that are missing at one or more stations. Supplementation is necessary, for instance, if one wishes to compare the mean rainfall on two drainage basins for a certain period and finds that the records are complete and satisfactory except for one storm. Such a record can be supplied by interpolation on an isohyetal map that has been prepared from records at adjacent stations. For example, the rainfall at station X in Fig. 29 would be estimated as 2.2 in.

For longer periods, as for instance a month or a year, it may be better to take into consideration the variation in the mean annual rainfall at the different stations. This can be done as follows. Suppose that for the period for which simultaneous records are available at A and B, the mean annual rainfall at A is 37.54 in. and at B it is 40.20 in. For the year in which the records are missing at A, the rainfall at B is 38.87 in. If we let P_A equal the rainfall at A for this year, then

$$\frac{P_A}{38.87} = \frac{37.54}{40.20}$$

and $$P_A = 36.30 \text{ in.}$$

If there are two or three other stations whose distance from A is about the same as that of B, we may follow the same procedure with them, thus obtaining three or four estimated values of P_A, the weighted mean of which may be taken as the most probable value.

Testing and Adjusting Precipitation Records

If it is known that a particular rain gage has been moved and that at one of the locations the records are likely to be inaccurate, perhaps owing to the presence of trees or buildings, it is desirable to test the accuracy of the records and adjust them if necessary. This may be done by plotting the accumulated rainfall at the gage in question against the average accumulated rainfall of a number of other nearby gages which are influenced by the same meteorological conditions.[16] An example of such a double-mass curve, presented by Kohler,[17] is

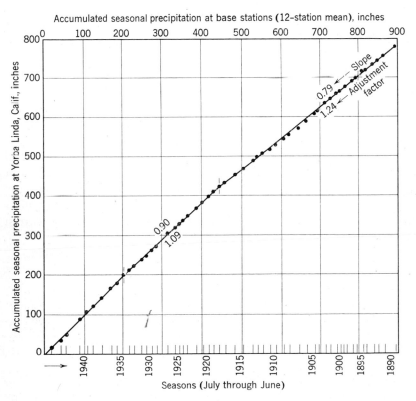

Fig. 31.

[16] C. F. Merriam, "A Comprehensive Study of the Rainfall of the Susquehanna Valley," *Trans. Am. Geophys. Union,* pp. 471–476, 1937.

[17] Max A. Kohler, "On the Use of Double-Mass Analysis for Testing the Consistency of Meteorological Records and for Making Required Adjustments," *Bull. Am. Meteorol. Soc.,* vol. 30, No. 5, pp. 188–189, 1949.

shown in Fig. 31. This curve shows two changes in slope, one at the end of 1917 and one near the end of 1934. If the rain gage was moved at about these dates, the curve can be expected to show the effects of the changes in location. It is, of course, necessary that the average of the group of gages used as a basis of comparison does not in itself have some inconsistency. Even though there is no reason to suspect that the values at one gage location are less accurate than those at another, it may be desirable to adjust the records to a single location for purposes of correlation with other hydrological data such as stream flow. In the example shown in Fig. 31, values from the earliest period of records were adjusted to the most recent period in the following manner. When the gage was in its final location, the rainfall at the gage was 0.98 (the slope of the line in Fig. 31 from 1935 to 1945) times the average for the 12 stations. At its original location the rainfall at the gage was only 0.79 times the average for the 12 stations. Therefore, the correction factor is 0.98/0.79 or 1.24.

Frequency of Intense Rainfalls

It often becomes necessary for the design of such structures as bridges, spillways, or culverts to determine the greatest rainfall that may be expected to occur with any given frequency. By frequency is meant the average recurrence interval of rains equal to or greater than a certain magnitude. For example, a 10-yr frequency for a 1-hr rain is that magnitude of hourly rainfall which can be expected to be equaled or exceeded ten times in 100 yr. It should not be construed that such rains will be separated by 10-yr intervals. It is much more likely that two or more will occur in any 10-yr period, and two or more may occur in one year or even in one month.

Rainfall frequency is determined at any location by arranging all of the larger rains of the selected duration in order of decreasing size, assigning the number one to the largest rain, two to the second largest, and so on. Then the frequency (T_r) of any rain is given by the equation

$$T_r = \frac{t}{m} \tag{3}$$

in which t is the total number of years of record and m is the number of the rain. For example, if there were 30 yr of records at a certain gage, the rain having the number ten was equaled or exceeded ten times in 30 yr, and its average recurrence interval was 30/10 or 3 yr.

It may be convenient to present the magnitudes and frequencies of a series of rains graphically. An example of such a graph is shown

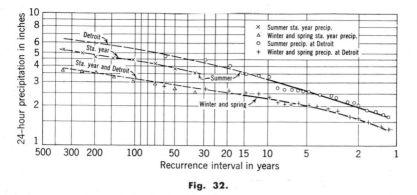

Fig. 32.

in Fig. 32. The values plotted are 24-hr summer rains and winter and spring rains at Detroit, Michigan. The magnitudes of the rains were determined from U. S. Weather Bureau records of daily precipitation in the manner described on page 98. The frequencies were determined from equation 3 as shown in Table 6, columns 1 through 4.

One of the difficulties in frequency determinations is that recurrence intervals for the larger rains cannot be accurately determined. As an illustration, the largest 24-hr summer rain at Detroit has a frequency of 58 yr according to equation 3, and is plotted in that position in Fig. 32. However, this value is based on only one 58-yr sample. If during the next 58-yr period no rain equal to or greater than this one were to occur, its frequency would be computed as 116 yr. If, on the other hand, two rains larger than this one were to occur during the next 58-yr period, its frequency would be 39 yr. Thus it may be seen that the frequency of the largest rain, as determined from equation 3, must be considered as an approximation, since it is known that the correct value could, with equal probability, be larger or smaller than the computed value.

Similar limitations apply in a decreasing degree to other rains having large recurrence intervals. In one study reported by the Weather Bureau,[18] frequencies were determined from 56 yr of records, but by using only the last ten of the 56 yr. The 2-yr frequency rain determined from ten years of records differed by 31 per cent from the value determined from the longer records. Furthermore, it was found that the magnitude of the rain which, on the basis of ten years of records, appeared to have a 2-yr frequency, had a recurrence interval of 4.5 yr on the basis of the entire 56 yr of records.

[18] U. S. Weather Bureau, "Rainfall Intensities for Local Drainage Design in the United States," *Tech. Paper* No. 24, Part I, 1955.

TABLE 6

Number of Rains (m)	Detroit $t = 58$ Years			Station-Year $t = 1744$ Years		
	Recurrence Interval (T_r) in Years	24-Hour Precip. in Inches		Recurrence Interval (T_r) in Years	24-Hour Precip. in Inches	
		Summer	Winter and Spring		Summer	Winter and Spring
(1)	(2)	(3)	(4)	(5)	(6)	(7)
1	58	4.75	2.79	1744	6.81	4.72
2	29	4.51	2.71	872	5.98	4.56
3	19.3	4.06	2.62	581	5.47	4.33
4	14.5	3.51	2.51	436	5.31	4.00
5	11.6	3.41	2.49	349	5.30	3.70
6	9.7	3.36	2.34	291	5.13	3.65
7	8.3	2.75	2.16	249	4.96	3.60
8	7.3	2.70	2.12	218	4.75	3.57
9	6.5	2.70	2.10	194	4.70	3.57
10	5.8	2.63	2.09	174	4.63	3.55
12	4.8	2.60	2.04	145	4.58	3.32
14	4.2	2.51	2.02	125	4.57	3.19
17	3.4	2.42	1.93	103	4.41	3.08
20	2.9	2.38	1.83	87	4.27	3.04
25	2.3	2.17	1.69	70	4.18	2.94
35	1.66	1.83	1.52	50	3.85	2.70
50	1.16	1.65	1.34	35	3.53	2.54

Statisticians have attempted to find methods of plotting frequency data so that they will fall in a straight line, in the hope that such a line, established by the lower values, could be extended to larger return intervals. A number of such procedures have been summarized by Chow.[19] Most methods of this kind are based on an assumed statistical distribution of the values. While any procedure which causes the plotted points to fall nearly on a straight line is helpful, it must be remembered that the points themselves represent the frequency relationship at a rain gage better than any assumed statistical arrangement. The authors have found the logarithmic plotting shown in Fig. 32 to be as satisfactory as any other method.

[19] V. T. Chow, "A General Formula for Hydrologic Frequency Analysis," *Trans. Am. Geophys. Union,* pp. 231–237, April 1951.

An extensive study of rainfall frequencies in the United States was made by the Department of Agriculture.[20] Figures **33** and **34** are reproductions of two isohyetal charts from this publication. Similar graphs for frequencies varying from 2 to 100 yr and for durations varying from 5 min to 24 hr were also prepared. More recently, frequency studies were made at selected locations by the Weather Bureau.[21,22] Care should be used in determining frequencies from generalized charts such as those shown in Fig. 33 and Fig. 34 or from studies at neighboring locations, because local conditions may cause differences in rainfall characteristics. If records are available, it is always better to make frequency studies with data obtained at the location where they are to be used.

The *station-year method*[23] has been used to estimate recurrence intervals which are longer than can be accurately derived from records of a single station. This method is based on the idea that all locations in a meteorologically homogeneous area (see page **91**) will experience similar rainfall frequencies, and that if these stations are widely enough separated the total of the rainfall experiences at all of the stations will be similar to the experience of any one station, over a period of records equal to the sum of the periods at the individual stations. As an example, the maximum summer rains and winter and spring 24-hr rains at **37** stations located within 100 miles of Detroit were arranged in decreasing order, as shown in Table 6, columns 6 and 7. The total duration of the records from the 37 gages was 1744 yr. The frequencies shown in column 5 were determined from equation 3 and plotted in Fig. 32. It is of interest to note that the summer station-year curve falls below the summer curve for Detroit, whereas the spring curves are in close agreement. This is because the summer rainfall at Detroit is greater than that of the surrounding locations. For example, the frequency curve for Port Huron, which is approximately 60 miles from Detroit, agrees very well with the station-year curve. Even though the summer station-year curve is not in close agreement with the Detroit curve, it is of great value as a guide in the extension of the Detroit curve to large recurrence

[20] David L. Yarnell, "Rainfall Intensity-Frequency Data," *U. S. Dept. Agr. Misc. Publ.* No. 204, 1935.

[21] U. S. Weather Bureau, "Rainfall Intensity-Duration-Frequency Curves," *Tech. Paper* No. 25, 1955

[22] U. S. Weather Bureau, "Rainfall Intensities for Local Drainage Design in the United States," *Tech. Paper* No. 24, Parts I and II, 1953 and 1954.

[23] Katharine Clarke-Hafstad, "Reliability of Station-Year Rainfall-Frequency Determinations," *Trans. A.S.C.E.,* p. 633, 1942.

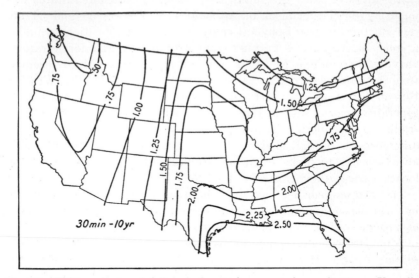

Fig. 33.   Thirty-minute rainfall, in inches, to be expected once in 10 yr.   Yarnell.

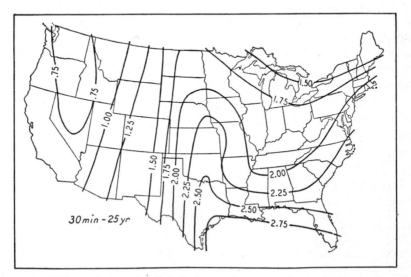

Fig. 34.   Thirty-minute rainfall, in inches, to be expected once in 25 yr.   Yarnell.

intervals. It should be noted that the largest rain plotted on the station-year curves has a recurrence interval of 349 yr, and that there are five 349-yr samples available for this analysis.

Relation between Storm Frequency and Mean Annual Rainfall

If throughout any area the probability of occurrence of a storm of any given intensity is the same at every point, that area is said to be *meteorologically homogeneous*. Everywhere in such an area the rainfall expectancy is the same. Inasmuch as the annual rainfall is the total depth of the rains of all different intensities, it necessarily follows that if everywhere throughout a given area or in two different areas the frequency of storms of all different intensities is the same, the average annual rainfall must also be the same at all points within such areas. The converse of this proposition is not necessarily true, however, because on two different areas having the same total annual rainfall those totals may be made up of an infinite number of combinations of depths of rains of different intensities. As an illustration, in southwestern United States and in north central Canada there are areas in each of which the mean annual rainfall is 20 in. In southwestern United States this total depth of 20 in. usually results from a few storms of short duration but of high intensity, whereas in north central Canada the corresponding total is usually the result of a much greater number of storms of longer duration but of lesser intensities. These two areas, therefore, have the same mean annual rainfall but are not meteorologically homogeneous.

The same factors affect and determine the mean annual rainfall of an area as affect its meteorological homogeneity. These factors are as follows:

1. Distance from the ocean.
2. Direction of prevailing winds.
3. Mean annual temperature.
4. Altitude.
5. Topography.

These influences are more or less interdependent. For instance, normally, with prevailing winds from the ocean, the mean annual rainfall will be high near the shore and, except when the topography is steep and precipitous, will decrease slowly toward the interior. However, if the prevailing winds are from the land to the sea, the mean annual rainfall will not be excessive even near the shore, and the effect of the ocean's presence will not be noticeable for any considerable distance inland.

The condition most favorable for a high mean annual rainfall and likewise for a high frequency of intense storms is found on the ocean side of a mountain range near the coast, in the tropics, at an altitude of 4000 to 5000 ft and with the prevailing winds from the sea. Without the mountain range or without the presence of the ocean, with lower mean annual temperature, with lower altitude, or with a different direction of prevailing winds, the frequency of intense storms and the mean annual rainfall would be correspondingly reduced.

Because of the interrelationship existing between these various influences it is impossible with our present limited knowledge to express quantitatively the effect that each of these factors has upon mean annual rainfall and frequency of intense storms. The best that can be done at present is to recognize the existence and character of these various influences and thereby, with the aid of mean annual rainfall records, determine whether or not two different areas are meteorologically homogeneous. In all probability if two stations have the same average annual precipitation and the same average number of days of rainfall per year, they are meteorologically homogeneous.

Intensity-Duration Curves

The use of precipitation data for hydrological purposes requires information concerning magnitudes of rains of various frequencies and for specific durations. The relationship between duration, intensity, and frequency at any location may be determined from an analysis of the rainfall records obtained at that location. First, the magnitudes of rains of various frequencies are derived in the manner previously described and illustrated in Table 6 for a number of selected durations, as for example, 5 min, 15 min, 30 min, 60 min, and so on. If, then, average intensity is plotted against duration *for a particular frequency,* a curve having a shape similar to one of those shown in Fig. 35 can be drawn through the points. For example, the No. 1.8 curve of Fig. 35 is approximately the 10-yr frequency curve for Ann Arbor, Michigan. Such a curve may be used to determine the average intensity of a 10-yr frequency rain for any desired duration. Such curves, called *intensity-duration* curves, provide one of the important tools for the prediction of runoff. The curves shown in Fig. 35 are generalized ones prepared by the U. S. Army Corps of Engineers. Curves derived for any particular location may differ somewhat from these.

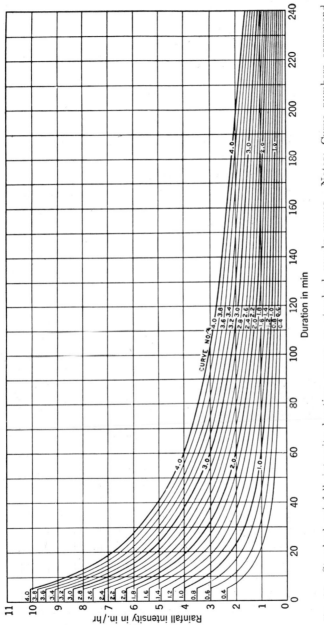

Fig. 35. Standard rainfall intensity–duration curves or standard supply curves. Notes: Curve numbers correspond to 1-hr values of rainfall or supply indicated by respective curves; all points on the same curve are assumed to have the same average frequency of occurrence. From *Engineering Manual* by Corps of Engineers, U. S. Army.

Intensity-duration curves can also be described by means of an equation of the following form,

$$p = \frac{A}{(t + B)^n} \tag{4}$$

in which p is the average rain intensity in inches per hour, t is the duration in minutes, and A, B, and n are constants. By taking the logarithms of both sides of this equation

$$\log p = \log A - n \log (t + B) \tag{5}$$

it can be seen that, if B is selected properly, the logarithms of p and $(t + B)$ should plot as a straight line having a slope equal to $-n$. The value of B is determined by plotting points with various assumed values of B until a straight line is established, after which A and n may be found graphically (see page 394).

A very important property of intensity-duration curves is that any one of the curves describes quite well the relation between maximum

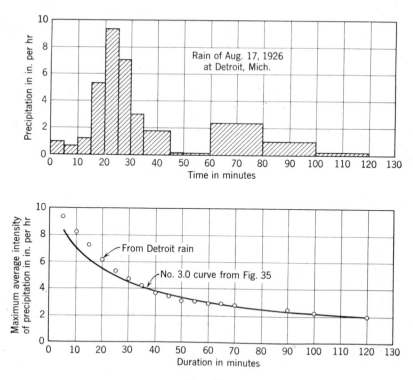

Fig. 36.

intensity and duration during an intense rainstorm. This is because, if the maximum hour of a rain has, let us say a 10-yr frequency, the maximum precipitation for other durations will also have about the same frequency. This is illustrated by the example shown in Fig. 36 in which actual intensities during a rainstorm are shown together with the intensity-duration curve derived from the same rain and the No. 3.0 curve from Fig. 35. The similarity between the points obtained from the single rainstorm and the generalized curve is apparent. Knowing that a typical intensity-duration curve can be derived from a single intense rain, we see that an intensity-duration curve may be used to determine a time-intensity pattern for a rain of any selected frequency. For example, suppose that a frequency study has shown that the 25-yr 30-min rain at a certain location has an intensity of 4.0 in. per hr. This rain falls on the 2.6 curve of Fig. 35. From this curve it may be seen that the probable average intensity during the maximum 60 min of a 25-yr rain would be 2.6 in. per hr, for the maximum 90 min, 2.0 in. per hr, and so on. The maximum 60 min of rain would include the maximum 30 min of rain, as well as the second largest

TABLE 7

Duration t, min	Precipitation Intensity p, in./hr	Accumulated Precipitation P, in.	Time Increments t, min	Precipitation during Time Increments P, in.	p in./hr
0					
			30	2.0	4.0
30	4.0	2.0			
			30	0.6	1.2
60	2.6	2.6			
			30	0.4	0.8
90	2.0	3.0			
			30	0.2	0.4
120	1.6	3.2			
0					
			10	1.05	6.3
10	6.3	1.05			
			10	0.55	3.3
20	4.8	1.60			
			10	0.40	2.4
30	4.0	2.00			

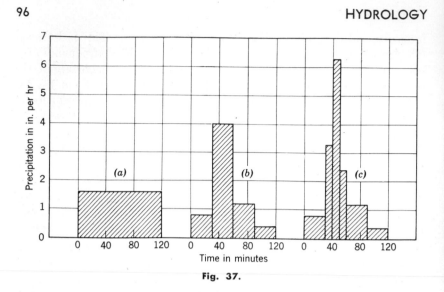

Fig. 37.

30-min period. The total rain during the maximum 30-min period would be $4.0 \times 30/60 = 2.0$ in. and during the maximum hour, $2.6 \times 60/60 = 2.6$ in. Therefore, the intensity during the second largest 30-min period would be $(2.6 - 2.0)/(30/60) = 1.2$ in. per hr. These computations as well as those for two additional 30-min periods are shown in Table 7. Also shown are computations of the average intensity during the three 10-min periods of heaviest rainfall for this same 25-yr rain. Results of these computations have been used to determine three possible intensity-time patterns, shown in Fig. 37, each of which is consistent with the 2.6 curve of Fig. 35. The arrangement of intensity-time patterns is arbitrary.

Time-Intensity Patterns for Daily Rainfall

In the previous section, the derivation of detailed time-intensity patterns was discussed. It is now the purpose to provide additional information concerning probable intensities and durations of rains which are designated as daily rains in the published records of the U. S. Weather Bureau. Daily rainfall values do not reveal the intensity patterns in sufficient detail to permit their use for many hydrologic purposes. This fact is well illustrated in the following example.

The published records of the daily rainfall at station 15–26 in the Muskingum basin show that 2.73 in. fell on June 27, 1939, and 1.96 in. on June 28. These records are for the 24-hr periods beginning at 8 A.M. on each of these days. If this rain fell at a uniform rate, its intensity might have been only slightly in excess of 0.1 in. per hr. Many soils are capable of absorbing such a rain and hence would yield no surface runoff. Consider, however, the intensity pattern, Fig. 38, which shows the depth of rainfall by 30-min periods. In the figure it is seen that during this storm there were two major periods of intense rainfall. During the first, 2.66 in. of rain fell in 4.5 hr, and during the second 1.86 in. fell in 1.5 hr. The average intensities during these periods were 0.59 in. per hr and 1.24 in. per hr respectively. Few soils are capable of absorbing such high rates of rainfall, and, therefore, because of this extremely variable rainfall pattern, surface runoff would occur.

Furthermore, instead of the picture presented by the daily records which show that 4.69 in. fell in 2 days, actually no rain fell on June 27, and 4.65 in. fell in a period of 17.5 hr on June 28. Nor is this an isolated example. A study of continuous gage records as shown either by a graph or by short-time-interval totals when compared with daily totals reveals the fact that usually the actual peak intensities are far greater than indicated by the published daily rainfall totals.

A study by Sherman[24] of the continuous rainfall records obtained at Chestnut Hill reservoir (Boston) extending over a period of 25 yr led him to the conclusion that the actual average duration of storms recorded as occurring in different numbers of days is as follows:

Recorded Duration	Actual Duration
1-day storms	13 to 14 hr
2-day storms	21 to 31 hr
3-day storms	43 to 47 hr
4-day storms	71 to 74 hr
5-day storms	83 to 84 hr

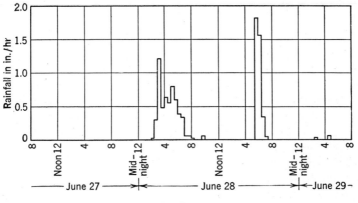

Fig. 38.

[24] C. W. Sherman, "Actual Duration of One-Day and Two-Day Rain Storms," *Civil Eng.*, March 1939.

He also found that the above relationships hold true regardless of the intensities of the storms.

Because the vast majority of the rainfall records that are available in any given locality were obtained by cooperative observers and give only the total rainfall for each 24-hr period prior to the time of observation, for the reasons stated above such records must be corrected before they are suitable for frequency-intensity studies. For this correction two general methods may be employed, viz., the recorded duration in days may be reduced to an estimated actual duration as indicated by Sherman's studies, or the recorded 1-day, 2-day, etc., storm depths may be corrected in some manner so that they will more nearly represent the actual maximum depths of rainfall occurring in any of these time periods.

If the first of these correction methods is employed, other studies similar to those made by Sherman in Boston should be carried on at various points throughout the country in order to determine whether the Boston relationships hold true generally. If it is found that they do not, such studies should determine the extent of the variations in different sections and the causes producing them.

The exact procedure to be followed in the correction of the recorded storm depth depends upon whether or not a recording gage was located within the storm area, preferably near the center. Two methods will be described. Their use will be illustrated in connection with a 2-day rainfall record.

1. If at least one continuous record is available, from this may be determined the maximum amount of rain that fell during any 24-hr period and also the percentage that this amount is of the total 2-day rainfall. This same percentage is then applied to the total 2-day rainfall as measured at each of the nonrecording stations located within the storm area. If, for instance, at the recording station 2.54 in. fell on the first day and 1.71 in. fell on the day following, and the graph shows that 3.74 in., or 88 per cent of the total, fell within a 24-hr period, and the record at a nonrecording station shows 2.45 in. on the first day and 3.70 in. on the second, then $0.88(2.45 + 3.70) = 5.41$ in., which is taken as the maximum 24-hr rainfall at this station. Although this value may not be correct, the chances are that it is much more nearly correct than the 3.70 in. as indicated by the records.

2. The second method, which is used only when no continuous record of the storm is available at any station, is based upon the law of probability. If the observer reads the gage at 6 p.m., a 24-hr rainfall is just as likely to start at 6 a.m. (or at any other hour) as at 6 p.m. If it begins at 6 a.m. and is of uniform intensity, this 24-hr rain having

a depth of, say, 6 in. will be recorded as a 2-day rain with 3 in. falling each day. With no continuous record available, however, it would be impossible to determine from the records whether this rain fell in 48 hr or in 24 hr or even in a much shorter period. As far as may be learned from the published records, it is possible that the maximum rainfall in any 24-hr period was 3 in. It is equally possible, however, that it was 6 in. These two figures therefore represent the minimum and the maximum depths of rain that could possibly have fallen at this station in any 24-hr period during this storm. The most probable value should be the mean of these two, or 4.5 in.

Therefore, if daily rainfall records indicate that rain fell on two or more successive days, in order to determine the probable maximum depth of rain that fell in any 24-hr period during that storm, to the maximum recorded total should be added one half of the larger total that fell on either the preceding or succeeding day, and so on for longer storms. For instance, suppose that the daily totals for three successive days are 1.20, 2.75, and 0.86 in. The maximum 24-hr total would be

$$2.75 + \tfrac{1}{2} \times 1.20 = 3.35 \text{ in.}$$

and the maximum 48-hr total would be

$$2.75 + 1.20 + \tfrac{1}{2} \times 0.86 = 4.38 \text{ in.}$$

Attention should be called to the fact, however, that often additional information concerning the time of beginning and end of rainfall may be obtained from the observer's notes, and when this is done the above approximation is unnecessary. Isochronal maps sometimes are of value in analyzing storm intensity patterns. These are further discussed in Chapter 9.

Variation of Average Precipitation with Area

Frequency-duration studies are usually made with point rainfall, i.e., the precipitation data from one gage. In applying precipitation data to drainage basins for the estimation of runoff it is necessary to estimate the average depth of precipitation on basins of various sizes. This may be accomplished by first determining magnitudes and frequencies of point rainfall within the basin and then reducing this value by an amount indicated by the areal distribution of major rains of record. Information regarding the average depth of individual rainstorms for areas of varying size has been collected and published by

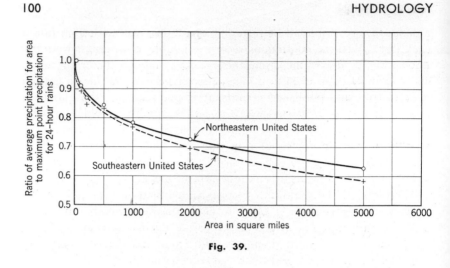

Fig. 39.

the Miami Conservancy District[25] and the U. S. Army Corps of Engineers.[26]

Fifty-one of the largest rains reported were analyzed to determine the ratio of the average precipitation for areas up to 5000 square miles and the maximum point rainfall for each storm. The maximum point rainfall for these 51 rains varied from 5.8 in. to 36.5 in. The rains were arranged in two groups, one for northeastern United States and one for the southeastern states. Averages of the ratios of average to maximum rainfall were determined for various areas. The results are shown in Fig. 39. It may be seen that both groups show a similar relationship, thus indicating that areal distribution patterns of individual rainstorms do not vary greatly with location. However, some individual storms differed greatly from the curves of Fig. 39, and it was noted that for several of the very largest rains of record the ratios decreased much more rapidly with area than the average trend shown by the curves. It was also found that ratios for rains of shorter durations than 24 hr fell slightly below the curves of Fig. 39, whereas for longer durations the values were somewhat larger. These curves may be used to estimate the average depth of rainfall for any area corresponding to a point rainfall of a selected magnitude and frequency. In using curves of this kind it is usually assumed that the point rainfall covers an area of 10 square miles.

Many studies have been made to determine the variation of maxi-

[25] Miami Conservancy District, "Storm Rainfall of Eastern United States," *Tech. Rept.,* Part V, Dayton, Ohio.
[26] U. S. Army Corps of Engineers, "Storm Rainfall in the United States." 1953.

mum or near-maximum precipitation with area.[27,28,29] Such studies
are based on envelope curves of all maximum rains of record, and the
decrease of average precipitation with area is likely to be greater than
for a typical large rainstorm. A series of studies relating point rainfall
at the geographical center of an area to average over the area has
been reported by Huff and Niell.[30]

Maximum Precipitation

For some purposes, as for example the design of the spillways of
large dams, it is necessary to estimate the maximum rainfall ever to
be expected. This may be done by transposing to the area of the
drainage basin the largest rains that have been recorded within the
region which is meteorologically homogeneous with the basin. Records
of such rains have been published in the references cited on page 101.
The Weather Bureau and the Corps of Engineers have estimated the
maximum probable precipitation for various durations and areas east
of the 105th meridian.[31] Their values are based on the transposition of
maximum storms, with adjustments for differences in elevation and
moisture content of the atmosphere. The largest recorded rains in
the United States for various durations are shown in Fig. 40.[32] A
method of storm transposition, known as the isopercental method,
which is especially applicable to mountainous areas, is described in
Chapter 9.

[27] Robert D. Fletcher, "A Relation between Maximum Observed Point and
Areal Rainfall Values," *Trans. Am. Geophys. Union*, June 1950, pp. 344–348.

[28] U. S. Weather Bureau and U. S. Army Corps of Engineers, "Seasonal Variation of the Probable Maximum Precipitation East of the 105th Meridian,"
Hydrometeorological Rept. No. 33, 1956.

[29] M. C. Boyer, "A Correlation of the Characteristics of Great Storms," *Trans.
Am. Geophys. Union*, April 1957, pp. 233–238.

[30] F. A. Huff and J. C. Niell, "Areal Representativeness of Point Rainfall,"
Trans. Am. Geophys. Union, June 1957, pp. 341–345.

[31] See note 27.

[32] U. S. Weather Bureau, "Maximum Recorded United States Point Rainfall,"
Tech. Paper No. 2, 1947.

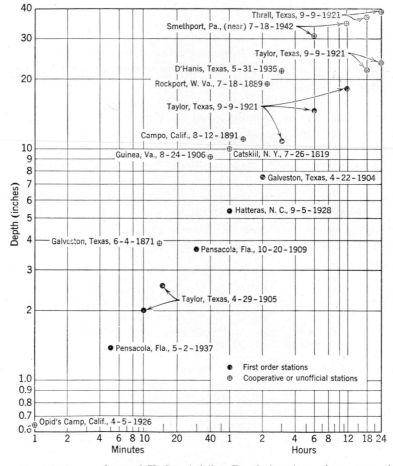

5

Infiltration and Soil Moisture

Precipitation reaching the ground surface may become either surface runoff or infiltration, depending on whether or not the rain intensity exceeds the infiltration capacity. That portion of the precipitation which infiltrates may add to the moisture content of the soil or may become ground water. Later chapters deal with surface runoff and ground water. This chapter is devoted to a discussion of infiltration and soil moisture.

INFILTRATION

Attention has already been called to the great diversity in the characteristics of the hydrographs of different streams. It has been shown that the flow of some is relatively steady throughout the year, whereas others are extremely fluctuating and some are intermittent. (See Fig. 5.) The most influential factor in determining the steadiness or variability of flow is the source of supply. If the principal source is from surface runoff, the stream is almost certain to have large floods and small rates of low-water flow. On the other hand, if the drainage basin is very permeable, as one having a coarse sandy soil, and if there is no relatively impervious stratum above the water table, there may be almost no surface runoff, and the flow will be well sustained and fairly uniform throughout the year.

The ability of a drainage basin to absorb and detain the water that falls upon it as rain or that comes to it from the melting of snows therefore provides a key to the character of the resulting hydrograph and becomes a matter of fundamental importance to the hydrologist. It appears that Horton was the first to recognize this fact and to suggest the theory of *infiltration capacity*.[1] This theory provides one of the most useful tools that we now have in the field of hydrology.

Definition

Infiltration is the process whereby water enters the surface strata of the soil and moves downward toward the water table. This water first replenishes the soil moisture deficiency, and thereafter any excess moves on downward and becomes ground water. The maximum rate at which a soil in any given condition is capable of absorbing water is called its *infiltration capacity* (f). For drainage basins upon which there is subsurface storm flow (see page 17), the true infiltration capacity is not measured by the ability of the surface strata to absorb water, but rather by the ability of the relatively impervious substratum to absorb water and transmit it downward.

Rain enters the soil at capacity rates only during and immediately following periods of rainfall excess, that is, periods during which the rainfall rate exceeds the infiltration capacity. When the rain intensity is less than the infiltration capacity, the prevailing infiltration rates are approximately equal to the rainfall rates.

Factors Affecting Infiltration Capacity

Infiltration capacities of most soils are characterized by extreme variability. The actual value at any time at a particular location is the combined result of the interaction of many factors. Some factors cause the infiltration capacity to differ from one location to another, whereas others produce variations from time to time at any location. Of this latter group, some factors cause the values to decrease during a rain as illustrated in Fig. 44, and some induce seasonal variations as illustrated in Figs. 41 and 42. There are some factors, such as vegetative cover, which may cause variation with both location and time. The various factors which affect the infiltration capacity are described in the following paragraphs.

Depth of Surface Detention and Thickness of Saturated Layer. The principal force which causes water to enter the soil is gravity. As a layer of soil near the surface has its interstitial spaces saturated,

---

[1] R. E. Horton, *Surface Runoff Phenomena,* Publ. 101, Edwards Bros., Ann Arbor, Mich.

the water flows through a series of tiny tubes of a length (l) approximately equal to the thickness of the saturated layer. At the top of each tube, the pressure is that produced by the depth of surface detention (D), and the total pressure head causing discharge is ($D + l$). The resistance is proportional to l. When l is large compared with D, changes in l have nearly equal effect on the force and the resistance, and the rate of infiltration is nearly constant. However, at the beginning of a rain, D and l may be of the same order of magnitude. Under such conditions the force is large compared with the resistance, and water will enter the soil very rapidly. This is one of the reasons why f is relatively large at the beginning of a rain.

Soil Moisture. The effect of soil moisture is twofold. (1) If the soil is quite dry at the beginning of a rain, the wetting of the top layer creates a strong capillary potential just under the surface which supplements the gravitational force in causing infiltration. This process is described in more detail later in this chapter. (2) When subjected to wetting, any colloids present in the soil swell and reduce the infiltration capacity during the initial period of rainfall. Soil moisture is usually high in winter and spring and low in summer and fall. This factor, therefore, is responsible for much of the typical seasonal variation, as well as for part of the rapid decrease in f during a rain.

Compaction Due to Rain. Mechanical compaction caused by raindrops greatly reduces the infiltration capacity in soils of fine texture. The surface of exposed clay soils can be worked into a virtually impermeable condition in this manner, whereas the infiltration capacity of a clean sandy soil is affected very little by rain compaction. Protection by vegetative cover can minimize or practically eliminate this effect, even in finely textured soils. This is another factor which causes the infiltration capacity to decrease rapidly during the initial portion of a rainstorm.

Inwash of Fine Material. When a soil becomes very dry, the surface often contains many fine particles. When infiltration begins, these fine particles are carried into the soil, which acts as a filter, and the fine material is deposited in the interstitial spaces, thus reducing the infiltration capacity. This factor also reduces f during a period of rainfall.

Compaction Due to Man and Animals. Where heavy pedestrian or vehicular traffic occurs on a soil, the surface is rendered relatively impervious. Examples of types of areas which have low infiltration capacities as the result of this factor are overgrazed pastures, playgrounds, and dirt roads.

Macrostructure of Soil. Several methods of compacting a soil and thereby reducing f have been described. It will now be shown that a permeable soil structure may be developed under certain conditions. This effect may be caused by several natural phenomena such as by burrowing animals and insects, by the decay of vegetable matter, particularly roots, by frost heaving, and by sun checking. Plowing and cultivation also produce a coarse soil structure. However, the higher infiltration capacities produced in this manner are often reduced very rapidly by compaction due to rain. In some soils the structure may be changed by the leaching out of soluble materials.

Vegetative Cover. This factor is related to many of those already mentioned, but it is of sufficient importance to warrant a separate discussion. The presence of a dense cover of vegetation, such as grass or forest, tends to promote rapid infiltration. The vegetative cover not only provides protection from compaction due to rain, but also provides a layer of decaying organic matter which promotes the activity of burrowing insects and animals.

In a study of the factors affecting the infiltration capacities of a dozen different soil types, Lewis and Powers[2] found that the effect of cover may be even more important than soil type. That this is true may easily be seen by a comparison of the condition of a barren clay or loamy soil with one that is thickly forested. The surface of the barren soil is hard and closely compacted from the successive beatings of rains and by the tread of animals. When protected by a thick covering of forest litter, however, the same kind of soil will be loose and pervious and will have a high infiltration capacity. A protected soil may have many times the infiltration capacity that it has when it is barren.

In a study quite similar to that discussed in the preceding paragraph, Duley and Kelly[3] found that there may be more variation in infiltration capacity resulting from surface conditions on a single soil, depending upon whether or not that soil is under cultivation, than would be found on different soils having the same surface conditions.

Transpiration by vegetation removes soil moisture and thus tends to provide a high f during initial periods of rain. Open crops, such as potatoes or corn, provide little protection from rain compaction and only a partial cover of organic matter, with the result that values of f may be relatively low in areas covered by such crops.

Temperature. Because flow in the interstitial spaces is nearly always laminar, changes in viscosity influence the rate of infiltration.

[2] M. R. Lewis and W. L. Powers, *Soil Sci. Soc. Am. Proc.*, 1938, pp. 334–339.

[3] F. I. Duley and L. L. Kelly, *Nebraska Agr. Expt. Sta. Research Bull.* 112, May 1939.

This factor causes values of f to be somewhat lower in winter and early spring than during the warmer weather of summer and early fall.

Effects of Freezing. When rain having a temperature only slightly above 32° F falls on very cold ground, the rain may be cooled sufficiently to form an impermeable layer of ice on top of the ground. However, it would be very unusual for such a layer of ice to persist during a rain large enough to cause a serious flood. This is because the heat of fusion given off by the water in freezing warms the soil and partially eliminates the conditions which caused freezing. Additional rainfall will then usually provide sufficient heat to melt the ice.

Freezing of the soil moisture, a condition referred to as frost penetration, also affects the infiltration capacity. Although very few data are available, it appears[4] that a frost penetration of several inches reduces the initial infiltration capacity, but that after the frozen soil moisture is melted by the penetration of the rain, the infiltration capacity equals that which would have followed a similar rainfall without frost penetration.

Entrapped Air. When infiltration occurs at nearly uniform rates over a large area, the air in the soil spaces may be trapped temporarily. The downward movement of the sheet of water entering the soil then compresses the air. This effect is particularly noticeable in areas where the ground is nearly horizontal such as, for example, portions of the Netherlands. The compression of the air in the ground forces air out through wells, sometimes with sufficient velocity to produce a whistling sound. Let us assume that the ground surface and the water table are parallel and that the soil is of uniform porosity throughout a given area, so that the entering water advances as a sheet of uniform thickness completely filling the voids. If the water table is at D feet below the ground surface, and the infiltering sheet of water has penetrated to a depth of d feet, the pressure in the entrapped air will be, from the laws of hydrostatics, neglecting capillarity,

$$p = 14.7 + 0.433d$$

Also, in accordance with Boyle's law,

$$14.7D = p(D - d)$$

Solving these two equations simultaneously gives

$$d = D - 34$$

From this equation it is seen that, under the assumed conditions, infiltration cannot occur unless the water table is more than 34 ft

[4] Leonard Schiff and F. R. Dreibelbis, "Infiltration, Soil Moisture, and Land-Use Relationships with Reference to Surface Runoff," *Trans. Am. Geophys. Union,* February 1949, pp. 75–88.

below the ground surface. Actually, however, the ground surface is seldom parallel with the water table. On the contrary it is irregular and contains countless ridges and mounds, and furthermore, instead of the infiltering water entering as a sheet of uniform thickness, it penetrates very unevenly. The tops of the ridges and mounds act as vents through which some of the compressed air escapes at the same time that water is penetrating throughout the adjacent area. There can be no question, however, but that compression of entrapped air does tend to retard infiltration and is one of the factors that cause a reduction in infiltration capacity as the storm progresses, although often it is of relatively minor importance.

Annual and Seasonal Changes

The average infiltration capacity of a drainage basin changes both annually and seasonally. The annual change results principally from changes in land use, from changes in the character of the annual vegetation, and from the advancing stage in the development of the perennial vegetation. Except for major changes in land use, these variations occur slowly and their effects become discernible only after a period of years. However, when an entire basin or any large portion of it is subjected to a sudden change in land use, such, for instance, as being deforested and put into agriculture, the resulting change in infiltration capacity may be marked.

In the preceding discussion it may have been observed that the various factors that affect infiltration capacity are not constant throughout the year. For instance, the moisture content of the soil reaches a maximum in spring and a minimum in fall. Also the changes in the macrostructures resulting from animal borings, from the decay of vegetal roots, from the condition of the vegetal cover, from cultivation, and from temperature affect infiltration capacity more or less seasonally. Figure 41 shows the seasonal variation of infiltration capacity on the Rouge River basin in Michigan. The curves were based on infiltration capacities determined from the analyses of 49 stream rises which occurred over a period of more than 20 yr. Relatively few of the stream rises occurred during the summer, and for some months only a single value was obtained, as indicated in Fig. 41. The average of all values, as well as the minimum value for each month, is shown. The solid line is representative of average conditions, whereas the dashed line is an envelope of minimum values. For coarse, sandy soils these two graphs would perhaps be closer together and would show considerably less seasonal variation, whereas for a compact clay they might be even more divergent and variable than here shown.

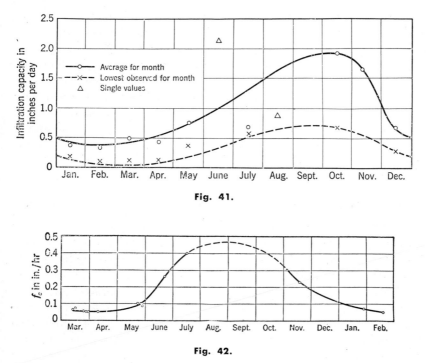

Fig. 41.

Fig. 42.

In Fig. 42 is shown a curve representing the seasonal variation of f during 1938–1939 for a small watershed at Edwardsville, Illinois, as derived by Horner and Lloyd.[5] A series of graphs of this type, drawn to scale and showing the maximum and minimum values of f for a variety of drainage basins of different physical characteristics and climatic conditions, would be of great practical use. It is hoped that, on the basis of the data now being collected by the various government agencies, this need will soon be filled.

Methods of Determining f

There are two general methods of determining infiltration capacity. The first is with an infiltrometer of which there are many different kinds, but in all of which water is artificially applied to a small area or sample plot, and the rate of infiltration is determined more or less directly. The second is by analysis of the hydrograph of runoff resulting from a natural rainfall on a drainage basin.

[5] W. W. Horner and C. Leonard Lloyd, "Infiltration-Capacity Values as Determined from a Study of an Eighteen-Month Record at Edwardsville, Ill.," *Trans. Am. Geophys. Union*, 1940, Part II, pp. 522–541.

The first of these methods is helpful in determining the effects of land use, slope, vegetal cover, and other variable factors over which it is desirable to have control in making studies on the prevention of soil erosion, flood reduction, underground storage, and similar problems in the solution of which hydrograph analysis often cannot be used. For reasons that will be explained presently, records obtained with infiltrometers are of value qualitatively rather than quantitatively. At least with our present limited knowledge they cannot be safely used for computing runoff from rainfall. On the other hand, infiltration capacities determined by hydrograph analysis are extremely useful for this purpose.

Infiltrometers

Infiltrometers are of two general classes: (1) those in which the rate of intake is determined directly as the rate at which water must be added to maintain a constant depth, usually about ¼ in., within the infiltrometer, and (2) rain simulators.

Under the first general class, the most common types consist either of two concentric rings or of a single tube. In the first type, two shallow concentric rings of sheet metal, usually ranging from 9 in. to 36 in. in diameter, are placed with their lower edges a few inches below the ground surface and with the upper portion projecting above, as shown in Fig. 43. Water is then applied in both compartments, a and b, and is always kept at the same level in both. The function of the outer ring is to prevent the water within the inner space from

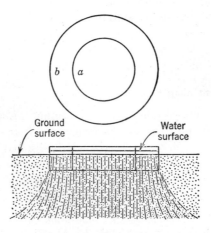

Fig. 43.

spreading over a larger area after penetrating below the bottom of the ring. From the rate at which water must be added to the inner ring in order to maintain a constant level, the infiltration capacity and its manner of variation are determined.

In the second type, a single tube is placed in the ground at a depth at least equal to that to which the water penetrates during the experiment, and therefore no spreading can occur. The rate at which water must be added to maintain a constant depth within the tube is then observed.

A number of other types of infiltrometers have been used, in which water is applied to a small enclosed area in the form of a sheet of water of definite thickness. Although these devices provide a simple and direct method of determining the capacity at which the ground is capable of absorbing water under those conditions, the results obtained are of value only in the determination of the influence of land use, vegetation, slope, and other physical variables. This is true because (1) the effect of the beating of raindrops, with the resulting compaction and inwash of fine materials, is absent; (2) the effect of compression of the entrapped air is absent because of lateral escape; (3) it is impossible to place a ring or tube in the ground without disturbing the soil structure near the boundary. Because of the small area contained within this type of infiltrometer, the disturbed area may be an appreciable percentage of the total, and the results are correspondingly affected.

Rain Simulators

In order to eliminate the foregoing objectionable features to as great an extent as possible, various types of infiltrometers have been devised in which water is applied by sprinkling at a uniform rate that, except perhaps for a brief initial period, is in excess of infiltration capacity. The area covered usually ranges from 1 sq ft to 0.01 acre. The varying rate of the resulting surface runoff is measured, and from these data the f curve is derived.

Horton was one of the first to use this type of infiltrometer. Even before World War I he determined infiltration capacities of small circular tracts about 10 ft in diameter to which water was supplied by a sprinkling system consisting of a number of radial horizontal pipes about 6 ft above the ground, rotating about a vertical axis, and driven by the reaction of a series of horizontal jets. In the more recent investigations that have been conducted by the Soil Conservation Service and other agencies, the water has been supplied through a system of stationary pipes designed to secure a practically uniform distribution of water over the plot, the proper size of drops, and the desired height of fall. Following are brief descriptions of some of the more commonly used types of infiltrometers of this general class.

Pearse. In this type the water is applied through a perforated pipe at the upper edge of a plot 1 ft square, and the runoff is collected at the lower edge. The rate of application is controlled by maintaining a constant elevation of water in the supply tank.

Modified North Fork. Water is applied through sprinklers to a rectangular area of 2.5 sq ft. The rate of application is measured by means of six rain gages, each 1 in. in diameter, and the runoff is collected at the lower end of the plot and measured.

Rocky Mountain. This instrument is quite similar to the modified North Fork infiltrometer except that the water is applied to a plot 2 ft by 4 ft and is measured by twelve 1-in. gages.

Modified Type F. This type of infiltrometer, also developed by the Soil Conservation Service, has perhaps been more commonly used than any other, and probably it measures the true infiltration capacity more accurately. Simulated rainfall is applied to an area approximately 6 ft by 12 ft and is measured in two trough gages, each 12 ft long and 1 in. wide, properly centered over the area. The runoff is automatically recorded.

Many other types of infiltrometers have been used, and unquestionably still more will be developed. Their use has not been standardized, and so it cannot be said that any particular type is best. The objections to the use of infiltrometers of the ring and tube type apply also to the sprinkling type, although to a lesser degree. It has been quite definitely established[6] that the results obtained by infiltrometers are qualitative and not quantitative. In other words, with infiltrometers it is possible to determine the relative effect of any change in land use or of any other controllable physical characteristic. It is not possible, however, to determine satisfactorily the runoff from a drainage basin by the direct use of infiltration capacities as determined by infiltrometers. This is because of the factors stated above and also because it is difficult to obtain sufficient samples to determine the average value of f for a large basin. For basins in which there is subsurface storm flow, values of f as determined by infiltrometers would in all probability give grossly misleading results. A typical hydrograph produced by a rain simulator is shown in Fig. 92, and a detailed discussion of the method of analysis used to derive the f curve from such a hydrograph is presented on pages 231 to 240.

[6] H. G. Wilm, "Methods for the Measurement of Infiltration," *Trans. Am. Geophys. Union,* 1941, pp. 678–686.

Hydrograph Analysis

Accurate data on the varying intensities of rainfall during any given storm, together with a continuous record of the resulting runoff, provide an excellent basis for the determination of infiltration capacity. Furthermore, infiltration capacities thus determined may, with confidence, be used to determine the hydrograph of runoff resulting from any given storm occurring on the same basin under similar conditions. Before explaining this method of determining infiltration capacity by hydrograph analysis, it may be well to review briefly the runoff process.

When rain starts falling on any particular basin, it does so at varying intensities over the area. In the beginning a portion is intercepted by trees, grasses, other vegetation, buildings, and so forth, and never reaches the ground surface. An additional portion flows into depressions, both small and large, and later either evaporates or soaks into the ground. The remainder starts flowing overland toward the stream channels, but in so doing a part of it infiltrates into the soil.

The rain that is not used up by either interception, depression storage, or infiltration eventually finds its way overland to the stream channels but only after some delay. In other words, there is a lag between the time when excess rainfall occurs and the time when that water appears as surface runoff at the outlet of the drainage basin. Furthermore this delay varies throughout the basin and throughout the storm period.

Because of this varying period of delay or lag between the time when rain falls on a basin and the time when the excess appears at the outlet as surface runoff, it is often difficult, and in large drainage basins it is usually impossible, to determine the exact manner in which infiltration capacity varies throughout a storm. For smaller basins in which the hydrograph is quick to respond to the varying intensities of rainfall, the actual manner in which f varies throughout the storm can often be quite accurately determined, but for larger basins it is possible to determine only the average infiltration capacity, f_a.

Determination of the f-Curve

A method of determining the infiltration-capacity curve for small drainage basins as suggested by Horner and Lloyd[7] will be explained and, with minor modifications, illustrated by the following example. In Fig. 44 is a graph showing the variation in rain intensity as it

[7] W. W. Horner and C. Leonard Lloyd, "Infiltration-Capacity Values as Determined from a Study of an Eighteen-Month Record at Edwardsville, Illinois," *Trans. Am. Geophys. Union*, 1940, pp. 522–541.

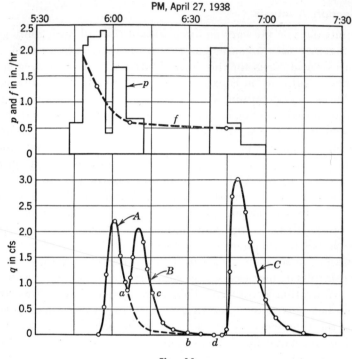

Fig. 44.

occurred on the Controlled Watershed,[8] at La Crosse, Wisconsin, on April 27, 1938, and the resulting hydrograph of surface runoff. The area of this watershed is only about 2.7 acres. Because of its small size, each period of intense rainfall produces a separate peak in the hydrograph. It will be observed, however, that the first two periods of intense rain occurred in such rapid succession that the resulting hydrographs overlap. The recession curve of A may be completed by drawing ab parallel with cd as shown in the figure. The areas beneath graphs A, B, and C when reduced to the proper units show depths of runoff on the basin of 0.10 in., 0.09 in., and 0.18 in. The depths of rain that occurred during these three periods of rainfall excess are, respectively, 0.355 in., 0.22 in., and 0.29 in. After deducting the respective depths of runoff from each of these values, the total infiltration, F, corresponding to each of these periods of intense rain is found to be 0.255 in., 0.13 in., and 0.11 in. Strictly speaking, these are not true

    [8] "Hydrologic Studies," Upper Mississippi Valley Conservation Experiment Station, La Crosse, Wis., *U. S. Dept. Agr. Soil Conserv. Serv. Tech. Paper* **29**, November 1939.

values of infiltration, for they include interception and depression storage. Nevertheless, inasmuch as it is impossible to determine the magnitude of interception and depression storage and since they never become surface runoff anyway, they may therefore conveniently be included with and considered as infiltration. Furthermore, by so doing, the values of f thus determined may be applied directly to any design storm to find the resulting runoff without the necessity of deducting values of interception and depression storage, which would have to be estimated.

In order to reduce these values of F to capacity rates, f, it is necessary to divide each by the average length of time during which infiltration was occurring at capacity rate over the entire basin. These periods of infiltration start at the beginning of excess rainfall and continue until some time after it ends. At the moment that excess rainfall ends, if the storm covers the whole area, infiltration is occurring at capacity rate over the entire basin, but soon thereafter this area starts shrinking from the outer boundaries toward the stream channels. Horton assumed that the equivalent period during which the same volume of residual infiltration would occur on the entire basin is equal to one third of the period that elapses from the end of excess rainfall until the end of overland flow. Horton[9] has called attention to the fact that overland flow ends about at the point of inflection on the recession side of the hydrograph. The reason that he selected this point is that, after the cessation of overland flow, the hydrograph represents only outflow from channel storage and is therefore an exhaustion curve and as such must be concave upward. By this method of determination, the durations of infiltration, t_a, t_b, and t_c, corresponding to each of these three periods of excess rainfall, were found to be 11, 13, and 13 min respectively. Therefore,

$$f_a = (0.355 - 0.10) \times \frac{60}{11} = 1.39 \text{ in. per hr}$$

$$f_b = (0.22 - 0.09) \times \frac{60}{13} = 0.60 \text{ in. per hr}$$

$$\text{and } f_c = (0.29 - 0.18) \times \frac{60}{13} = 0.51 \text{ in. per hr}$$

Plotting each of these values at a time $t/2$ after the beginning of excess rainfall for each of these periods, the f curve, shown in Fig. 44, is obtained.

[9] R. E. Horton, *Surface Runoff Phenomena*, Publication 101, Edwards Bros., Ann Arbor, Mich., p. 34.

For large basins, the method described here cannot be readily applied because there is no relation between the recession curve of the hydrograph and the period of residual infiltration. Furthermore, for larger basins the period of residual infiltration is small compared with the period of rainfall excess and may be neglected. Consequently the assumption is made that the rainfall excess, which is the area of the precipitation graph above the f_a curve, is equal to the surface runoff. Based on this assumption, the average infiltration capacity is determined for each stream rise by computing the rainfall excess for various assumed values of f_a, until the volume of rainfall excess is equal to the volume of surface runoff determined from the hydrograph. The values of f_a determined in this manner for stream rises A, B, and C in Fig. 44 are 1.61, 0.65, and 0.55 in. per hr respectively. Additional examples of this method of deriving f_a are given in Chapter 8.

The f curve, derived above and shown in Fig. 44, is a typical infiltration-capacity curve. It starts with a high value, f_0, because of the initial soil conditions and the heavy initial demands of interception and depression storage which are here included with infiltration; then it drops rapidly during the early stages of the storm and finally levels off and approaches a constant value, f_c. In this particular case, f_0 is nearly four times as great as f_c. For different basins this ratio has, however, a wide range, depending upon the amount of interception and depression storage and upon the type, texture, and condition of the soil. Horton[10] has called attention to the fact that this curve is of the exhaustion type, that it approaches a constant value, usually after a period of 1 to 3 hr, and that it may be represented by an equation of the form

$$f = f_c + (f_0 - f_c)e^{-kt}$$

in which e is the Napierian base, k is a constant for a given curve, and f is the infiltration capacity in inches per hour at any time, t, in hours. (For an explanation of methods of determining f_0 and k in this equation see page 238.)

Attention should be called to the fact that the infiltration-capacity curve shown in Fig. 44 is, in reality, not an f curve but, rather, it is an f_a curve. In other words, it does not represent instantaneous values of infiltration capacity as it existed throughout the storm period, but instead it represents the average infiltration capacity for each of the several periods of high storm intensity. It is possible that, during

[10] R. E. Horton, "Analysis of Runoff Plat Experiments with Varying Infiltration Capacity," *Trans. Am. Geophys. Union*, 1939, Part IV, p. 693.

the period between showers, from 6:12 to 6:38 P.M., some recovery in infiltration capacity may have occurred, and, if such was the case, this curve should be made to dip and then rise again. In no case is it possible to determine the exact behavior because of the variable period of delay between the time when water falls as rain and the time when it appears as surface runoff at the outlet of the drainage basin. However, the divergence of the f curve shown in Fig. 44 and the true f curve is probably of minor significance.

Infiltration Capacity of Very Large Basins

For drainage basins that are larger than those for which the rain intensity may be considered as being uniform over the entire area, Horton[11] proposed the following method for determining the average infiltration capacity, f_a, that existed during any given storm. The procedure presumes that enough rainfall records are available on the basin to represent the rainfall variation satisfactorily and also that at least one of these records was obtained by an automatic recording gage. The fact should be brought out at this point and emphasized that, for drainage basins in which there is subsurface storm flow (see page 17), any value of f_a obtained by this method is not the infiltration capacity of the ground surface, but for all practical purposes it is the average infiltration capacity of the relatively impervious substratum. Therefore, values so derived may be directly applied to any design storm to determine surface runoff from that same basin, but should not be used for runoff studies on any other basin on which subsurface conditions are probably quite different.

This method is based upon two assumptions: first, the fact that, in great general storms producing major floods on large basins, the rain intensity patterns at adjacent stations are very similar; second, the fact that surface runoff approximately equals the difference between the rainfall and the infiltration that occurs during the period of rainfall excess. In other words, the rain that falls during and immediately following the period of rainfall excess, but infiltrates during the subsequent period of overland flow, is ignored.

Even after the above assumptions are made, and even though the infiltration capacity were uniform over the entire basin, it still would not be permissible to divide the difference between the total rainfall and the total runoff by the duration of rainfall excess as shown by the recording gage, because the period of rainfall excess varies throughout the basin and is different at the various stations. This fact must

[11] R. E. Horton, "Determination of Infiltration Capacity for Large Drainage Basins," *Trans. Am. Geophys. Union,* 1937, Part II, pp. 371–385.

be taken into consideration or the result would not represent the true infiltration capacity at all. The method herein described consists of finding a value of f that, when multiplied by the period of rainfall excess and subtracted from the total rainfall for the same period, will leave a remainder equal to the total surface runoff.

It is further assumed that the periods of rainfall, but not of rainfall excess, are approximately the same at all stations, although not necessarily simultaneous. For a method of correcting for the varying duration of rainfall that is likely to occur at the different stations during a convectional rain, or during a storm accompanying a rapidly moving cold front, reference should be made to the original paper.

The station at which the recording gage is located will be called the base station, and those at which only 24-hr total rainfall records are available will be called substations. It is first necessary to determine which rainfall stations should be considered. This may be done by the Thiessen method as described on page 81. The daily rainfall records at the various stations are then adjusted to a common 24-hr basis as explained on page 72.

The average infiltration capacity may first be approximated by subtracting the total surface runoff from the total rainfall as recorded at the base station and dividing the difference by the period of rainfall at the base station. In doing this, one should ignore any period of light rainfall, either at the beginning or at the end. The percentage of the total rainfall that fell during each hour at the base station is then computed. Next, a total rainfall of some whole number of inches that is about equal to the average depth for the given storm is assumed. Then the depth of rain falling each hour at the base station is determined by multiplying this assumed depth by the various percentages as above determined. The results of a set of these computations as given by Horton in the original paper are shown in Table 8. In column 2 are shown the hourly depths of rainfall, and in column 3 are shown the percentages of the total. In column 4 are shown the corresponding depths of rain that would fall during each hour of a 4-in. storm having an intensity pattern similar to that of the recorded storm. In columns 5, 6, 7, 8, and 9 are shown the depths of rainfall excess that would occur each hour as a result of this same storm, but for infiltration capacities of 0.1, 0.2, 0.3, 0.4, and 0.5 in. per hr, respectively.

In Fig. 45, the total rainfall excesses as shown in columns 5, 6, 7, 8, and 9 are plotted against a storm rainfall of 4 in. Similar tables are prepared for storms having depths of 2 in., 3 in., 5 in., and 6 in., and the results are plotted, producing the curves shown in the figure. It

TABLE 8

Recorded Rainfall at Base Station				$P = 4.0$ in.				
		Portion	Total	Infiltration Capacity f,				
	Amount,	of	Amount,	in./hr				
Hour	in.	Total	in.	0.10	0.20	0.30	0.40	0.50
(1)	(2)	(3)	(4)	(5)	(6)	(7)	(8)	(9)
					Rainfall Excess			
5 A.M.	0.05	0.013						
6	.05	.013						
7	.03	.008						
8	.02	.005						
9	.05	.013						
10	.05	.013						
11	.07	.019						
12 M.	.08	.022	0.088	0				
1 P.M.	.20	.054	.216	0.116	0.016	0	0	0
2	.20	.054	.216	.116	0.016	0	0	0
3	.13	.035	.140	.040	0	0	0	0
4	.12	.032	.128	.028	0	0	0	0
5	.03	.008						
6	.02	.005						
7	.15	.040	.160	.060	0	0	0	0
8	.15	.040	.160	.060	0	0	0	0
9	.35	.094	.376	.276	0.176	0.076	0	0
10	.35	.094	.376	.276	0.176	0.076	0	0
11	.35	.094	.376	.276	0.176	0.076	0	0
12 P.M.	.35	.094	.376	.276	0.176	0.076	0	0
1 A.M.	.25	.068	.272	.172	0.072	0	0	0
2	.25	.068	.272	.172	0.072	0	0	0
3	.15	.040	.160	.060	0	0	0	0
4	.15	.040	.160	.060	0	0	0	0
5	.05	.013						
6	.05	.013						
7	.02	.005						
8	.01	.003						
Totals	3.73	1.000		1.988	0.880	0.304	0	0

should be noted that Table 8 shows that for storms of this pattern having a total depth of 4 in. there would be no surface runoff if the infiltration capacity is 0.4 in. per hr or more.

From the curves shown in Fig. 45, the rainfall excess for the various infiltration capacities can be determined for any total depth of rain. In Table 9, column 2, are shown the total depths of rainfall at each

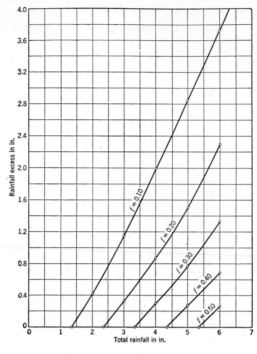

Fig. 45.

TABLE 9

Station (1)	Total Rainfall, in. (2)	Rainfall Excess for Values of f in in./hr of		
		0.10 (3)	0.20 (4)	0.30 (5)
A	5.91	3.65	2.22	1.27
B	3.81	1.82	0.77	0.20
C	3.76	1.76	0.74	0.18
D	4.13	2.08	0.95	0.35
E	4.01	2.00	0.90	0.30
F	4.09	2.05	0.93	0.33
G	4.92	2.76	1.48	0.74
H	6.05	3.77	2.32	1.35
Averages	4.58	2.49	1.26	0.59

of the substations within the basin during this storm. In columns 3, 4, and 5 are shown values of rainfall excess as obtained from the curves in Fig. 45 for each of these depths of total rainfall. The average of the values in any column represents the average excess rainfall on the entire basin. In Fig. 46 these averages are plotted against infiltration capacity. From this curve, if the rainfall excess is known, the infiltration capacity is readily found.

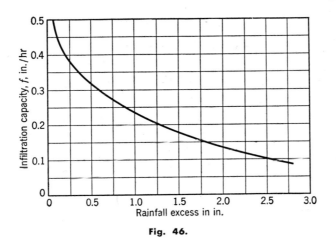

Fig. 46.

Greater accuracy could be obtained by weighting the rainfall excess at each of the various stations by the Thiessen method, but this is not considered necessary unless there are only a few records available or if the rainfall is very nonuniformly distributed over the basin.

SOIL MOISTURE

Soil moisture is the term applied to the water held in the soil by means of molecular attraction. It forms a film around the soil particles, fills the small wedge-like spaces between soil particles, and may completely fill the smaller interstitial spaces. This moisture is held so tightly that it strongly resists any forces tending to displace it. The degree of its resistance to movement is expressed by its *capillary tension* or the synonymous term *capillary potential*, which is a measure of the force required to remove this moisture from the soil. It is most conveniently expressed in terms of depth of water having an equivalent pressure. Its value is negative with respect to atmospheric pressure. When its absolute value is less than one atmosphere it may be deter-

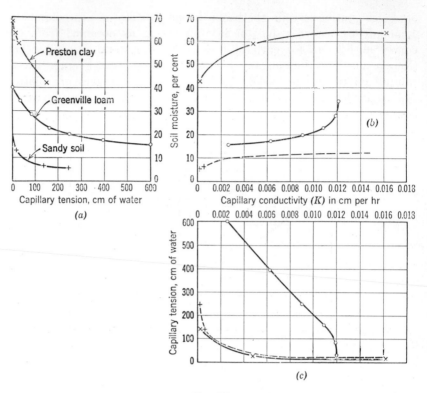

Fig. 47.

mined by means of a tensiometer (described on page 124). For greater tensions its value may be determined by means of a centrifuge. Capillary potential is related to the soil moisture content, but this relationship is different for soils of different textures, as illustrated by data determined by Richards[12] and plotted in Fig. 47a.

Movement of Moisture in Unsaturated Soils

Soil moisture moves under the influence of the gravitational force and the force resulting from differences in capillary potential. The equation for discharge may be written[13]

$$Q = KIa \qquad (1)$$

[12] L. A. Richards, "Capillary Conductivity Data for Three Soils," *J. Am. Soc. Agron.,* vol. 28, 1936, p. 297.

[13] L. A. Richards, "Capillary Conduction of Liquids through Porous Mediums," *Physics,* vol. 1, 1931, p. 318.

which is similar to the equation for ground-water discharge (see page 148). Q is the discharge through the area a, K is a coefficient of conductivity, and I is the sum of the capillary potential gradient and the gradient of the gravitational force. If capillary potential is expressed in centimeters of water (h), its gradient would be $\Delta h/l$ where l is the length of travel. The gradient of the gravitational force in similar units would be $\Delta z/l$, where Δz is the difference in elevation at the two ends of the length l. If K is expressed in centimeters per hour and a in square centimeters, Q will have the units cubic centimeters per hour. For downward flow, the two motivating forces act in the same direction. When flow is upward, the gravitational component of I must be subtracted from the capillary potential component.

For horizontal flow the gravitational component is zero. The coefficient of conductivity increases as the soil moisture increases, as shown in Fig. 47b. This increase is to be expected because the liquid films form the conduits through which the moisture flows. It can be seen from equation 1 and Fig. 47b that moisture will move from moist regions to drier ones under the influence of the capillary potential. Thus, after a rain the top soil becomes wet from infiltration and the soil moisture will move downward under the combined influence of the capillary and gravitational forces. This process has been investigated by Colman,[14] who found that moisture advanced downward in what he described as a "wetting zone" in which the capillary potential gradient was very steep. It was found that this wetting zone had to extend 12 to 30 in. below the ground surface, depending upon the type of soil, before the surface soil attained a moisture content as great as the field capacity (see page 19). As the wetting zone continued downward beyond these limiting depths, the layer of top soil which had attained field capacity gradually increased in thickness. This phenomenon has also been discussed by Richards and Moore.[15]

Another important application of the laws of soil moisture movement is the case in which soil moisture is being removed from the soil surface by evaporation. The decrease in moisture near the surface reduces the capillary potential, and a potential gradient is established, which readily becomes greater than the gravitational potential and results in an upward movement of the moisture. At first the moisture will be drawn from the soil moisture itself, but if the water table is

[14] E. A. Colman, "The Dependence of Field Capacity upon the Depth of Wetting of Field Soils," Soil Sci., vol. 58, 1944, p. 43.

[15] L. A. Richards and D. C. Moore. "Influence of Capillary Conductivity and Depth of Wetting on Moisture Retention in Soil," Trans. Am. Geophys. Union, August 1952, p. 531.

not too far below the ground surface, the moisture will be drawn from the ground water. This problem has been studied by Remson and Fox,[16] who assumed that some of Richard's data relating K to capillary potential (Fig. 47c) could be represented by a straight line. With this assumption, the rate of upward movement of water was computed for various depths to the water table. At present, the practical applications of such results are limited by the meager amount of data available as to the relationship between K and the capillary potential for actual field soils in situ.

Measurement of Soil Moisture

The quantity of soil moisture present in a given soil sample may be expressed in various ways. The methods commonly used are the ratio of the weight of water to the weight of the dry soil, or the percentage of water by volume. It is often convenient to express the soil moisture deficiency at any location in terms of inches depth of water. The most basic method of measuring the moisture content of a soil is by weighing samples of soil before and after removing the moisture. This method has certain disadvantages, the most important being that a continuous record cannot be obtained at any one location because of the necessity of removing the samples from the ground for laboratory testing.

A number of methods[17] of obtaining continuous records of soil moisture have been developed, all of which must be calibrated by the use of the soil sample method described above. However, once calibrated, all of these methods permit continuous soil moisture determination without disturbing the soil. There follows a brief description of five methods of measuring soil moisture.

1. *The use of porous sorption blocks.* These blocks are kept in close contact with the soil but may be readily removed and weighed. The moisture content of the blocks is related to that of the surrounding soil.

2. *The use of tensiometers.*[18,19] Tensiometers are porous cups which are filled with water and embedded in the soil. A pressure gage

[16] Irwin Remson and G. S. Fox, "Capillary Losses from Ground Water," *Trans. Am. Geophys. Union,* April 1955, p. 304.

[17] Omer J. Kelley, Albert S. Hunter, Howard R. Haise, Clinton H. Hobbs, "A Comparison of Methods of Measuring Soil Moisture under Field Conditions," *J. Am. Soc. Agron.,* vol. 38, September 1946, pp. 759–784.

[18] L. A. Richards and Willard Gardner, "Tensiometers for Measuring the Capillary Tension of Soil Water," *J. Am. Soc. Agron.,* vol. 28, 1936, pp. 352–358.

[19] L. A. Richards, "Soil Moisture Tensiometer Materials and Construction," *Soil Sci.,* vol. 53, 1942, pp. 241–248.

or U-tube is used to measure the capillary potential or tension between the water and the soil. The soil tension is related to the moisture content for any particular soil.[20]

3. *Methods based on the relation between thermal conductivity of the soil and the soil moisture content.*[21] An electrical resistance, which constitutes one leg of a Wheatstone bridge, is placed in the soil. When the soil moisture is high, heat will be conducted rapidly away from this resistance, whereas for dry soil the heat conductivity of the soil is low, and the resistance element will become hotter, thus increasing its resistance and throwing the bridge farther out of balance.

4. *Methods based on the relation of the electrical resistance of porous dielectric materials to their moisture content.* When such materials are placed in close contact with the soil, they rather quickly develop a moisture content which is in equilibrium with that of the surrounding soil. Two electrodes are embedded in the material, and the electrical resistance between the electrodes is measured by means of a Wheatstone bridge. The materials that have been used are gypsum,[22] fiberglass,[23] fiberglass embedded in gypsum,[24] nylon,[25] and nylon embedded in gypsum.[26] The gypsum block was found to lack sensitivity in the very wet range, but the other three materials gave reliable calibration curves for moisture contents in the range from the wilting point to complete saturation.

5. *A method using emanations from radioactive materials.*[27] Such a method has been developed and seems to hold promise for practical

[20] L. A. Richards and J. Sterling, "Soil Moisture Content Calculations from Capillary Tension Records," *Soil Sci. Soc. Am. Proc.,* vol. 3, 1939, pp. 57–64.

[21] Byron Shaw and L. D. Baver, "An Electrothermal Method for Following Moisture Changes in the Soil in Situ," *Soil Sci. Soc. Am. Proc.,* vol. 4, 1939, pp. 78–83.

[22] G. J. Bouyoucos and A. H. Mick, "An Electrical Method for the Continuous Measurement of Soil Moisture under Field Conditions," *Mich. Agr. Expt. Sta. Tech. Bull.* 172, 1940.

[23] E. A. Colman, "The Place of Electrical Soil-Moisture Meters in Hydrologic Research," *Trans. Am. Geophys. Union,* vol. 27, December 1946, pp. 847–853.

[24] R. E. Yonker and R. E. Dreibelbis, "An Improved Soil-Moisture Measuring Unit for Hydrologic Studies," *Trans. Am. Geophys. Union,* vol. 32, June 1951, pp. 447–449.

[25] G. J. Bouyoucos and G. A. Crabb, Jr., "Measurement of Soil Moisture by the Electrical Resistance Method," *Agr. Eng.,* December 1949.

[26] G. J. Bouyoucos, "Newly Developed Nylon Units for Measuring Soil Moisture in the Field," *Highway Research Abstr.,* January 1954.

[27] Wilford Gardner and Don Kirkham, "Determination of Soil Moisture by Neutron Scattering," *Soil Sci.,* vol. 73, 1952, pp. 391–401.

applications.[28,29] The method depends on the fact that hydrogen slows fast neutrons more than other common elements and that most of the hydrogen in a soil is in the water. The apparatus consists of a source of fast neutrons and a slow neutron counter. For a high moisture content the slow neutron count will be high, whereas for dry soil the count will be lower. This method differs from the others in that the average moisture content over a layer more than one foot thick is determined, rather than the actual amount of moisture at a specific depth. The thickness of the layer affecting the results varies somewhat with the moisture content of the soil and with the vertical location of the instruments.

    [28] D. F. Belcher, T. R. Cuykendall, and H. S. Sack, "Nuclear Meters for Measuring Soil Density and Moisture in Thin Layers," *Civil Aeronaut. Admin., Tech. Div. Rept.* 161, 1952.
    [29] C. H. M. van Bavel, E. E. Hood, and N. Underwood, "Vertical Resolution in the Neutron Method for Measuring Soil Moisture," *Trans. Am. Geophys. Union,* vol. 35, August 1954, pp. 595–600.

6

Ground Water

John G. Ferris

Chapter 6 presents certain phases of ground-water hydrology with special reference to the laws governing the movement of ground water. It is not intended to present a complete discussion of either the general or the quantitative phases of ground-water hydrology, which is beyond the scope of this book. For more complete discussions of the occurrence and movements of ground water, the reader is referred to the papers listed at the end of the chapter.

Our study of the waters of the earth progresses from the more familiar fields of atmospheric water and surface water to the third province of hydrology, which deals with the study of subsurface or ground water. Among the many prerequisites necessary to the study of ground-water hydrology, probably the one most neglected in the training of engineers is the subject of geology. Inasmuch as it would be impossible to correct this deficiency in any single chapter, it is necessarily assumed that the student has sufficient background training in this field to recognize the degree to which geology controls the occurrence and movement of ground water.

Although man has long been familiar with the development of small water supplies from wells, it is only since the demands upon our

This chapter is published with the permission of the Director of the U. S. Geological Survey. The author is Research Engineer of the Ground Water Division, U. S. Geological Survey.

ground water have become heavy that much thought has been directed to the hydraulics of ground-water flow. The great advances made since the turn of the century in the improvement of well-drilling methods and pumping equipment, particularly in the development of the deep-well turbine pump, have resulted in a marked upward trend in the use of ground water for domestic, rural, municipal, and industrial water supply. It is of interest to note that in 1939 it was estimated[1] that, in the United States, about 9100 public water supplies were derived from ground water and about 3300 from surface sources. Superimpose on this established upward trend the demands of industry awakened to the economic advantages of ground water for air temperature and humidity control and as a relatively constant quality source lending itself to almost fixed treatment. Notwithstanding the magnitude of the total withdrawal of ground water for all the above uses, this total is exceeded by the present demand for ground water in irrigation.

An ever-increasing number of problems has attended the rapid growth in the use of ground water. Those engaged in the search for answers to these problems are handicapped by the deficiencies in hydrologic research and the lack of trained technicians in this field. Our ground-water reserves have, too frequently, been called inexhaustible. Advances in hydrology show the fallacy of such a belief. Equally unfavorable, however, is the dissemination of discouraging opinions by those who have experienced water shortages that result from overdevelopment. It becomes increasingly evident that a wiser and fuller use of this great national resource can be achieved only by the sound and rational methods of the trained hydrogeologist and hydrogeological engineer.

The earth's crust, composed of its myriad and varied hard rocks and the unconsolidated overburden, serves as a vast underground reservoir for the storage and transmission of percolating ground waters. The rocks comprising the earth's crust are seldom if ever solid throughout. They contain numerous openings called interstices that vary through a wide range of sizes and shapes. Although these interstices may reach cavernous size in some rocks, it should be noted that most of them are very small. Generally, they are interconnected, permitting movement of the percolating waters, but in some rocks they are isolated, preventing the transmission of water between interstices. Accordingly, then, the mode of occurrence of ground water in the rocks of a given area is largely determined by the geology of that area.

[1] "Inventory of Water Supply Facilities," *Eng. News-Record*, 1939, vol. 123, p. 414.

Porosity

The physical property of a rock that defines the degree to which it contains interstices is termed its *porosity* and is expressed quantitatively as the percentage that the interstitial volume is of the total. The porosity of a material is dependent on the interrelation of size, shape, and manner of sorting of its component parts in unconsolidated or pervious sedimentary material; or on the size, shape, and pattern of channeling in relatively soluble rock such as limestone; or on the size, shape, and pattern of fracturing in the dense sedimentary, igneous, and metamorphic rocks. Some idea of the relation of porosity to rock texture and particle sorting may be gained by reference to Fig. 48.

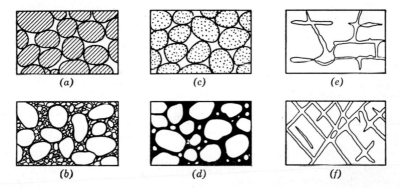

Fig. 48. Diagram showing several types of rock interstices and the relation of rock texture to porosity. *a*, Well-sorted sedimentary deposit having high porosity; *b*, poorly sorted sedimentary deposit having low porosity; *c*, well-sorted sedimentary deposit consisting of pebbles that are themselves porous, so that the deposit as a whole has a very high porosity; *d*, well-sorted sedimentary deposit whose porosity has been diminished by the deposition of mineral matter in the interstices; *e*, rock rendered porous by solution; *f*, rock rendered porous by fracturing. After Meinzer, *U. S. Geological Survey Water-Supply Paper* 489, 1923, Fig. 1, p. 3.

The porosity of rock or unconsolidated material may range from considerably less than 1 per cent to more than 50 per cent. However, a porosity in excess of 40 per cent is rare, except in soils or poorly compacted materials. In general, we may consider a porosity greater than 20 per cent as large, between 5 and 20 per cent as medium, and less than 5 per cent as small.

There are a number of methods in use for determining the porosity of rocks or soils which are based on either volumetric or specific-gravity measurements of dry versus saturated samples. The relation of the factors most commonly required for porosity tests is summarized by the following equation,[2]

$$p = 100\left(\frac{W}{V}\right) = 100\left(\frac{V - v}{V}\right) = 100\left(\frac{S - a}{S}\right) = 100(b - a) \quad (1)$$

where p is porosity, W volume of water required to saturate dry sample of rock or soil, V volume of sample, v aggregate volume of solid particles comprising the sample, S weighted average of specific gravities of minerals composing the soil or rock, a specific gravity of dry samples, and b specific gravity of saturated sample.

Rather elaborate core-sampling apparatus have been devised to obtain samples in an undisturbed condition. However, the removal of any sample from its original environment is certain to disturb the sample to some extent. There is no positive assurance that any laboratory procedure reproduces the original regimen of pressure, temperature, or volume. Furthermore, in the final analysis the sample represents only an infinitesimal section of the soil or rock formation.

Specific Yield

Another physical characteristic which is of importance in the hydrology of ground water is the *specific yield*. When saturated rocks or soils are drained under the action of gravity, it is found that the volume of water yielded by draining is less than the volume of void space indicated by the total porosity of the material because of the pellicular water that is retained by molecular attraction. The quantity of water yielded by gravity drainage from saturated water-bearing material is termed the specific yield and is expressed as a percentage of the total volume of the material drained. The quantity of water retained by the material against the pull of gravity is termed the *specific retention* or *field capacity* and is again expressed as a percentage of the total volume of the material. A somewhat similar term, moisture equivalent,[3] is frequently used to represent the moisture retained by a saturated sample when subjected to an arbitrary centrifugal force. It is evident that the sum of the specific yield and the specific retention of a material is equal to its porosity.

If evaporation is prevented, the greater part of the water retained by a column of rock or sand and gravel, after draining for 24 hr, will

---

[2] O. E. Meinzer, "The Occurrence of Ground Water in the United States," *U. S. Geol. Survey Water-Supply Paper* 489, 1923, p. 12.

[3] L. J. Briggs and J. W. McLane, "The Moisture Equivalent of Soils," *U. S. Dept. Agr. Bur. of Soils Bull.* 45, 1907.

be retained almost indefinitely as a film held by molecular adhesion on the walls of the interstices. The greater the amount of total interstitial surface in a rock or unconsolidated material the greater is its specific retention. As would be expected, it is found that, as the effective diameter of grain decreases, the specific retention generally increases because the total exposed surface area increases with decreasing grain size.

Although the total porosity of a clay or fine sand might be equivalent to the total porosity of a coarse gravel, it follows from the foregoing statements that the large specific retention of the clay would result in a very small specific yield, whereas the reverse would be true for the coarse gravel. For practical purposes, a water-bearing formation of coarse gravel would supply large quantities of water to wells, whereas clay formations, although saturated and of high porosity, would be of little value in this respect. Accordingly, we find that specific yield is termed by some as the effective or practical porosity.

Determinations of the specific yield or specific retention by laboratory methods are limited by the difficulties of securing undisturbed and representative samples that are noted under permeability determinations by laboratory methods. In addition, the short sample columns used in the laboratory cannot duplicate the very long capillary tubes that probably exist in the thick sections found in the field. As for permeability, the most satisfactory determinations of specific yield are made in the field through the medium of pumping tests.

Permeability and Transmissibility

The vertical percolation of ground water through capillary interstices results in the build-up of a hydraulic gradient with consequent lateral percolation of water through interconnecting interstices. The capacity of a formation for transmitting water is measured by its *coefficient of permeability*, which is defined by Meinzer[4] as the rate of flow of water in gallons per day through a cross-sectional area of 1 sq ft under a hydraulic gradient of 1 ft per ft at a temperature of 60° F.

The term *coefficient of transmissibility* introduced by Theis[5] is coming into popular usage in ground-water hydrology. The coefficient of transmissibility is defined as the rate of flow of water in gallons per

[4] N. D. Stearns, "Laboratory Tests on Physical Properties of Water-Bearing Materials," *U. S. Geol. Survey Water-Supply Paper* 596, 1927, p. 148.

[5] C. V. Theis, "The Relation between the Lowering of the Piezometric Surface and the Rate and Duration of Discharge of a Well Using Ground Water Storage," *Trans. Am. Geophys. Union*, 1935, p. 520.

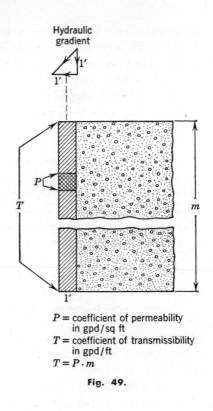

P = coefficient of permeability
in gpd / sq ft
T = coefficient of transmissibility
in gpd / ft
$T = P \cdot m$

Fig. 49.

day through a vertical strip of the aquifer 1 ft wide and extending the full saturated height under a hydraulic gradient of 100 per cent at a temperature of 60° F. The difference between the coefficients of permeability and transmissibility is shown in diagrammatic form by Fig. 49.

The permeability of granular material varies with the diameter and degree of assortment of the individual particles. A well-sorted gravel has a much higher permeability than a well-sorted coarse sand. However, gravel with a moderate percentage of medium- and fine-grained material may be considerably less permeable than a uniformly sized coarse sand. In graded material, the particles of moderate size fill the pore spaces between the larger particles, and in turn the resultant pore spaces are filled by the fine materials, thus forming a compactly knit and impervious mass such as is obtained in good concrete.

Measurements of the permeability of rocks and unconsolidated materials may be made by either field or laboratory methods as described by Muskat[6] and by Wenzel.[7] Laboratory determinations of the coefficient of permeability are made by measuring the discharge or the time rate of change in head, for the percolation of measured quantities of water through a known area and volume of soil sample. Devices used for this purpose are termed *permeameters* and include a supply reservoir or tank from which water is discharged through a percolation cylinder under either a constant or a variable head. The percolation cylinder is accurately machined to a fixed diameter and is equipped with a base screen which supports the soil sample and permits free inflow of water. Manometer tubes in the supply and receiving reservoirs are used to determine the loss of head that occurs for the vertical percolation of known quantities of water through the soil cylinder at measured rates. A schematic representation of the more common types of permeameter is shown in Fig. 50.

The use of permeameters to determine the permeability of unconsolidated material is invalidated to a large degree because of the great errors introduced in repacking a disturbed sample. Inasmuch as the packing arrangement is a critical factor in determining the permeability of an incoherent material, it would seem advisable to apply laboratory methods only to consolidated materials or cores of unconsolidated material. Further caution should be exercised because the volume of material used in permeameter tests represents only an infinitesimal sample of a formation that is generally quite heterogeneous. Accordingly, to be of value permeameter programs should include many samples collected at frequent depth intervals and at numerous locations within the area.

Field determinations of permeability are made by either the velocity or the potential method. In the velocity method one well is used for the injection of salt, dye, or an electrolyte. Two or more wells are used as observation stations to determine the time rate of travel of the injected substance through the water-bearing material. Fluorescein is generally used for the dye method and can be detected by eye or in more dilute form by colorimeter. The chemical or salt method requires periodic sampling and analysis of water from each observation well to determine the time of arrival of the salted solution. The electrolyte method requires periodic readings of the electric conductivity of the water in each observation well. Measurements of

[6] Morris Muskat, *Flow of Homogeneous Fluids through Porous Media,* McGraw-Hill, 1937.

[7] L. K. Wenzel and V. C. Fishel, "Methods for Determining Permeability of Water-Bearing Materials," *U. S. Geol. Survey Water-Supply Paper* 887, 1942.

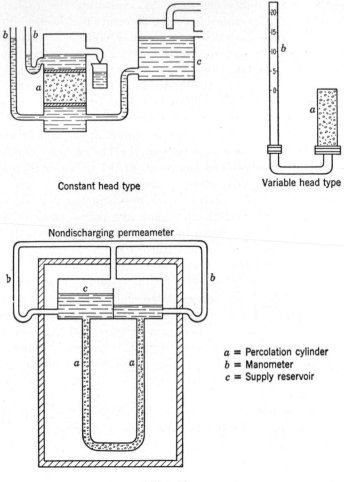

Fig. 50.

the water-table gradient, the distance between observation wells, and the time of travel of the injected material provide the basis for determining the permeability of the material over the path of travel. A sketch of the equipment setup for one form of the velocity method is shown in Fig. 51.

Inasmuch as the velocity of flow through most ground-water aquifers is measured in terms of a few feet per day, it is necessary that velocity observations be confined to small areas in order to secure results within a reasonable time. This method measures the velocity of the fastest thread of water that happens to intersect the two wells and not necessarily the average velocity between the wells. This method would be impractical for sampling adequately any heterogeneous aquifer that has large variations in vertical and horizontal permeability.

Potential methods of determining permeability are based on measurements of the amount and rate of drawdown or recovery of water level in observation wells at different distances from a well that is either pumping or recovering from pumping, respectively. The principles and application of this method are covered in detail under the discussion of ground-water hydraulics. A distinct advantage of the potential method is its ability to sample large areas of the undisturbed aquifer within a limited time and at a minimum of expense.

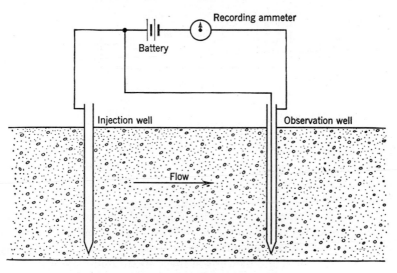

Fig. 51.

The Ground-Water Reservoir

The classification of the earth's crust with reference to its properties as a reservoir for the storage and transmission of percolating ground waters and the subdivision of this reservoir into its component parts is shown in Fig. 52. Interstices are probably absent in the zone of rock flowage, because the stresses are beyond the elastic limit, and the rock is in a state of plastic flow. Water in this zone is classified as internal water and is not in the realm of the hydrologist. The depth at which rocks undergo permanent deformation is not known accurately but is generally estimated as many miles.

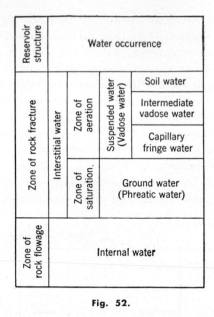

Fig. 52.

In the zone of rock fracture, the stresses are below the elastic limit, and interstices can exist in the rocks. Water in this zone is stored in the soil or rock interstices and accordingly is termed interstitial water. Although there is no direct relation between porosity and depth, in general, the porosity decreases with depth, the large openings particularly being absent at great depths. In crystalline rocks most of the water is encountered within 300 ft of the surface.[8] In sedimentary rocks, such as limestone and sandstone, porous zones that yield water readily are encountered in some places at depths of more than 6000 ft, although most wells in these strata find little water below a depth of 2000 ft. The decrease in size of interstices with increased depth is caused in part by the increased pressure at great depth, which tends to close the pore spaces or crevices, and in part by the cementation of interstices by the heavier and more highly mineralized waters.

The zone of aeration is that part of the earth's crust where the water present is not under hydrostatic pressure, except temporarily, and for the most part the interstices are filled with atmospheric gases. Water retained in this zone is held by molecular attraction and is termed pellicular, suspended, or vadose water. The thickness of the zone of aeration varies considerably depending on the geology, hy-

[8] E. E. Ellis, "Occurrence of Water in Crystalline Rocks," *U. S. Geol. Survey Water-Supply Paper* 160, 1906, pp. 19–28.

drology, and topography of the area. It may be virtually nonexistent in lowland areas adjacent to bodies of surface water as in marsh lands, or it may be as much as 1000 ft thick as in arid regions of great topographic relief.

The belt of soil water consists of the soil and other unconsolidated materials in which the root systems of plants, grasses, and trees are developed and from which water is discharged to the atmosphere by evaporation or transpiration. Evaporation occurs largely at the surface, except in tight clay soils under prolonged drying, where shrinkage cracks develop and permit air circulation to some depth. Although water may be brought to the evaporation areas by capillarity, in general water is not discharged in appreciable quantities by evaporation below depths of a few feet. As to transpiration, note that, although the root penetration of most common grasses and field crops is seldom more than a few feet, records indicate root development for wheat to depths of 7 ft; for alfalfa as much as 30 ft;[9] and for some perennials in arid regions as much as 50 ft.[10]

The capillary fringe is the belt overlying the zone of saturation and containing interstices, some or all of which are filled with water that is in connection with and is a continuation of the zone of saturation, being held above that zone by capillarity acting against the force of gravity. The thickness of the capillary fringe in granular material is a function of the effective particle size and generally increases as the grain size decreases. The fringe thickness may range from a few inches in coarse gravel to 8 ft in silty material and is probably much greater in very fine-grained sediments. The capillary fringe in a given material may vary slightly in thickness from summer to winter because of changes in water temperature. The surface tension of water increases as the temperature decreases, and within the range of 60° to 32° F it increases about 3 per cent. Although the density of water varies with temperature, this change is negligible. Accordingly, then, the thickness of the capillary fringe would be somewhat greater in late winter and spring, the period of lowered ground-water temperature.

Beneath the capillary fringe lies the zone of saturation. It is this zone that is of importance to the hydraulic engineer and well driller as the source of water for wells and springs. It is of importance to the hydrologist as the reservoir that provides the closing link in the hydrologic cycle by serving as the mechanism for the intake, trans-

[9] W. W. Burr, "The Storage and Use of Soil Moisture," *Nebraska Univ. Research Bull.* 5, 1914, p. 9.

[10] O. E. Meinzer, "Plants as Indicators of Ground Water," *U. S. Geol. Survey Water-Supply Paper* 577, 1927, p. 77.

port, and return of underground waters and to the surface and the atmosphere. The upper surface of the zone of saturation is called the *water table*.

Water Table and Artesian Aquifers

Although idealized conditions such as are shown in Fig. 85 are found frequently in the field, usually an actual cross section of a valley is more complex than indicated by this diagram. Field reconnaissance may reveal more than one water-bearing formation with considerable variation in the character of each stratum. The many geologic processes involved, coupled with the great variations in intensity and duration of the forces in action during each stage of development leading up to the existing structures, have resulted in an infinite number of variations in the geologic and hydrologic dimensions of the ground-water reservoir. The "hodge-podge" assortment of the drift cover in glaciated areas typifies these complexities. However, the heterogeneous nature of the surficial materials does not invalidate the fundamental principles but merely complicates their application.

A stratum or formation of permeable material that will yield gravity ground water in appreciable quantities is termed an *aquifer*. The term "appreciable quantity" is relative because, where ground water is obtained with difficulty, even fine-grained, poorly productive materials may be classed as principal aquifers. If an aquifer is overlain by a confining bed of impervious material and if the water level in a tightly cased well penetrating the aquifer rises above the bottom of the confining bed, the aquifer is termed *artesian*. The overlying confining bed is an *aquiclude*. The artesian aquifer differs from the water-table aquifer in that the surface, formed by contouring or connecting the heights of the water level in tightly cased wells tapping the aquifer, is not a free surface exposed to the soil atmosphere but is an imaginary pressure surface standing above the body of the aquifer. Consequently it receives the name of piezometric surface. Although the term piezometric surface can be applied also to the water-table surface, the reverse is not true. Contours drawn on the piezometric surface are referred to as isopiestic lines. A diagrammatic cross section illustrating the application of the above terminology is shown in Fig. 53.

The water level in well 1, which taps aquifer *A*, coincides with the water table or surface of the zone of saturation in this aquifer, and consequently well 1 is a nonartesian or water-table well. The water levels in wells 2, 3, and 4 stand above the base of the overlying aqui-

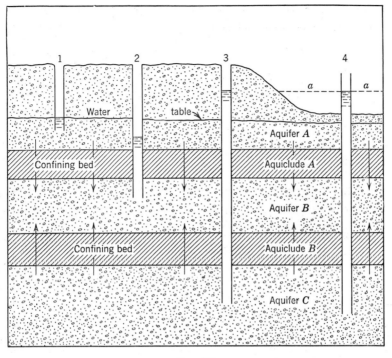

Fig. 53.

clude, and aquifers B and C are artesian. Region a–a is an area of artesian flow, and well 4 is a flowing well. The lower static level in aquifer B indicates that water is moving from aquifer A or C into aquifer B through a distant break in aquiclude A or B or by vertical leakage through the aquicludes. The high head in wells 3 and 4 indicates that the recharge or intake area of aquifer C is at a relatively high elevation, probably above the land surface shown in the cross section. Aquifers like B and C, which contain confined ground water, are pressure conduits and exhibit interesting elastic phenomena.

Elastic Properties of Artesian Aquifers

It is a common observation that wells in some areas will undergo changes of water level during periods of large fluctuation in barometric pressure. A representation of the mechanism causing the change of water level under varying air pressure and a hydrograph from a well exhibiting this effect are shown in Fig. 54. As the barometric pressure increases, the water level in the well casing tends to be depressed. An equal effect is exerted on the soil column and on the shallow water

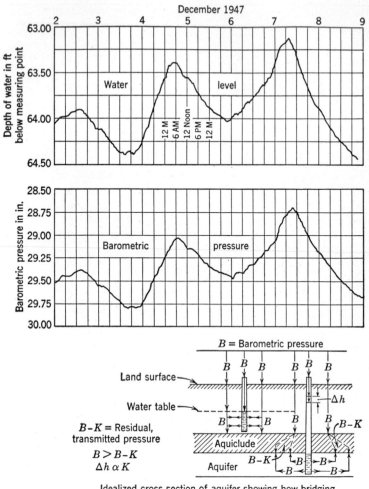

Idealized cross section of aquifer showing how bridging action of overlying aquiclude sets up pressure differential in the underlying aquifer which is balanced by a change in hydrostatic head.

Fig. 54.

table with a resultant balance of the pressure inside and outside the well tapping the shallow aquifer, and consequently no net change in water level occurs. In the deeper aquifer, however, the overlying aquiclude is competent to some degree in resisting the load imposed by the rising barometer and does not transmit the full effect of the air pressure change. Consequently, the water level in the well tapping confined ground water is depressed an amount equal to the proportion of the barometric pressure change that is not transmitted by the aquiclude. The ratio of water-level change to the barometric change, in equivalent units, is termed the barometric efficiency of the well. Note that the effect is inverse, that is, as the barometric pressure rises the water level declines.

Inasmuch as the increased hydrostatic pressure in the aquifer, which accompanies a rise in barometric pressure, exceeds the residual pressure transmitted through the aquiclude, a net positive pressure is exerted on the aquiclude. As a result of this pressure, the aquiclude is compressed slightly, or, conversely, the aquifer expands a small amount. The slight increase in aquifer volume accommodates the water displaced from the well casing by the increased pressure on the water surface. Changes in barometric pressure are generally of very short duration compared to the time required for the displaced water to move through the formation for any distance. Consequently, barometric fluctuations are recorded in confined aquifers if the overlying aquiclude is competent to resist pressure and extends over an appreciable area. Wells located near an outcrop area or near a break in the aquiclude, where contact with the surface or surface formations occurs within close proximity to the well, will not exhibit barometric effects.

Reports of blowing and sucking wells which exhibit pronounced updraft or downdraft of air at the well mouth may be explained by the barometric effects noted above. These reports are especially prevalent where an extensive aquiclude occurs some distance above the water table, so that there is a body of air confined between the water table and the aquiclude, which communicates with the atmosphere only through wells. Also the frequent reference to noticeable cloudiness or color in the well water preceding a storm might be explained in part by the rapid rise of water level, which would accompany a barometric low and would bring into the well silty or fine material, as a result of the quick inrush of water through the screen. Some cloudiness may also be caused by gas that escapes from solution when the atmospheric pressure is lowered.

Superimposed loads on the earth's crust also produce changes of water level in wells tapping confined ground water, as indicated in Fig. 55, which shows an autographic record of water-level fluctuation caused by railroad trains passing within 100 ft of the observation well. The alternate loading and unloading of the earth's crust by ocean tides in the coastal areas results in a corresponding cycle of water-level fluctuation in wells as shown in Fig. 56. In these cases, the resultant of the impressed pressure that is transmitted to the

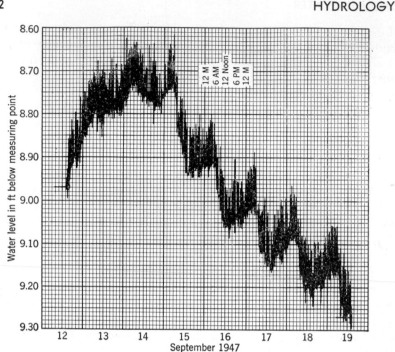

Fig. 55. Hydrograph from automatic water-stage recorder in operation on well tapping Marshall sandstone at Battle Creek, Michigan. Short-period vertical displacements superimposed on curve are water-level fluctuations caused by artesian loading from passing railroad trains.

aquifer, because of the incompetency of the aquiclude to resist entirely the increase in pressure, causes a rise in water level in the well casing, and the ratio of this rise to the total load impressed is termed the tidal efficiency of the aquifer. Inasmuch as the tidal efficiency is a measure of the incompetency of the aquiclude and the barometric efficiency is a measure of its competency, it is evident that the sum of the barometric and tidal efficiencies of an aquifer must equal unity, as demonstrated mathematically by Jacob.[11]

Subsurface Leakage

The presence of aquicludes or confining layers of considerable thickness and of dense, compact texture has probably served to further the somewhat popular but quite erroneous belief that the artesian aquifers are insulated strata containing connate waters. In this connection, it should be noted that many of our highly developed artesian aquifers would be dry today if such insulation were general.

Fortunately, however, most aquifers receive recharge either through direct infiltration on outcrop areas, through permeable breaks in the confining aquicludes, or by means of leakage through the aquiclude itself. Like many physical terms, the word impervious is only relative and not absolute because air or water will permeate most materials if sufficient time and pressure are involved.

To demonstrate the possible magnitude of aquiclude leakage, there is represented in Fig. 57 an idealized cross section of a geologic condition that is found frequently in the field. It is assumed that the average coefficient of permeability is 2000 gal per day per sq ft for aquifer B and 0.2 gal per day per sq ft for aquiclude A, or a ratio of 10,000 to 1. The permeability value selected for the aquifer is representative of the average obtained for many sand and gravel

[11] C. E. Jacob, "On the Flow of Water in an Elastic Artesian Aquifer," *Trans. Am. Geophys. Union,* 1940, p. 583.

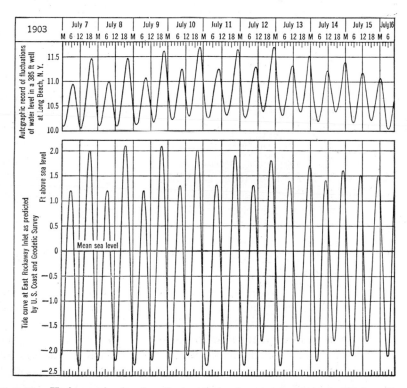

Fig. 56. Hydrograph showing fluctuations of water level in a 386-ft well at Long Beach, N. Y., as compared to the tide at East Rockaway Inlet, N. Y. From Plate 4 of *U. S. Geological Survey Water-Supply Paper 155.*

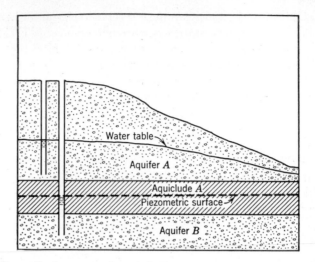

Fig. 57. Generalized cross section of shallow and deep aquifer showing differential hydrostatic head.

formations. The value selected for the aquiclude corresponds to a sample of clayey silt tested in the hydrologic laboratory[12] of the U. S. Geological Survey. The mechanical analysis for this material indicates clay, 49.3 per cent, silt, 45.3 per cent, and material larger than silt but less than 0.50 mm, 5.4 per cent; the porosity was 55.5 per cent. Assume that the water table in the shallow aquifer has a head 50 ft greater than the piezometric surface in the deeper aquifer. Assign a thickness of 50 ft for aquiclude A. With the foregoing conditions, it is calculated that the leakage through the aquiclude from the shallow to the deep aquifer would occur at the rate of 0.2 gal per day per sq ft of aquiclude area. This seems a minor item at first consideration, but for each square mile the leakage totals 5.6 million gal per day, or enough to supply a community of 56,000 people at an average rate of 100 gal per capita per day. When we consider the many square miles of contributing area available to most large aquifers, it is evident that the assumed aquiclude can contain even less pervious material and still pass appreciable quantities of water.

For the assumed conditions with a porosity of 56 per cent, the movement of water through the aquiclude would occur at the rate of 0.6 in. per day or require about 3 yr for a traverse through the 50-ft

[12] L. K. Wenzel and V. C. Fishel, "Methods for Determining Permeability of Water-Bearing Materials," *U. S. Geol. Survey Water-Supply Paper* 887, 1942, p. 13.

section. Accordingly, then, an aquifer recharged only by leakage from adjacent aquicludes will not show water-level fluctuations in response to short period changes in precipitation rate.

In addition to the dewatering problems in subsurface construction where aquifers are exposed by excavation, other difficult problems may arise in deep excavation into an overlying aquiclude. Prior to excavation, the stresses in an aquiclude would be in equilibrium with the total force exerted by the underlying aquifer. Assume that at the site the aquifer has a large hydrostatic head and a high transmissibility. The aquiclude over a long period of time has compacted to a thickness that provides the inherent stability to balance the upward pressure from the aquifer. Although detailed information is not available, it would seem probable that any excavation to appreciable depth in the aquiclude might disturb the force balance to an extent that might result in upheaval of the pit floor and general instability. If rupture of the aquiclude occurred or if permeable zones were exposed, large boils or springs might develop. A condition of this type might be remedied by a few properly spaced wells that penetrate the deep aquifer and are pumped at a rate sufficient to reduce the pressure and restore an equilibrium state.

Underflow

To all who are acquainted with the construction of blind drains, the type of ground-water flow termed underflow will strike a familiar chord. The geologic "horse" in sedimentary rock and the buried kames, eskers, alluvium, and outwash channels in the drift mantle are examples of nature's large-scale underdrains. Underflow may occur under either water-table or artesian conditions as shown in Fig. 58. Inasmuch as the word channel is generally used in surface-water terminology for flow with a free surface, the term underflow channel can be assigned for the water-table condition because a free surface exists. In a similar manner, underflow conduit can be used for the artesian condition because the term conduit generally implies confined flow.

In periods of extended drought many stream channels, though dry with reference to surface flow, may carry appreciable quantities of water as underflow. In view of the vast network of preglacial and interglacial stream channels throughout the glaciated areas of the United States, plus the evidence that many of these buried channels are very large, it becomes evident that the underflow in channels filled with very permeable material may be an appreciable part of the base

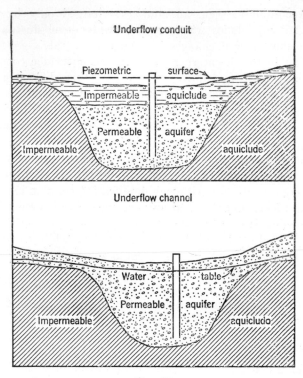

Fig. 58.

flow from some drainage basins. Although the velocity of such under-flow would be very much less than surface flow, the total discharge becomes appreciable if large areas are involved.

Seepage

The movement of water between ground-water aquifers and surface sources is termed seepage. It is further classified as influent seepage, which is recharge from surface bodies of water, and effluent seepage, which is discharge to surface bodies of water. Thus surface streams are influent streams if the stream contributes water to the ground-water reservoir and effluent streams if water is received from the water table. A sketch of conditions existing in each type is shown in Fig. 59. The local build-up of head on the water table underlying an influent stream is termed a ground-water mound. The so-called base flow of surface streams is the effluent seepage from the drainage basin. During periods of prolonged drought, when the total flow of a stream is restricted to the base flow, the stream is functioning solely as a

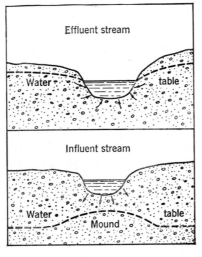

Fig. 59.

drain. Accordingly, the collection of pertinent data concerning the volume of discharge and the time rate of water-table decline for baseflow periods, which is one phase of present field investigations conducted by the U. S. Geological Survey, will provide in time the basis for application of drain formulas and the ultimate forecast of base flow for major streams.

Ground-Water Hydraulics

Although the first studies of the flow of water through capillary tubes by Hagen[13] and Poiseuille[14] indicated that the rate of flow is proportional to the hydraulic gradient, it was Darcy[15] who confirmed this law and applied it to the flow of water percolating through filter sands. Darcy's law is expressed as follows, in the system of units of general usage,

$$v = \frac{PI}{p} \tag{2}$$

where v is velocity in feet per day, P coefficient of permeability in

[13] G. Hagen, "Ueber die Bewegung des Wassers in engen cylindrischen Rohren," *Ann. Physik Chem.*, Leipzig, 1839, vol. 46, pp. 423–442.

[14] J. L. M. Poiseuille, "Recherches expérimentales sur le mouvement des liquides dans les tubes de tres petit diamètre," *Roy. Acad. Sci. Inst. France Math. Phys. Sci. Mem.*, 1846, vol. 9, p. 433.

[15] Henri Darcy, *Les Fontaines publiques de la ville de Dijon*, Paris, 1856.

cubic feet per day per square foot, I hydraulic gradient in feet per foot, and p porosity expressed as a ratio.

In most ground-water problems, the total volume of flow is required, rather than the velocity, and consequently equation 2 is modified to the form

$$Q = PIA \qquad (3)$$

where Q is discharge in cubic feet per day, P coefficient of permeability in cubic feet per day per square foot, I hydraulic gradient in feet per foot, and A area of flow cross section in square feet.

This formula may be adapted for use with the more convenient coefficient of transmissibility by noting the distinction between its definition and that of the coefficient of permeability

$$Q = TIW \qquad (4)$$

where Q and I are defined as above, T is the coefficient of transmissibility in cubic feet per day per foot, and W the width of flow cross section in feet.

Either equation 3 or 4 may be used for determining the discharge of ground water through underflow channels or conduits or for computing the discharge across a given length of a contour on the water table or the piezometric surface. Most underflow problems can be greatly simplified by assuming an idealized rectangular cross section that closely approximates the actual section. An approximation of this type is shown in Fig. 60, with appropriate notations concerning the application of the foregoing terminology. A sample computation is made using the following assumed values, which are representative of average conditions for a sand and gravel filled channel.

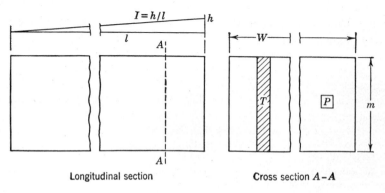

Longitudinal section   Cross section $A-A$

Assumptions:

$$P = 270 \text{ cu ft per day per sq ft}$$

Hₒ gradient $$I = 10 \text{ ft per mile}$$

$$A = mW$$

where $m = 100$ ft, average thickness of aquifer, and $W = 5000$ ft, average width of aquifer; then by equation 3

$$Q = PIA$$

$$= 270 \cdot \left[\frac{10}{5280}\right] \cdot (100 \times 5000)$$

$$Q = 255,000 \text{ cu ft per day}$$

or by equation 4

$$Q = TIW$$

where

$$T = P \cdot m = 270 \cdot 100 = 27,000$$

$$Q = 27,000 \cdot \left[\frac{10}{5280}\right] \cdot 5000$$

$$Q = 255,000 \text{ cu ft per day}$$

Although the formulas above are of considerable value in under-flow determinations, their application requires a knowledge of the permeability or transmissibility of the aquifer. The first application of Darcy's law to the analysis of the hydraulics of wells was made by Dupuit[16] in 1863. His equation was derived for a discharging well located at the center of a highly idealized circular island and thus quite limited in its application. A modification of the Dupuit analysis was developed by Thiem[17] in 1906 that utilized for the first time two or more observation wells to determine the field coefficient of permeability. The derivation of Thiem's formula may be set up from the profile section through the cone of depression shown in Fig. 61. From Darcy's law, the flow through any concentric cylindrical section of the water-bearing material is given by equation 3

$$Q = PIA$$

[16] Jules Dupuit, *Études théoretiques et pratiques sur le mouvement des eaux*, Paris, second ed., 1863.
[17] Gunter Thiem, *Hydrologische Methoden*, J. M. Gebhardt, Leipzig, 1906, 56 pp.

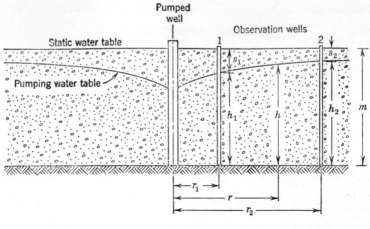

Fig. 61.

Using cylindrical coordinates, we take r as the radius of any cylinder and h as the height of the cone of depression at the distance r from the well. Then

$$I = \frac{dh}{dr} \tag{5}$$

and the flow area

$$A = 2\pi rh \tag{6}$$

Therefore

$$Q = P \cdot \frac{dh}{dr} \cdot 2\pi rh \tag{7}$$

Rewriting and setting up the integral between the limits r_1 and r_2, the respective distances to observation wells 1 and 2, we have

$$\int_{r_1}^{r_2} \frac{dr}{r} = \frac{2\pi P}{Q} \int_{h_1}^{h_2} h \, dh \tag{8}$$

Integrating and inserting the limits, we obtain

$$\log_e \frac{r_2}{r_1} = \frac{2\pi P}{2Q} [h_2{}^2 - h_1{}^2] = \frac{\pi P}{Q} [h_2{}^2 - h_1{}^2] \tag{9}$$

But

$$h_2{}^2 - h_1{}^2 = [h_2 + h_1][h_2 - h_1] \tag{10}$$

and

$$h_2 - h_1 = s_1 - s_2 \tag{11}$$

If the amount of drawdown is small compared to the saturated thickness of the water-bearing material, h_2 and h_1 are nearly equal and approximate the saturated thickness, m, or

$$h_2 + h_1 = 2m \tag{12}$$

$$\log_e \frac{r_2}{r_1} = \frac{\pi P}{Q} \cdot 2m(s_1 - s_2) = \frac{2\pi Pm}{Q}(s_1 - s_2) \tag{13}$$

but

$$T = Pm$$

therefore

$$\log_e \frac{r_2}{r_1} = \frac{2\pi T}{Q}(s_1 - s_2) \tag{14}$$

Converting the logarithm to the base 10 and transposing to solve for T, we have

$$T = \frac{2.30Q \log_{10} \dfrac{r_2}{r_1}}{2\pi(s_1 - s_2)} \tag{15}$$

where T is the coefficient of transmissibility in cubic feet per day per foot, Q is discharge of pumped well in cubic feet per day, r_1 and r_2 are the respective distances of observation well from pumped well in feet, and s_1 and s_2 are the respective drawdown or recovery in observation well in feet.

The derivation of the Thiem formula is based on the following assumptions, and its successful application is dependent on the degree to which these qualifications are satisfied by the field conditions: (1) the aquifer is homogeneous, isotropic, and of infinite areal extent; (2) the discharging well penetrates and receives water from the entire thickness of the aquifer; (3) the coefficient of transmissibility is constant at all places and at all times; (4) pumping has continued at a uniform rate for a time sufficient for the hydraulic system to reach an equilibrium stage or a steady flow condition; (5) the flow lines are radial; and (6) flow is laminar. Despite the limiting assumptions, Thiem's formula is widely applicable to ground-water problems, and, as will be demonstrated, many of the above limitations can be removed by appropriate adjustment.

As shown by Wenzel,[18] the equilibrium formulas used by Slichter,

[18] L. K. Wenzel and V. C. Fishel, "Methods for Determining Permeability of Water-Bearing Materials," *U. S. Geol. Survey Water-Supply Paper* 887, 1942, pp. 79–82.

Turneaure and Russell, Israelson, and Muskat are essentially modified forms of Thiem's method. Furthermore, Jacob[19] demonstrated that Wenzel's "limiting formula" and "gradient formula" are also specialized forms of the Thiem method. Accordingly, all the foregoing formulas are limited by the same assumptions used in deriving Thiem's formula. Several of the previously mentioned equilibrium formulas entail the determination of R, the distance from the pumped well at which the drawdown is inappreciable, and necessarily assume that the drawdown cone has reached a state of equilibrium over the entire area of influence. The use of R arises when observation wells are not available, and the required two points for the equilibrium formula are (1) the pumped well where r and s are measurable and (2) the point of zero drawdown at the radius of influence. Arbitrary values have been assigned to R by several investigators: Slichter[20] gives 600 ft; Muskat[21] 500 ft; and Tolman[22] 1000 ft. Turneaure and Russell[23] indicate that adequate estimates can be made in many instances by assuming R to be approximately 1000 ft. When it is recognized that measurable drawdowns were observed by Leggette[24] at distances as great as 7.1 miles from a pumped well, it appears that under certain conditions the previous estimates for R may be low. A ground-water reservoir tends toward a state of equilibrium with natural discharge balancing natural recharge. Consequently, the development of a well disturbs this balance, and the new equilibrium state is reached by the propagation of the cone of depression to an extent where the natural recharge is increased or the natural discharge is decreased by an amount equal to the withdrawal by the well. In some instances the radius of the cone necessary to reach the areas of natural recharge or discharge may be many times greater than the values cited or estimated by the investigators mentioned above.

[19] C. E. Jacob, "Notes on Determining Permeability by Pumping Tests under Water-Table Conditions," U. S. Geological Survey, mimeographed report, June 1944.

[20] C. S. Slichter, "Theoretical Investigation of the Motion of Ground Water," U. S. Geol. Survey 19th Ann. Rept., 1899, Part 2, p. 360.

[21] Morris Muskat, Flow of Homogeneous Fluids through Porous Media, McGraw-Hill, 1937, p. 95.

[22] C. F. Tolman, Ground Water, McGraw-Hill, 1937, p. 387.

[23] F. E. Turneaure and H. L. Russell, Public Water Supplies, John Wiley, fourth ed., 1940, p. 270.

[24] R. M. Leggette, "The Mutual Interference of Artesian Wells on Long Island, N. Y.," Trans. Am. Geophys. Union, 1937, p. 493.

The Nonequilibrium Formula

A major advancement in ground-water hydraulics was made by Theis[25] in 1935 with his development of the nonequilibrium formula which introduces the time factor and the specific yield or coefficient of storage. This formula was derived by analogy between the flow of ground water and the flow of heat by conduction. Later, Jacob[26] demonstrated the derivation of this formula using hydraulic concepts directly.

A generalized free-body diagram of the flow system in the vicinity of a discharging well is shown by Fig. 62. Assuming that impermeable planes bound the system on top and bottom and all flow is radial, we find from the principle of the conservation of matter that the difference in the rate of flow through the inner and outer faces of the cylindrical shell must be drawn from storage within the shell.

$$Q_1 - Q_2 = \frac{dv}{dt} \qquad (16)$$

From equation 4 the flow through the inner face is

$$Q_1 = T I_1 W_1 = \frac{-T \, \partial s 2\pi r}{\partial r} \qquad (17)$$

Since the second derivative defines the rate of change in slope, we can determine the slope or gradient of the piezometric surface at the outer face of the cylinder.

$$I_2 = I_1 + \frac{\partial^2 s}{\partial r^2} \, dr$$

$$= \frac{\partial s}{\partial r} + \frac{\partial^2 s}{\partial r^2} \, dr \qquad (18)$$

Then the flow through the outer face is

$$Q_2 = -T \left(\frac{\partial s}{\partial r} + \frac{\partial^2 s}{\partial r^2} \, dr \right) 2\pi (r + dr) \qquad (19)$$

The rate of change in volume within the cylindrical shell is expressed as

$$\frac{dv}{dt} = 2\pi r \, dr \, \frac{\partial s}{\partial t} \, S \qquad (20)$$

[25] C. V. Theis, "The Relation between the Lowering of the Piezometric Surface and the Rate and Duration of Discharge of a Well Using Ground-Water Storage," *Trans. Am. Geophys. Union*, 1935, pp. 519–524.

[26] C. E. Jacob, "On the Flow of Water in an Elastic Artesian Aquifer," *Trans. Am. Geophys. Union*, 1940, pp. 574–586.

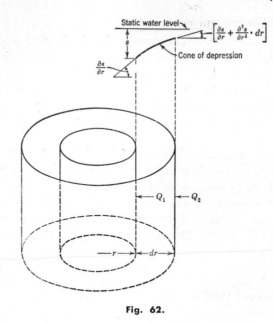

Fig. 62.

where S is the coefficient of storage. For water-table conditions, S is equivalent to the specific yield of the materials dewatered by pumping. For artesian conditions, where water is drawn from storage by the compression of the aquifer, S is equal to the water obtained from a column of water-bearing material with a base one foot square and a height equal to the thickness of the aquifer.

Substituting the above values in equation 16 gives us

$$-T\frac{\partial s}{\partial r}2\pi r + T\left(\frac{\partial s}{\partial r} + \frac{\partial^2 s}{\partial r^2}\,dr\right)2\pi(r + dr) = 2\pi r\,dr\,\frac{\partial s}{\partial t}\,S$$

$$-T\frac{\partial s}{\partial r}2\pi r + T\left[2\pi r\frac{\partial s}{\partial r} + 2\pi r\,dr\,\frac{\partial^2 s}{\partial r^2} + 2\pi\,dr\,\frac{\partial s}{\partial r} + 2\pi(dr)^2\,\frac{\partial^2 s}{\partial r^2}\right]$$

$$= 2\pi r\,dr\,\frac{\partial s}{\partial t}\,S$$

Dividing through by $2\pi r T\,dr$ and neglecting differentials higher than first order, we have

$$\frac{\partial^2 s}{\partial r^2} + \frac{1}{r}\frac{\partial s}{\partial r} = \frac{S}{T}\frac{\partial s}{\partial t} \tag{21}$$

This is the differential equation for the radial flow of water in an elastic artesian aquifer. For a constant pumping rate Q, the solution of this equation is given by

$$s = \frac{Q}{4\pi T} \int_{r^2S/4Tt}^{\infty} \frac{e^{-u}}{u} \, du \qquad (22)$$

where $u = \dfrac{r^2S}{4Tt}$ (23)

t = time since pumping started in days

Q = discharge of pumped well in cubic feet per day

The expression in equation 22 is not directly integrable as an elementary function, but its value can be computed by the following series:

$$\int_{r^2S/4Tt}^{\infty} \frac{e^{-u}}{u} \, du$$

$$= W(u) = -0.577216 - \log_e u + u - \frac{u^2}{2.2!} + \frac{u^3}{3.3!} \cdots \qquad (24)$$

As noted above, the exponential integral is written symbolically as $W(u)$, which in this usage is generally read "well function of u." Tables of the value of this exponential integral have been published.[27] Values of $W(u)$ for values of u from 10^{-15} to 9.9 as tabulated by Wenzel[28] are given in Table 10. Values in the table are values of $W(u)$ for different values u equal to N (columns 1 and 18), multiplied by 10 to the various powers shown at the top of each remaining column. For example, when u has the value 5.0, $W(u)$ is determined from the line having $N = 5$ and column 17 as 0.001148, or, when u has the value 0.005, $W(u)$ is 4.7261 (from the same line and column 14). Inspection of equations 22 and 23 reveals that, if s can be measured for one or more values of r and for several values of t, and if the discharge Q is known, S and T can be determined. However, the presence of two unknowns and the nature of the exponential integral make it impossible to effect an exact analytical solution. Inasmuch

[27] *Smithsonian Physical Tables*, Table 32, eighth revised ed., 1933; the values to be used are those given for Ei $(-x)$, with the sign changed.

[28] L. K. Wenzel and V. C. Fishel, "Methods for Determining Permeability of Water-Bearing Materials," *U. S. Geol. Survey Water-Supply Paper* 887, 1942, facing p. 89.

TABLE 10

Values of W(u) for Nonequilibrium Formula

1	2	3	4	5	6	7	8	9
N	$N \times 10^{-15}$	$N \times 10^{-14}$	$N \times 10^{-13}$	$N \times 10^{-12}$	$N \times 10^{-11}$	$N \times 10^{-10}$	$N \times 10^{-9}$	$N \times 10^{-8}$
1.0	33.9616	31.6590	29.3564	27.0538	24.7512	22.4486	20.1460	17.8435
1.1	33.8662	31.5637	29.2611	26.9585	24.6559	22.3533	20.0507	17.7482
1.2	33.7792	31.4767	29.1741	26.8715	24.5689	22.2663	19.9637	17.6611
1.3	33.6992	31.3966	29.0940	26.7914	24.4889	22.1863	19.8837	17.5811
1.4	33.6251	31.3225	29.0199	26.7173	24.4147	22.1122	19.8096	17.5070
1.5	33.5561	31.2535	28.9509	26.6483	24.3458	22.0432	19.7406	17.4380
1.6	33.4916	31.1890	28.8864	26.5838	24.2812	21.9786	19.6760	17.3735
1.7	33.4309	31.1283	28.8258	26.5232	24.2206	21.9180	19.6154	17.3128
1.8	33.3738	31.0712	28.7686	26.4660	24.1634	21.8608	19.5583	17.2557
1.9	33.3197	31.0171	28.7145	26.4119	24.1094	21.8068	19.5042	17.2016
2.0	33.2684	30.9658	28.6632	26.3607	24.0581	21.7555	19.4529	17.1503
2.1	33.2196	30.9170	28.6145	26.3119	24.0093	21.7067	19.4041	17.1015
2.2	33.1731	30.8705	28.5679	26.2653	23.9628	21.6602	19.3576	17.0550
2.3	33.1286	30.8261	28.5235	26.2209	23.9183	21.6157	19.3131	17.0106
2.4	33.0861	30.7835	28.4809	26.1783	23.8758	21.5732	19.2706	16.9680
2.5	33.0453	30.7427	28.4401	26.1375	23.8349	21.5323	19.2298	16.9272
2.6	33.0060	30.7035	28.4009	26.0983	23.7957	21.4931	19.1905	16.8880
2.7	32.9683	30.6657	28.3631	26.0606	23.7580	21.4554	19.1528	16.8502
2.8	32.9319	30.6294	28.3268	26.0242	23.7216	21.4190	19.1164	16.8138
2.9	32.8968	30.5943	28.2917	25.9891	23.6865	21.3839	19.0813	16.7788
3.0	32.8629	30.5604	28.2578	25.9552	23.6526	21.3500	19.0474	16.7449
3.1	32.8302	30.5276	28.2250	25.9224	23.6198	21.3172	19.0146	16.7121
3.2	32.7984	30.4958	28.1932	25.8907	23.5881	21.2855	18.9829	16.6803
3.3	32.7676	30.4651	28.1625	25.8599	23.5573	21.2547	18.9521	16.6495
3.4	32.7378	30.4352	28.1326	25.8300	23.5274	21.2249	18.9223	16.6197
3.5	32.7088	30.4062	28.1036	25.8010	23.4985	21.1959	18.8933	16.5907
3.6	32.6806	30.3780	28.0755	25.7729	23.4703	21.1677	18.8651	16.5625
3.7	32.6532	30.3506	28.0481	25.7455	23.4429	21.1403	18.8377	16.5351
3.8	32.6266	30.3240	28.0214	25.7188	23.4162	21.1136	18.8110	16.5085
3.9	32.6006	30.2980	27.9954	25.6928	23.3902	21.0877	18.7851	16.4825
4.0	32.5753	30.2727	27.9701	25.6675	23.3649	21.0623	18.7598	16.4572
4.1	32.5506	30.2480	27.9454	25.6428	23.3402	21.0376	18.7351	16.4325
4.2	32.5265	30.2239	27.9213	25.6187	23.3161	21.0136	18.7110	16.4084
4.3	32.5029	30.2004	27.8978	25.5952	23.2926	20.9900	18.6874	16.3948
4.4	32.4800	30.1774	27.8748	25.5722	23.2696	20.9670	18.6644	16.3619
4.5	32.4575	30.1549	27.8523	25.5497	23.2471	20.9446	18.6420	16.3394
4.6	32.4355	30.1329	27.8303	25.5277	23.2252	20.9226	18.6200	16.3174
4.7	32.4140	30.1114	27.8088	25.5062	23.2037	20.9011	18.5985	16.2959
4.8	32.3929	30.0904	27.7878	25.4852	23.1826	20.8800	18.5774	16.2748
4.9	32.3723	30.0697	27.7672	25.4646	23.1620	20.8594	18.5568	16.2542
5.0	32.3521	30.0495	27.7470	25.4444	23.1418	20.8392	18.5366	16.2340
5.1	32.3323	30.0297	27.7271	25.4246	23.1220	20.8194	18.5168	16.2142
5.2	32.3129	30.0103	27.7077	25.4051	23.1026	20.8000	18.4974	16.1948
5.3	32.2939	29.9913	27.6887	25.3861	23.0835	20.7809	18.4783	16.1758
5.4	32.2752	29.9726	27.6700	25.3674	23.0648	20.7622	18.4596	16.1571
5.5	32.2568	29.9542	27.6516	25.3491	23.0465	20.7439	18.4413	16.1387
5.6	32.2388	29.9362	27.6336	25.3310	23.0285	20.7259	18.4233	16.1207
5.7	32.2211	29.9185	27.6159	25.3133	23.0108	20.7082	18.4056	16.1030
5.8	32.2037	29.9011	27.5985	25.2959	22.9934	20.6908	18.3882	16.0856
5.9	32.1866	29.8840	27.5814	25.2789	22.9763	20.6737	18.3711	16.0685
6.0	32.1698	29.8672	27.5646	25.2620	22.9595	20.6569	18.3543	16.0517
6.1	32.1533	29.8507	27.5481	25.2455	22.9429	20.6403	18.3378	16.0352
6.2	32.1370	29.8344	27.5318	25.2293	22.9267	20.6241	18.3215	16.0189
6.3	32.1210	29.8184	27.5158	25.2133	22.9107	20.6081	18.3055	16.0029
6.4	32.1053	29.8027	27.5001	25.1975	22.8949	20.5923	18.2898	15.9872
6.5	32.0898	29.7872	27.4846	25.1820	22.8794	20.5768	18.2742	15.9717
6.6	32.0745	29.7719	27.4693	25.1667	22.8641	20.5616	18.2590	15.9564
6.7	32.0595	29.7569	27.4543	25.1517	22.8491	20.5465	18.2439	15.9414
6.8	32.0446	29.7421	27.4395	25.1369	22.8343	20.5317	18.2291	15.9265
6.9	32.0300	29.7275	27.4249	25.1223	22.8197	20.5171	18.2145	15.9119
7.0	32.0156	29.7131	27.4105	25.1079	22.8053	20.5027	18.2001	15.8976
7.1	32.0015	29.6989	27.3963	25.0937	22.7911	20.4885	18.1860	15.8834
7.2	31.9875	29.6849	27.3823	25.0797	22.7771	20.4746	18.1720	15.8694
7.3	31.9737	29.6711	27.3685	25.0659	22.7633	20.4608	18.1582	15.8556
7.4	31.9601	29.6575	27.3549	25.0523	22.7497	20.4472	18.1446	15.8420
7.5	31.9467	29.6441	27.3415	25.0389	22.7363	20.4337	18.1311	15.8286
7.6	31.9334	29.6308	27.3282	25.0257	22.7231	20.4205	18.1179	15.8153
7.7	31.9203	29.6178	27.3152	25.0126	22.7100	20.4074	18.1048	15.8022
7.8	31.9074	29.6048	27.3023	24.9997	22.6971	20.3945	18.0919	15.7893
7.9	31.8947	29.5921	27.2895	24.9869	22.6844	20.3818	18.0792	15.7766
8.0	31.8821	29.5795	27.2769	24.9744	22.6718	20.3692	18.0666	15.7640
8.1	31.8697	29.5671	27.2645	24.9619	22.6594	20.3568	18.0542	15.7516
8.2	31.8574	29.5548	27.2523	24.9497	22.6471	20.3445	18.0419	15.7393
8.3	31.8453	29.5427	27.2401	24.9375	22.6350	20.3324	18.0298	15.7272
8.4	31.8333	29.5307	27.2282	24.9256	22.6230	20.3204	18.0178	15.7152
8.5	31.8215	29.5189	27.2163	24.9137	22.6112	20.3086	18.0060	15.7034
8.6	31.8098	29.5072	27.2046	24.9020	22.5995	20.2969	17.9943	15.6917
8.7	31.7982	29.4957	27.1931	24.8905	22.5879	20.2853	17.9827	15.6801
8.8	31.7868	29.4842	27.1816	24.8790	22.5765	20.2739	17.9713	15.6687
8.9	31.7755	29.4729	27.1703	24.8678	22.5652	20.2626	17.9600	15.6574
9.0	31.7643	29.4618	27.1592	24.8566	22.5540	20.2514	17.9488	15.6462
9.1	31.7533	29.4507	27.1481	24.8455	22.5429	20.2404	17.9378	15.6352
9.2	31.7424	29.4398	27.1372	24.8346	22.5320	20.2294	17.9268	15.6243
9.3	31.7315	29.4290	27.1264	24.8238	22.5212	20.2186	17.9160	15.6135
9.4	31.7208	29.4183	27.1157	24.8131	22.5105	20.2079	17.9053	15.6028
9.5	31.7103	29.4077	27.1051	24.8025	22.4999	20.1973	17.8948	15.5922
9.6	31.6998	29.3972	27.0946	24.7921	22.4895	20.1869	17.8843	15.5817
9.7	31.6894	29.3868	27.0843	24.7817	22.4791	20.1765	17.8739	15.5713
9.8	31.6792	29.3766	27.0740	24.7714	22.4688	20.1663	17.8637	15.5611
9.9	31.6690	29.3664	27.0639	24.7613	22.4587	20.1561	17.8535	15.5509

(From *U. S. Geological Survey Water-Supply Paper 887*.)

TABLE 10 (Continued)

Values of W(u) for Nonequilibrium Formula

10	11	12	13	14	15	16	17	18
$N \times 10^{-7}$	$N \times 10^{-6}$	$N \times 10^{-5}$	$N \times 10^{-4}$	$N \times 10^{-3}$	$N \times 10^{-2}$	$N \times 10^{-1}$	N	N
15.5109	13.2383	10.9357	8.6332	6.3315	4.0379	1.8229	0.2194	1.0
15.4456	13.1430	10.8404	8.5379	6.2363	3.9436	1.7371	.1860	1.1
15.3586	13.0560	10.7534	8.4509	6.1494	3.8576	1.6595	.1584	1.2
15.2785	12.9759	10.6734	8.3709	6.0695	3.7785	1.5889	.1355	1.3
15.2044	12.9018	10.5993	8.2968	5.9955	3.7054	1.5241	.1162	1.4
15.1354	12.8328	10.5303	8.2278	5.9266	3.6374	1.4645	.1000	1.5
15.0709	12.7683	10.4657	8.1634	5.8621	3.5739	1.4092	.08631	1.6
15.0103	12.7077	10.4051	8.1027	5.8016	3.5143	1.3578	.07465	1.7
14.9531	12.6505	10.3479	8.0455	5.7446	3.4581	1.3098	.06471	1.8
14.8990	12.5964	10.2939	7.9915	5.6906	3.4050	1.2649	.05620	1.9
14.8477	12.5451	10.2426	7.9402	5.6394	3.3547	1.2227	.04890	2.0
14.7989	12.4964	10.1938	7.8914	5.5907	3.3069	1.1829	.04261	2.1
14.7524	12.4498	10.1473	7.8449	5.5443	3.2614	1.1454	.03719	2.2
14.7080	12.4054	10.1028	7.8004	5.4999	3.2179	1.1099	.03250	2.3
14.6654	12.3628	10.0603	7.7579	5.4575	3.1763	1.0762	.02844	2.4
14.6246	12.3220	10.0194	7.7172	5.4167	3.1365	1.0443	.02491	2.5
14.5854	12.2828	9.9802	7.6779	5.3776	3.0983	1.0139	.02185	2.6
14.5476	12.2450	9.9425	7.6401	5.3400	3.0615	0.9849	.01918	2.7
14.5113	12.2087	9.9061	7.6038	5.3037	3.0261	.9573	.01686	2.8
14.4762	12.1736	9.8710	7.5687	5.2687	2.9920	.9309	.01482	2.9
14.4423	12.1397	9.8371	7.5348	5.2349	2.9591	.9057	.01305	3.0
14.4095	12.1069	9.8043	7.5020	5.2022	2.9273	.8815	.01149	3.1
14.3777	12.0751	9.7726	7.4703	5.1706	2.8965	.8583	.01013	3.2
14.3470	12.0444	9.7418	7.4395	5.1399	2.8668	.8361	.008939	3.3
14.3171	12.0145	9.7120	7.4097	5.1102	2.8379	.8147	.007891	3.4
14.2881	11.9855	9.6830	7.3807	5.0813	2.8099	.7942	.006970	3.5
14.2599	11.9574	9.6548	7.3526	5.0532	2.7827	.7745	.006160	3.6
14.2325	11.9300	9.6274	7.3252	5.0259	2.7563	.7554	.005448	3.7
14.2059	11.9033	9.6007	7.2985	4.9993	2.7306	.7371	.004820	3.8
14.1799	11.8773	9.5745	7.2725	4.9735	2.7056	.7194	.004267	3.9
14.1546	11.8520	9.5495	7.2472	4.9482	2.6813	.7024	.003779	4.0
14.1299	11.8273	9.5248	7.2225	4.9236	2.6576	.6859	.003349	4.1
14.1058	11.8032	9.5007	7.1985	4.8997	2.6344	.6700	.002969	4.2
14.0823	11.7797	9.4771	7.1749	4.8762	2.6119	.6546	.002633	4.3
14.0593	11.7567	9.4541	7.1520	4.8533	2.5899	.6397	.002336	4.4
14.0368	11.7342	9.4317	7.1295	4.8310	2.5684	.6253	.002073	4.5
14.0148	11.7122	9.4097	7.1075	4.8091	2.5474	.6114	.001841	4.6
13.9933	11.6907	9.3882	7.0860	4.7877	2.5268	.5979	.001635	4.7
13.9723	11.6697	9.3671	7.0650	4.7667	2.5068	.5848	.001453	4.8
13.9516	11.6491	9.3465	7.0444	4.7462	2.4871	.5721	.001291	4.9
13.9314	11.6289	9.3263	7.0242	4.7261	2.4679	.5598	.001148	5.0
13.9116	11.6091	9.3065	7.0044	4.7064	2.4491	.5478	.001021	5.1
13.8922	11.5896	9.2871	6.9850	4.6871	2.4306	.5362	.0009086	5.2
13.8732	11.5706	9.2681	6.9659	4.6681	2.4126	.5250	.0008086	5.3
13.8545	11.5519	9.2494	6.9473	4.6495	2.3948	.5140	.0007198	5.4
13.8361	11.5336	9.2310	6.9289	4.6313	2.3775	.5034	.0006409	5.5
13.8181	11.5155	9.2130	6.9109	4.6134	2.3604	.4930	.0005708	5.6
13.8004	11.4978	9.1953	6.8932	4.5958	2.3437	.4830	.0005085	5.7
13.7830	11.4804	9.1779	6.8758	4.5785	2.3273	.4732	.0004532	5.8
13.7659	11.4633	9.1608	6.8588	4.5615	2.3111	.4637	.0004039	5.9
13.7491	11.4465	9.1440	6.8420	4.5448	2.2953	.4544	.0003601	6.0
13.7326	11.4300	9.1275	6.8254	4.5283	2.2797	.4454	.0003211	6.1
13.7163	11.4138	9.1112	6.8092	4.5122	2.2645	.4366	.0002864	6.2
13.7003	11.3978	9.0952	6.7932	4.4963	2.2494	.4280	.0002555	6.3
13.6846	11.3820	9.0795	6.7775	4.4806	2.2346	.4197	.0002279	6.4
13.6691	11.3665	9.0640	6.7620	4.4652	2.2201	.4115	.0002034	6.5
13.6538	11.3512	9.0487	6.7467	4.4501	2.2058	.4036	.0001816	6.6
13.6388	11.3362	9.0337	6.7317	4.4351	2.1917	.3959	.0001621	6.7
13.6240	11.3214	9.0189	6.7169	4.4204	2.1779	.3883	.0001448	6.8
13.6094	11.3068	9.0043	6.7023	4.4059	2.1643	.3810	.0001293	6.9
13.5950	11.2924	8.9899	6.6879	4.3916	2.1508	.3738	.0001155	7.0
13.5808	11.2782	8.9757	6.6737	4.3775	2.1376	.3668	.0001032	7.1
13.5568	11.2642	8.9617	6.6598	4.3636	2.1246	.3599	.00009219	7.2
13.5530	11.2504	8.9479	6.6460	4.3500	2.1118	.3532	.00008239	7.3
13.5394	11.2368	8.9343	6.6324	4.3364	2.0991	.3467	.00007364	7.4
13.5260	11.2234	8.9209	6.6190	4.3231	2.0867	.3403	.00006583	7.5
13.5127	11.2102	8.9076	6.6057	4.3100	2.0744	.3341	.00005886	7.6
13.4997	11.1971	8.8946	6.5927	4.2970	2.0623	.3280	.00005263	7.7
13.4868	11.1842	8.8817	6.5798	4.2842	2.0503	.3221	.00004707	7.8
13.4740	11.1714	8.8689	6.5671	4.2716	2.0386	.3163	.00004210	7.9
13.4614	11.1589	8.8563	6.5545	4.2591	2.0269	.3106	.00003767	8.0
13.4490	11.1464	8.8439	6.5421	4.2468	2.0155	.3050	.00003370	8.1
13.4367	11.1342	8.8317	6.5298	4.2346	2.0042	.2996	.00003015	8.2
13.4246	11.1220	8.8195	6.5177	4.2226	1.9930	.2943	.00002699	8.3
13.4126	11.1101	8.8076	6.5057	4.2107	1.9820	.2891	.00002415	8.4
13.4008	11.0982	8.7957	6.4939	4.1990	1.9711	.2840	.00002162	8.5
13.3891	11.0865	8.7840	6.4822	4.1874	1.9604	.2790	.00001936	8.6
13.3776	11.0750	8.7725	6.4707	4.1759	1.9498	.2742	.00001733	8.7
13.3661	11.0635	8.7610	6.4592	4.1646	1.9393	.2694	.00001552	8.8
13.3548	11.0523	8.7497	6.4480	4.1534	1.9290	.2647	.00001390	8.9
13.3437	11.0411	8.7386	6.4368	4.1423	1.9187	.2602	.00001245	9.0
13.3326	11.0300	8.7275	6.4258	4.1313	1.9087	.2557	.00001115	9.1
13.3217	11.0191	8.7166	6.4148	4.1205	1.8987	.2513	.000009988	9.2
13.3109	11.0083	8.7058	6.4040	4.1098	1.8888	.2470	.000008948	9.3
13.3002	10.9976	8.6951	6.3934	4.0992	1.8791	.2429	.000008018	9.4
13.2896	10.9870	8.6845	6.3828	4.0887	1.8695	.2387	.000007185	9.5
13.2791	10.9765	8.6740	6.3723	4.0784	1.8599	.2347	.000006439	9.6
13.2688	10.9662	8.6637	6.3620	4.0681	1.8505	.2308	.000005771	9.7
13.2585	10.9559	8.6534	6.3517	4.0579	1.8412	.2269	.000005173	9.8
13.2483	10.9458	8.6433	6.3416	4.0479	1.8320	.2231	.000004637	9.9

as one of the unknowns, T, occurs twice in the equation, once in the argument of the function and again as a divisor of the exponential integral, solution by trial would be most laborious. However, a graphical method of superposition, devised by Theis, makes a simple solution of the equation possible. The first step in this method is the plotting of a "type curve," on logarithmic coordinate tracing paper, which represents the evaluation of the exponential integral or series of equation 24. From Table 10 values of $W(u)$ are plotted against the argument u to generate the type curve which is shown by a solid line in Fig. 63.

Rearranging equations 22 and 23 gives us

$$s = \left[\frac{Q}{4\pi T}\right] W(u) \tag{25}$$

and

$$\frac{r^2}{t} = \left[\frac{4T}{S}\right] u \tag{26}$$

If a constant withdrawal rate is maintained, that is, if Q is constant, the bracketed portions of equations 25 and 26 are constant for a given pumping test. Note that s is related to r^2/t in a manner that is similar to the relation of $W(u)$ to u. Consequently, if values of the drawdown or recovery, s, are plotted against r^2/t on logarithmic coordinate tracing paper, to the same scale as the type curve, $W(u)$ versus u, the curve of observed data will be similar to the type curve.

The circles on Fig. 63 represent the successive values of drawdown as computed from periodic measurements of the water-level decline in an observation well 48 ft from a well that was pumped at the constant rate of 250 gpm. In practice, the computed values of s and r^2/t are plotted on a separate sheet of logarithmic tracing paper, and this graph of observed data is superimposed on the graph of the type curve. When the coordinate axes of the two curves are held parallel, the data curve is translated to a position which represents the best fit of the field data to the type curve. With both graph sheets at the best match position, an arbitrary point on the top curve is selected and pricked through or otherwise marked on the lower curve. The coordinates of this common point are noted for the upper and the lower graph. The trace of the type curve, for the match position, is shown as a dashed line through the field data, on Fig. 63. The coordinates of the match point are recorded, and the use of these data with equations 25 and 26 to solve for T and S is also shown.

The determination of the coefficients of transmissibility and storage for an aquifer, by the discharging-well method, is somewhat similar to

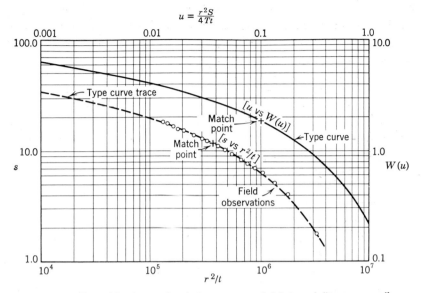

$$u = \frac{r^2 S}{4Tt}$$

Fig. 63. Logarithmic graph of the exponential integral "type curve."

$Q = 250$ gpm or 48,000 cu ft per day

Match-point coordinates

$u = 0.1 \; W(u) = 1.82$

$r^2/t = 3.75 \times 10^5 \qquad s = 11.6$

$$T = \frac{Q \cdot W(u)}{4\pi s} = \frac{48,000 \times 1.82}{4\pi \times 11.6} = 600 \text{ ft}^2/\text{day}$$

$$S = \frac{4uT}{r^2/t} = \frac{4 \times 0.1 \times 600}{3.75 \times 10^5} = 6.4 \times 10^{-4}$$

the testing procedure of measuring beam deflections under a given load to determine the elastic properties of a structural material. As for the beam, we can predict the drawdown or deflection of the water level at any point or for any load from a knowledge of its behavior under a known load at known points of observation.

Assume that a well of 300-gpm capacity is to be drilled in the comparatively poor aquifer covered by the pumping test of Fig. 63 and that the following conditions apply for this example:

Total depth of well	= 200 ft
Screen setting	= 170 to 200 ft
Diameter of well	= 12 in.
Proposed yield	= 300 gpm or 57,600 cu ft per day
Static depth to water	= 5 ft below grade

The problem is to predict the performance of this well for 30 days of continuous operation at peak capacity with total withdrawal from storage, that is, no recharge from rainfall or other sources. From the foregoing conditions we may set up the known quantities as follows:

$$Q = 57,600 \text{ cu ft/day} \qquad\qquad r = 6 \text{ in.} = 0.5 \text{ ft}$$
$$t = 30 \text{ days} \qquad\qquad\qquad T = 600 \text{ ft}^3/\text{day}$$
$$S = 6.4 \times 10^{-4}$$

Then from equation 23

$$u = \frac{(0.5)^2 6.4}{4 \times 600 \times 30 \times 10^4} = 2.2 \times 10^{-9}$$

The value of $W(u)$ corresponding to the above value of u is read from Table 10 as

$$W(u) = 19.4$$

From equation 25

$$s = \frac{57,600 \times 19.4}{4\pi \times 600} = 148 \text{ ft}$$

The pumping level at the end of the 30-day period is

Static level	=	5 ft below grade
Drawdown	=	148 ft
Pumping level	=	153 ft below grade

The estimated pumping level is only 17 ft above the top of the well screen by the end of the 30-day period, if the well is pumped continuously at the maximum rate. Consequently, it is advisable to examine the performance of this proposed well over longer periods of pumping. In the manner outlined above for the computation of the 30-day pumping level, the levels for other periods are computed and plotted as the lowermost curve on Fig. 64. As indicated by this curve, the pumping level will reach the top of the well screen after 9 months of continuous pumping at the 57,600 cu ft per day rate. We assume that the aquifer is completely penetrated[29] and that the top of it will coincide with the top of the well screen. Accordingly, the lowering of the water level in the pumped well below the top of the aquifer results in partial dewatering of the aquifer. This reduction in saturated thickness proportionately reduces the transmissibility and thereby increases the drawdown and furthers the decline of pumping

[29] The discharge Q will be smaller for a partially penetrating well. For a discussion of the effect of partial penetration on well yield, see reference 18 at the end of this chapter.

level for the given discharge rate. Extensive dewatering of an aquifer develops a "vicious cycle" of increased drawdown followed by decreased aquifer thickness, a condition which occasions additional drawdown and further reduction in aquifer capacity until the well fails at the excessive pumping rate. If the rate of pumping is reduced, the water level in the pumped well will recover in proportion to the reduction in discharge. For the foregoing example, reducing the pumping rate to 48,000 cu ft per day raises the pumping level to 28 ft above the top of the well screen at the time when the 57,600 cu ft per day rate would start dewatering the aquifer.

In the previous example, the original assumption that all water would be withdrawn from storage without replenishment results in a progressive decline of water level to infinite time. Such calculations are of value in estimating minimum performance of wells under adverse conditions of extended drought. Under normal conditions, as pumping continues, the cone of depression deepens and expands until (1) it intercepts a surface stream which is adequate to support the well discharge under the given conditions, (2) it encompasses an area that will support the well yield under the prevailing rate of surface infiltration, or (3) it intercepts areas of discharge and reduces this discharge by an amount equal to the well withdrawal. Most frequently, the well yield is obtained from a combination of two or more of these sources. If the total water available from the several sources is less than the pumping rate, progressive decline of water level may occur to a degree determined by the excess of discharge over recharge. Ultimately the net discharge cannot be greater than the available recharge from all sources.

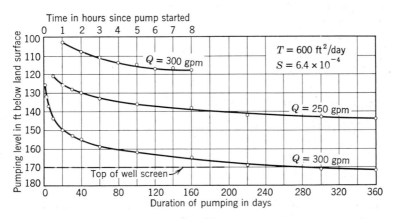

Fig. 64.

As indicated in the previous example, excessive dewatering of an aquifer is to be avoided, but it does not follow that all dewatering is objectionable. In any water-table aquifer it is of course necessary to dewater the aquifer partially, in order to induce flow toward the well. Sometimes it may be advisable to reduce the saturated thickness to provide storage capacity for the intake of percolating waters when infiltration occurs. If the cone of depression is maintained at a high stage and a shallow depth below land surface, then, when recharge occurs, all water in excess of the limited storage capacity will be rejected. The problem of determining proper pumping levels and well yields is one of engineering economics, which must be solved for each particular well field.

It is of interest to note that the majority of well installations to date were rated or sized without benefit of long-term drawdown predictions. In the most general and widespread method for determining well capacity, a brief and generally inadequate pumping test is made. Measurements are taken of the well discharge and drawdown through this short pumping period. Water levels are measured by an air line and altitude gage and are accurate to perhaps the nearest foot. If the pumping level remains relatively steady during the latter part of the test period, as it generally does when the pumping rate is constant because the decline is rather slow after several hours, it is quite common practice to assume that the well will continue to pump at the observed rate for an infinite time. The pumping levels for the example above are computed for an 8-hr period and a discharge of 57,600 cu ft per day, and plotted as the uppermost curve on Fig. 64. The level from the sixth to the eighth hour inclusive does not decline more than 2 ft, and air-line readings would probably show little or no change in drawdown for this period. Thus, in accord with the practice mentioned above, it is assumed that this well will deliver 57,600 cu ft per day or more for any period. The fallacy of this reasoning is better understood after examination of the modified form of the nonequilibrium formula.

Modified Nonequilibrium Formula

Jacob[30] recognized that the sum of the terms in the series of equation 24 beyond $\log_e u$ is not of appreciable magnitude when u becomes small. From the form of equation 23 it is noted that u decreases as the time, t, increases. Accordingly, for large values of t,

[30] C. E. Jacob, "Drawdown Test to Determine Effective Radius of Artesian Well," *Trans. A.S.C.E.*, vol. 112, 1947, pp. 1047–1070.

the terms beyond $\log_e u$ in the exponential series may be neglected and equation 25 may be written

$$s = \frac{Q}{4\pi T} W(u) = \frac{Q}{4\pi T} [-0.5772 - \log_e u]$$

or

$$s = \frac{Q}{4\pi T} \left[\log_e \left(\frac{1}{u} \right) - 0.5772 \right] \tag{27}$$

but

$$u = \frac{r^2 S}{4Tt} \quad \text{and} \quad \frac{1}{u} = \frac{4Tt}{r^2 S}$$

then

$$s = \frac{Q}{4\pi T} \left[\log_e \left(\frac{4Tt}{r^2 S} \right) - 0.5772 \right] \tag{28}$$

In applying equation 28 to measurements of the drawdown or recovery of water level in a particular observation well, the distance r will be constant and there follows

at time t_1

$$s_1 = \frac{Q}{4\pi T} \left[\log_e \left(\frac{4Tt_1}{r^2 S} \right) - 0.5772 \right]$$

at time t_2

$$s_2 = \frac{Q}{4\pi T} \left[\log_e \left(\frac{4Tt_2}{r^2 S} \right) - 0.5772 \right]$$

then the change in drawdown from time t_1 to t_2

$$s_2 - s_1 = \frac{Q}{4\pi T} \log_e \left(\frac{t_2}{t_1} \right) \tag{29}$$

Converting to logarithms to the base 10 gives us

$$s_2 - s_1 = \frac{2.30Q}{4\pi T} \log_{10} \left(\frac{t_2}{t_1} \right) \tag{30}$$

where Q and T are as previously defined, t_1 and t_2 are time in days since pumping started, and s_1 and s_2 are respective drawdowns at noted times, in feet.

The most convenient procedure for application of the foregoing equation is to plot the observational data for each well on semi-logarithmic coordinate paper as shown by Fig. 65, which is based on the same test data used in Fig. 63. From this curve make an arbitrary choice of t_1 and t_2 and note the corresponding values of s_1 and s_2. For convenience t_1 and t_2 are chosen one log cycle apart; then

$$\log_{10}\left(\frac{t_2}{t_1}\right) = 1$$

and

$$s_2 - s_1 = \Delta s = \frac{2.30Q}{4\pi T} \qquad (31)$$

or

$$T = \frac{2.30Q}{4\pi\,\Delta s} \qquad (32)$$

where Δs is the drawdown difference per log cycle, in feet.

Although the absolute value of the drawdown increases as the logarithm of the time of pumping, it follows from equation 31 that the drawdown per log cycle of time varies directly with the discharge Q, and inversely as the coefficient of transmissibility T.

Extrapolating the straight line of the semilog curve to its intersection with the zero-drawdown axis permits computation of S, the storage coefficient, as follows.

When $s = 0$, equation 28 yields

$$s = 0 = \frac{Q}{4\pi T}\left[\log_e\left(\frac{4Tt_0}{r^2 S}\right) - 0.5772\right]$$

$$\log_e\left(\frac{4Tt_0}{r^2 S}\right) = 0.5772 \qquad \text{or} \qquad \frac{4Tt_0}{r^2 S} = e^{0.5772}$$

and

$$S = \frac{4Tt_0}{r^2 e^{0.5772}} = \frac{2.25Tt_0}{r^2} \qquad (33)$$

where S, T, and r are as previously defined and t_0 is time intercept on zero-drawdown axis, in days.

The curvature of the semilog graph where time t is small indicates that the approximation is not valid in this region. Caution should be exercised in the use of this method to make certain that pumping has continued until t becomes large and all plotted points fall on a straight line. For moderate distances from the pumped well, this condition is generally satisfied within an hour or less for artesian conditions, but for water-table aquifers 12 hr or more may be required because of the time lag due to slow draining of the interstices.

It is advisable in any test to plot both the log-log graph for the type curve application and the semilog plot for the modified formula. The

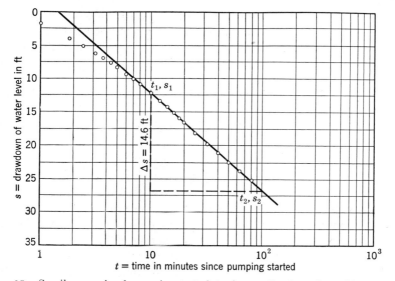

Fig. 65. Semilog graph of pumping test data for application of modified Theis formula.

$$Q = 250 \text{ gpm} \quad \text{or} \quad 48,000 \text{ cu ft/day}$$

$$r = 48 \text{ ft}$$

$$T = \frac{2.30Q \cdot \log_{10} t_2/t_1}{4\pi(s_2 - s_1)}$$

$$T = \frac{2.30 \times 48,000 \times \log_{10} 100/10}{4\pi(26.8 - 12.2)}$$

$$T = 600 \text{ ft}^2/\text{day}$$

$$S = \frac{2.25Tt_0}{r^2}$$

$$S = \frac{2.25 \times 600 \times \dfrac{1.46}{1440}}{48^2}$$

$$S = 6.0 \times 10^{-4}$$

semilog plot, as indicated previously, is an approximation method which yields a straight-line graph in the region where this approximation is justified. As shown in Fig. 65, when t is small and u is appreciable, the field observations fall beneath the selected line. As the distance, r, increases, the time required for the field data to become asymptotic to the limiting value of the slope also increases. Thus, for an observation well at a considerable distance from the pumped well, there is a greater risk in selecting the tangent prematurely. Assurance is gained by comparison with the result given by the log-log plot and by mutual agreement with the results from other observation wells. The interference effect of other pumping wells, the limitation of geologic boundaries, and other extraneous effects may distort the plotted data in a manner that makes the straight-line selection unreliable. The semilog plot does, however, present certain advantages in pumping-test analysis, and its use is well justified as long as proper caution is observed. If analysis of the data is correct, the values of T and S determined by either method should agree within a small percentage.

In general, it is not possible to determine the storage coefficient, S, from observations within the pumping well, by either of the foregoing methods because the effective radius of the well is not known. For a well finished in rock, the effective radius may approach the nominal radius. However, this situation is not necessarily so, since the existence of large crevices, the overreaming action of the drill bit, or local cementation of the bore face may result in an effective radius greater or smaller than the nominal size. In a well finished in unconsolidated materials, the water level in the pumped well is lower than the water level in an equivalent uncased hole by the amount of friction loss through the screen. If development of the well is incomplete, the packing of fine material in the formation adjacent to the screen can greatly reduce the permeability and result in an effective radius which is considerably less than the nominal drilled size. A method of determining the effective radius for any well has been developed by Jacob.[31]

Noting from equation **28** that the drawdown varies with the logarithm of the time of pumping, we can recognize the fallacy in determining well capacity from the short-duration type of pumping test which was outlined previously. Any linear plot of drawdown level versus pumping time, on a time scale extended to fit an 8-hr pumping test as shown by the uppermost curve of Fig. 64 will invariably give the deceptive picture of the approach to a fixed pumping level. This flattening of slope is representative of a logarithmic relation when plotted to rectangular coordinates. If the pumping levels for the 8-hr test were plotted to the compressed time scale of the lower graph, there would appear to be a nearly vertical decline of operating level for the 8-hr period. When we consider that a well user may plan to pump a well continuously for the total of **8760** hr per yr and for many years, it is evident that the 8-hr or other short-term acceptance test is not only inadequate but quite misleading unless supported by quantitative methods such as those outlined above.

[31] C. E. Jacob, "Drawdown Test to Determine Effective Radius of Artesian Well," *Trans. A.S.C.E.*, vol. 112, 1947, pp. 1047–1070.

Adjustment of Test Data for Thin Aquifers

One of the basic assumptions in the derivation of the Thiem and the Theis formulas is the stipulation of a constant value of transmissibility. However, under water-table conditions the drawdown of water level by a discharging well reduces the saturated thickness of the aquifer, and, if this reduction in thickness is appreciable, the transmissibility is not constant but decreases with time. The following method, described by Jacob,[32] permits the correction of observed data to compensate for this effect. Appreciable reduction in saturated thickness voids the relation expressed by equation 12, and consequently equation 9 must be reduced to the drawdown form in some other manner. From Fig. 61 note that

$$h = m - s \tag{34}$$

then

$$h_2{}^2 = m^2 - 2ms_2 + s_2{}^2$$

$$h_1{}^2 = m^2 - 2ms_1 + s_1{}^2$$

and

$$h_2{}^2 - h_1{}^2 = -2ms_2 + 2ms_1 + s_2{}^2 - s_1{}^2$$

$$= 2ms_1 - s_1{}^2 - (2ms_2 - s_2{}^2)$$

$$h_2{}^2 - h_1{}^2 = 2m \left[\left(s_1 - \frac{s_1{}^2}{2m} \right) - \left(s_2 - \frac{s_2{}^2}{2m} \right) \right] \tag{35}$$

Substituting the expression above in equation 9 gives us

$$\log_e \frac{r_2}{r_1} = \frac{\pi P}{Q} 2m \left[\left(s_1 - \frac{s_1{}^2}{2m} \right) - \left(s_2 - \frac{s_2{}^2}{2m} \right) \right]$$

but

$$T = Pm$$

then

$$\log_e \frac{r_2}{r_1} = \frac{2\pi T}{Q} \left[\left(s_1 - \frac{s_1{}^2}{2m} \right) - \left(s_2 - \frac{s_2{}^2}{2m} \right) \right] \tag{36}$$

Converting to logarithms to the base 10 and transposing equation 36, we have

$$T = \frac{2.30Q \log_{10} r_2/r_1}{2\pi[(s_1 - s_1{}^2/2m) - (s_2 - s_2{}^2/2m)]} \tag{37}$$

[32] C. E. Jacob, "Notes on Determining Permeability by Pumping Tests under Water-Table Conditions," U. S. Geological Survey, mimeographed report, June 1944.

The above equation should be used in lieu of equation 15 if the saturated thickness of the aquifer is appreciably diminished by the declining water level. Note that if the drawdowns s_1 and s_2 are very small compared to the original saturated thickness, m, the correction fraction may be omitted, and equation 37 reduces to equation 15. Compensation of the drawdown data by subtracting the factor $(s^2/2m)$ should result in a straight-line graph for the semilog plottings of the Thiem or modified Theis method.

The Method of Images

The assumption of infinite areal extent for an aquifer, which is necessary for the development of either the equilibrium or the non-equilibrium formula, is essentially fulfilled by a few major aquifers of sedimentary rock, such as the Dakota sandstone described by Meinzer.[33] However, in most areas the existence of formation boundaries or of folds and faults or the dissection by surface streams serves to limit the continuity of consolidated strata to distances of a few miles or more. In the unconsolidated materials and particularly in the glaciated areas the prerequisite of infinite areal extent is seldom satisfied. Consequently, it is necessary to make appropriate adjustment for the effect of these geologic boundaries before the foregoing formulas can be applied to problems of flow in areally limited aquifers.

Inasmuch as an impervious formation detracts from the contributing area of the aquifer it bounds, we refer to its contact as a negative boundary. In a similar manner, we use the term positive boundary where an aquifer is intersected by a perennial stream or other body of surface water with sufficient flow to prevent development of the cone of depression beyond the surface source. Several possible types of geologic boundaries are shown in generalized form by Fig. 66.

It is recognized that, except for some faulted structures, most geologic boundaries do not occur as abrupt straight-line demarcations but rather as tapered and irregular terminals. In general, however, the area covered by a well-field or pumping-test site is relatively small compared to the area of even the limited aquifers, and it is often possible to treat the geologic boundary as an abrupt discontinuity. The greater the distance to the boundary from the well site, the smaller would be the error involved by this approximation. Where conditions permit the assumption of a straight-line demarcation for a geologic

[33] O. E. Meinzer and H. A. Hard, "The Artesian-Water Supply of the Dakota Sandstone in North Dakota, with Special Reference to the Edgeley Quadrangle," U. S. Geol. Survey Water-Supply Paper 520, 1925, pp. 73–95.

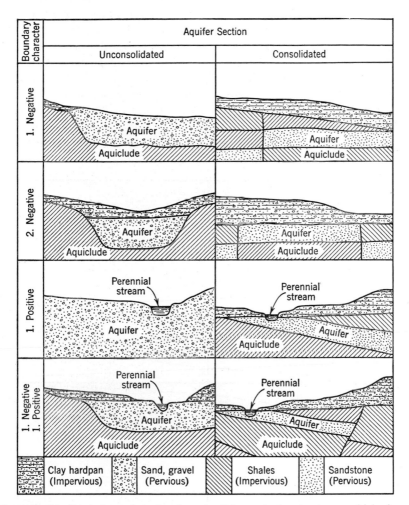

Fig. 66. Idealized examples showing possible geologic structures which form definite bounding conditions for the flow systems in aquifers. The term negative is used for boundaries formed by impermeable materials which do not contribute flow to the system. Positive boundaries refer to the intersection of the aquifer by sources of water which sustain the hydrostatic head and stop the growth of the drawdown cone.

boundary, it is possible to solve the flow problem by the substitution
of a hypothetical system that satisfies the limits of the real system.

The method of images devised by Lord Kelvin in his work on
electrostatic theory is a convenient tool for the solution of boundary
problems. An idealized section of an aquifer that is intersected and
bounded by a surface stream is shown in Fig. 67. To be effective as
a boundary, the stream flow must equal or exceed the withdrawal of
the well, because any flow below the well yield would result in drying
up of the stream and elimination of the boundary. Assume the stream
to be of infinitesimal width or the equivalent of a line source. In a
rigid analysis it would be necessary also that the stream extend the full
depth of the aquifer to justify fully the use of unidimensional method.

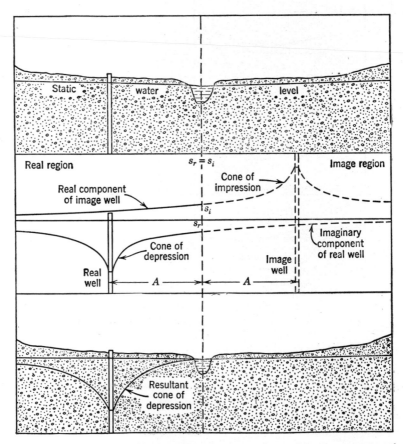

Fig. 67. Idealized section of an aquifer which is intersected by a stream together
with a hypothetical well system for the solution of this type of flow problem.

However, reasonable estimates can be made by this method when observation wells are available at distances that are sufficient to minimize the effect of vertical flow components. If the stream cannot be depleted, the boundary limit requires that there shall be zero drawdown at the line source. Any system that can satisfy this boundary limit is a solution of the real problem. As shown by the central diagram of Fig. 67, the real and bounded aquifer is replaced by an imaginary aquifer of infinite areal extent, and an imaginary recharging well is placed on the opposite side of and equidistant from the boundary. As illustrated, the imaginary recharge well returns water to the aquifer at the same rate as it is withdrawn by the real discharge well. Consequently, the image well produces a build-up of water level at the boundary that is exactly equal to and cancels the drawdown of the real well. This system results in zero drawdown at the boundary which satisfies the limit of the real problem.

The real components of the cone of depression of the real well and the cone of impression of the image well are shown as solid lines in the region of real values. To secure the resultant cone of depression or to evaluate the drawdown at any point in the real region, it is necessary to add algebraically the real components of the several depression cones. The resultant cone of depression is steepened on the riverward side of the well and flattened on the landward side. This point should be recognized in drawing or examining contour maps of the water-table or piezometric surface for aquifers of this type.

An aquifer bounded by impervious strata is shown in idealized section by Fig. 68. The boundary is approximated as before by a sharp line of demarcation. Inasmuch as the impervious strata cannot contribute water to the pumped well, the limit imposed by the barrier is that there shall be no flow across the boundary line. As shown by the image setup in the central diagram, an imaginary discharging well is placed across the boundary at a right angle to and equidistant from the boundary. The drawdown of the image well at the boundary is equal to the effect of the real well, and the symmetrical drawdown cones produce a ground-water divide everywhere along the boundary. The image system produces a normal derivative equal to zero along the divide, and, as there can be no flow across a divide, this image system satisfies the limit of the real problem and is therefore a solution.

The real components of the cones of depression of the image well and the real well are shown as solid lines in the region of real values. Again, the resultant cone of depression or the drawdown at any point in the aquifer is determined by adding the real component of each depression cone. The resultant cone of depression for this example is flattened on the side adjacent to the boundary and steepened on the opposite side of the well.

An example of an aquifer bounded by impervious strata on two sides is shown by the idealized section of Fig. 69. The setup of the primary images to balance the effect of the real well at each boundary is

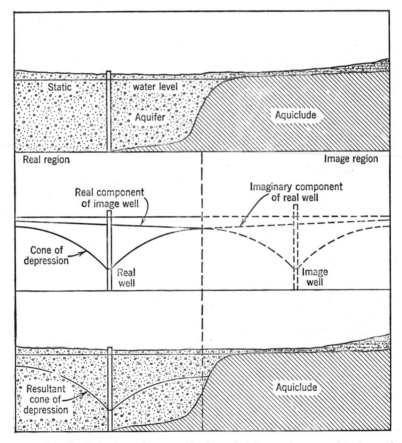

Fig. 68. Idealized section of an aquifer bounded by an impermeable formation together with a hypothetical well system for the solution of this type of flow problem.

similar to the previous examples. The real component of each cone of depression is shown as a solid line in the region of real values. Although these primary images balance the effect of the real well at their respective boundaries, each image produces an unbalanced draw-down at the farther boundary. These unbalanced drawdowns at the boundaries theoretically produce a gradient and consequent flow across the boundary. Thus it is necessary to add a secondary set of image wells at the appropriate distances to balance the residual effect of the primary images. Each image well in the secondary set will again disturb the balance at the farther boundary, and all successive sets of

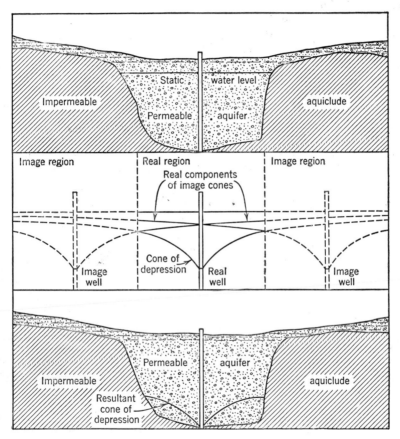

Fig. 69. Idealized section of underflow channel bounded by impermeable formation and setup of hypothetical well system used for solution of flow problems under this condition.

images to infinity will leave residuals at the boundaries. In practice it is necessary only to add image pairs until the residual effects are negligible in comparison with the total effect.

The modified nonequilibrium formula illustrated in Fig. 65 is particularly advantageous for the analysis of image or boundary effects because it is easier to recognize changes in slope of a straight line than to detect changes in curvature of a log-log curve. Equation 31 indicates that $\Delta s/1$, the slope of the semilog graph, is dependent only on the pumping rate and the transmissibility of the aquifer. For a specific aquifer the transmissibility is a constant and the rate of pumping may be held constant. Under these conditions the graph of drawdown versus the logarithm of time since the pump started will show successive changes in slope as pumping continues. The water level will draw down at an initial rate under the influence of the real well that is nearest to the observation well. When the cone of depression of the nearer image well affects the observation well, the rate of drawdown will be doubled after r^2/t becomes small, because the total rate of withdrawal is then equal to the rate of the real well plus one image well, or twice the rate of the real well. The effect of the farther image triples the slope of the semilog graph after r^2/t becomes small for this image, because the total rate for the real well plus two image wells is three times as great as the rate of the real well.

As previously mentioned, the use of Jacob's approximate method should be restricted to small values of u, which occur when the distance r is small and the time t is large. Frequently image distances are large in relation to the distance from an observation well to a pumping well. If a single image is involved, the semilog plotting of drawdown versus time shows a two-limbed graph. The transition from the first limb to the second limb follows a curved path through the region where the values of u for the image well are large. When t becomes sufficiently large in relation to r^2, the value of u for the image well becomes small and the observed data follow the straight line of the second segment of the graph.

If more than one image well occurs and if the image wells are at comparable distances, the effect of second-, third-, or higher-order image wells may reach an observation well before sufficient time has elapsed for u to become small enough to warrant the application of this method to the effect of the first image well. Under these circumstances, the observed data follow a path of increasing curvature. An example of a semilog graph for an observation well affected by second- and higher-order image wells is shown as Fig. 70.

Approximate values for the location of the image wells are obtained by drawing tangents to the observed-data graph at the appropriate slope values. If the divergence of each line of Fig. 70 were noted, the graph could be separated and replotted as three separate lines with each component having the same slope and intercepting the zero-drawdown axis at its respective value of time. The time intercept on

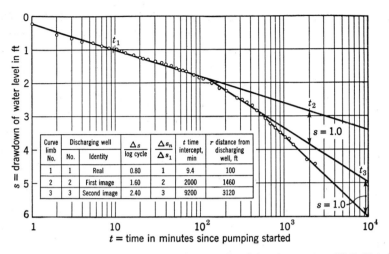

Fig. 70. Graph showing drawdown of water level in observation Well E-1 by pumping tests on Test Well 36 at Hemphill Road and Saginaw Street, at southern city limits of Flint, Mich.

this axis permits the calculation of the storage coefficient by equation 33. Inasmuch as the coefficient of storage, S, is constant for a given aquifer the following relation obtains.

$$S = \frac{2.25Tt_1}{r_1^2} = \frac{2.25Tt_2}{r_2^2} = \frac{2.25Tt_3}{r_3^2}$$

or

$$\frac{t_1}{r_1^2} = \frac{t_2}{r_2^2} = \frac{t_3}{r_3^2} \tag{37}$$

It follows from the equation above that, if the time intercepts are known for all wells, real or imaginary, and if the distance from the observation well to the real well is known, the distance to any image well can be determined from the data on the semilog graph.

The determination of the image distance from the time intercept of the semilog graph on the zero-drawdown axis may involve considerable error if the observational data are dispersed and if the slope is small, because the intercept is poorly defined for small slopes. In addition, this intercept generally occurs at very small values of time, and consequently small errors in the intercept locus result in appreciable errors in the distance values.

The following method avoids the objections of the intercept method. Assume two observation wells at distances r_1 and r_2 from a discharging

well, and from equation 28 the drawdown in each well is calculated
as follows.

$$s_1 = \frac{Q}{4\pi T}\left[\log_e\left(\frac{4Tt_1}{r_1{}^2 S}\right) - 0.5772\right]$$

$$s_2 = \frac{Q}{4\pi T}\left[\log_e\left(\frac{4Tt_2}{r_2{}^2 S}\right) - 0.5772\right]$$

From the semilog graph for one well record the value of the time
for a particular value of s, and from the graph for the second well
record the time value for the same value of s. Then when $s_1 = s_2$

$$\log_e\left(\frac{4Tt_1}{r_1{}^2 S}\right) = \log_e\left(\frac{4Tt_2}{r_2{}^2 S}\right)$$

or

$$\frac{t_1}{r_1{}^2} = \frac{t_2}{r_2{}^2} \tag{38}$$

This relation is identical with equation 37. From the form of
equations 37 and 38 it follows that for a given aquifer the times of
occurrence of zero drawdown or of equal drawdown vary directly as
the squares of the distances from the observation well to the discharging well and are independent of the rate of pumping. The equal-
drawdown method was used for the data on Fig. 70.

The time values at the tangent intersections determine only the
approximate distances to the image wells. The time intercepts so
determined will be too small and the calculated image distances will
therefore be smaller than the correct distances. These preliminary
estimates of the image distances may be corrected by trial. The
method is to assume locations of the image wells based on the values
computed by the first approximation. Using equations 25 and 26, we
can determine the drawdown component resulting from each image
well. The time-drawdown graph is obtained by adding these components. Successive adjustments may be made in the image distances
until the computed and observed graphs are in agreement.

If a pumping test is run without prior knowledge of geologic boundaries and if the semilog graphs for all observation wells show evidence
of image reflections, it would be possible to locate such boundaries by
calculating the distance from each observation well to each image well.
By scribing this distance as an arc from the respective observation
well, the image well is located at the intersection of the arcs. The
boundary is located at the midpoint of a line joining the real well and
the image well.

The field layout and the image arc intersections for a test of the
foregoing type are shown in Fig. 71. Theoretically the arcs should

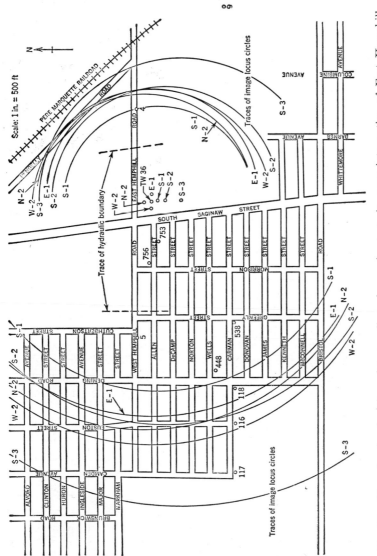
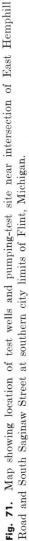

Fig. 71. Map showing location of test wells and pumping-test site near intersection of East Hemphill Road and South Saginaw Street at southern city limits of Flint, Michigan.

intersect at a common point, but deviations of the real aquifer from
the vertically bounded aquifer assumed in the derivation of the
method of images result in a dispersion of the arcs and their intersections. As shown in Fig. 71, the east image well is quite definitely
located by the arc intersections in the vicinity of East Hemphill Road,
notwithstanding the fact that the observation wells are concentrated
in a rather small area. With few or no arc intersections, the location
of the image well may be taken at the center of the arc band where
arcs are most closely grouped. It therefore appears from Fig. 71 that
the west image well is near the intersection of the arc band with West
Hemphill Road. Without a knowledge of the geology of the area, it
may be necessary to describe the complete circles in order to determine the location of the narrowest portion of the arc band. The
dispersion of the arcs for the west image suggests that the west
boundary may be less abrupt than the east boundary. For comparison,
Fig. 72 shows the geologic cross section of the aquifer as determined
by test drilling, and the trace of the computed boundaries are shown
thereon as dashed lines. Recall that the boundaries determined by
the pumping-test data represent a rectangular aquifer section which is
equivalent hydraulically to the real aquifer.

Under favorable conditions, which justify the several assumptions
embodied in the foregoing methods, these principles properly applied
permit the location of geologic boundaries within sufficient limits to
reduce greatly the number of test wells required for their confirmation.
In any problem, the pumping-test analysis must conform with the
geologic evidence if both are sound. Any disagreement between the
hydraulic data and the geologic data is untenable and points to incorrect analysis of either or both sets of data. It should also be
recognized that long-term extrapolation of pumping-test results hinges

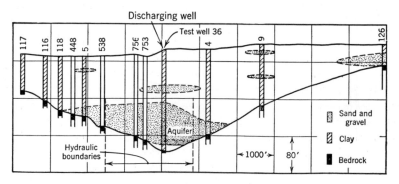

Fig. 72.

on the loose assumption that the conditions observed over a short period of pumping will continue to prevail over the extrapolated period. Consequently, it is advisable for the purpose of long-term predictions to reinforce the data by a number of pumping tests at several sites, to obtain an adequate sampling of the area that will be affected by long-continued pumping.

Application of the Storage Equation to an Aquifer

The general hydrologic equation groups all parts of ground-water movement under the broad term of ground-water increment. With the knowledge of ground-water occurrence and mechanics now available, it is feasible to set up the storage equation for an aquifer as follows:

$$F + R_S + R_U + R_L + R_W = E + D_S + D_U + D_L + D_W \pm \Delta S \quad (39)$$

where F = recharge from infiltration
$\quad R_S$ = recharge from surface bodies of water
$\quad R_U$ = recharge from lateral underflow
$\quad R_L$ = recharge by leakage through an aquiclude
$\quad R_W$ = recharge by wells, trenches, or other infiltration devices

and

$\quad E$ = discharge by evapo-transpiration
$\quad D_S$ = discharge to surface bodies of water
$\quad D_U$ = discharge by lateral underflow
$\quad D_L$ = discharge by leakage through an aquiclude
$\quad D_W$ = discharge by wells
$\quad \Delta S$ = increase or decrease in storage volume

Quantitative field investigations to evaluate the magnitude of the several terms in equation 39 for our major aquifers represent one phase of the work of the U. S. Geological Survey and its cooperating agencies. The extent of these surveys to date, however, has been so limited that very few areas are adequately covered by records of sufficient length to permit appraisal of all the factors suggested previously.

Estimates of the portion of rainfall that may enter an aquifer are generally made by an analysis of fluctuations in ground-water level as the result of specific storms or on the basis of long-term correlations between water-level hydrographs and precipitation records. The intensity, frequency, and time of occurrence of the rainfall greatly influence the amount of ground-water recharge. Short periods of heavy precipitation may result in considerable overland runoff, but their duration may be so short that the rain may do no more than wet the upper part of the soil. Conversely, a rain of light intensity but long duration is conducive to slow, continued percolation that ultimately saturates the soil and permits considerable recharge to the underlying water table. Inasmuch as the soil-moisture deficiency may absorb a large part of the percolating waters as they pass through the soil zone to the underlying water table, it follows that light rainfalls of short duration are of little benefit unless they occur with sufficient frequency to overcome the depletion of soil moisture.

The most favorable period for recharge from precipitation is the nongrowing season, extending from the first killing frosts in fall to the last killing frosts in spring. During this period, the moisture demands of vegetation are generally negligible, and the soil evaporation is greatly reduced. Accordingly, then, a large portion of the precipitation penetrates to the water table until the soil belt is frozen. In this connection, it is of interest to note that snow cover provides relatively good insulation from frigid temperatures. Consequently, early snowfall of sufficient depth may protect the soil zone from frost formation and may permit appreciable percolation into the soil during periods of snow melt. Especially favorable is a spring period of gradual snow melt over unfrozen soil with precipitation occurring at intensities that limit surface runoff.

Topography is also a controlling factor in determining the opportunity and amount of recharge to an aquifer from infiltration. In areas of great relief the steep slopes accelerate the rate of overland runoff. However, in areas having flat slopes the surface runoff is sluggish and there is appreciable ponding or surface storage for lengthy periods and thus greater opportunity for ground-water recharge. In regions where the water table is close to the surface, the volume of storage space available for recharge intake is limited by the shallow depth to the water table. When the reservoir is filled, the excess recharge is rejected and the water is discharged as surface runoff.

The amount of water-table rise for a given rainfall may vary considerably within any area because of differences in porosity of the aquifer, in both vertical and horizontal directions. In material of low porosity, a moderate rainfall may result in very large rises of water level, although the total volume of water recharged is quite small. Generally, these high heads result in rapid discharge of the stored water after the rain ceases. Throughout a period of recharge, there is continued discharge by the aquifer. Consequently, in correlating records of ground-water level with precipitation, it should be recognized that the recorded rise in water level represents the net difference between the simultaneous recharge and discharge.

A portion of the hydrograph for a shallow observation well located near Grayling, Michigan, is reproduced as Fig. 73. This well is finished in sand and gravel at a depth of 8 ft and is located in an area that is densely covered by small oak and pine trees. It is of interest to note that the water level in this well recovered from a near-record low stage in January 1947 to a near-record high stage by May 1947 as the result of a short period of above-normal precipitation, which occurred during the latter part of the nongrowing season.

The determination of recharge from or discharge to surface bodies of water is generally made by stream-discharge measurements at selected cross sections. For areas where stream-gaging stations are established, it may be possible to secure continuous records of discharge and to utilize these data during base-flow periods. The amount of seepage per foot of channel may be small in comparison with the total discharge of the stream. Consequently, discharge measurements must be made with great precision and repeated on numerous occasions at various stages. It may be necessary to gage the stream flow at several widely distant sections to introduce sufficient seepage length to detect measurable differences in discharge. If gaging sections must be spaced at long intervals, the geologic reconnaissance must be made in sufficient detail to evaluate the effect of underflow channels, faults, or other discontinuities that may intersect the stream between gaging sections.

Considerable attention has been directed to methods of determining and forecasting effluent seepage, or discharge to surface bodies of water, because it represents the base flow of our surface streams. Inasmuch as the water table throughout a drainage basin is a hydraulic

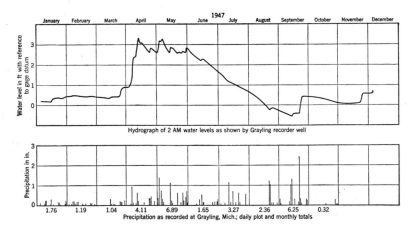

Fig. 73.

unit, it seems probable that a definite law could be developed that would properly weight the geologic characteristics of the basin and would express the rate of effluent seepage in terms of the water-table height at known points in the basin. With such a relationship, it would be feasible to forecast accurately the effluent seepage for any position of the water table at a given point. By selection of appropriate observation wells, which introduce time lag in proportion to their distance from the stream, these forecasts could be made for prolonged periods. A contribution toward this analysis was made by Jacob,[34] who outlined an experimental technique for research into this field. A formula developed by Theis[35] for the flow of water to a drain holds considerable promise for the prediction of effluent seepage from water-table elevation and forms the basis for interpretation of experimental evidence now being collected.

The development of agricultural drainage to lower regional water tables by increasing effluent seepage may lead to detrimental conditions through a part of the growing season. There are shown in Table 11 the average hydrologic conditions that prevail during the

TABLE 11

Summary of Average Hydrologic Conditions That Prevail in Many Areas

Average Condition Prevailing in the Season Noted

Factor	Winter–Spring	Summer–Fall
Soil moisture content	High	Low
Water table	High stage	Low stage
Vegetation demand	Minimum	Maximum
Ground-water flow	Cold and viscous water	Warm and less viscous water
Surface water	High stages and peak flows	Low stages and base flows

spring and summer seasons. It is evident that the spring season is one in which all or nearly all the factors contributing to poor drainage are at their maximum or worst condition. Drains designed to meet this extreme condition are not only more than adequate through the balance of the year, but may even cause overdrainage through the growing season. Through the summer and fall seasons such over-

[34] C. E. Jacob, "Correlation of Ground-Water Levels and Precipitation, Long Island, N. Y.," *Trans. Am. Geophys. Union,* 1944, p. 939.

[35] C. V. Theis, "Ground-Water in the Middle Rio Grande Valley of New Mexico," *U. S. Geol. Survey Rio Grande Joint Investigation,* 1937, p. 44.

drainage may deplete the regional ground-water body to such an extent that the capillary zone is drawn beyond the reach of the plant rootlets, and large soil-moisture deficiencies may develop. This practice may account for the large loss of top soil evidenced in some overdrained muckland areas. It would seem reasonable that in some areas drainage ditches should be blocked and the water should be used for irrigation in the season of low water table.

The measurement of recharge or discharge by underflow is based on observation of ground-water gradients that prevail across key cross sections of the underflow channel or conduit. From drilling records it may be possible to estimate the size and shape of the underflow channel at several points. If feasible, pumping tests should be conducted to determine the channel capacity at the control section. Observation wells, strategically located, provide the basis for making long-term measurements of the changes in water-table gradients across the control sections. From a knowledge of the channel area, transmissibility, and water-table gradient it is possible to determine the quantity of underflow at each time of water-level observation.

The studies of recharge and discharge from adjacent aquicludes are thus far of limited scope. Considerable research in this field is required, both in the collection of field data and in the development of applicable mathematical techniques. As previously mentioned, the rates of ground-water movement through the aquicludes are small and the collection of experimental data may be handicapped by long time lags. It would seem desirable, however, to obtain water-level records for wells tapping the aquicludes at varying depths and particularly to observe the fluctuations in areas of heavy withdrawal or reduction in aquifer pressure. For the present, the leakage factor can only be estimated and such estimates would be difficult to defend.

The withdrawal of water by wells in any area can be estimated by a comprehensive canvass of all well owners to determine their rate of pumping and the extent to which this rate fluctuates daily, weekly, and annually. Many well installations are not metered, but reasonable estimates can usually be made by correlation of water use with a convenient unit of production that is measured. Where water use is not related to a particular unit of output, it may be correlative with total pay rolls, total operating expenses, or total net or gross income. It is generally possible to secure fair to good records of total pumpage by the foregoing methods. From the pumpage inventory, a map of the type shown in Fig. 74[36] may be drawn to show the amount and dis-

[36] W. T. Stuart, "Ground-Water Resources of the Lansing Area, Michigan," *Progress Report* 13, Michigan Department of Conservation, June 1945.

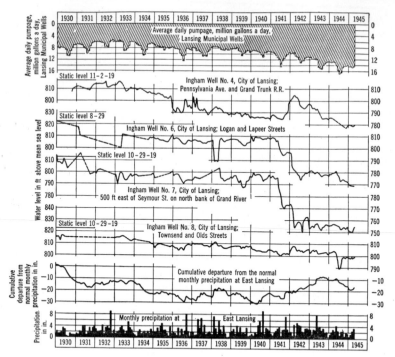

Fig. 75. Graphs showing pumpage, fluctuations of water levels, and precipitation, Lansing, Mich.

tribution of pumping at the time of the inventory. This map serves as a guide to the interpretation of the water-level contour map, as regions of large withdrawal should correspond with the areas of low water level and regions of little or no pumping should be areas of high water level. Deviations from the general correspondence between the pumpage-distribution map and the water-level contours may indicate the presence of zones of natural recharge or discharge or may reveal the existence of geologic boundaries or inhomogeneities. In addition to this areal correlation of pumpage and water level, it is necessary to plot pumpage versus time to determine the seasonal and long-term trends in withdrawal and correlate these data with the water-level hydrographs as shown in Fig. 75.[36]

Artificial recharging of ground-water reservoirs is finding ever-increasing use as a method of water conservation. Recharge is accomplished either by water spreading or by diffusion wells. Water spreading may be accomplished by (1) the flooding method, (2) the basin method, or (3) the ditch or furrow method. The flooding method

Fig. 74. — Distribution and mortality

Fig. 74. Distribution and magnitude

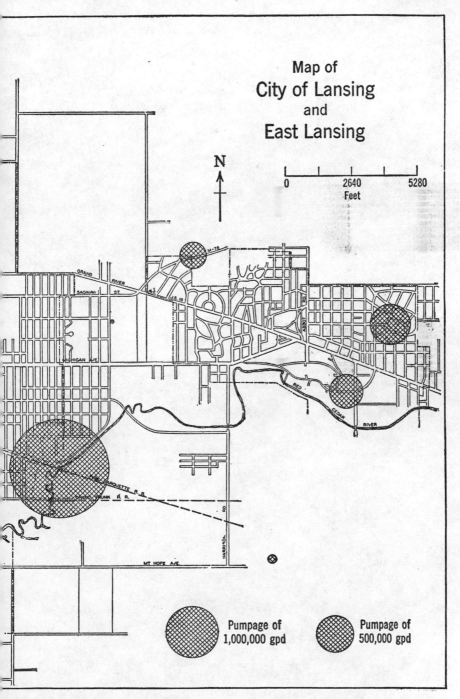

Map of
City of Lansing
and
East Lansing

N

| 0 | 2640 | 5280 |

Feet

Pumpage of
1,000,000 gpd

Pumpage of
500,000 gpd

page from wells, Lansing, Mich., 1944.

is restricted to topography which lends itself to surface ponding under conditions that permit prolonged retention of the surface waters. The basin and ditch methods require periodic maintenance to remove the accumulated silt from the percolation areas. A plan of the Canyon Basin spreading ground[37] in the San Gabriel Valley, California, is shown in Fig. 76. Well hydrographs showing the effect of this spreading operation are shown in Fig. 77.

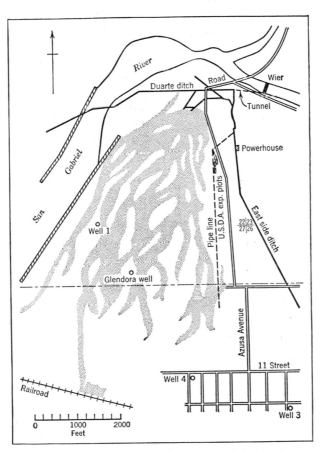

Fig. 76. Spreading ground of Canyon Basin, San Gabriel River, near Azusa, Calif. The general outline of the debris cone overlying the basin is shown. The Duarte ditch which supplies water for artificial spreading, the location of the experimental plots of the Bureau of Agricultural Engineering, and the location of key wells are also shown.

[37] A. T. Michelson and Dean C. Muckel, "Spreading Water for Storage Underground," *U. S. Dept. of Agr. Tech. Bull.* 578, 1937, pp. 26–31.

Recharge of underground reservoirs by diffusion wells is practiced on a large scale in Kings and Queens Counties on Long Island, New York, as the result of conservation legislation which requires that new air-conditioning and cooling wells with a capacity greater than 100,000 gallons per day must return the water to the aquifer from which it is drawn. During the summer of 1944 more than 200 recharge wells and basins returned water at a combined rate of 60,000,000 gpd.[38] Diffusion wells require periodic surging and development to remove the accumulation of silt and other fine materials. Although the unit volume cost of recharging with diffusion wells may greatly exceed that of the spreading method, in the highly industrialized and urbanized areas this may be the only possible method. An example of the solution of a problem of critical water shortage by recharging through diffusion wells is found in the experience of several large distillers in Louisville, Kentucky, during the summer of 1944.[39] Faced with an imminent water shortage the distillers, at the suggestion of the U. S. Geological Survey, converted to city water during cold weather, permitted the wells to rest, and used the cold surface water from the city supply to recharge the aquifer. Recharging started on March 10, 1944, and continued until the latter part of May 1944. By utilizing city water and ground water it was possible for the distilleries to continue full operation during the summer.

Provision is made in the storage equation, page 179, to add the contribution by artificial recharge. This quantity is determined by a pumpage inventory in the case of diffusion wells and by surface-water measurement in the case of water spreading.

The changes in storage volume within an aquifer are based on periodic observations of changes in water level for a selected network of observation wells. Contours of the water table or piezometric surface are drawn and used for estimates of change in storage volume.

The collection of detailed records of the same nature as above is a function of the U. S. Geological Survey and many cooperating state agencies. Although the scope of these surveys is still quite limited, the upward trend of investigatory surveys of ground-water conditions in recent years indicates a gradual realization by engineers, geologists, and hydrologists that a real and practical solution of ground-water problems can be made.

[38] M. L. Brashears, "Artificial Recharge of Ground Water on Long Island, New York," *Econ. Geol.,* vol. 41, No. 5, August 1946, pp. 503–516.

[39] W. F. Guyton, "Artificial Recharge of Glacial Sand and Gravel with Filtered River Water at Louisville, Kentucky," *Econ. Geol.,* vol. 41, No. 6, September-October 1946, pp. 644–658.

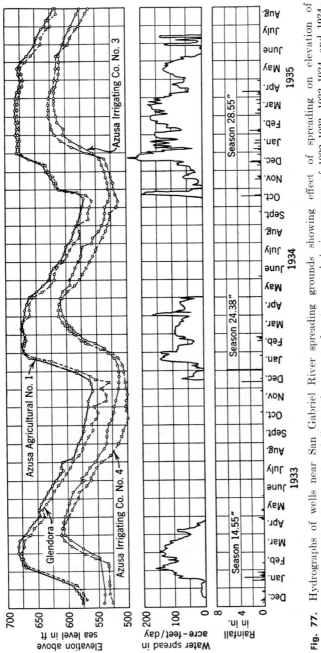

Fig. 77. Hydrographs of wells near San Gabriel River spreading grounds showing effect of spreading on elevation of underground water table, also showing daily total amount of water spread during seasons of 1932–1933, 1933–1934, and 1934–1935, and daily rainfall for these seasons.

It remains a common practice to adjudge the merits of a ground-water supply on the basis of a short capacity test on a single test well, no observational data being recorded except the discharge and drawdown of the well. Frequently, these measurements are made at random intervals and under widely varying conditions. Interruptions in pumping, which permit recovery of the water table, may invalidate the meager data collected and may lead to quite erroneous conclusions, but they seem of little importance to the untrained observer. The influence of geologic boundaries is oftentimes not recognized, and as a result unexpected well failure may occur.

Considerable optimism is warranted in facing future problems when one recognizes the advances made in ground-water hydrology since the development of the nonequilibrium formula by Theis in 1935. Although the mathematical tools are still limited, the awakened interest in the field will in time develop new methods and techniques. The collection of observational data will uncover the required evidence to interpret more clearly many ground-water phenomena that are now recorded but not understood.

When we recognize that the great majority of our ground-water developments in this country are based on meager and obsolete knowledge of the principles of ground-water hydrology, it is evident that a large field of opportunity lies ahead for adequately trained hydrologists.

BIBLIOGRAPHY[40]

1. Adam, N. K., *The Physics and Chemistry of Surfaces*, 3rd ed., London, Oxford University Press, 1941.
2. Blaney, H. F., C. A. Taylor, and A. A. Young, *Rainfall Penetration and Consumptive Use of Water in Santa Ana River Valley and Coastal Plain*, California Department Public Works, Division Water Resources, 1930.
3. Briggs, L. J., and H. L. Shantz, "The Wilting Coefficient for Different Plants and Its Indirect Determination," *U. S. Dept. Agr. Bur. Plants Industry Bull.* 230, 1912.
4. Brown, J. S., "A Study of Coastal Ground Water, with Special Reference to Connecticut," *U. S. Geol. Survey Water-Supply Paper* 537, 1925.
5. Chamberlin, T. C., "The Requisite and Qualifying Conditions of Artesian Wells," *U. S. Geol. Survey 5th Ann. Rept.*, Pt. C, pp. 125–173, 1885.
6. Collins, W. D., "Temperature of Water Available for Industrial Use in the United States," *U. S. Geol. Survey Water-Supply Paper* 520-F, 1923–1924.
7. Collins, W. D., "Notes on Practical Water Analysis," *U. S. Geol. Survey Water-Supply Paper* 596-H, 1928.

[40] This bibliography provides references which were not included in the text.

8. Cooper, H. H., Jr., and C. E. Jacob, "A Generalized Graphical Method for Evalutating Formation Constants and Summarizing Well-Field History," *Trans. Am. Geophys. Union,* vol. 27, No. 4, pp. 526–534, August 1946.

9. Darton, N. H., "Geothermal Data of the United States," *U. S. Geol. Survey, Bull.* 701, 1920.

10. Dole, R. B., "Use of Fluorescein in the Study of Underground Water," *U. S. Geol. Survey Water-Supply Paper* 160, 1906.

11. Eisenhart, L. P., *Differential Geometry of Curves and Surfaces,* Ginn and Co., 1909.

12. Ferris, J. G., *Memorandum Concerning a Pumping Test at Gas City, Ind., with a Detailed Discussion of the Methods Used in the Quantitative Analysis of Water-Well Interference Problems,* Indiana Dept. Cons., Div. Water Resources, Indianapolis, Ind., April 1945.

13. Fishel, V. C., "Further Tests of Permeability with Low Hydraulic Gradients," *Trans. Am. Geophys. Union,* pp. 499–503, August 1935.

14. Fishel, V. C., and O. E. Meinzer, "Tests of Permeability with Low Hydraulic Gradients," *Trans. Am. Geophys. Union,* pp. 405–409, June 1934.

15. Guyton, W. F., and N. A. Rose, "Quantitative Studies of Some Artesian Aquifers in Texas," *Econ. Geol.,* vol. 40, No. 3, pp. 123–226, May 1945.

16. Jacob, C. E., "Correlation of Ground-Water Levels and Precipitation on Long Island, N. Y.," Part 2, Correlation of data, *Trans Am. Geophys. Union,* 1944, pp. 928–939, May 1945.

17. Jacob, C. E., "Recovery Method of Determining Permeability, Empirical Adjustment for," U. S. Geol. Survey, mimeographed report, November 10, 1945.

18. Jacob, C. E., "Adjustments for Partial Penetration of Pumping Well," U. S. Geol. Survey, mimeographed report, August 10, 1945.

19. Kazmann, R. G., "Some Field Applications of Water Transmissibilty and Storage Coefficients," *Agr. Eng.,* vol. 25, No. 8, Dallas, Tex., August 1944.

20. King, F. H., "Principles and Conditions of the Movements of Ground Water," *U. S. Geol. Survey 19th Ann. Rept.,* Pt. 2B, pp. 59–294, 1899.

21. Meinzer, O. E., "Outline of Ground-Water Hydrology," *U. S. Geol. Survey Water-Supply Paper* 494, 1923.

22. Meinzer, O. E., "Large Springs in the United States," *U. S. Geol. Survey Water-Supply Paper* 557, 1927.

23. Meinzer, O. E., "Outline of Methods for Estimating Ground-Water Supplies," *U. S. Geol. Survey Water-Supply Paper* 638-C, 1932.

24. Meinzer, O. E., "Ground Water in the United States, a Summary of Ground-Water Conditions and Resources, Utilization of Water from Wells and Springs, Methods of Scientific Investigation, and Literature Relating to the Subject," *U. S. Geol. Survey Water-Supply Paper* 836-D, 1939.

25. Meinzer, O. E., "Compressibility and Elasticity of Artesian Aquifers," *Econ. Geol.,* vol. 23, No. 3, pp. 263–291, May 1928.

26. Meinzer, O. E., "Ground Water—a Vital National Resource," *J. Am. Water Works Assoc.,* vol. 34, No. 11, pp. 1595–1605, November 1942.

27. Meinzer, O. E., "Problems of the Perennial Yield of Artesian Aquifers," *Econ. Geol.,* vol. 40, No. 3, pp. 159–163, May 1945.

28. Meinzer, O. E., "General Principles of Artificial Ground-Water Recharge," *Econ. Geol.,* vol. 41, No. 3, pp. 191–201, May 1946.

29. Meinzer, O. E., "Hydrology in Relation to Economic Geology," *Econ. Geol.*, vol. 41, No. 1, pp. 1-12, January-February, 1946.

30. Meinzer, O. E., *Hydrology* (Physics of the Earth—9), New York, McGraw-Hill Book Co., June 1942.

31. Meinzer, O. E., and N. D. Stearns, "A Study of Ground Water in the Pomperaug Basin, Conn.," *U. S. Geol. Survey Water-Supply Paper* 597-B, 1929.

32. Piper, A. M., "Notes on the Relation Between the Moisture Equivalent and the Specific Retention of Water-Bearing Materials," *Trans. Am. Geophys. Union*, pp. 481-487, June 1933.

33. Piper, A. M., "A Graphic Procedure in the Geochemical Interpretation of Water Analyses," *Trans. Am. Geophys. Union*, pp. 914-928, May 1945.

34. Slichter, C. S., "Field Measurements of the Rate of Movement of Under-Ground Waters," *U. S. Geol. Survey Water-Supply Paper* 140, 1905.

35. Stearns, N. D., "The Geology and Ground-Water Hydrology of the Experimental Area of the U. S. Public Health Service at Fort Caswell, N. C.," U. S. Pub. Health Service, *Hygienic Lab. Bull.* 147, Washington, D. C., 1927.

36. Stearns, N. D., H. T. Stearns, and G. A. Waring, "Thermal Springs in the United States," *U. S. Geol. Survey Water-Supply Paper* 679-B, 1937.

37. Stiles, C. W., H. R. Crohurst, G. E. Thomson, and N. D. Stearns, "Experimental Bacterial and Chemical Pollution of Wells via Ground Water, with a Report on the Geology and Ground-Water Hydrology of the Experimental Area at Fort Caswell, N. C.," U. S. Pub. Health Service, *Hygienic Lab. Bull.* 147, 1927.

38. Theis, C. V., "Equation for Lines of Flow in Vicinity of Discharging Artesian Well," *Trans. Am. Geophys. Union,* pp. 317-320, June 1932.

39. Theis, C. V., "The Significance and Nature of the Cone of Depression in Ground-Water Bodies," *Econ. Geol.*, vol. 33, No. 8, pp. 889-902, December 1938.

40. Theis, C. V., "The Source of Water Derived from Wells," *Civil Eng.*, vol. 10, No. 5, pp. 277-280, May 1940.

41. Theis, C. V., "The Effect of a Well on the Flow of a Nearby Stream," *Trans. Am. Geophys. Union,* pp. 734-738, August 1941.

42. Thompson, D. G., and A. G. Fiedler, "Some Problems Relating to Legal Control of Use of Ground Waters," *J. Am. Water Works Assoc.*, vol. 30, No. 7, pp. 1049-1091, July 1938.

43. Todd, D. K., *Ground Water Hydrology*, New York, John Wiley, 1959.

44. Tolman, C. F., and J. F. Poland, "Ground Water, Salt-Water Infiltration, and Ground-Surface Recession in Santa Clara Valley, Santa Clara County, Calif.," *Trans. Am. Geophys. Union,* pp. 23-35, July 1940.

45. Unklesbay, A. G., and H. H. Cooper, Jr., "Artificial Recharge of Artesian Limestone at Orlando, Fla.," abstr. in *Econ. Geol.*, vol. 40, No. 1, p. 95, January-February 1945.

46. Veatch, A. C., "Fluctuations of the Water Level in Wells," *U. S. Geol. Survey Water-Supply Paper* 155, 1906.

47. Wenzel, L. K., "The Thiem Method for Determining Permeability of Water-Bearing Materials and Its Application to the Determination of Specific Yield, Results of Investigations in the Platte River Valley, Nebr.," *U. S. Geol. Survey Water-Supply Paper* 679-A, 1936.

48. Wenzel, L. K., and A. L. Greenlee, "A Method for Determining Transmissibility and Storage Coefficients by Tests of Multiple Well Systems," *Trans. Am. Geophys. Union*, 1943, pp. 547–564, January 1944.

49. Werner, P. Wilh., "Notes on Flow-Time Effects in the Great Artesian Aquifers of the Earth," *Trans. Am. Geophys. Union*, pp. 687–708, October 1946.

50. White, W. N., "A Method of Estimating Ground-Water Supplies Based on Discharge by Plants and Evaporation from Soil—Results of Investigations in Escalante Valley, Utah," *U. S. Geol. Survey Water-Supply Paper* 659-A, 1932.

7

Water Losses

Most of the problems that the hydrologist is called upon to answer may be divided into two general classes: (1) a determination of the maximum flood that may be expected with a certain frequency and (2) a determination of the monthly, seasonal, annual, or long-term average yield that may be anticipated from any given basin. Classification 2 includes problems pertaining to the low water flow and its probable duration and frequency of occurrence.

For the solution of these two types of problems entirely different techniques are employed. For the first, a detailed study of the characteristics of the hydrograph of surface runoff from the basin is required, together with a knowledge of infiltration capacity and its variations. Evaporation, transpiration, and other losses are ordinarily ignored because of the short period during which they are effective. For the solution of problems of the second type, the relative importance of these two kinds of data is reversed. Several different procedures have been suggested for determining long-term yield. The best use of any of them requires a knowledge of water losses and the many factors that affect and determine those losses. One of the oldest methods of determining the yield of a basin for which no runoff records were available was to estimate the losses and then deduct them from the total precipitation. Although the authors believe that in most cases a better procedure is available for determining monthly, seasonal, or annual yield, they recognize the value of a knowledge of water losses in the application of all these methods and therefore present the following discussion of this subject.

Water losses are here defined as the difference between the total precipitation and the total runoff from any given area. This may at once be recognized as being an engineer's definition of water losses, for the reason that the engineer is usually interested in the utilization of water for power, navigation, water supply, and so forth, and, therefore, he considers that portion of the rainfall that is not available for those purposes as lost. On the other hand, the agriculturist who is interested in seeing that water is available for transpiration by his crops would probably define water losses as being the difference between precipitation and transpiration. The topics discussed in this chapter are the fundamental basis for sound conservation and watershed management practices.

Although nearly all water losses are, in the final analysis, evaporative, they may be subdivided as follows:

1. Interception.
2. Evaporation from water surfaces.
3. Plant transpiration.
4. Soil or land evaporation.
5. Watershed leakage.

These losses occur in successive and overlapping stages, starting with the beginning of precipitation and continuing until all the water that fell as precipitation has left the watershed.

In the determination of the water losses from a drainage basin any part of which is irrigated, that water which is artificially applied to the land must be considered an integral part of the precipitation. If this fact is kept in mind, no special discussion will be necessary to make the following principles applicable to irrigated areas. It has become customary to speak of the water that is used by interception, transpiration, and evaporation during the growth of any particular crop as being the *consumptive use* for that type of vegetation. When these losses are made to cover all such losses occurring in the valley or drainage basin, they are then called the *valley consumptive use*. This quantity is equal to the total water losses except for those basins from which there is watershed leakage.

The water that is intercepted by vegetation, buildings, and other objects and does not reach the ground is evaporated and returned to the air as water vapor. In a similar manner, the water that goes to depression storage and does not later infiltrate into the soil is returned to the air by evaporation. Especially in summertime when the ground surface has been heated, the rate of evaporation from that surface during the period immediately following precipitation is unusually high and continues at a diminishing rate for a long time after rainfall ceases. Even that water which infiltrates into the soil and joins the ground-water table is often subject to these losses, for, if the capillary fringe that lies just above the water table extends up to the ground surface, water will continuously be drawn up to the ground surface and evaporated therefrom; or, if the capillary water is not within reach of ground surface evaporation but is within reach of the roots of trees and other vegetation, it will be subject to the transpirational demands of that vegetation.

These different losses are interwoven to such an extent that they cannot be easily segregated to permit the separate and independent measurement of each. Fortunately, however, the interrelationship between these losses which makes separate measurement difficult tends to make their total more nearly constant for any particular region and climate and, therefore, reduces the importance and the necessity for their separate measurements. For instance, the presence of vegetation affects and reduces the rate of evaporation from the ground surface, and, in turn, the evaporation from the ground surface reduces the moisture available for transpiration, thereby making their sum more nearly uniform over any given basin, regardless of the variation in vegetal cover.

The actual amount of the loss on any drainage basin depends upon the following factors:

1. The nature of the precipitation.
2. The type and development of the vegetation.
3. The area covered by buildings, pavements, and other objects.
4. The climatological factors such as temperature, humidity, and wind velocity.

INTERCEPTION

The interception rate expressed, for example, in inches per hour, is greatest at the beginning of storms and decreases with their duration. At first the surfaces of the leaves, branches, and trunks of trees and the stems of vegetation are dry and capable of retaining a considerable amount of moisture as interception storage, but after they have once become thoroughly wetted, the interception rate becomes equal to the

evaporation rate from those surfaces for the remainder of that particular shower.

Many storms consist of a series of showers separated by intervals
of varying length. Upon the cessation of any shower, evaporation
begins to deplete the interception storage and continues until all the
available moisture has been returned to the air in the form of vapor
or until another shower occurs. Thus it appears that the total interception during different storms is constant neither in quantity nor in
percentage of total rainfall. For any given area and condition of
vegetation the equation is of the form

$$x = a + bt \qquad (1)$$

in which x represents the total interception in inches depth on basin, a
is the interception storage capacity in inches depth on basin, b is the
evaporation rate in inches per hour, and t is the duration of the shower
in hours. The equation above is, of course, applicable only to storms
exceeding the interception storage capacity, a.

As indicated by the formula, the total amount of interception increases with the duration of the storm, and since depth of precipitation
increases with duration there is a general correlation between total interception and total rainfall although there is little difference between
the losses resulting from a heavy downpour and from a light rain of
the same duration. However, the percentage of the total precipitation
that is lost through interception decreases as the amount of precipitation increases. As an illustration, for 0.25 in. rainfall in a dense forest
perhaps 0.2 in., or 80 per cent, is intercepted and never reaches the
ground, whereas for a rainfall of 1 in. perhaps 0.3 in., or 30 per cent,
is intercepted, and for heavier rains the percentage is still less.

For coniferous trees the amount of interception is greater than for
deciduous trees even in full leaf; the difference as given by various
writers ranges from zero to 100 per cent. For any given depth of precipitation, winter and summer losses appear to be about the same for
conifers, but for deciduous trees summer losses are two or three times
as great as winter losses. For dense grasses, shrubs, and grains approaching full growth, the interception loss is nearly as great as for
deciduous trees in full leaf, but their season is short and as a result
their total annual interception is considerably less than for deciduous
trees.

Figure 78 shows the results of measurements of interception for two
types of fairly dense forest cover made by the U. S. Forest Service,
Southeastern Forest Experiment Station, Asheville, North Carolina.
The values of interception plotted in the graphs were obtained by

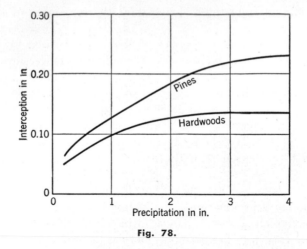

Fig. 78.

subtracting the ground rainfall plus tree-bole drainage from the total precipitation. The tree-bole drainage amounted to 10 to 30 per cent of the total interception. Hoover[1] has reported that measurements made on a 10-year-old planting of loblolly pine located near Union, S. C., showed that an average of 86 per cent of the rain reached the ground.[2]

EVAPORATION FROM WATER SURFACES

Evaporation is the process by which a liquid or a solid is changed into a vapor. The exact laws governing this process are not clearly understood. To obtain the best conception of this phenomenon and of the laws governing it, it may be desirable first to review briefly the physical structure of water.

Any body regardless of its size is made up of a large number of molecules, each of which is constantly in motion at varying velocities and in different directions. The average velocity of all the molecules

[1] Marvin D. Hoover, "Interception of Rainfall in a Young Loblolly Pine Plantation," Station Paper No. 21, Southeastern Forest Expt. Sta., 1953.

[2] A number of other investigations of rainfall interception are:

R. E. Horton, "Rainfall Interception," *Monthly Weather Rev.*, 1919, vol. 47, 603–623.

H. W. Beall, "The Penetration of Rainfall through Hardwood and Softwood Forest Canopy," *Ecology*, 1939, vol. 15, pp. 412–415.

J. Kittredge, H. S. Loughhead, and A. Mazurak, "Interception and Stemflow in a Pine Plantation," *J. Forestry*, 1941, vol. 39, pp. 505–522.

C. H. Niederhof and H. G. Wilson, "Effect of Cutting Mature Lodgepole-Pine Stands on Rainfall Interception," *J. Forestry*, 1943, vol. 41, pp. 57–61.

comprising any given mass determines its temperature. At absolute zero temperature all molecular activity is supposed to cease. In any given mass every molecule is attracted to every other one by a force that is inversely proportional to the square of the distances between them and directly proportional to the product of their masses. Those molecules that happen to be nearest to the free surface of a liquid are, therefore, acted upon by more of these forces from underneath than from above. Molecules that are near the surface, therefore, must overcome this additional force in order to escape into the air as water vapor. It thus appears that only the more rapidly moving molecules escape. Hence, the remaining mass will have a lower average temperature than before. Evaporation is therefore a cooling process.

Although molecules are continuously leaving the water surface, others are returning, and the rate of evaporation is determined by the excess rate of those leaving over those returning. If more are returning than are leaving, condensation is said to be taking place. Immediately adjacent to the water surface is a thin layer of air whose temperature is the same as that of the water. This film quickly becomes saturated with water vapor (see page 59). If, in the air above, the vapor pressure is the same as in the film, there can be no further evaporation. If, however, the vapor pressure in the air above is less than that in the film, through diffusion, convection, and wind action the vapor near the water surface will be dispersed and evaporation will continue. The rate of evaporation depends upon the difference between these two vapor pressures or, in other words, upon the pressure gradient. This principle, known as Dalton's law, is expressed by the formula

$$E = C(p_w - p_a) \tag{2}$$

in which E is the rate of evaporation in inches per day; p_w is the vapor pressure in the film of air next to the water surface or, in other words, the maximum vapor pressure corresponding to the temperature of the water; p_a is the vapor pressure in the air above; and C is a coefficient that is dependent upon barometric pressure, wind velocity, and perhaps other variables.

Influence of Depth

Depth has a very pronounced influence upon the rate of evaporation from any large body of water. The explanation of this phenomenon can be found in a comparison of the cycle of events that occurs in a shallow lake with that which occurs in a deep lake.

In late winter or early spring the temperature of an entire body of shallow water will be at or near 32° F. As the temperature of the air rises, the temperature of the water on the surface also rises, but as it does so, the weight of the water increases, and the warmer water sinks to the bottom as the colder but lighter water rises to the top. At the surface it in turn is warmed to a still higher temperature and greater density, and the turnover process is repeated. This continues until the temperature of all the water becomes 39.2° F, the temperature corresponding to the maximum density of water. From then on, as the surface water becomes warmer it also becomes less dense and therefore remains on the surface. The water below the surface heats more slowly by direct radiation and conduction, as well as by mechanical mixing produced by currents and wave action.

In autumn the overturning process is repeated in reverse. When the surface water cools below the temperature of the lower water it becomes heavier and sinks to the bottom, and the warmer water at the bottom rises to the surface. This continues until the entire body of water has a temperature of 39.2° F. After that, as the surface water cools further it becomes lighter and remains on the surface. This explains why, for a given reduction in air temperature, the surface-water temperature will drop much more quickly from 39° to 32° F than from 46° to 39° F.

Consider now a deep body of water. Either in spring or autumn, after the temperature of the entire mass has reached 39.2°, further changes resulting from radiation, conduction, and mixing are slow and extend only to a limited depth. Below 200 ft the temperature remains at or near 40° F throughout the year. However, the amount of heat that is required to raise the temperature of a large mass of water from 39.2° F to the temperature which it attains by autumn is enormous, and as a result there is a considerable lag between the temperature of the water and that of the air. The temperature of the water is lower than the air temperature in summer and higher in winter, whereas in shallow bodies of water the mean daily temperatures of the air and water do not differ so greatly.

This lag in the temperature of the water in deep lakes behind the temperature of the air above exerts two important influences on the rate of evaporation from such lakes, both of which combine to reduce the summer evaporation below and increase the winter evaporation above the observed rates on shallow lakes. The first of these influences is apparent from a consideration of Dalton's law (see page 197). Inasmuch as E varies with $(p_w - p_a)$, any reduction in the

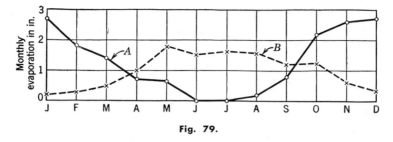

Fig. 79.

temperature of the water reduces p_w, $(p_w - p_a)$, and likewise E. Also in winter an increase in the temperature of the water increases p_w, $(p_w - p_a)$, and E. The second influence results from the fact that in summertime the colder the water is with respect to the air, the colder, heavier, and therefore the more stable will be that vapor-laden film of air that is in direct contact with the water. Because of this increased stability of the air adjacent to the water, the effect of wind action is partially nullified. On the other hand, in early winter the saturated layer of air next to the water is considerably warmer than the air above. Therefore, being unstable, it rises even without the aid of wind action and is replaced by other air of lower humidity. In Fig. 79 are shown monthly variations in the rate of evaporation from deep and shallow lakes. Graph A represents the rate of evaporation from Lake Superior as determined by Rohwer's formula, equation 3, page 202, using average mean monthly air and water temperatures as given by Hickman.[3] Graph B represents the rate of evaporation from a shallow lake as determined by this same formula, using the same air temperatures as before but assuming the water temperatures to be the same as those of the air. This means that in winter the lake surface would freeze over, and the evaporation from the ice would be given by equation 3. Although the latter assumption may not be exactly true, Rohwer found that it is approximately correct.

Methods of Determining Evaporation

Several methods may be used to determine the rate of evaporation from the water surface of reservoirs, natural lakes, or rivers. These methods include the use of:

1. The storage equation.
2. Auxiliary pans.

[3] H. O. Hickman, "Hydrology of the Great Lakes, a Symposium," *Trans. A.S.C.E.*, 1940, vol. 105, p. 813.

3. Evaporation formulas.

4. Humidity and wind velocity gradients.

5. The energy budget.

Storage Equation Method. The first of these methods involves the equation

$$P + I \pm U = E + O \pm \Delta S$$

in which P is the precipitation on the water surface, I the surface inflow, U the net underground inflow or outflow, E the evaporation from the water surface, O the surface outflow, and ΔS is the change in storage. This last quantity is positive for an increase and negative for a decrease in storage. The quantities are usually expressed as inches depth on the water area for some convenient time interval.

The chief disadvantage of this method is that these quantities may be determined with only varying degrees of accuracy. All the errors in measurement are combined and thrown into the resulting value of E. It is particularly difficult to make accurate measurements or estimates of the underground flow. In some cases this quantity is negligible, whereas in others it is an important factor. Large springs may occur in the lake bed, or, if the bed and surrounding area are highly permeable, the direct underground inflow may be large. In other instances, and especially is this true of artificial reservoirs, large underground seepage losses may occur. Small basins are sometimes constructed with impervious linings in order to eliminate seepage losses.

Little is known of the magnitude of underground flow into or out of large lakes. In his study of Lake Superior,[4] Pettis concluded that the inflow was quite large. The discussion of the same article by Meinzer[5] provides additional information on this subject.

Pan Measurements. Because of the ease with which accurate measurements can be made with small pans, a tremendous amount of work has been done by this method. However, it has been found that the rate of evaporation from a small pan is not the same as from a large body of water; nor is the rate of evaporation the same for all pans, since it is affected by such factors as size, depth, and location. Hence, for any given type of pan installation, it is necessary not only to measure the rate of evaporation under all different conditions but also to determine the coefficient or coefficients to be used in reducing the pan results to what may be anticipated from a lake or reservoir.

[4] Col. C. R. Pettis, "Hydrology of the Great Lakes, a Symposium," *Trans. A.S.C.E.*, vol. 105, p. 795.

[5] O. E. Meinzer, "Hydrology of the Great Lakes, a Symposium" (Discussion), *Trans. A.S.C.E.*, vol. 105, p. 834.

The following are brief descriptions of some of the more commonly used types of pans:

1. *Class A. U. S. Weather Bureau Land Pan.* This pan is 4 ft in diameter, 10 in. deep, and the bottom is raised 6 in. above the ground surface. The water surface is supposed to be at least 2 in. and never more than 3 in. below the top of the pan.

2. *U. S. Bureau of Plant Industry Sunken Pan.* This pan is 6 ft in diameter, 2 ft deep, and buried in the ground within 4 in. of the top. The water surface in the pan is supposed to be not more than $\frac{1}{2}$ in. above or below ground level.

3. *Colorado Sunken Pan.* The Colorado Experiment Station has developed a pan 3 ft square, with a depth ranging from less than 18 in. to 3 ft, and buried in the ground within about 4 in. of the top. The water is supposed to be maintained within 1 in. of ground level.

4. *U. S. Geological Survey Floating Pan.* Because it was believed that the evaporation from a pan floating in a large body of water would be nearly the same as from the surrounding water, the U. S. Geological Survey has used a pan 3 ft square by 18 in. deep, supported by drum floats in the center of a raft 14 ft by 16 ft. The water level in the pan is supposed to be at the same elevation as that of the surrounding body, with the sides of the pan projecting 3 in. above.

5. On a number of occasions U. S. Weather Bureau land pans have been mounted on rafts and used as floating pans. However, they appear to have no particular advantage over the U. S. Geological Survey floating pan.

After a thorough study of the results obtained by each of these different types of pans, the Subcommittee on Evaporation, of the Special Committee on Irrigation Hydraulics, of the American Society of Civil Engineers, recommended the U. S. Weather Bureau Class A land pan as their first choice. Next in order of preference was the Colorado sunken pan, and third was the U. S. Geological Survey floating pan. In their summary for and against the use of the U. S. Weather Bureau land pan they state:[6]

The advantages are:

1. More data on this pan are available for comparison than on any other particular type of pan.
2. The coefficient has been found to be about the same for this pan in comparison with large water surfaces in many locations and under many conditions.
3. It is easy of access for observations.

[6] Carl Rohwer, Robert Follansbee, and others, "Symposium on Evaporation from Water Surfaces," *Trans. A.S.C.E.,* 1934, vol. 99, pp. 673–747.

4. It is not subject to uncertainty due to inward or outward wash of water as is the case for a floating pan.

5. It is raised above reasonable drift of dirt, debris, and snow.

6. It is reasonable in cost of installation.

The disadvantages are:

1. The coefficient is considerably less than unity; that is, the rate of evaporation is much greater from the pan than from a reservoir surface.

2. For the data available, coefficients for certain months vary greatly from those for other months. This inconsistency, however, is true for all types of pans thus far studied.

Perhaps a more important disadvantage is that the coefficient depends upon so many factors that vary from time to time and from place to place, that it is practically impossible to determine it accurately.

As a coefficient to be applied to the observed evaporation from a Class A U. S. Weather Bureau land pan for the determination of the evaporation from a lake or reservoir, this committee recommended 0.70, with a range between 0.60 and 0.82. For the Colorado sunken pan they recommended 0.78 with a range between 0.75 and 0.86, and for the U. S. Geological Survey floating pan they recommended 0.80, with a range from 0.70 to 0.82. For a more complete discussion of this subject see the article by Rohwer and Follansbee previously cited.[6] This same article gives the results of numerous evaporation measurements, some of which are shown in Table 12. Additional evaporation data have been summarized by the Weather Bureau.[7]

Evaporation Formulas. Most of the evaporation formulas that have been proposed are based upon Dalton's law and therefore are of the general form of equation 2, in which a value of C has been derived from observed evaporation from small pans. Therefore, to determine the evaporation from large bodies of water, a carefully selected coefficient (see preceding article and reference page 201) must be applied to the results obtained by means of any of these formulas.

As a result of studies made by the Bureau of Agricultural Engineering of the U. S. Department of Agriculture,[8] Rohwer derived the formula

$$E = 0.771(1.465 - 0.0186B)(0.44 + 0.118V)(p_w - p_a) \qquad (3)$$

in which E is the evaporation from lakes or reservoirs in inches per day, B is the mean barometric pressure in inches of mercury at 32° F,

[7] U. S. Weather Bureau, "Mean Monthly and Annual Evaporation from Free Water Surface," *Tech. Paper* No. 13, 1950.

[8] C. Rohwer, "Evaporation from Free Water Surfaces," *U. S. Dept. of Agr. Tech. Bull.* 271, December 1931.

TABLE 12

Summary of Evaporation Records Reduced to Reservoir Surface Evaporation*

Station	Elevation in Ft.	Years	Temperature of Air in ° F.	Wind Velocity at the Pan, in Miles/Hr	Relative Humidity (%)	Reservoir Surface Evaporation in In. April–September	Annual	Maximum per Month
Gardiner, Me.	100	1915–24	45	2.2	..	18.10	24.26	4.56
Ithaca, N. Y.	800	1918–30	47	1.8	78	17.11	22.54	4.17
Pleasantville, N. J.	40	1924–30	51	2.9	74	23.02	31.81	5.40
Washington, D. C.	280	1915–17	54	2.3	69	23.52	34.53	4.87
Chapel Hill, N. C.	500	1921–30	61	1.1	69	20.03	28.56	4.71
Birmingham, Ala.	650	1910	63	...	72	32.18	42.99	6.25
Grand River Lock, Wis.	780	1905–12	46	...	..	21.64	28.57	5.75
Madison, Wis.	860	1906–11	46	...	75	12.91	19.82	3.04
Centerville, Minn.	880	1919–27	45	4.0	..	24.11	30.97	7.37
Iowa City, Iowa	610	1907–10	46	...	..	19.59	30.08	5.36
Columbus, Ohio	763	1918–30	52	2.0	74	19.21	26.81	4.94
Cincinnati, Ohio	520	1910	54	...	68	29.46	38.19	6.02
Clarksburg, W. Va.	1030	1923–30	53	2.6	79	20.65	26.00	6.05
Columbia, Mo. #1	750	1916–27	54	1.5	71	20.28	28.13	5.31
Columbia, Mo. #2	750	1916–26	54	2.9	71	26.31	35.82	6.85
Silverhill, Ala.	250	1918–30	67	1.8	78	25.35	38.27	5.73
Crowley, La.	21	1910–19	68	2.8	77	30.76	46.90	7.18
Williston, N. Dak.	1875	1909–16	39	5.5	74	32.12	38.79	8.45
Rapid City, S. Dak.	3240	1916–21	46	2.0	58	25.61	36.43	7.02
Lincoln, Nebr.	1250	1917–30	51	4.1	69	32.06	42.04	9.92
Wichita, Kans.	1300	1918–27	56	4.2	68	34.60	49.62	9.27
Lawton, Okla.	1111	1916–20	61	6.4	..	41.75	54.35	11.42
San Antonio, Tex.	700	1907–12	70	...	68	43.46	63.71	10.14
Spur, Tex.	....	1922–30	61	6.0	61	42.84	62.44	10.80
El Paso, Tex.	3700	1889–93	64	...	36	49.95	71.16	10.79
Bozeman, Mont.	4754	1918–30	41	2.7	..	24.72	33.77	7.58
Shoshone Reservoir, Wyo.	5390	1916–29	46	...	..	31.70	43.27	9.46
Fort Collins, Colo.	4998	1887–1927	46	1.7	68	30.41	42.19	6.12
Wagonwheel Gap, Colo.	9610	1920–24	34	2.0	64	16.12	22.32	3.22
Santa Fe, N. Mex.	7010	1917–30	48	2.6	54	33.66	44.82	8.46
Elephant Butte, N. Mex.	4265	1916–30	60	3.9	..	47.24	66.99	11.75
Arrowrock, Idaho	3220	1916–30	49	0.8	..	20.32	40.09	8.07
Salt Lake City, U.	4250	1928–30	52	3.6	50	40.67	50.94	10.10
Fallon, Nev.	3970	1908–30	51	3.0	52	44.50	56.74	11.10
Tucson, Ariz.	2400	1929–30	67	1.3	40	41.82	60.26	9.39
Walla Walla, Wash.	1000	1917–30	53	2.0	58	29.68	36.85	8.64
Yakima, Wash.	1060	1910	50	...	..	35.07	47.25	7.41
Warm Springs Reservoir, Oreg.	....	1927–30	47	2.5	..	38.39	54.04	10.42
Klamath Falls, Oreg.	4100	1924–29	48	...	..	24.08	36.71	6.33
Corvallis, Oreg.	235	1922–30	52	1.5	..	21.88	30.68	5.92
Tahoe, Calif.	6230	1916–30	42	3.0	..	22.34	32.09	6.67
E. Park Reservoir, Calif.	1200	1911–29	59	4.0	..	39.48	50.84	9.51
Oakdale, Calif.	215	1918–30	60	5.2	..	45.75	56.89	11.76
Chula Vista, Calif.	9	1918–30	59	3.8	..	26.84	42.26	5.45
Keewatin, Ont.	....	1913–28	36	...	72	11.24	14.29	3.84
Saskatoon, Sask.	....	1918–30	..	...	..	23.51	28.89	7.14
Edmonton, Alta.	....	1918, '21–22	..	...	..	18.65	24.00	5.46
San Juan, Puerto Rico	82	1919–30	78	...	78	31.34	55.29	6.54
Gatun, Canal Zone	85	1912–30	80	7.1	84	22.47	48.38	7.03
Maunawili, Oahu	250	1921–30	72	1.9	..	17.23	30.92	3.80
Alexandria, Egypt	....	1920–29	68	...	72	.....	28.76	....
Atbara, Sudan	....	1905–29	83	...	29	.....	123.67	....

* Data taken from "Evaporation from Reservoir Surfaces" by Robert Follansbee, *Trans. A.S.C.E.*, 1934, 99.

V is the mean velocity of the wind in miles per hour about 6 in. above the ground, p_w is the pressure of saturated vapor at the mean temperature of the water surface in inches of mercury, and p_a is the average vapor pressure in the air in the same units. This equation is based on extensive observations and has been checked under various conditions. For application to small pans, the term 0.771 should be omitted.

Many other formulas have been proposed by different experimenters for the determination of the rate of evaporation from free water surfaces. For a more complete discussion of this subject reference should be made to the article cited previously.

Inasmuch as wind velocity in most of these formulas refers to the velocity at a point about 6 in. above the ground, it is usually necessary to reduce measured velocities to ground velocities. Investigations by the Department of Agriculture provide extensive information concerning the variation in wind velocity near the ground. A year of wind velocity records was obtained at Arlington, Virginia,[9] for elevations of 1, 7, 13, and 25 ft, together with temperatures at elevations of 2 ft and 24.5 ft. A number of careful observations were also made at New Philadelphia, Ohio.[10] Here the wind velocity was measured at twelve points, with the lowest at 0.5 ft above the ground and the highest at 28 ft above the ground.

Various sets of data from the latter publication are plotted in Figs. 80 and 81. The ordinates are elevations above the ground (z), plotted logarithmically. In Fig. 80 the abscissas are wind velocities (v_z), whereas in Fig. 81 the abscissas are the ratios of the velocities at the various elevations to the velocity at 1 ft. It may be noted that curves A, B, and C of Fig. 81 were obtained at various times during the same day. This is a typical variation. Curve D shows the most uniform velocity gradient, and curve E the steepest gradient of the 97 complete sets given in the paper. The difference in the slopes and the curvatures of the various curves is due in part to the effect of the temperature gradient.

When the upper air is warmer than the lower air, during a temperature inversion, the air is relatively stable since there is little tendency for the upper air to mix with lower layers. As a result the velocity gradient tends to remain steep. Such a condition as shown by curves C and E of Fig. 81 quite regularly prevails at night. During the daytime the lower air is warmed and a temperature lapse rate greater

[9] C. W. Thornthwaite and Benjamin Holzman, "Measurement of Evaporation from the Land and Water Surfaces," *U. S. Dept. of Agr. Tech. Bull.* 817, 1942.

[10] C. W. Thornthwaite and Paul Kaser, "Wind Gradient Observations," *Trans. Am. Geophys. Union,* 1943, p. 166.

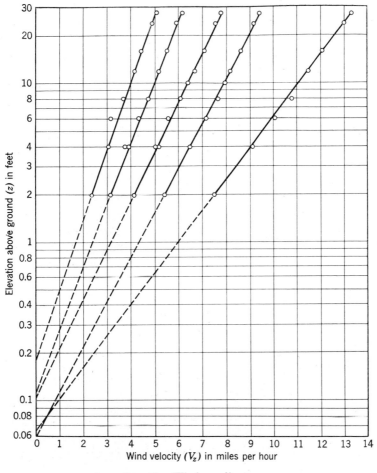

Fig. 80.   Wind gradients.

than the normal adiabatic rate is often established.   At such times
the heavier upper air tends to fall and mix with the slower-moving
lower air.   The result is a tendency for a more uniform velocity at all
elevations.   Curves A and D of Fig. 81 illustrate these conditions.
Curves B, C, and F, as well as those shown in Fig. 80, are typical of
those which occur during normal adiabatic lapse rates.

When the curves are straight lines, they can be represented by a
logarithmic equation of the form suggested by Prandtl,

$$V_z = \frac{V_*}{K} \ln \frac{z}{z_0} \tag{4}$$

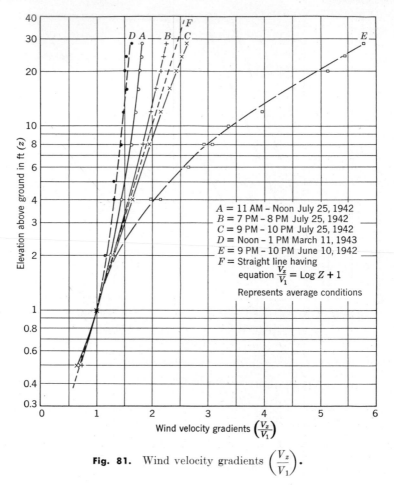

Fig. 81. Wind velocity gradients $\left(\dfrac{V_z}{V_1}\right)$.

in which V_* is the friction velocity, K is a constant and z_0 is the elevation above the ground at which the velocity becomes zero. The shear velocity varies with the magnitude and gradient of the wind but may be assumed constant for all values of z. Although z_0 is closely related to the magnitude and nature of the roughness in pipes, this relationship does not appear to be as consistent for wind gradients. This fact is illustrated by the gradients in Fig. 80, where it may be seen that, in general, z_0 decreases as the wind velocity increases.

If equation 4 is written for $z = 1$, then

$$V_1 = \frac{V_*}{K} \ln \frac{1}{z_0} \qquad (4a)$$

From equations 4 and 4a the following expression for the ratio V_z/V_1 may be derived

$$\frac{V_z}{V_1} = \frac{\log z}{-\log z_0} + 1 \qquad (4b)$$

This equation may be used to represent the straight lines plotted on Fig. 81. The equation for curve F of Fig. 81 is

$$\frac{V_z}{V_1} = \log z + 1 \qquad (4c)$$

which corresponds to $z_0 = 0.1$ ft. According to values of z_0 presented by Sutton,[11] this value of z_0 should occur over grass which is between 10 and 50 cm high.

Several methods have been devised to account for the effect of temperature gradients on the velocity profiles.[12,13] Unfortunately, temperature gradients are not often available at locations where evaporation is to be computed. However, the variations in wind profiles resulting from differences in z_0 can be corrected in an approximate manner because of the relation of z_0 to the wind velocity. This is illustrated in Fig. 82 where values V_{25}/V_1 are plotted against V_1 for 220 observations selected at random from *Bulletin* 817,[9] together with the 97 values of V_{24}/V_1 taken from *Wind Gradient Observations*. The two groups of ratios, i.e., V_{25}/V_1 and V_{24}/V_1, were plotted together since the difference between the two is small compared with experimental errors and the influence of other factors. It may be seen that there is a tendency for the velocity gradient between the 1-ft and the 25-ft levels to be steep for low values of V_1 and flat for high values.

The average value of the ratio for all the points plotted in Fig. 82 was found to be 2.33. If this value is plotted at an elevation of 24.5 ft on Fig. 81, it will be seen that curves B and F very nearly represent average conditions.

As a practical method of reducing the wind velocity at any elevation to the velocity at 6 in. above the ground, it is suggested that the ratios be computed from equation 4 or read from curve F. For example, if V is measured at a point 10 ft above the ground (V_{10}) and

[11] O. G. Sutton, *Micrometeorology*, McGraw-Hill, New York, 1953.

[12] E. L. Deacon, "Vertical Diffusion in the Lower Layers of the Atmosphere," *Quart. J. Roy. Meteorol. Soc.*, January 1949, pp. 81–103.

[13] David N. Keast and Francis M. Wiener, "An Empirical Method for Estimating Wind Profiles over Open, Level Ground," *Trans. Am. Geophys. Union*, October 1950, pp. 858–864.

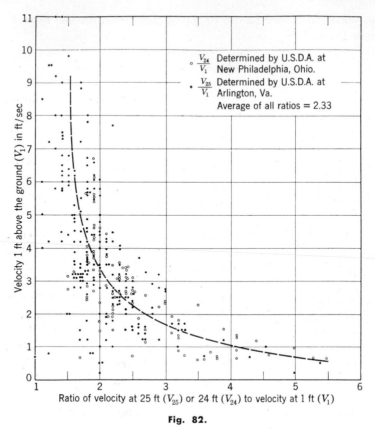

Fig. 82.

found to be 5 ft per sec, equation 4 becomes $V_{10}/V_1 = (\log 10) + 1$ or $V_{10}/V_1 = 2$. Also, $V_{0.5}/V_1 = (\log 0.5) + 1$ or $V_{0.5}/V_1 = 0.70$. The ratio of the wind velocity at 10 ft (V_{10}) to the velocity at the ground ($V_{0.5}$) may then be found by combining the above values as follows: $V_{10}/V_{0.5} = V_{10}/V_1 \times V_1/V_{0.5} = 2 \times 1/0.70 = 2.86$. Using the value of 5 ft per sec for V_{10}, $V_{0.5} = 5/2.86 = 1.75$ ft per sec. All the ratios determined in the above example from equation 4 could also have been read from curve F, Fig. 81.

A greater degree of refinement may be obtained by first solving for the velocity at 1 ft from curve F, then from Fig. 82, checking for the corresponding V_{25}/V_1. If this is far different from 2.4, the ratios may be redetermined from another curve of the family of curves in Fig. 81. If in the example above, V_{10} had been 8 ft per sec, the ratios should have been determined from curve D rather than curve F.

It should be understood that many other factors also influence the wind velocity pattern. Such factors as the roughness and slope of the ground and the presence of buildings or trees in the vicinity may cause great fluctuations in the velocity. It would, for example, be difficult to decide whether an anemometer placed 4 ft above the roof of a 20-ft building should be corrected for an elevation of 4 ft or 24 ft. Neither is likely to give the proper result, owing to the presence of eddies and cross currents which exist under such conditions.

It should also be noted that over large bodies of water, the roughness due to waves increases as the wind velocity increases.[14] This roughness causes the friction velocity, as well as z_0, to increase as the wind velocity increases. For low wind speeds over exceptionally smooth surfaces the profiles are influenced by the fluid properties, and the equations presented here would not apply.

Use of Humidity and Wind Velocity Gradients. The fourth method of measuring evaporation is based on the premises (1) that, if a moisture gradient exists in the air, water vapor will move toward points of lower moisture content, and (2) that the rate of movement of the water vapor is accentuated by the intensity of turbulence in the air. This method has the great advantage of being applicable to both natural land and water surfaces. The difficulty involved in its use is the fact that sensitive and relatively expensive equipment is required. The humidity gradient may be determined from simultaneous measurements of the moisture content of the air at two elevations above the ground with some type of hygrometer. The intensity of turbulence is determined from corresponding measurements of wind velocity gradients. The development of a relationship between the two quantities and the rate of evaporation is based upon the assumption that water vapor will be transported in a manner similar to the interchange of momentum by the turbulent mixing process. The formula for evaporation also includes a turbulence constant that must be evaluated experimentally. The U. S. Department of Agriculture has been conducting an extensive series of tests[15] involving this method. Hourly evaporation-transpiration records covering nearly a year have been obtained for a meadow in Arlington, Virginia. The reference cited above gives a review of the theoretical background for this method, including a derivation of the formula as well as a description of the instruments and methods used in its application.

[14] N. K. Wagner, "An Analysis of Over-Water Wind Profile Measurements," *Trans. Am. Geophys. Union*, October 1958, pp. 845–852.

[15] C. W. Thornthwaite and Benjamin Holzman, "Measurement of Evaporation from Land and Water Surfaces," *U. S. Dept. of Agr. Bull.* 817, May 1942.

Energy Budget Method.　The fifth method of determining evaporation is based on the idea of conservation of heat energy within a body of water. For any given body of water a balance must exist between (1) insolation; (2) heat transferred from the water surface by radiation, conduction, or convection; (3) heat energy acquired or lost in raising or lowering the temperature of the water; and (4) heat dissipated or acquired by evaporation or condensation. If items (1), (2), and (3) are measured, the evaporation or condensation may be determined. This relation between evaporation and insolation was suggested by A. Angstrom[16] in 1920. A method of utilizing this principle to determine evaporation from a natural water surface has been presented by Richardson,[17] and also by Cummings.[18] Its application requires records of air temperatures above lakes, temperature gradients within lakes, and clearness of the atmosphere. The Weather Bureau has in operation a number of pyrheliometer stations in the United States which are providing data regarding the amount of solar energy reaching the earth under different conditions. Tests conducted at Lake Hefner in Oklahoma City[19] have provided additional information needed for practical use of this method of estimating evaporation. An interesting application has been described by Neumann and Rosenan,[20] who also have provided a useful bibliography for those interested in a more detailed study of this procedure.

Control of Reservoir Evaporation

In regions of low rainfall, evaporation rates from water surfaces are usually high and conservation of water is of major importance. Southwestern United States and parts of Australia provide good illustrations of these conditions. For instance, at Stevens Creek Reservoir, which impounds part of the water supply for Broken Hill, Australia, it is reported[21] that 3 gal of water are evaporated for every gallon pumped. In a region such as this, which has an annual precipi-

---

[16] *Geografiska Annala*, 1920, H. 3, p. 237

[17] Burt Richardson, "Evaporation as a Function of Insolation," *Trans. A.S.C.E.*, 1931, vol. 95, 996.

[18] N. W. Cummings, "The Evaporation-Energy Equations and Their Practical Application," *Trans. Am. Geophys. Union*, 1940, pp. 512–522.

[19] E. R. Anderson, "Energy Budget Studies in Lake Hefner Studies," *Tech. Rept., Water-Loss Investigations*, vol. 1, pp. 71–119, *U. S. Geol. Survey Circ.* 229, 1952.

[20] J. Neumann and N. Rosenan, "The Black Sea: Energy Balance and Evaporation," *Trans. Am. Geophys. Union*, October 1954, pp. 767–774.

[21] W. W. Mansfield, "Influence of Monolayers on the Natural Rate of Evaporation of Water," *Nature*, vol. 175, 1955, p. 247.

tation of less than 10 in., evaporational losses of this magnitude are of great concern. If the evaporation could be reduced by one third, the available water supply would be doubled.

Scientists have known for some time of certain chemical compounds which spread in monomolecular layers over water surfaces and inhibit evaporation. Because of the increasing need for conservation of water, an interest has developed in the use of such substances for controlling evaporation in reservoirs. Mansfield[21] is credited with first testing hexadecanol (acetyl alcohol), which seems to be the most promising compound. More recent tests at the Stevens Hill Reservoir[22] indicate that during a 14-wk period the evaporation from this 2000-acre reservoir was reduced about 37 per cent, at a cost of about one penny per 1000 gal saved. Experimental work conducted in Illinois has shown a reduction in evaporation of approximately 33 per cent during the warmest summer periods and 11 per cent during cooler periods.[23] The Bureau of Reclamation made studies to determine the effect of a hexadecanol film on taste, color, odor, and biological quality, and no deleterious effects were observed.[24]

TRANSPIRATION

Transpiration is the process whereby the moisture that has circulated through the plant structure is returned to the atmosphere, principally in the form of water vapor. For any given plant the rate of transpiration varies throughout the 24 hours of the day; it varies from one day to another depending upon the temperature, sunlight, moisture available, and other atmospheric conditions; for annual plants it varies throughout their period of growth, and for perennial plants it varies from year to year, depending upon their stage of development.

Some of these factors influence transpiration and evaporation in a very similar manner; others do not. For instance, temperature seems to exert the same influence on both; in other words, the rate of transpiration is doubled for approximately every 18° F rise in temperature. Also relative humidity, wind velocity, and perhaps barometric pressure appear to exert almost the same effect upon transpiration as they do

[22] K. B. Moulton, "Evaporation Control at Broken Hill," *Weather,* July 1957, Royal Meteorol. Soc., London, Eng.

[23] W. J. Roberts, "Evaporation Suppression from Water Surfaces," *Trans. Am. Geophys. Union,* October 1957.

[24] G. Earl Harbeck, Jr., "Some Recent Studies of Evaporation and Evapotranspiration by the U. S. Geological Survey," *Proc. Conf. on New Research Methods in Hydrol.,* Scripps Institute of Oceanography, 1957.

upon evaporation from free water surfaces. On the other hand, transpiration is to a considerable extent influenced and controlled by the amount of sunlight, moisture available, and stage of plant development.

Sunlight

Although the rate of evaporation from a free water surface is usually lower at night than in daytime, the reduction is principally due to the lower night temperature of the air and to the resulting increase in relative humidity. Transpiration rates, however, experience a much greater variation between day and night, principally because transpiration varies directly with plant growth, which is almost wholly dependent upon sunlight. As a result, transpiration is virtually restricted to daylight hours.

A striking illustration of the effect of transpiration and of its variations between day and night is provided in Figs. 83 and 84. In Fig. 83 is shown the variation in flow July 7 to 14, 1938, for stream 14, which drains an area of 152 acres in Coweeta Experimental Forest of the Southeastern Forest Experiment Station near Asheville, North Carolina. In Fig. 84 are shown the fluctuations in ground-water level September 19 to 26, as recorded in Well G–2 which is located in the valley bottom of a dry cove where the water table is 10.5 ft below the ground surface. The water level in Well G–1 is also shown. This well is about 30 ft from G–2, where the water table is about 16.5 ft from the ground surface. Dr. C. R. Hursh, Senior Forest Ecologist at the station, explains these fluctuations in the following manner.

A much greater density of trees and shrubs exists near the banks of the streams and in the valley bottoms than is to be found farther back and nearer the divide. The roots of this vegetation penetrate into the capillary fringe, thus lowering the water table in the immediate vicinity during the daylight hours when transpiration is most active. Back farther from the stream channel the water table is so far below the ground surface that the plant roots cannot reach the capillary fringe. As a result, in this region there is no transpirational draft during the daytime followed by a night recovery, but instead there is only a continuous decline in the water table until it is replenished from precipitation. These conditions are illustrated in Fig. 85, in which abc represents the water level in the stream and adjacent ground water in the morning, before the effects of transpiration are felt. To a greatly exaggerated scale, $a'b'c'$ shows the water surface in the stream and the adjacent water table at the end of a day's transpiration. During the following night, water from cd flows in and

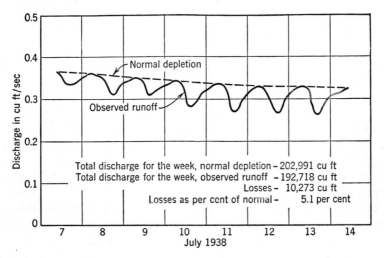

Fig. 83. Stream hydrograph reflecting transpiration draft. Stream 14, drainage area, 152 acres, Coweeta Experimental Forest, Southeastern Forest Experiment Station, Asheville, N. C.

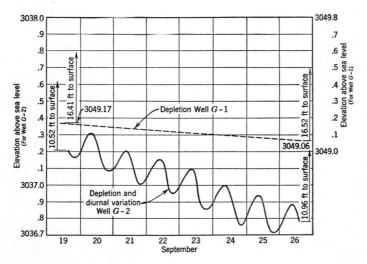

Fig. 84. Ground-water elevations, Coweeta Experimental Forest, Southeastern Forest Experiment Station, Asheville, N. C.

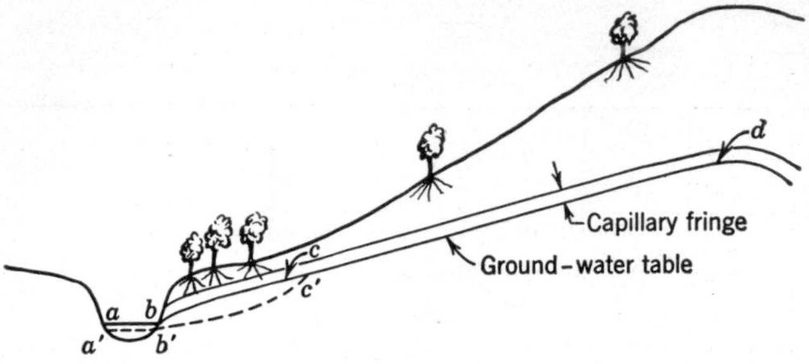

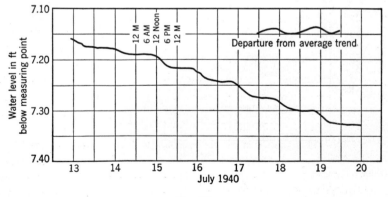

Fig. 85.

restores the lower portion of the water table almost but not quite to its initial level, *abc*.

A portion of the record obtained from an automatic water-stage recorder in operation in a shallow well near Roscommon, Michigan, is reproduced as Fig. 86.[25] Detailed examination of this diagram shows the consistent daily drawdown of water level through the sunlight period. A time difference is noted at each end of the cycle, in that the drawdown period generally starts about 8:00 A.M. each day or about 2½ hr after sunrise, and the recovery of water level or cessation of drawdown starts shortly before 6:00 P.M. or more than 2 hr before sunset. The maximum rate of drawdown of water level occurs during the noon period, when the sun is at the zenith. The periods of so-called recovery are represented by the intervals of decreased drawdown rate and in this example do not imply an actual rise in water

Fig. 86.

[25] Figure supplied by John G. Ferris.

level.   During the growing season, the general trend of water level is downward, and the transpiration phenomenon is superimposed on this downward trend.   To show the effect more clearly, a portion of the graph is reproduced by replotting the departure of the curve from the average downtrend.

The effect of transpiration draft as shown in Figs. 83 and 84 is most frequently observed in small headwater streams and even then only when the water table or capillary water in the adjacent banks is within reach of the roots of vegetation.   It is less distinctly seen in hydrographs of large streams because of the ironing-out effect produced by the large number of inflowing tributaries, each having a different timing.

Moisture Available

Quite naturally the amount of moisture that is used by vegetation is limited to the amount that is available.   Except for aquatic and aerial vegetation, plants have the following possible sources of moisture supply: gravity water, pellicular water, and capillary water.   Gravity water is available only for short periods during and immediately following rains, and under the action of gravity it is always moving downward toward the water table.   Pellicular water exists above the capillary fringe as a thin film covering the soil grains, and is held there against the action of gravity.   Vegetation whose roots do not penetrate into the capillary fringe is, therefore, principally dependent upon pellicular water for its moisture supply.   Vegetal roots are incapable of drawing all the pellicular water from the soil, and in this respect various types of plants seem to differ little.   Assuming an average depth of penetration of plant roots of 5 ft, Tolman[26] estimated a moisture content of a little less than 1 ft of water in this depth for a soil of average texture.   Throughout a growing season most vegetation requires 6 in. to 24 in. of water or more.   Therefore those plants whose roots do not penetrate to the capillary fringe are dependent upon frequent replenishment of soil moisture by rains.   When the available moisture has been exhausted to the point at which permanent wilting occurs, the ratio of the weight of the remaining moisture to the weight of the dry soil is called the *wilting coefficient* for that soil.   Its value varies inversely with the sizes of the soil grains and ranges from less than 1 per cent for coarse sand to 25 or 30 per cent for heavy clay.

Plants whose roots penetrate into the capillary fringe are not so directly dependent upon rains for the replenishment of their supply, for, as this moisture is drawn off, it is continuously replenished from

[26] C. F. Tolman, *Ground Water,* McGraw-Hill, 1937, p. 31.

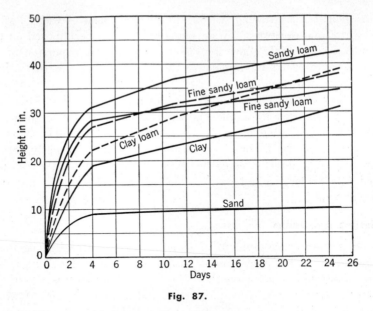

Fig. 87.

the water table. The rate of replenishment, however, depends upon the sizes of the soil grains and upon the height to which the water must be raised. If, for instance, the capillary fringe is 4 ft in thickness and the roots penetrate halfway through or to within 2 ft of the water table, the rate of replenishment will be very much greater than if the depth of penetration were only a few inches. In Fig. 87 are shown the rates of capillary rise in a number of California soils as determined by W. A. Packard in an unpublished research reported by Tolman.[27] In this figure it will be noted that the average height of rise in the first 4 days is about 75 per cent of the total height observed in 25 days.

Raising or lowering the water table may be either a benefit or a detriment to vegetation. If, for instance, the water table is at such an elevation that the natural penetration of the roots is well into the capillary fringe but not into the water table, the conditions for plant growth are at their best. If the water table is lowered, the plants will at times suffer from lack of moisture, and if it is raised for any great length of time the submerged roots will be killed by drowning. On the other hand, if the water table is naturally so low that the capillary water is beyond the reach of the roots, a proper amount of raising will benefit vegetation; and, if it is naturally so high that the

[27] By permission from *Ground Water,* by C. F. Tolman, copyrighted by McGraw-Hill, 1937.

roots can penetrate only to an insufficient depth without being drowned, a certain amount of lowering will prove beneficial.

Stage of Plant Development

In addition to the diurnal variation in transpiration that has already been discussed, there are also seasonal and annual variations depending upon the stage of development and rate of growth. All plants grow more rapidly at certain seasons of the year than at others. The fact is quite well established that for any particular type of vegetation the rate of transpiration varies with the weight of dry matter produced. Inasmuch as the production of dry matter is the result of growth, it varies directly with vegetative activity. In other words, transpiration is restricted to the growing season and is most rapid during the period when vegetation is growing the fastest.

Transpiration Ratio

From month to month there are large variations in the rate of growth for different types of vegetation, and as a result, the monthly changes in transpiration are correspondingly large. Because of the difficulties encountered in measuring monthly changes in ground-water and soil-moisture storage, few data are available on monthly transpiration. Nor is much known about the changes from year to year resulting from the growth and development of annual plants. For any particular kind of vegetation, the ratio between the weight of water consumed and the weight of dry matter produced is called its transpiration ratio. In determining this factor, the weight of the dry matter of the entire plant, exclusive of the roots, should be used. Sometimes, however, to make the results more generally useful, only the marketed crop is used, such as the grain of wheat, corn, beans, and rice, the tubers of potatoes and sugar beets, and so on.

For any type of plant the transpiration ratio varies widely, depending upon the kind of soil, available moisture, relative humidity, and other climatic factors. In Table 13 are given the usual range and approximate average values for some of the more common types of vegetation.[28] These transpiration ratios are based upon the weight

[28] For detailed results of experimental investigations see the following references: L. J. Briggs and H. L. Shantz, *U. S. Dept. Agr. Bur. Plant Industry Bull.* 285, 1913.

L. J. Briggs and H. L. Shantz, *J. Agr. Research,* vol. 3, No. 1, pp. 1–63, 1914.

H. L. Shantz and L. N. Piemeisel, *J. Agr. Research,* vol. 34, No. 12, pp. 1093–1190, 1927.

O. E. Meinzer, "Physics of the Earth, IX," *Hydrology,* Chapter 8 by C. H. Lee, McGraw-Hill, 1942, pp. 283–288.

TABLE 13

| Plant | Transpiration Ratios | |
	Usual Range	Average
Alfalfa	700–1000	850
Wheat	300– 550	450
Oats	400– 650	500
Corn	250– 350	300
Rye	400– 600	500
Barley	300– 600	450
Rice	600– 800	700
Cotton		600
Red clover	300–1000	800
Buffalo grass	250– 350	300
Weeds	200–1000	600
Potatoes	300– 600	500
Sugar beets	300– 500	400

of dry matter produced rather than upon the weight of the marketed product.

Measurement of Transpiration

Although a number of laboratory methods of measuring transpiration have been used, especially by botanists, the one that has met with most favor by engineers, foresters, and agriculturists has been the *closed-phytometer method*. This instrument consists of a watertight tank containing sufficient earth to nourish the plant. A cover is sealed on to prevent any rain from entering or any water from escaping from the tank except through plant transpiration. Means are provided for adding water as desired. The transpirational losses for any period are equal to the original weight plus the weight of water added, minus the final weight. This method is, of course, restricted to plants having relatively small root systems.

In column 5, Table 14, are shown some transpiration ratios determined from experiments by Briggs and Shantz. These values are based upon the weight of the dry matter contained in the marketed product. The weights and depths shown in columns 6 and 7 were computed by applying these ratios to the average yields shown in column 2. These experiments were conducted at Akron in eastern Colorado and do not necessarily represent the transpiration requirements of crops grown under different soil and climatic conditions.

TABLE 14

Crop (1)	Bu per acre (2)	Lb per bu (3)	Lb per acre (4)	Transpiration Ratio§ (5)	Lb of water per acre (6)	Depth in in. (7)
Wheat	30	60	1800	1000–1600	1,800,000– 2,880,000	8–12.5
Oats	50	32	1600	1100–1900	1,760,000– 3,040,000	8–13.5
Barley	35	48	1680	950–1250	1,600,000– 2,050,000	7–9
Rye	25	56	1400	1800	2,520,000	11
Corn	80	35	2800	850–1240	2,240,000– 3,470,000	10 15
Potatoes	100	60	1320†	1380–2200	1,820,000– 2,900,000	8–13
Sugar Beets	10*		2400‡	570	1,360,000	6
Alfalfa	1.5*		3000	420–1060	1,260,000– 3,180,000	5.5–14
Red Clover	1.5*		3000	720–1020	3,060,000	9.5–13.5

* Tons per acre.
† Dry matter taken as 22% of total weight.
‡ Dry matter taken as 12% of total weight.
§ Based upon the results of experiments by Briggs and Shantz, *J. Agr. Research*, vol. 3, No. L, pp. 1–63, 1914.

In fact, they do not truly represent the water uses of crops grown in eastern Colorado under actual field conditions. All these plants were grown in closed phytometers and in screened shelters. The experimenters concluded that the shelters caused a reduction in the water requirement of approximately 20 per cent. The extent of the influence of the phytometers upon the water consumption is unknown.

Another method of determining transpiration is by means of watershed studies. This method requires a period of intensive study of rainfall and runoff, after which the vegetative cover on the drainage basin is changed or removed. The effect of removing the vegetative cover can then be determined from subsequent measurements. One method of evaluating the effect of the changes is by means of a correlation of runoff between the basin being studied and an adjacent drainage basin. The correlation is established by making careful rainfall and runoff measurements on both basins during the period before the change is made. It is assumed that this same relationship would have continued during the following period and that any deviations can be ascribed to the change. The effect of removing vegetation can also be determined by computing the total annual water losses before and after the change, by means of the storage equation, as described on page 226. In addition to measuring precipitation and runoff, this method requires that continuous records of soil moisture, water-table elevations, and ground-water movement be made. Complete meteorological records should also be maintained to permit the correlation of the results with climatic factors and also to detect any unusual differences in these factors for the periods before and after making the change in land use. Correction may also have to be made because the water-use rate of perennial vegetation, such as a forest, changes as it matures, so that the basis for comparison with original conditions may not remain constant during the years following the removal of the vegetation.

Although the foregoing methods enable us to make an accurate analysis of the change in water yield of a drainage basin, it may not be possible to determine exactly the corresponding change in transpiration, since the rate of soil evaporation may have also undergone a change. The increased exposure due to the removal of dense vegetation usually increases the evaporation opportunity of the soil. However, this effect is complicated by the fact that soil evaporation is dependent on the presence of soil moisture, and soil moisture is also influenced by the removal of vegetation. If vegetation is removed without disturbing the infiltration capacity (page 106), more soil moisture will be available for evaporation, whereas, if soil is left unprotected, the infiltration capacity will be greatly decreased, and soil moisture will be less than before the cutting.

Two outstanding examples of watershed studies for the determination of transpiration were conducted by the Southeastern Forest Experiment Station of the U. S. Forest Service at the Coweeta Hydrological Laboratory.[29,30] This laboratory is located in the southern Appalachian Mountains of western North Carolina near the Georgia boundary. The experimental work reported here originated under the direction of Dr. C. R. Hursh, formerly Senior Forest Ecologist for the Station. In one experiment, a rather dense forest was completely cut on a 32.8-acre basin in 1941, and, except for 3 years, the sprouts and

[29] M. D. Hoover, "Effect of Removal of Forest Vegetation upon Water-Yields," *Trans. Am. Geophys. Union*, Part VI, 1944, pp. 969–977.

[30] Robert E. Dils, "The Coweeta Hydrologic Laboratory," Southeastern Forest Experiment Station, Asheville, N. C., 1957.

shrubs were cut back annually through 1955. Special care was used to maintain the original condition of the ground surface by leaving fallen logs in place. The annual precipitation on this basin is about 70 in., and the growing season extends from April through September. During the first year after cutting, the water yield was increased by about 17 in. It may be assumed that the transpiration of the original vegetative cover was somewhat greater, perhaps 20 in. per yr. After the cutting, many herbaceous plants began to invade the area and reduce the water yield. After several years, the changes in water yield were stabilized at rates that were about 11 in. per yr higher than the original rates.

A similar complete cutting was made on another Coweeta watershed, but in this experiment vegetation was allowed to grow back naturally. The increase in runoff was again about 17 in. during the first year. Fifteen years after the cutting, the yield was still 4 in. per yr greater than the yield expected under original conditions. Other tests in this experimental area, which included farming and grazing, also produced increased runoff but caused much higher peak flows and serious erosion.

A similar study[31] was made in Utah in a region having an annual precipitation of about 53 in. This area was covered by aspen with a herbaceous understory. Removal of the aspen increased stream flow by 4 in. per yr. The later removal of the herbaceous cover increased the stream flow another 4 in., but the annual soil loss also increased. Additional studies similar to those described will provide the basis for future land-use management.

Two other promising methods of determining evapotranspiration rates are the use of humidity and wind velocity gradients and the energy budget method, which were described in the previous section dealing with evaporation from water surfaces. A procedure for applying the energy budget method has been presented by Penman.[32]

SOIL EVAPORATION

Soil evaporation, or land evaporation, is the loss of moisture through direct evaporation from the individual soil grains located at and near the ground surface. Its rate is governed by the same factors that

---

[31] A. R. Croft, and L. V. Monninger, "Evapotranspiration and other Water Losses on Some Aspen Forest Types," *Trans. Am. Geophys. Union*, August 1953, pp. 563–574.

[32] H. L. Penman, "Estimating Evaporation," *Trans. Am. Geophys. Union*, February 1956, pp. 43–50.

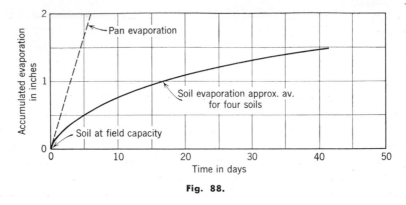

Fig. 88.

affect the rate of evaporation from a free water surface, plus a factor which Horton has called "evaporation opportunity." This factor, as its name implies, is a measure of the opportunity or of the possibility of the occurrence of evaporation from the ground surface. It may be expressed as the percentage that the actual evaporation from the ground surface is of the rate of evaporation from a free water surface. It is principally controlled by the amount of moisture present in the surface strata of the soil and ranges from zero for a thoroughly dry ground surface to 100 per cent or more for a bare soil immediately after a rain. Under a hot sun, with a relatively low humidity and a high wind velocity, this evaporation will continue at a high rate for some time after the cessation of rainfall, until the ground surface starts drying. It will then decrease as the surface of the ground dries, until a constant rate is reached which is dependent on the depth to the water table and the nature of the soil.

This behavior is illustrated in Fig. 88, which is based on data reported by Veihmeyer and Brooks.[33] The curve shows a typical relationship between accumulated soil evaporation and time, during a period without replenishment of the soil moisture from rainfall or from the water table. The straight line shows the comparable evaporation from a 12-ft pan. This example illustrates that whereas soil evaporation is high in regions having a high annual rainfall that is well distributed throughout the year, in regions of low annual rainfall, or where the precipitation is largely concentrated in one season, the soil evaporation is much less. The rate of decrease in soil evaporation which occurs after the soil has been brought to field capacity is much more rapid than is the rate of decrease in transpiration losses, which

[33] F. J. Veihmeyer and F. A. Brooks, "Measurement of Cumulative Evaporation from Bare Soil," *Trans. Am. Geophys. Union,* August 1954, pp. 601–607.

continues at near-maximum speed until the soil moisture has been depleted almost to the wilting point.

Influence of High or Low Water Table

If the water table is at or near the ground surface, the evaporation rate is approximately the same as the rate from a free water surface. As the water table is lowered, the rate of evaporation decreases by an amount that is dependent on the nature of the soil. This fact is illustrated in Fig. 89, which is based on tests conducted by Veihmeyer and Brooks.[34] Values shown in this figure are obtained from measurements on soil-filled tanks in which the water tables are held at constant levels. The value for zero depth to the water table is determined from a standard Weather Bureau evaporation pan.

Water is raised from the water table to the ground surface in two ways. If the capillary fringe extends to the ground surface (see Fig. 87), water is carried upward at relatively rapid rates in the capillary tubes. In addition, soil moisture moves from moist soil to dry soil under the influence of the capillary potential gradient, described more fully in Chapter 5, page 121.

In most drainage basins are certain areas in which the ground surface is never within the capillary fringe and throughout which the rate of soil evaporation is extremely variable, ranging from a maximum immediately after rains to zero during dry periods. In other areas the ground surface is always being supplied with capillary water, and the

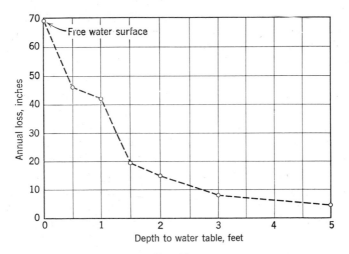

Fig. 89.

[34] See note 33.

soil-evaporation rate is continuous and much more nearly uniform. When these areas are artificially drained, the water table is lowered, and the soil evaporation is greatly reduced. The effect of drainage upon flood and low water flows was discussed in Chapter 3. (See page 55.) Intermediate between these two areas is a third area, throughout which, during a portion of the year, the ground surface is within the capillary fringe, and the soil evaporation is continuous and fairly uniform. During the remainder of the year, the ground surface is above the capillary water, and the evaporation rate is discontinuous. Depending on the size of this intermediate area and upon the length of time each year when the ground surface is within the capillary fringe, soil evaporation will vary one year from another, even though all other factors such as temperature, humidity, and precipitation remain the same.

Measurement of Soil Evaporation

From the foregoing statement it appears that experiments to determine soil evaporation must be conducted under two different sets of conditions, namely, (1) for a freely draining soil and (2) for a soil whose surface is constantly being supplied with capillary water and which, therefore, has a higher evaporation opportunity.

For measuring soil evaporation under the first of these conditions, lysimeters are commonly used. A lysimeter is a tank, usually 4 to 6 ft square and 3 to 6 ft deep, filled with earth, and embedded with the surface almost flush with the ground. The bottom is funnel shaped and drains into a closed receptacle located in an underground gallery or passageway. The soil evaporation is the difference between the rainfall and the drainage.

To measure the evaporation from a soil whose surface is within the capillary fringe, tanks may be used that are equipped to maintain the water table at any desired elevation. The soil evaporation is determined by weighing the tanks at stated intervals and knowing the amount of water that was added in the interim.

In general, experiments that are designed to isolate and determine separately plant transpiration and soil evaporation must necessarily be conducted under conditions that rarely exist in nature. These two quantities are so interdependent that they cannot easily be separated. Vegetation reduces soil evaporation in two ways: first, by using some of the moisture that would otherwise be available for soil evaporation and, second, by reducing the wind velocity and thereby increasing the relative humidity at the ground surface. On the other hand, soil evaporation removes moisture that would otherwise be available for transpiration. Consequently any figures on soil evaporation and transpiration that have been determined separately are of little practical value, for they cannot be added in determining the total water losses from any basin.

The humidity gradient and the energy budget methods of determining evaporation from water surfaces described on pages 209 and 210 are ideally suited to measuring combined evaporation and transspiration rates. It may be hoped that carefully controlled applications of these methods under various conditions will provide valuable information in regard to both soil evaporation and combined evaporation-transpiration rates.

WATERSHED LEAKAGE

The geological formation under many drainage basins is such that precipitation falling on one basin finds its way underground through fissures and water-bearing strata to an outlet, either in a nearby or a remote drainage basin, or directly to the sea. This is called *watershed leakage*. Although it is believed to occur quite commonly, in many cases it is relatively unimportant, and the losses from one basin are frequently balanced by accretions from another.

Occasionally, however, these losses are large and may constitute a major loss from a basin, as in the north branch of the Thunder Bay River and in the Rainy River in northern Michigan. Both these basins are underlain with limestone. Sinkholes are numerous, and much of the runoff finds its way into them and thence, in all probability, to Lake Huron. Similar conditions are known to occur in Wisconsin and in many other states.

A thorough knowledge of the geology of the basin usually provides the best evidence as to the probability of such leakage. Without such information, runoff records from the basin in question should be compared with records from similar basins nearby. The results of this comparison together with a study of the rainfall records and a knowledge of the soil, topography, and vegetal cover should give a good indication of the probability of any appreciable amount of watershed leakage. A more detailed discussion of this topic may be found in Chapter 3, pages 53 and 54.

TOTAL WATER LOSSES

As stated early in this chapter the total water losses from any drainage basin consist of interception, evaporation from land and

water surfaces, transpiration, and ground-water outflow. Ordinarily
these losses for any given drainage basin can be either measured or
estimated more accurately and more easily collectively than separately. The relationship between these collective losses and rainfall,
runoff, ground-water discharge, and storage, is expressed by the
equation

$$L = P - Q - U \pm \Delta S \tag{5}$$

in which L is the total losses for the period, P the total precipitation
for the period, Q the total runoff for the period, U the net ground-water
outflow for the period, and ΔS the increment in surface and subsurface storage during the period. The sign is plus for a decrease in
storage and minus for an increase. All these quantities are expressed
in inches depth on the drainage basin. The quantity ΔS is made up
of three separate factors: (1) the increment in surface storage in
lakes, ponds, swamps, and streams; (2) the change in ground-water
storage below the water table, which for any given area and period
is equal to the product of the average change in level and the average
porosity of the soil; and (3) the change in field moisture above the
water table.

For any region, a study of the rainfall and ground-water records
reveals the fact that well-defined cycles are maintained for each of
these phenomena throughout the year. As an illustration, in southern
Michigan about 18 per cent of the annual precipitation occurs in
winter, 27 per cent in spring, 29 per cent in summer, and 26 per cent
in fall. It is not to be inferred that these percentages hold rigidly
each year, but rather that they represent the average values and indicate the general cyclic variation in precipitation throughout the
year.

Also the ground-water level usually reaches its maximum stage
about the first of May and then is subjected to a more or less general
decline until the latter part of September or the first of October.
Furthermore, although during the year there may be fluctuations
amounting to several feet or even more, the observed level on
October 1 of any year does not ordinarily differ greatly from the
long-term mean elevation for that date, except as a result of unnatural
changes or developments made within the basin. Also at this time of
year the amount of surface storage and the soil-moisture deficiency
do not usually vary much one year from another. Because of these
facts, the average annual water loss for any period of 5 yr or longer,
beginning and ending with October 1, may be determined from
equation 5 ignoring ΔS. If the values of P and Q have been accurately

determined for the period, the average annual water loss should be correct within an inch or two at the most.

If the water loss for a single year is determined in this same manner, the error will be considerably greater, depending upon the value of ΔS for that year. For instance, if the water table on October 1 of any year is 18 in. higher or lower than it was on the same date for the preceding year, and the average soil porosity is $33\frac{1}{3}$ per cent, the change in ground-water storage alone amounts to 6 in., which added to the changes in soil-moisture and surface storage would probably give a total value for ΔS of 8 or 10 in. This large error should, however, be detected, and at least partial correction should be made. This is possible because, except during a period of surface runoff immediately following a storm, all the stream flow is derived from ground water and from surface storage. Inasmuch as the surface storage and the soil-moisture content also vary more or less in parallel with the ground-water storage, it is seen that, except when surface runoff is occurring at the end of the water year, the stream flow at that time provides a good index of ΔS for that year. If, for example, on October 1 of two successive years the entire flow is apparently coming from ground water and if that flow is approximately the same on those dates, the value of ΔS is negligible for that year. If, however, the flow is considerably greater or less at the end of the year than it was at the beginning, ΔS must be taken into account and correction must be made for it, or the annual loss for such a year will be correspondingly in error. The best procedure to be followed in making this correction depends upon the character of the data at hand in each case. If, for instance, sufficient ground-water levels are available, this change in ground-water storage can be approximated fairly well, depending upon knowledge of the average soil porosity. If this change represents an increase in storage, in all probability there will also be increases in the amounts of soil moisture and surface storage. On the basis of a knowledge of surface-storage conditions, depth and character of soil, and also the antecedent rainfall, these quantities may be estimated and added to the change in ground-water storage to determine the total value of ΔS.

The value of ΔS in equation 5 may also be determined from a normal depletion curve of a stream (see page 20). Because the depletion curve represents the rate of depletion of ground-water storage, ΔS is equal to the area beneath the portion of the curve bounded by the discharge rates occurring at the beginning and the end of the period for which ΔS is being determined.

The underground flow is usually small. However, sometimes there may be watershed leakage (page 40) or indirect drainage (page 53) which must be included in the computations. In some drainage basins there may be a considerable amount of ground-water outflow from aquifers lying beneath the river draining the basin. It may be necessary to determine the magnitudes of such flows by methods described in Chapter 6, before concluding that they are negligible.

If ground-water discharge may be neglected, the average annual water loss over a long period of years can be determined quite accurately from only precipitation and runoff records. This is because the storage term in equation 5 becomes small with respect to P and Q under such conditions. On the other hand, for the accurate determination of annual water losses, ΔS must be taken into account, and its value may be at least closely approximated for each successive year from ground-water levels or from the hydrograph. For seasonal or monthly losses, the determinations will be less accurate.

Factors Affecting Total Water Losses

The total water losses for any year are the combined result of the influence of many factors, the principal of which are the total annual precipitation, its intensity and distribution throughout the year, temperature, humidity, and wind velocity. Of the last three factors, temperature is perhaps the most important.

In *U. S. Geological Survey Water-Supply Paper* 846 are given the results of a study made to determine the annual water losses on a large number of drainage basins in many of the eastern and central states. In this paper an attempt is also made to correlate water loss and temperature. Figure 90 has been reproduced from this paper. In this figure the isothermals are shown heavy, and the lighter lines are generalized lines of mean annual water loss. It will be observed that in a general way these two sets of lines are nearly parallel east of the Mississippi River, but, because of reduced precipitation and the resultant reduction in evaporation opportunity at points not far west of the Mississippi, the water-loss lines dip to the south and cross the isothermal lines nearly at right angles.

In Fig. 91 are shown the annual water losses from the drainage basins of the south branch of the Nashua River and of the Sudbury River, as given in this paper, each plotted against the mean temperature for the corresponding years. This figure shows a general lack of correlation between annual water loss and annual temperature. There are two reasons for this. In the first place the quantities that are plotted as annual water loss are in fact annual water loss plus or minus ΔS. It has been shown that for yearly periods ΔS may be as

much as 8 or 10 in. Furthermore, in addition to temperature, water
losses are influenced by amount and distribution of rainfall, depth to
water table, humidity, wind velocity, and other factors.

The part that water losses play in the determination of yield will
be discussed in Chapters 8 and 9.

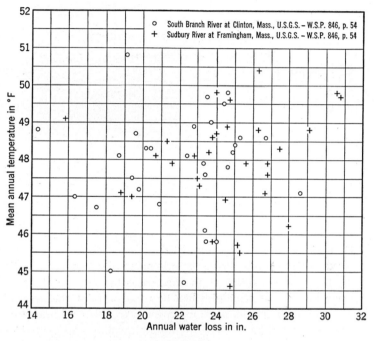

Fig. 91.

8

Runoff

The practical objective of the science of hydrology is to provide a means of determining the characteristics of the hydrograph that may be expected for a stream draining any particular basin. The basic principles have been explained in the preceding pages. It remains to be shown how those principles can be used best for the determination of (1) the maximum flood flow expected to occur with any stated frequency for a given basin; (2) the minimum flow anticipated under a given set of conditions; and (3) the monthly, annual, or average long-term yield.

Before the solution of these several problems is taken up, attention should be called to the fact that the first is concerned almost entirely with surface runoff; in the second, ordinarily only ground-water flow is involved; and in the third, it is the sum of surface runoff and ground-water flow, without reference to the source.

SURFACE RUNOFF

In the determination of the maximum flood flow or any of the other characteristics of surface runoff, the very nature of the available data depends to a considerable extent upon the size of the area drained. We will, therefore, first consider the surface runoff from small plots, because small plots provide a simple basic understanding of the runoff process. The methods developed for small plots may be used for determining the runoff from subdivisions of drainage systems when no runoff data are available on the larger areas. Then the surface runoff of small watersheds having areas varying from a few acres to perhaps 10 square miles will be studied. These are of the size encountered in the design of culverts, storm sewers, airports, and small bridges. Finally, methods will be discussed for determining the characteristics of the flood hydrographs that may be expected from larger drainage basins such as those involved in flood studies, power development, irrigation, and water supply.

Runoff from Small Plots

Overland flow occurs after the rate of precipitation exceeds the infiltration capacity for sufficient time to fulfill the demands of depression storage and establish an initial quantity of surface detention. In order to produce surface runoff it is necessary that areas in which surface detention and overland flow exist be connected with the stream by means of surface channels. It is possible, for example, to have surface runoff from a relatively impervious portion of the ground surface pass over a more pervious soil and be completely absorbed before reaching the stream. When rain falls on a ground surface over which surface runoff has not recently occurred, there are obstacles that hinder the formation of the small ephemeral channels which exist during fully established overland flow. It is often necessary for surface detention at local points to be built up to a considerable depth before it can by-pass or remove twigs, grass, and other litter from these tiny stream paths. The presence of dusty earth will in itself cause the formation of large globules of water held in place by surface tension. After this preliminary phase has been completed, surface runoff will be established in a definite network of rills and rivulets that will carry the water toward the larger drainage channels. During fully developed surface runoff, the storage equation may be written for a watershed. If a very small runoff plot is selected, fairly detailed information on conditions existing during surface runoff can be obtained. Tests on small plots are usually made with rain simulators. (See page 111.) An analysis of rainfall and runoff is first made to determine the shape of the infiltration capacity curve and the relation between surface detention and rate of runoff. Second, the information gained from the analysis may be used to synthesize a hydrograph of runoff that would occur from any other precipitation pattern. This second step is the important practical result that may be obtained from any such study. It is, for example, the operation which on a larger scale is required for designing spillways, storm sewers, culverts, or other structures that must permit the safe passage of storm water.

An example of such an analysis and synthesis will be presented here to illustrate the procedure. The experiment selected for presentation was conducted by the U. S. Department of Agriculture Soil Conservation Service.[1] Figure 92a shows the hydrograph resulting from a 60-min application of rain at the uniform rate of 3.333 in. per hr to a 6 by 24 ft plot. This test is listed as run 90, site 18. The plot has a slope in its long dimension of 3.32 per cent. The soil is Mohave sandy clay loam, which supported a sparse weed cover at the time of the test.

The storage equation may be written for any time increment of Δt hours during this rain as follows, neglecting evaporation:

$$D_1 + p_a\,\Delta t - q_a\,\Delta t - \frac{(f_1 + f_2)}{2}\,\Delta t = D_2 \qquad (1)$$

In this equation the subscripts 1 and 2 represent the beginning and end, respectively, of a time interval. D is the average depth of surface detention in inches on the plot; p_a is the average rate of precipitation during an interval, in inches per hour; q_a is the average rate of surface runoff from plot during an interval, in inches per hour; f is the infiltration capacity at any time, t, in inches per hour.

When precipitation ends, the surface detention or storage existing on the plot is disposed of partly as residual surface runoff and partly as residual infiltration. The portion of surface detention that becomes residual runoff may be evaluated from the recession side of the hydrograph as follows: Starting at the end of the runoff and working backward in small time increments, we may determine the volume of residual runoff, Q_r, in inches for each increment as shown in Table 15, columns 1 to 6. Values of Q_r were then plotted against rate of runoff, q, as shown in Fig. 92b. From this curve the volume of residual runoff corresponding to any rate of runoff during the recession side of this hydrograph can be determined. The relation of q to Q_r is precisely true only for the particular value of minimum infiltration capacity, f_c, for which it was derived. It must be recognized that, since the total surface detention is disposed of by the combination of overland flow and infiltration, their periods must end simultaneously. A variation in f_c may have a noticeable effect on the time required for the storage to be dissipated. The condition is comparable to a

[1] E. L. Beutner, R. R. Gaebe, and R. E. Horton, "Sprinkled Plat Runoff and Infiltration Experiments on Arizona Desert Soils," SCS-TP-38, September 1940.

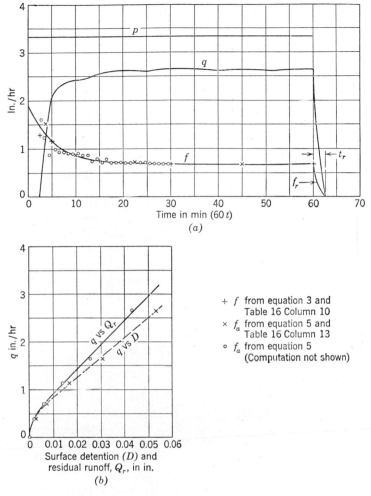

Fig. 92.

tank of water emptying through two orifices. If the size of one orifice is increased, the total time required for a given quantity of water to discharge will be decreased, and the relation between storage and discharge will change for each orifice. In most cases f_c is relatively small compared with q, so that the effect of a change in f_c is not of great importance.

The portion of the surface detention that becomes residual infiltration may be taken (see page 115) as $\frac{1}{3} f_c t_r$, and the total volume of surface detention existing at the end of precipitation is therefore

TABLE 15

1 Time before End of SRO, min	2 Δt, min	3 q, in./hr	4 q_{av}, in./hr	5 ΔQ_r, in.	6 Q_r, in.	7 f_r, in./hr	8 $f_r(av)$, in./hr	9 ΔF_r, in.	10 $\Delta Q_r + \Delta F_r = \Delta D$, in.	11 D, in.
0		0			0	0				0
	0.57		0.195	0.00185			0.030	0.00028	0.00213	
0.57		0.39			0.00185	0.060				0.00213
	0.50		0.545	0.00455			0.095	0.00079	0.00534	
1.07		0.70			0.00640	0.130				0.00747
	0.50		0.915	0.00763			0.190	0.00158	0.00921	
1.57		1.13			0.0140	0.250				0.0167
	0.50		1.390	0.0116			0.315	0.00263	0.0142	
2.07		1.65			0.0256	0.380				0.0309
	0.50		2.150	0.0179			0.530	0.00442	0.0223	
2.57		2.65			0.0435	0.680				0.0532

$D = Q_r + \frac{1}{3}f_ct_r$. The value of D at the end of surface runoff in Fig. 92 is then

$$0.0435 + \frac{0.68 \times 2.57}{3 \times 60} = 0.0435 + 0.0097 = 0.0532 \text{ in.}$$

In order to determine the relationship between D and q for the recession side of the hydrograph, a residual infiltration curve, f_r, was sketched on Fig. 92a from a value of 0.68 at a time of 60 min to zero at a time of 62.57 min. This curve was sketched by trial so that the area beneath it is $\frac{1}{3}f_ct_r$. Increments of residual infiltration may then be determined in the same manner as for residual runoff as shown in Table 15, columns 7 to 9. These increments are then added to corresponding increments of Q_r to give increments D, which when added cumulatively give the values of D shown in columns 10 and 11. Values of D are plotted against q in Fig. 92b. The relationship represented by these points will be required in the process of synthesizing a hydrograph and will be discussed in more detail later.

The relations of Q_r to q, and of D to q, derived from the recession side of the hydrograph, must now be assumed to apply to the rising side as well, in order to derive the infiltration capacity curve. The same assumption must be made again later in synthesizing a hydrograph. There is little doubt that these relations for the rising side of the hydrograph are somewhat different from the ones derived from the falling side. There is some question of the magnitude of this difference. Tests made by Izzard and Augustine[2] show reasonably close agreement of the relation between D and q for the two legs of the hydrograph. Actually, this difference may be unimportant in the final result, since the curve determined on the basis of this assumption is also used in synthesizing a hydrograph from rainfall.

On the basis of the assumption that $D_1 = Q_{r1} + \frac{1}{3}f_1t_{r1}$, equation 1 may now be written in the following form:

$$Q_{r1} + \frac{1}{3}f_1t_r + p_a \Delta t - q_a \Delta t - \frac{1}{2}f_1 \Delta t - \frac{1}{2}f_2 \Delta t = D_2 \qquad (2)$$

The equation above may be solved for values of f_1 by starting at the end of precipitation and working backward through successive time intervals. It must be assumed that at the end of precipitation the infiltration capacity has become practically constant, so that f_2 for the first interval (from $t = 30$ min to $t = 60$ min) is equal to $p_2 - q_2$. It is also assumed that at any time the value of t_r may be determined

[2] C. F. Izzard and M. T. Augustine, "Preliminary Report on Analysis of Runoff Resulting from Simulated Rainfall on a Paved Plot," Trans. Am. Geophys. Union, 1943, Part II, p. 500.

from the recession side of the hydrograph and the value of Q_r from Fig. 92b. To facilitate the solution, the equation may be rearranged as follows:

$$f_1 = \frac{D_2 + q_a \, \Delta t + \frac{1}{2} f_2 \, \Delta t - Q_{r1} - p_a \, \Delta t}{\frac{1}{3} t_{r1} - \frac{1}{2} \, \Delta t} \tag{3}$$

In this form all the quantities in the right member are known, and the value of f_1 may be determined. This fact is illustrated by an application to the hydrograph shown in Fig. 92a.

The solution is summarized in Table 16, columns 1 to 12. Arbitrary time intervals are selected and indicated in column 2. Care should be used to insure that values of $t/2$ and $\frac{1}{3} t_r$ are of entirely different magnitude, to avoid extremely small and sensitive denominators. Values of q and corresponding values of Q_r and t_r are determined from Figs. 92a and 92b. The value of f_2 for the first time interval is 0.68 in. per hr, and the corresponding value of D_2 is 0.053 in., as shown in Table 15, column 11. The solution then becomes

$$f_1 = \frac{0.053 + 1.325 + 0.170 - 0.044 - 1.665}{(0.857/60) - (15/60)} = \frac{-0.161}{-0.236} = 0.68 \text{ in./hr}$$

and D_1 is then computed as follows:

$$D_1 = Q_{r1} + \frac{1}{3} f_1 t_{r1} = 0.044 + 0.010 = 0.054 \text{ in.}$$

The values of f so determined are shown in column 10 of Table 16 and are plotted in Fig. 92a.

If it is assumed that residual infiltration is unimportant and may be neglected, then $D_2 = Q_{r2}$, $D_1 = Q_{r1}$, and equation 2 becomes

$$Q_{r1} + p_a \, \Delta t - q_a \, \Delta t - f_a \, \Delta t = Q_{r2} \tag{4}$$

where $f_a = (f_1 + f_2)/2$. Equation 4 may be rearranged as follows to permit the determination of f_a for successive time intervals.

$$f_a = \frac{Q_{r1} - Q_{r2} + p_a \, \Delta t - q_a \, \Delta t}{\Delta t} \tag{5}$$

Equation 5 is obviously easier to use than equation 3. It is the one suggested by Horton[3] and used by the Soil Conservation Service in *Technical Paper* 38. The simplifying assumptions made in connection with equations 4 and 5 influence the values of f_a so obtained only where f is changing rapidly. Even then the difference in the results is small, and the additional work involved when using equation 3 may not be justified. Values of f_a for the time increments used in the

[3] R. E. Horton," Analysis of Runoff Plot Experiments with Varying Infiltration Capacity," *Trans. Am. Geophys. Union*, 1939, Part IV, p. 693.

TABLE 16

1 Time from Beginning of Precipitation, min (60t)	2 $\Delta t \times 60$, min	3 q, in./hr	4 q_a, in./hr	5 $q_a \Delta t$, in.	6 $p_a \Delta t$, in.	7 Q_r, in.	8 $t_r \times 60$, min	9 $\frac{t_r}{3} \times 60$, min	10 f (Eq. 3), in./hr	11 $\frac{f\Delta t}{2}$ in.	12 D in.	13 f_a (Eq. 5), in.
60		2.65				0.044	2.57	0.857	0.68	0.170	0.053	
	30		2.65	1.325	1.665							0.68
30		2.65				0.044	2.57	0.857	0.68	0.085	0.054	
	15		2.61	0.651	0.833							0.72
15		2.56				0.043	2.54	0.847	0.77	0.064	0.055	
	10		2.32	0.387	0.555							0.87
5		2.08				0.033	2.35	0.783	1.17	0.025	0.046	
	2.58		1.04	0.045	0.143							1.51
2.42		0				0	0	0	1.25	0.029	0	

previous numerical example have been computed by means of equation 5. These values are shown in Table 16, column 13, and are plotted in Fig. 92a. Also shown in Fig. 92a are values of f_a obtained by means of equation 5 when 1-min intervals are used during the first 30 min.

In order to extend the f curve to time $t = 0$, and thus determine the initial value of infiltration capacity, f_0, it is necessary to include initial detention in the storage equation for the time interval extending from beginning of precipitation to the beginning of surface runoff. The problem is further complicated by the fact that, although the values of f probably will continue to rise as a continuous curve, if this curve rises above the precipitation curve, it becomes discontinuous as far as application of the storage equation is concerned. Specifically, the sum of the end values of f divided by two would no longer approximate the average value of infiltration rate for the interval. One method of overcoming this difficulty would be to determine an equation for the known portion of the curve and then extend this curve to a time of zero. Horton[3] found that the points agree very closely with an equation of the form

$$f = f_c + (f_0 - f_c)e^{-kt} \tag{6}$$

in which k is a constant and t is the time from the beginning of precipitation, in hours.

By choosing any two sets of values of f and t from the f curve and placing them in the equation above, two equations with two unknowns, namely f_0 and k, are obtained. The equations may then be solved by successive approximations. The numerical values obtained in this manner depend a great deal on what particular sets of values are taken from the f curve. For example, in Fig. 92a, for $f = 1.44$, $t = 2.42$ min, and $f = 0.77$, $t = 15$ min, the value of k is 10.2 and the value of f_0 is 1.85 in. per hr; whereas, for $f = 1.44$, $t = 2.42$ min, and $f = 0.98$, $t = 5$ min, $k = 21.6$ and $f_0 = 2.51$ in. per hr.

Another method of solving for the constants in this equation, which leads to more definite results, is suggested when the equation is rearranged as follows:

$$f - f_c = (f_0 - f_c)e^{-kt}$$

and written in logarithmic form,

$$\log (f - f_c) = \log (f_0 - f_c) - kt \log e$$

and solving for t,

$$t = \frac{1}{k \log e} \log (f_0 - f_c) - \frac{1}{k \log e} \log (f - f_c) \tag{7}$$

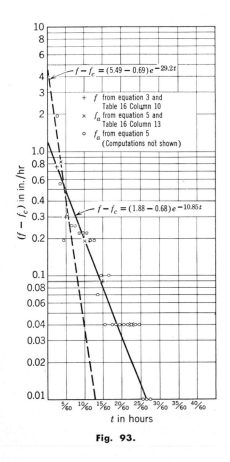

Fig. 93.

It may be seen that in this form the equation is that of a straight line in which t and log $(f - f_c)$ are the variables. The slope of the line is $-1/k$ log e. Therefore, if an equation of this type correctly represents the form of the f curve, a straight line should be obtained when values of log $(f - f_c)$ are plotted against t. The values derived for the example under discussion have been plotted in this manner in Fig. 93. A straight line is shown that represents the general trend of the values. The slope of this line is -0.212; therefore, $-1/k$ log $e = -0.212$, and $k = 10.85$. When $t = 0$, f is equal to f_0. The value of $(f - f_c)$ at $t = 0$ is 1.20 and therefore $f_0 = 120 + 0.68 = 1.88$ in. per hr. The solid line plotted through the f values in Fig. 92a is based on these values of k and f_0. If all but the very highest values of f are ignored, a much larger value of f_0 is obtained. For example, the values of f_0 and k derived in *Soil Conservation Service Technical*

Paper 38,[4] for this hydrograph are 5.49 and 29.2 respectively. The curve determined by these values is shown by the dashed line on Fig. 93.

When a value of f_0 is decided upon, the value of initial detention, D_i, may be computed. In this example, if f_0 is taken as 1.88 in. per hr, the value of D_i is

$$(p_a - f_a)t_i = \left(3.33 - \frac{1.88 + 1.47}{2}\right)\frac{2.42}{60} = 0.067 \text{ in.}$$

Although the value of f_0 and, therefore, the value of D_i are subject to some uncertainty owing to the personal judgment involved in plotting the line on Fig. 93, the error introduced in utilizing these values to predict runoff from another rain is small because, when f_0 is large, D_i is correspondingly small, and vice versa, so that the sum of initial infiltration and initial detention remains about the same.

The Relation between Surface Detention and Discharge. There has been determined from the recession side of the hydrograph a series of corresponding values of q and D as shown in Table 15 and plotted in Fig. 92b. Such a relationship may usually be represented by an equation having the form

$$q = KD^m \tag{8}$$

When plotted logarithmically, an equation of this type is represented by a straight line having the slope m.

The value of m in equation 8 depends upon whether flow is laminar or turbulent. For laminar flow it may be shown both theoretically and experimentally that the value of m is 3. For turbulent flow experimental evidence indicates that m is approximately $\frac{5}{3}$. Typical experimental results obtained for uniform steady flow on smooth concrete[5] are plotted in Fig. 94a. Lines having slopes of 3 and $\frac{5}{3}$ respectively are drawn on the figure to illustrate that the plotted points fall very nearly along these slopes. In the transition zone it may be noted that the slope reduces rapidly from 3 to less than 1 and then increases gradually to $\frac{5}{3}$. Instead of steady uniform flow, runoff from rainfall is unsteady, nonuniform, and spatially variable. Furthermore, the velocity distribution is likely to differ from normal flow because of the incoming raindrops and outgoing infiltration. Consequently one

[4] F. L. Beutner, R. R. Gaebe, and R. E. Horton, "Sprinkled Plat Runoff and Infiltration Experiments on Arizona Desert Soils."

[5] "Studies of River Bed Materials and their Movement, with Special Reference to the Lower Mississippi River," *Paper* 17, U. S. Waterways Expt. Sta., Vicksburg, Miss., January 1935.

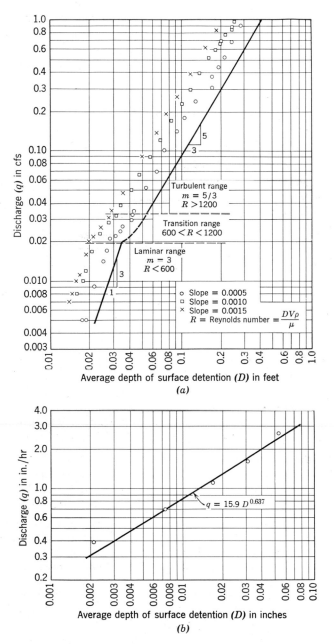

Fig. 94.

cannot safely conclude that runoff from rainfall will have exactly the same characteristics exhibited by the data plotted in Fig. 94a. However, experimental results obtained by Izzard[6] for runoff resulting from the application of artificial rainfall on paved and turfed surfaces show that m is 3 for the laminar range. Until additional experimental evidence is secured, it can only be assumed that flow in the transition and turbulent ranges will also be similar to that shown in Fig. 94a. It must be recognized that the Reynolds number for turfed plots, based on the average depth and velocity, is quite likely not comparable with a Reynolds number similarly determined for pavements. This is because the average depth and velocity may occur over only a small percentage of a turfed runoff area. The major portion of the area is likely to have depths and velocities less than the average, whereas the bulk of the runoff occurs in small rivulets having a depth and velocity greater than the average.

The value of K in equation 8 varies with the surface roughness, the Reynolds number, the slope of the plot, and the units of D and q. Its value may be readily determined from a set of experimental data, either analytically or by extending the straight line in a logarithmic plotting to $D = 1$. It has been suggested that K might be determined from the Manning formula.[7,8] The Manning formula arranged for flow in thin sheets is shown in equation 9, Q_1 being discharge in cubic feet per second per foot of width.

$$Q_1 = \frac{1.486}{n} D^{5/3} S^{1/2} \qquad (9)$$

When the value of m in equation 8 is $5/3$, equations 8 and 9 are comparable, and K is seen to be equal to $1.486 S^{1/2}/n$. It may be assumed that the slope of the energy gradient, S, is nearly equal to the slope of the ground surface. Values of K so obtained may be expected to give fairly adequate results for turbulent flow but could not be used for laminar flow or for flow in the transition range. For laminar flow, the exponent of S is 1 instead of $1/2$ and n is no longer a function of the roughness but of Reynolds number. The values of K and m

[6] C. F. Izzard, "The Surface-Profile of Overland Flow," *Trans. Am. Geophys. Union*, 1944, Part VI, p. 959.

[7] R. E. Horton, "Hydrologic Interrelations of Water and Soils," *Soil Science Soc. of Am. Proc.*, 1937, vol. 1, p. 401.

[8] R. E. Horton, "The Interpretation and Application of Runoff Plot Experiments with Reference to Soil Erosion Problems," *Soil Science Soc. of Am. Proc.*, 1938, vol. 3, p. 340.

TABLE 17

1 Time (t), min	2 Precipitation (p), in./hr	3 Inf. Cap. (f), in./hr	4 Precip. Exc. $(p-f) = (p_e)$, in./hr	5 p_{ea}, in./hr	6 $p_{ea} \cdot \Delta t$, in.	7 $\Sigma\ p_{ea} \cdot \Delta t$, in.	8 Run-off (q), in./hr
0	2.00	1.88	0.12				
				0.21	0.003		
1	2.00	1.70	0.30			0.003	
				0.39	0.007		
2	2.00	1.52	0.48			0.010	
				0.545	0.009		
3	2.00	1.39	0.61			0.019	
				0.675	0.011		
4	2.00	1.26	0.74			0.030	
				0.785	0.013		
5	2.00	1.17	0.83			0.043	
	3.00		1.83				
				1.87	0.031		
6	3.00	1.09	1.91			0.074	0.55
				1.98	0.066		
8	3.00	0.95	2.05				1.78
				2.085	0.069		
10	3.00	0.88	2.12				1.99
				2.15	0.072		
12	3.00	0.82	2.18				2.11
				2.20	0.073		
14	3.00	0.78	2.22				2.16
				1.235	0.041		
16	1.00	0.75	0.25				1.47
				0.26	0.009		
18	1.00	0.73	0.27				0.35
				0.28	0.009		
20	1.00	0.71	0.29				0.26

Other Methods of Determining Runoff from Small Plots. A method of developing an equation for the rising side of the hydrograph has been suggested by Horton.[9,10] This method involves writing equation 10 in the following differential form:

$$p_e \, dt - q \, dt = dD \tag{13}$$

If equation 13 is solved for dt and the value of q from equation 8 is introduced, the following expression is obtained:

$$dt = \frac{dD}{p_e - KD^m} \tag{14}$$

By assuming p_e to be constant, equation 14 may be readily integrated for selected whole number values of m, although the form of the resulting equations would be mathematically incorrect because p_e should be included as a function of time. For the particular case of $m = 2$, the resulting equation is

$$q = p_e \tanh^2 \tfrac{3}{2} \sqrt{K p_e} \, t \tag{15}$$

For values of m of 1 and 3, an equation of a different form is obtained, whereas for other exponents of D the difficulties of integration, even assuming p_e to be constant, preclude the development of an equation similar to equation 15. Horton suggested that it might be possible to find an equation similar to equation 15 which could be expected to give good results for all values of m. Until that equation is found, it is believed that a direct approach to the problem, such as that given on the preceding pages, must be used.[11]

A basic analytical approach to the problem of surface runoff from a plane surface has been made by Keulegan.[12] Methods of designing urban and airport drainage facilities have been presented by Horner and Jens.[13,14] Many other noteworthy publications are brought to the reader's attention by references given in the articles cited in this

[9] R. E. Horton, "Hydrologic Interrelations of Water and Soils," *Soil Science Soc. of Am. Proc.*, 1937, vol. 1, p. 401.

[10] R. E. Horton, "The Interpretation and Application of Runoff Plot Experiments with Reference to Soil Erosion Problems," *Soil Science Soc. of Am. Proc.*, 1938, vol. 3, p. 340.

[11] For a more detailed discussion of equation 15 see S. W. Jens, "Drainage of Airport Surfaces—Some Basic Design Considerations," discussion by E. F. Brater in *Trans. A.S.C.E.*, 113, 785, 1948.

[12] G. H. Keulegan, "Spatially Variable Discharge over a Sloping Plane," *Trans. Am. Geophys. Union,* 1944, Part VI, p. 956.

[13] W. W. Horner and S. W. Jens, "Surface Runoff Determination from Rainfall without Using Coefficients," *Trans. A.S.C.E.*, 1942, vol. 107, p. 1039.

[14] S. W. Jens, "Drainage of Airport Surfaces—Some Basic Design Considerations," *Trans. A.S.C.E.*, 113, 785, 1948.

chapter. No discussion of this subject should omit reference to the publication by Horton of his *Surface Runoff Phenomena*.[15]

The Unit Hydrograph

In 1932 LeRoy K. Sherman presented his now almost universally accepted theory of the unit hydrograph.[16] This new concept of surface runoff is one of the most important contributions ever made to the science of hydrology. Along with Bernard's distribution graph,[17] it provides a most useful tool for the determination of the hydrograph of surface runoff that results from any given amount of rainfall excess.

The following principles constitute the unit hydrograph theory:

1. A unit hydrograph is a hydrograph of surface runoff resulting from a relatively short, intense rain, called a unit storm.

2. A *unit storm* is defined as a rain of such duration that the period of surface runoff is not appreciably less for any rain of shorter duration. Its duration is equal to or less than the *period of rise* of a unit hydrograph, that is, the time from the beginning of surface runoff to the peak. For all unit storms, regardless of their intensity, the period of surface runoff is approximately the same.

3. A *distribution graph* is a graph having the same time scale as a unit hydrograph and ordinates, which are the per cent of the total surface runoff that occurred during successive, arbitrarily chosen, uniform time increments. Alternative and interchangeable units for the ordinates are cubic feet per second per square mile per inch of surface runoff. The most important concept involved in the unit hydrograph theory is that all unit storms, regardless of their magnitudes, produce nearly identical distribution graphs. Thus, once a distribution graph is derived for a drainage basin, it serves as a means of converting any expected volume of surface runoff into a hydrograph of river discharge.

Although it can be easily proved theoretically that the foregoing relationships cannot possibly hold true rigidly, the error is so trivial that from a practical viewpoint they may be considered as being correct.

The authors have found that the duration of a unit storm must not exceed the period of rise. This is substantially in agreement with

15 R. E. Horton, *Surface Runoff Phenomena,* Part I—Analysis of the Hydrograph, Publication 101, Horton Hydrological Lab., Voorheesville, N. Y., February 1935.

16 L. K. Sherman, "Streamflow from Rainfall by Unit-Graph Method," *Eng. News Rec.,* 1932, p. 501.

17 Merrill M. Bernard, "An Approach to Determinate Stream Flow," *Trans. A.S.C.E.,* vol. 100, 1935, p. 347.

Sherman's statement to the effect that the duration must be less than the time of concentration. The time of concentration is probably only a little longer than the period of rise. The authors believe that the period of rise is more easily defined and determined than the time of concentration. For large watersheds, the duration of a unit storm may be less than the period of rise, possibly no more than half as long.

It must be emphasized that there is no relation between the duration of rainfall excess that produces a unit hydrograph and the time intervals into which the unit hydrograph is divided for the purpose of obtaining a distribution graph. The selection of the magnitude of these intervals depends entirely upon how accurate a reproduction of the hydrograph is desired and upon the time available for the work.

Small Watersheds

The term "small watersheds" is here used to designate drainage basins varying in area from a few acres to approximately 10 square miles. Most of the watersheds for which culverts and storm sewers are designed fall within this category. The subject is treated by first

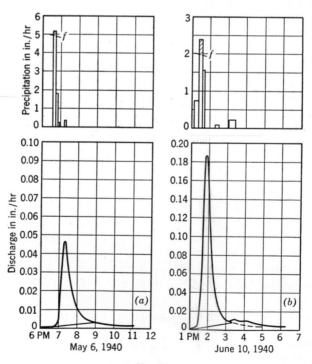

Fig. 96.

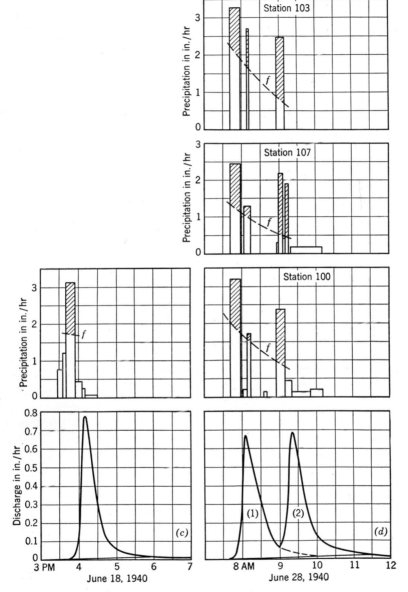

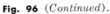

Fig. 96 (*Continued*).

determining unit hydrographs and infiltration-capacity curves for several watersheds, followed by a demonstration of the usefulness of these tools in predicting runoff from rainfall. Although originally devised for use on large watersheds for which "unit storms" could be determined from daily rainfall records, the principle is applicable to small drainage basins as well.[18,19] Some data will also be presented for the purpose of permitting the reader to evaluate the reliability of the unit-hydrograph principle when applied to small watersheds.

Unit hydrographs are determined for any basin by examining the flood hydrographs of record on the basin, together with the intensity graphs of the rains which produced the floods. All single-peaked hydrographs produced by short, intense rains are selected, and distribution graphs are derived. Similar analyses applied to floods produced by rains of longer duration reveal the maximum rainfall duration which still produce consistent distribution graphs. Five unit hydrographs and the corresponding rain-intensity graphs for a drainage basin having an area of 76.5 acres are shown in Fig. 96.[20]

The first step in deriving distribution graphs from unit hydrographs is to separate surface runoff from ground-water discharge. It has been shown that the line making this separation may rise or fall during a flood rise, depending on the amount of ground-water accretion (page 26). The behavior of the ground-water inflow to a stream during stream rises and methods of establishing the line of separation were discussed in Chapter 2, page 28. Usually there is no difficulty in selecting the point of the beginning of surface runoff, because of the abrupt fashion in which hydrographs rise. The end of surface runoff may also be indicated by a break in the slope of the recession curve. If not, one of the methods previously suggested may be used, or the point may be arbitrarily selected on the basis of judgment.

Although the actual length of the base of the surface-runoff hydrograph may be changed considerably by various reasonable selections of the end point, the more important properties of the hydrograph, namely, the total volume of surface runoff and the magnitude of the larger ordinates, vary little. It becomes evident during the following

[18] W. W. Horner and F. L. Flynt, "Relation between Rainfall and Run-off from Small Urban Areas," *Trans. A.S.C.E.*, 1936, vol. 101, p. 140.

[19] E. F. Brater, "The Unit Hydrograph Principle Applied to Small Watersheds," *Trans. A.S.C.E.*, 1940, vol. 105, p. 1154.

[20] Data for these graphs were obtained from "Hydraulic Data," *Hydrologic Bulls.* 1 and 2, North Appalachian Experimental Watershed, Coshocton, Ohio, Soil Conservation Service, U. S. Department of Agriculture.

discussion that the actual method of selecting a base line separating surface runoff from ground-water flow is not as important as being consistent in its use, that is, using the same method in the synthesis of a hydrograph as was used in the analysis of the data. It is sometimes desirable to separate two overlapping unit hydrographs into single graphs as illustrated in Fig. 96d. The separating line is determined by assuming that the recession curve of the first unit hydrograph would be the same as that for the second.

Having separated base flow from surface runoff, the next step is to divide the surface-runoff graph into convenient time units, usually at least ten in number, and determine the average rate of surface runoff during each interval. It is well to select the largest interval that still gives a reasonably accurate integration of the hydrograph, in order to keep the number of computations at a minimum. Ten-minute intervals are used in the hydrographs shown in Fig. 96. The values are tabulated in Table 18, column 2. Each individual average rate could be converted to volume, but time is saved by converting only the sum of the individual averages to total volume. The percentages of the total discharge that appear during each time interval are obtained by dividing each 10-min average successively by the sum of the averages, and multiplying by 100. These values, shown in Table 18, column 3, are the ordinates of the distribution graphs. In addition to the average values, the peak surface runoff must be recorded and the corresponding peak percentage determined. This is the most important value of all, because it is used to compute the maximum rate of runoff expected from another rain. Although the peak percentage is an instantaneous value, it may be derived and used in the same manner as the percentages derived from average values of discharge.

Sometimes the alternative units for the ordinates of distribution graphs, cubic feet per second per square mile per inch of surface runoff, are more convenient. As an illustration, both types of distribution graph ordinates are derived for the June 10 storm. In Table 19, the surface runoff rates, expressed as average cfs for each 10 min time interval, are shown in column 2, and the distribution graph percentages determined as described above are shown in column 3. The total volume of surface runoff for this storm, expressed in inches depth on the drainage basin, is determined from the summation of column 2 as follows:

$$\frac{\text{Volume}}{\text{Area}} = \frac{(45.11 \times 10 \times 60) \text{ ft}^3}{(76.5 \times 43,560) \text{ ft}^2} \times 12 \frac{\text{in.}}{\text{ft}} = 0.0975 \text{ in. on basin}$$

TABLE 18*

1 10-min Interval	May 6		June 10		June 18		June 28 (1)		June 28 (2)	
	2 Discharge, in./hr	3 Distribution Graph, percentages	2 Discharge, in./hr	3 Distribution Graph, percentages	2 Discharge, in./hr	3 Distribution Graph, percentages	2 Discharge, in./hr	3 Distribution Graph, percentages	2 Discharge, in./hr	3 Distribution Graph, percentages
1	0.001	0.6	0.003	0.5	0.02	0.9	0.06	2.7	0.07	3.2
2	0.013	7.7	0.042	7.2	0.31	14.4	0.43	19.3	0.47	21.3
3	0.040 (0.045)	23.8 (26.8)	0.118 (0.186)	20.1 (31.8)	.72 (0.77)	33.3 (35.7)	0.59 (0.67)	26.5 (30.0)	0.59 (0.65)	26.8 (29.6)
4	0.040	23.8	0.176	30.1	0.53	24.6	0.43	19.3	0.40	18.2
5	0.027	16.1	0.120	20.5	0.26	12.0	0.31	13.9	0.23	10.4
6	0.017	10.1	0.056	9.6	0.13	6.0	0.17	7.6	0.14	6.4
7	0.011	6.4	0.032	5.5	0.07	3.2	0.08	3.6	0.09	4.1
8	0.008	4.8	0.018	3.1	0.05	2.3	0.05	2.2	0.06	2.7
9	0.005	3.0	0.010	1.7	0.03	1.4	0.04	1.8	0.05	2.3
10	0.003	1.8	0.006	1.0	0.02	0.9	0.03	1.3	0.04	1.8
11	0.002	1.2	0.003	0.5	0.01	0.5	0.02	0.9	0.03	1.4
12	0.001	0.6	0.001	0.2	0.01	0.5	0.01	0.5	0.02	0.9
							0.01	0.4	0.01	0.5
Σ	0.168	100.0	0.585	100.0	2.16	100.0	2.23	100.0	2.20	100.0

* Values in parentheses are peak values.

TABLE 19

(1) 10-Min Interval	(2) Av. Rate of SRO, cfs	(3) Distribution Graph, per cent	(4) Distribution Graph, cfs per sq mi per in. of surface runoff
1	0.23	0.5	20
2	3.24	7.2	278
3	9.10	20.1	780
	(14.34)	(31.8)	(1230)
4	13.57	30.1	1160
5	9.25	20.5	790
6	4.32	9.6	370
7	2.47	5.5	210
8	1.39	3.1	120
9	0.77	1.7	66
10	0.46	1.0	39
11	0.23	0.5	20
12	0.08	0.2	7
	45.11	100.0	

The distribution ordinates shown in column 4 are obtained by dividing the values in column 2 (cfs) by the surface runoff (0.0975 in.) and the area of the basin (0.1195 square mile).

The fact that the two types of units of the distribution graph are comparable may be demonstrated by deriving one of the values in column 4 from the corresponding percentage in column 3. The conversion is made for the third time interval for which the distribution graph percentage is 20.1. The volume of surface runoff during this interval, converted to cu ft, is

$$\frac{20.1\%}{100} \times \frac{0.0975 \text{ in.}}{12 \frac{\text{in.}}{\text{ft}}} \times 0.1195 \text{ mile}^2 \times 5280^2 \frac{\text{ft}^2}{\text{mile}^2}$$

The corresponding average rate of surface runoff in cubic feet per second during this time interval is obtained by dividing by the number of seconds in a time interval (600). Dividing also by the area in square miles and the surface runoff in inches, we obtain the corresponding value in column 4,

$$\frac{20.1\%}{100} \times \frac{0.0975 \text{ in.}}{12 \dfrac{\text{in.}}{\text{ft}}} \times 0.1195 \text{ mile}^2 \times 5280^2 \frac{\text{ft}^2}{\text{mile}^2} \times \frac{1}{600 \text{ sec}}$$

$$\times \frac{1}{0.1195 \text{ mile}^2} \times \frac{1}{0.0975 \text{ in.}} = 780 \frac{\text{ft}^3}{\text{sec} \times \text{mile}^2 \times \text{in.}}$$

It may be noted that the area terms as well as the surface runoff terms disappear from the above conversion. The only remaining variables are the percentage (20.1) and the number of seconds in a time interval (600), which appear as a ratio. That this ratio is a constant for any drainage basin may be demonstrated as follows: Consider the percentages derived by using some time interval Δt. If the same unit hydrograph is divided into twice as many time intervals having the magnitude $\Delta t/2$, all percentages are approximately half as large, because the same volume of surface runoff is divided into twice as many portions, and the peak percentage is exactly half as large, and therefore the values of $\% \div \Delta t$ remain the same. Thus, the conversion from one unit to the other is not only independent of the area of the basin and the size of the flood, but is also independent of the magnitude of the time intervals selected for the derivation of the distribution graphs. Also, any distribution-graph ordinate expressed in per cent is equivalent to one particular value expressed in cubic feet per second per square mile per inch.

To complete the analysis of the hydrograph, it is necessary to determine values of infiltration capacity. The two hydrographs of Fig. 96d provide an excellent opportunity to determine the effect of previous precipitation upon the infiltration capacity and will be used as an example to illustrate the procedure. The total surface runoff from these two storms is $2.23 \times {}^{1}\%_{60} = 0.37$ in., and $2.20 \times {}^{1}\%_{60} = 0.37$ in., respectively. The values 2.23 and 2.20 were obtained from Table 18, column 2, for the rain of June 28. It is now necessary to establish infiltration-capacity curves that cut the rain intensity graphs in such a manner that the shaded portion of the graphs have an area of 0.37 in. Methods of determining f_a are described in Chapter 5. In Fig. 96d are shown the records from three intensity gages that are applicable to this watershed. The f curves that satisfy the above conditions are shown for each precipitation record. When the f curve cuts off more than a single segment, the location of the curve can best be determined by trial. Since the three f curves differ somewhat, it is necessary to determine an average value. In doing so, the several curves may be weighted according to the Thiessen method (page 81).

Infiltration capacities determined by the above method usually differ from those obtained from small plots for several reasons. In the first place, observed surface runoff from small watersheds may include subsurface storm flow (see page 17), whereas, from small plots, it does not. Part of the area of every basin is impermeable because of pavements, buildings, rock outcrops, and so on. Furthermore, the portion of a drainage basin that is covered by the streams and connecting lakes also acts as if it were an impervious surface. In the determinations above no deduction is made for such areas, whereas small plots are usually so chosen that they have no such areas. Also in the foregoing method no consideration is given to the fact that infiltration continues on an ever-decreasing area after the period of excess rainfall ends. On small plots this subsequent period of infiltration is negligible. Furthermore, because of the variation in rainfall intensity and distribution and because of the usually great distances between gages, the correct average rainfall pattern cannot ordinarily be determined for a large basin. The variation of the three intensity graphs shown in Fig. 96d is not at all unusual. In more mountainous regions, greater variations than this are common. Obviously this factor can cause computed values of f to be either too high or too low.

The Variation in Distribution Graphs for a Watershed. In the following pages it is suggested that distribution graphs of the type derived in the previous example be used to predict runoff, not only from the basin for which they were derived, but also for other watersheds having similar physical characteristics. It has been stated previously that from a purely theoretical viewpoint the principle of the unit hydrograph cannot be strictly true. To use with confidence a procedure of this type it is desirable to determine the degree of accuracy expected from its application. An indication of this accuracy may be observed from the variations between distribution graphs obtained from any particular watershed. The data for the five distribution graphs presented in Table 18, column 3, are typical. These graphs are shown superimposed on each other in Fig. 97. The values of peak percentage provide the most sensitive basis of comparison. The ratio of the largest peak percentage to the smallest is 1.34, as compared with a corresponding ratio of maximum to minimum peak discharge of 16. It may be noted from Fig. 96 that the duration of rainfall excess varies from 32 to 8 min.

Various characteristics of nine distribution graphs determined for Watershed 97,[21] which has an area of 4581 acres, are shown in Table 20 (pages 258 and 259). Rain intensity and infiltration

[21] Data for these graphs were obtained from Hydrologic Data, *Hydrologic Bulls.* 1 and 2, U. S. Department of Agriculture Soil Conservation Service, North Appalachian Experimental Watershed, Coshocton, Ohio.

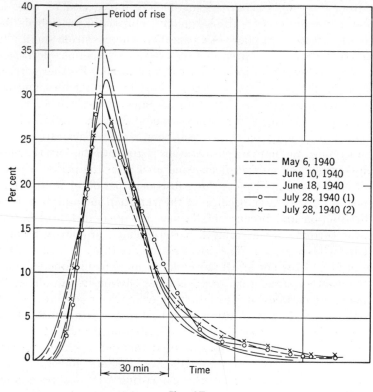

Fig. 97.

capacity values are determined from averages of three to five recording gages. In order to give an indication of the variation within each column, the ratio of the largest value to the smallest is given at the bottom of many of the columns. It may be noted that the smallest variations occur for the values of peak percentage and period of rise. These ratios are 1.4 and 1.75 respectively, whereas the ratio of largest to smallest values of total precipitation, total surface runoff, and peak rate of surface runoff are 2.8, 19.1, and 18.3 respectively. Attention may also be called to the duration of effective precipitation shown in column 10. The largest is 92 min and the smallest 13 min, with a ratio of 7. Some indication of the timing and distribution of the rainfall for each of the nine storms is given by data in columns 11 and 12. It is believed that the variations in distribution graphs resulting from unit storms on any particular watershed are mainly the result of rainfall distribution and timing. Especially in long narrow watersheds, rains moving up the valley produce much lower peaks than rains moving down the valley. This is strikingly illustrated by two points plotted in Fig. 98a (see note on Fig. 98a).

In each of the two groups of distribution graphs presented, the maximum variation of the peak percentage from the average for the group is approximately 20 per cent. Similar variations are noted on many other streams. In predicting maximum flood flow for design purposes, the effect of this variation is eliminated to some extent by choosing the higher peaked unit hydrographs in making the estimate.

Comparison of Distribution Graphs from Similar Watersheds. Average values of the various properties of the distribution graphs from eight watersheds having areas varying from 74.2 acres to 4581 acres are shown in Table 21. These watersheds are located adjacent to each other on the North Appalachian Experimental Watershed, and consequently they are of a similar type. It may be noted from column 7, that when peak percentages are based on an interval equal to one tenth of the base length, they are nearly of the same magnitude. On the other hand, values in column 5 show that when peak percentages are based on a uniform time interval, 10 min in this example, they vary inversely with the area. These values of peak percentage are plotted against area in Fig. 98a, in which their trend is represented by the solid straight line. Similar values for five other groups of watersheds are also shown in Fig. 98a. All the groups exhibit a similar trend. Although size is by no means the only characteristic of a watershed that influences the shape of the unit hydrograph, Fig. 98a indicates that it is one of the principal ones. It is expected that as more experimental data become available, it will be possible to evaluate the effect of shape, stream density, slope, and other factors in a similar manner. Curves of the type shown in Fig. 98a serve as a basis for the determination of peak runoff from small watersheds by methods to be discussed presently.

Critical Rainfall Duration. In order to predict runoff from any watershed, it is first necessary to determine the expected maximum precipitation. However, since both magnitude and intensity of precipitation vary with the duration, it is necessary to estimate the critical rainfall period for each basin. The data shown in Table 20, as well as other similar studies on small watersheds, indicate that a volume of rainfall excess may be converted to runoff by means of a single application of the distribution graph, if its duration is no longer than the period of rise. The graph resulting from a longer rain must be derived by successive applications of the distribution graph to unit durations of rainfall excess (see page 270). However, because rains of a given

TABLE 20

1	2	3	4	5	6	7	8
Date	Precip-itation, in.	Surface Runoff, in.	Maximum Rate of Surface Runoff, in./hr	Peak Percentage of Distribution Graph	Period of Rise, min	Average Infiltra-tion Capacity, in./hr	Per Cent of Precipitation Appearing as Surface Runoff
July 8, 1939	0.80	0.080	0.039	23.0	90	1.45	10.0
July 8, 1939	0.60	0.172	0.079	20.8	110	1.54	28.7
May 6, 1940	0.50	0.025	0.009	18.25	90	2.00	5.0
June 10, 1940	1.065	0.168	0.061	18.2	100	2.40	15.8
June 11, 1940	0.67	0.214	0.088	20.5	100	0.96	31.9
June 18, 1940	1.05	0.268	0.112	20.9	110	2.00	25.5
June 23, 1940	0.87	0.066	0.024	17.95	95	1.95	7.6
June 28, 1940	1.39	0.476	0.165	17.35	140	0.93	34.2
Aug. 28, 1940	1.40	0.181	0.088	24.3	80	1.53	12.9
Ratio of Maximum to Minimum	2.8	19.1	18.3	1.4	1.75	2.6	6.8

frequency decrease in intensity with duration, the intensity may become equal to or less than the infiltration capacity. This situation may even occur for durations less than the period of rise. As a result, it is usually found that very little additional contribution to surface runoff occurs when the duration is extended beyond the period of rise. In fact, often most of the surface runoff is caused by the most intense

TABLE 20 (Continued)

9	10	11	12	13	14	15	16
Duration of Precipitation			Distribution	Time	Time	Time from	Time from
Average Duration of Total Precipitation, min	Average Duration of Effective Precipitation, min	Time of Beginning and End of Effective Precipitation*	of Precipitation Approximate Percentage of Average Precipitation*	of Beginning of Surface Runoff	of Peak of Hydrograph	Beginning of Effective Precipitation to Peak, min	End of Effective Precipitation to Peak, min
36	9–24†	7:30–7:39 7:40–7:50 7:30–7:54	50 160 120	7:40	9:10	97	82
35–120†	9–36†	12:20–12:30 12:45–12:54 12:24–1:00	100 135 80	12:50	2:40	130	102
50	19	None 6:33–6:53 6:34–6:52	35 100 175	6:35	8:05	94	75
99–311†	18	1:10–1:34 1:06–1:22 1:06–1:32	81 100 118	1:20	3:00	110	92
77	13	1:14–1:28 1:05–1:20 1:17–1:26	78 112 100	1:15	2:55	100	87
76	14	3:35–3:45 3:33–3:42 3:43–3:58	87 109 95	4:00	5:50	131	117
99	15	8:14–8:35 8:20–8:35 8:18–8:32	92 103 100	8:40	10:15	117	102
158	92	7:40–9:08 7:39–9:15 7:40–9:16	72 111 125	7:50	10:10	150	58
147–421†	17	10:05–10:16 9:53–10:14 9:57–10:11	72 100 111	10:00	11:20	83	68
3.2	7.0					1.8	2.8

* The upper value was taken from a typical station near the upper end of the basin, the next two from the central and lower portions, respectively.

† In some cases the variation was so great that the range of values rather than the average is given.

portion of the rain, which has a duration considerably less than the period of rise. Therefore, for the sake of simplicity and at little sacrifice in accuracy, it is assumed that for small watersheds, the critical rainfall period may be taken equal to the period of rise.

TABLE 21

1	2	3	4	5	6	7	8
Water-shed Number	Area, acres	Period of Rise, min	Length of Base, min	Peak Percent-age Based on 10-min Intervals	Peak Ex-pressed in cfs/sq mi/in.*	Peak Percent-age based on Intervals Equal to 0.1 of Base	Ratio of Length of Base to Period of Rise
183	74.2	27	95	32.7	1270	31.0	3.5
177	75.6	25	124	30.8	1195	38.2	5.0
10	122	27	130	25.1	974	33.4	3.7
196	303	32	200	18.4	715	36.8	6.2
20	373	42	210	17.3	671	36.4	5.0
92	920	72	300	10.5	407	31.5	3.6
95	2569	64	283	12.1	470	34.2	4.2
97	4581	102	563	6.7	250	37.7	5.5

* See pages 15 and 16.

Values of period of rise are plotted against watershed area for two groups of basins in Fig. 98b. Again there is a noticeable trend among the points for each group. The relationship is by no means exact, because all the watershed characteristics except size are ignored.

Prediction of Runoff from Rainfall. If there are sufficient, continuous records available on a stream so that unit hydrographs and distribution graphs can be determined, the runoff can be predicted with assurance by applying the distribution-graph percentages to units of rainfall excess. Runoff from watersheds similar to those upon which records are available also can be predicted with satisfactory accuracy by means of curves such as are plotted in Fig. 98. In either instance the prediction of the volume of rainfall excess involves the selection of rainfall and infiltration rates by methods described in Chapters 4 and 5.

As an example, suppose it is desired to predict the flood peak resulting from a 10-yr rain on a 1,500-acre watershed located in central Ohio. It is assumed that the topography, soil, vegetative cover, and other watershed characteristics are similar to those of the North Appalachian Experimental Watershed for which curves are plotted in Fig. 98. From Fig. 98b, the period of rise is found to be approximately 64 min. The next step is to determine the maximum rainfall of this duration which will be equaled or exceeded once in 10 yr. This computation may best be made by analyzing local rainfall records (see Chapter 4, page 86). If there are no adequate records, or if such accuracy is not desired, an approximate value may be obtained from the frequency curves shown on page 90. This rain falls between the 2.0 and 2.2 curves of Fig. 35. The intensities given in column 2 of Table 21 were obtained by interpolation between these curves. Column 6 shows the computed precipitation rates which are plotted in an arbitrary arrangement in Fig. 99a. This method of determining a typical intensity-time pattern is explained more fully in Chapter 4, page 94. Figure 99b shows the same volume of precipitation, with the intensity assumed to be uniform during the entire 64-min duration.

It is now necessary to determine the minimum value of f expected at the time of this rain. This information may be gained from a study of multiple-peaked hydrographs produced by rains of long duration. For the purpose of this problem, it is assumed that f_c is 0.5 in. per hr. Also, for the sake of simplicity, it is assumed that f is constant for the duration of the rain. In applying this value of f_c to the two intensity graphs of Fig. 99, it becomes apparent that the volume of infiltration is the same and that, therefore, the volume of rainfall excess, P_e, is also the same. The volume of rainfall excess from Fig. 99b is $(2.05 - 0.50)64/60 = 1.65$ in. The value of P_e from Fig. 99a is computed in columns 8 and 9 of Table 22. If some portion of the precipitation graph were below the f curve, the value of P_e, computed from a single block of rainfall such as Fig. 99b, would be too small. Also, where runoff is being computed from a rain having a duration greater than the period of rise, the single block graph may not be substituted for a typical rainfall pattern.

The final step is to compute the maximum runoff rate. The precipitation excess is first converted to cubic feet as follows:

$$\frac{1.66}{12} \times 1500 \times 43,560 = 9,050,000 \text{ cu ft}$$

Because the peak percentages used in Fig. 98a are based on 10-min intervals, the volume of runoff must next be converted to cubic feet per second for 10 min, by dividing by the number of seconds in 10 min as follows:

$$\frac{9,050,000}{10 \times 60} = 15,100 \text{ cfs for 10 min}$$

Finally, the peak rate of runoff is obtained by multiplying by the peak percentage divided by 100. The peak percentage is found from Fig. 98a to be approximately 11 per cent. Therefore, the peak rate of runoff is $15,100 \times 11/100 = 1660$ cfs.

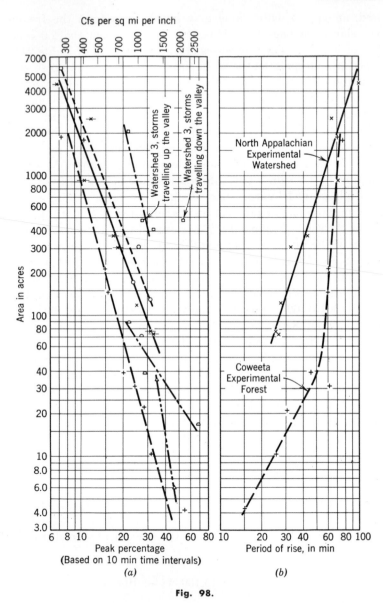

Fig. 98.

If it were desirable to design for the absolute maximum flood ever likely to occur, in addition to using a correspondingly greater rainfall excess, it would be desirable to determine values of peak percentage from a curve similar to the one in Fig. 98a, but showing maximum peaks instead of average values.

Fig. 98.

North Appalachian Experimental Watershed, Coshocton, Ohio. (Horizontal lines show range of individual values.)

Data taken from Hydrologic Data, *Hydrologic Bull.* 2, 1942, U. S. Department of Agriculture Soil Conservation Service,* Blacklands Experimental Watershed, Waco, Texas.

Data taken from Hydrologic Data, *Hydrologic Bull.* 3, 1942, U. S. Department of Agriculture Soil Conservation Service,* Central Great Plains Experimental Watershed, Hastings, Nebr.

Data taken from Hydrologic Studies, Compilation of rainfall and runoff from the watersheds of the Red Plains Conservation Experiment Station, Guthrie, Oklahoma, U. S. Department of Agriculture Soil Conservation Service.*

Coweeta Experimental Forest, Appalachian Forest Experiment Station, Asheville, N. C., U. S. Department of Agriculture Forest Service.†

Bent Creek Experimental Forest, Appalachian Forest Experiment Station, Asheville, N. C., U. S. Department of Agriculture Forest Service.†

---

* Computations made by R. E. Snell, a student in the University of Michigan. Horace H. Rackham School of Graduate Studies.

† E. F. Brater, "The Unit Hydrograph Principle Applied to Small Watersheds," *Trans. A.S.C.E.*, vol. 105, pp. 1154, 1940.

Large Watersheds

The preceding paragraphs dealt with watersheds varying in area from a few acres to approximately 10 square miles. The term "large watersheds" applies to basins having an area greater than 10 square miles. However, the distinguishing feature of large watersheds is not

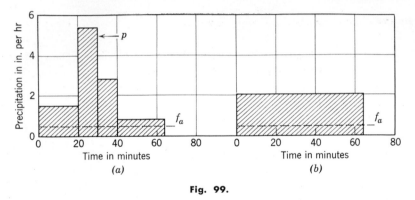

Fig. 99.

that their area is greater than some arbitrary limit, but rather that they are of such size that, within the basin, there are likely to be major differences in rainfall duration and intensity and in soil permeability. On large watersheds, major floods are frequently the result of high rates of surface runoff from only a portion of the basin. Consequently, it is usually necessary to determine unit hydrographs for several different rainfall distribution patterns. Also, in finding the average infiltration capacity for large basins, appropriate methods such as Horton's (see page 117) must be used. Finally, in correlating distribution graphs from different large watersheds, it is usually necessary to take into account other watershed characteristics in addition to size.

TABLE 22

1	2	3	4	5	6	7	8	9
Dura- tion	Precipi- tation Inten- sity	Accumu- lated Precipi- tation	Time Incre- ments	Precipitation during Time Increments			Precipitation Excess during Time Increments	
t, min	P, in./hr	p, in.	Δt, min	ΔP, in.	p, in./hr	f, in./hr	pe, in./hr	ΔPe, in.
			10	0.90	5.40	0.50	4.90	0.82
10	5.4	0.90						
			10	0.47	2.82	.50	2.32	0.39
20	4.1	1.37						
			20	0.50	1.50	.50	1.00	0.33
40	2.8	1.87						
			24	0.32	0.80	.50	0.30	0.12
64	2.05	2.19					$P_e =$	1.66

Determination of Unit Hydrographs. The selection of unit hydrographs requires judgment that may be gained only by experience. The procedure usually followed is to scan the runoff records for isolated hydrographs resulting from intense rains. These hydrographs are then plotted with the rain intensity records from various portions of the basin, as illustrated in Fig. 100. It is desirable to have an isohyetal map for each storm to show the rainfall distribution pattern. Those hydrographs that appear suitable may then be converted to distribution graphs, in the manner described on page 250. For any basin, the larger ordinates of distribution graphs obtained from similar rainfall patterns should agree closely, but the smaller ordinates may differ considerably. If there are no great variations in rainfall characteristics, an agreement as good or better than that in Fig. 97 may be expected.

The Youghiogheny River at Connellsville, Pennsylvania, is used for an example of runoff prediction on a large basin. The drainage area above Connellsville is 1326 square miles. Three hydrographs, together with average rain-intensity patterns, are shown in Fig. 100. The surface runoff is separated from ground-water discharge as shown in the figure. The average surface runoff rate for each 12-hr period, together with the instantaneous peak rate, is given for each graph in Table 23, column 3. Also shown in column 3 is the total surface runoff for each graph. The average infiltration capacity for each storm is determined and plotted in Fig. 100.

The distribution graphs are derived by converting each of the values in column 3, including the peak, to percentages of the total. These percentages are given in column 4, Table 23, and values in cubic feet per second per square mile per inch are shown in column 5.

The three distribution graphs are superimposed in Fig. 100 to show their similarity.

Another illustration of the expected degree of consistency of distribution graphs from the same basin is given in Table 24. Here are shown peaks of 27 distribution graphs for a watershed of 193 square miles which drains a highly urbanized area in and adjacent to Detroit, Michigan. The rains which produced these unit hydrographs varied considerably in their areal distribution pattern. Table 24 shows that peak discharges of the unit hydrographs vary from 720 cfs to 12,580 cfs and that the duration of the rainfall excess varies from 6 to 24 hr. However, only 4 of the 27 distribution-graph peaks differ from the average by more than 20 per cent.

The average distribution-graph peak for this gaging station and also the values for three other locations in the same drainage basin

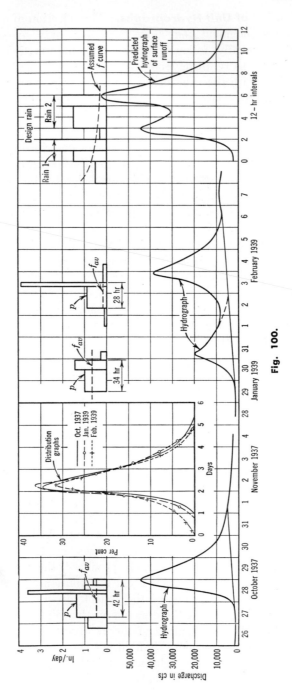

Fig. 100.

TABLE 23

1 Date	2 12-Hr Time Intervals	3 Surface Runoff, cfs	4 Distribution Graphs percentage	5 cfs per sq mi per in.
Oct. 1937	1	200	0.2	0.1
	2	4,500	3.7+	2.0
	3	35,000	29.1	15.7
	(pk)	(41,500)	(34.5)	(18.6)
	4	36,000	30.0	16.2
	5	22,000	18.3	9.9
	6	12,500	10.4	5.6
	7	6,000	5.0	2.7
	8	3,000	2.5	1.3
	9	1,000	0.8	0.4
		120,200 cfs for 12 hr or 1.68 in.	100.0	
Jan. 1939	1	1,800	3.6	1.9
	2	8,000	16.1	8.7
	3	15,500	31.2	16.9
	(pk)	(17,500)	(35.3)	(19.1)
	4	11,000	22.2	12.0
	5	7,000	14.1	7.6
	6	4,000	8.1	4.4
	7	2,000	4.0	2.2
	8	300	0.6	0.3
		49,600 cfs for 12 hr or 0.70 in.	99.9	
Feb. 1939	1	700	0.7	0.4
	2	2,000	2.0	1.1
	3	5,000	4.9	2.6
	4	11,000	10.8	5.8
	5	28,000	27.6	14.9
	(pk)	(32,000)	(31.5)	(17.0)
	6	26,000	25.6	13.8
	7	16,000	15.8	8.5
	8	8,000	7.9	4.3
	9	3,500	3.5+	1.9
	10	1,200	1.2	0.6
		101,400 cfs for 12 hr or 1.40 in.	100.1	

TABLE 24

Hydrographs and Distribution Graphs for the River Rouge at Plymouth Road

1	2	3	4	5	6
		Pk. Rate	Duration	Pk. of Distr. Graph,	Difference from Avg.
	SRO,	of SRO,	of Rainfall	cfs per sq mi	Peak,
Date	in.	cfs	Excess, hr	per in.	%
May '33	1.00	3700	24*	19.3	4.3
Feb. '35	0.76	2450	6	16.7	−9.7
Feb. '39	1.85	5940	24	16.7	−9.7
May '43	1.08	3890	12	18.6	0.5
May '45	0.38	1230	6	16.8	−9.2
Apr. '47	2.54	12580	18	25.6	38.3
Mar. '48	0.69	2240	12	16.8	−9.2
Feb. '49	0.39	1360	12	17.9	−3.2
Feb. '49	0.50	2050	18	21.2	14.6
Mar. '49	0.48	1950	6	21.0	13.5
Jan. '50	0.17	720	24*	22.2	20.0
Jan. '50	0.20	740	24*	18.9	2.2
Feb. '50	0.82	2250	18	14.1	−23.8
Apr. '50	0.96	3350	18	18.0	−2.7
Dec. '50	0.29	1000	18	17.9	−3.2
Dec. '50	0.45	1650	12	18.9	2.2
Jan. '52	0.37	1200	24*	16.5	−10.8
Jan. '52	0.32	1120	24*	18.3	−1.1
Jan. '52	0.30	960	24*	16.5	−10.8
Feb. '52	0.32	1100	24*	17.6	−4.9
Mar. '52	0.54	1900	24	18.2	−1.6
Apr. '52	0.48	1350	24	14.5	−21.6
Mar. '54	0.62	2820	12	23.3	25.9
Apr. '54	0.22	800	12	18.4	−0.5
Oct. '54	0.34	1350	6	20.6	11.3
Oct. '54	0.30	950	18	16.2	−12.4
Apr. '56	1.06	3940	48*	19.2	3.8
				Sum 499.9	
				Avg. 18.5	

* Duration equal to or less than these values. Exact duration not determined.

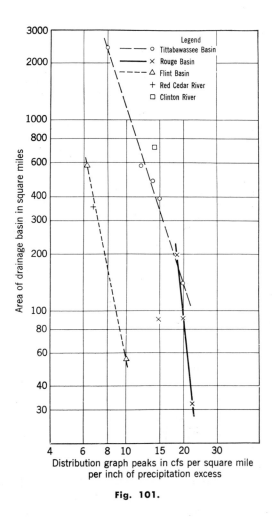

Fig. 101.

are plotted in Fig. 101, where it may be seen that the variation of peak with area of basin is similar to that of smaller watersheds in Fig. 98. It will be noted that three of the points for the Rouge River basin fall on a straight line and that one has a peak value smaller than that indicated by the trend of the other three. The difference is accounted for by the fact that this tributary, the Middle Rouge River, passes through an extensive system of lakes which modify the shape of the hydrograph. Also in Fig. 101 are distribution-graph peaks for two watersheds having two or more gaging stations and peaks for two other rivers located in the same region. By plotting values in this manner, for a particular region, we can predict distribution-graph peaks for locations where no gaging stations exist.

Predicting Runoff from Rainfall. When sufficient stream-flow records are available so that a representative distribution graph may be obtained, the construction of a hydrograph may be carried out with considerable assurance for any assumed rate of rainfall excess. No other procedure developed so far, approaches in accuracy that which may be obtained by this method, even when only a few records are available. If the period of assumed rainfall excess is about the same as that which produced the unit hydrographs, the procedure is to multiply the volume of rainfall excess by successive distribution graph percentages to obtain the increment of volume expected at the outlet during each time interval. Each increment of volume must then be converted to cubic feet per second. If the duration of rainfall excess is greater than that which will produce a single unit hydrograph, the rainfall excess must be divided into portions of shorter duration and the foregoing procedure applied to each portion. The final hydrograph may then be obtained by adding the various increments of runoff contributed to each time interval by the various portions of rainfall excess.

In reproducing or synthesizing hydrographs by this method, the best results are obtained if the rainfall excess is divided at points of sudden change in intensity, rather than at arbitrarily selected time intervals. The distribution graph is not a sufficiently precise tool to be sensitive to differences in the duration of rainfall excess that are small compared with the period of rise. For example, if the period of rise for a stream is 3 days, it is probable that periods of rainfall excess of 6, 12, or even 18 hr will produce nearly the same distribution graph. Further research is necessary before enough experimental evidence is available to establish the nature of the variation for such small changes in duration. Any refinements in the use of the distribution graph that may result from future research must include the effect of all the factors that influence the shape of the graph. (See page 31.) Such a refinement may be hoped for, but, while experimental evidence is accumulating, the distribution graph must be used with full cognizance of its limitations.

The distribution graphs developed for the Youghiogheny River will be used in an example of the application of the unit-hydrograph principle, to predict flood discharge from the assumed "design rain" shown in Fig. 100. For the purpose of this example an f curve is assumed and is shown superimposed on the design rain. The volume of rainfall excess for rains 1 and 2 is then determined as 1.68 in. or

120,000 cfs for 12 hr and 2.02 in. or 143,000 cfs for 12 hr, respectively. It is deemed necessary to apply the distribution graph to the two parts of the design rain separately, because the total duration of this rain is 72 hr, whereas the average period of rise of the three distribution graphs is only about half this much. It may be noted that the duration of rainfall excess for the three distribution graphs varies from 28 hr to 42 hr. Often an average-distribution graph is determined from a group such as is shown in Fig. 100. In this case the one for the

TABLE 25

1	2	3	4	5	6
		Runoff		Ground-	Total
12-Hr	First	Second		Water	Stream
Time	Rain,	Rain,	Total,	Flow,	Flow,
Intervals	cfs	cfs	cfs	cfs	cfs
1	200		200	2000	2,200
2	4,500		4,500	2300	6,800
3	35,000		35,000	2600	37,600
	(41,500)		(41,500)		(44,200)
4	36,000	300	36,300	2900	39,200
5	22,000	5,300	27,300	3200	30,500
6	12,500	41,600	54,100	3500	57,600
		(49,200)	(58,500)		(62,100)
7	6,000	42,800	48,800	3800	52,600
8	3,000	26,200	29,200	4100	33,300
9	1,000	14,900	15,900	4400	20,300
	Σ (120,200)				
10		7,200	7,200	4700	11,900
11		3,600	3,600	5000	8,600
12		1,100	1,100	5300	6,400
		Σ 143,000	Σ 263,200		

October 1937 storm is selected to apply to the design rains. These percentages are applied to the corresponding volumes of rainfall excess to obtain the values shown in columns 2 and 3 of Table 25. The values in column 3 are started 36 hr after those in column 2, to agree with the timing of the rain as shown in Fig. 100. Column 4 is the sum of columns 2 and 3 and gives the predicted surface runoff. It is still necessary to superimpose these values upon some assumed ground-water flows such as are shown in column 5. These values are combined with the surface runoff to obtain the values of column 6 which are plotted in Fig. 100.

The importance of carrying along the peak percentages cannot be overemphasized. All other percentage values are determined from average discharges during the selected time intervals. Only for extremely large basins would the average value for the maximum interval approach the value of the peak. In this example, an error of approximately 4500 cfs in the peak discharge would result if the peak percentage were ignored. As a result, the predicted hydrograph would have an incorrect shape.

As another example, let us assume that we desire to predict the peak discharge resulting from a maximum spring rain falling on the Youghiogheny basin. The maximum 48-hr March rain that can be expected on this basin is estimated as 10.4 in.[22] A rain of 48-hr duration is chosen because the actual duration of a 2-day rain is estimated to be less than 31 hr (see page 96), and thus less than the duration of the unit storms which produce the unit hydrographs in Fig. 100. It is assumed that this March rain is accompanied by a snow melt of one inch. Based on the values of f_a determined for the three hydrographs analyzed, it may be assumed that the March value of f_a is 0.2 in. per day. Then the total surface runoff is $(10.4 + 1.0 - 2 \times 0.2)$, or 11.0 in. The average of the three distribution-graph peaks is 17.2 cfs per square mile per in. The predicted peak rate of surface runoff is then,

$$11.0 \times 1326 \times 17.2 = 250,000 \text{ cfs}$$

A typical ground-water discharge value should be added to this value to obtain the peak discharge.

Often it is necessary to estimate the hydrograph at a point where no discharge records are available. There are many variations in the conditions under which this problem arises. Sometimes, for example, there may be gaging stations at other points on the stream from which unit hydrographs may be obtained. These may then be converted to the desired location by a flood-routing procedure (page 349). At other times there may be records on a number of other nearby basins having such similar watershed characteristics that a similarity between distribution graphs may be assumed.

In general, it is desirable to synthesize a hydrograph only on the basis of a thorough study of the graphs obtained at all available

[22] U. S. Weather Bureau and U. S. Army Corps of Engineers, "Seasonal Variation of the Probable Maximum Precipitation East of the 105th Meridian," Hydrometeorological Rept. No. 33, 1956.

nearby stations. Because of the wide variety of rainfall and physical characteristics that are likely to exist on large watersheds, it is usually not possible to find a group so similar that peaks may be compared on the basis of size alone. This is demonstrated by the values plotted in Fig. 101, in which even those from contiguous groups show a rather wide scattering. Some of the factors that cause the shape of the distribution graph to vary on any particular watershed are the rainfall-intensity pattern, the rainfall-distribution pattern, the direction of the storm path, the rainfall duration, the conditions of the soil at the beginning of the rain, the condition of the vegetation, the quantity of channel storage present at the beginning of the rain, the presence of ice in the stream, and the amount of vegetative growth in the stream. Some of the factors that cause variations in the distribution graphs for different basins are size, shape, slope of stream, slope of ground, stream density, roughness of stream channel, and the presence of natural or artificial channel storage.

The correlation of all these factors with the peak, period of rise, and base length of distribution graphs presents a difficult problem. Obviously, it is necessary to select only the more important factors for study. From an intensive study of the Connecticut River system, McCarthy[23] found that the distribution graph characteristics could be determined with the following watershed characteristics as a basis: (1) area, (2) slope of area-elevation graph, and (3) the stream pattern expressed as the number of major stems of a watershed. The area-elevation graph as used by McCarthy is similar to the hypsometric chart shown in Fig. 13, page 45.

From a study of streams draining the Appalachian Highlands, Snyder[24] found that he needed only to consider size and shape of watersheds in order to correlate the properties of distribution graphs. He found that the distance, L, measured along the principal stream from the outlet to a point adjacent to the geographical center of the basin, could be used as a measure of the effect of shape on the properties of the hydrograph. He was able to determine the relation of both the "lag" and peak of the hydrograph to this distance, L. The term "lag" is defined by Snyder as "the time between center of mass of surface-runoff-producing rain of a specified type of storm and the occurrence of resulting peak discharge at the location being studied." If some stream-flow data are available from which to obtain certain

[23] Gerald T. McCarthy, U. S. Engineer Office, Providence, R. I., *The Unit Hydrograph and Flood Routing*, 1939 (mimeographed report).

[24] Franklin F. Snyder, "Synthetic Unit-Graphs," *Trans. Am. Geophys. Union*, 1938, Part I, p. 447.

coefficients, the relations developed by Snyder may be used to estimate the shape of a distribution graph for a watershed.

For the purpose of making a similar study in the upper Ohio basin it was reported[25] that neither of the methods mentioned above was entirely satisfactory but that a combination of the two was found useful. Perhaps no single universally applicable approach to this complex problem can be found. It must be expected that oftentimes when unit hydrographs are to be developed new problems may arise, the solution of which requires ingenuity and good judgment. Nevertheless, the unit hydrograph is by far the most dependable tool for predicting flood runoff that has been developed so far.

Transference of Peak Flows. Rarely are discharge records available at the exact point on a stream where they are needed.

Suppose, for instance, that a flood of 5000 cfs is recorded at a point above which the drainage area is 100 square miles. It is desired to find the corresponding peak flow at some other point—let us say where the drainage area is 200 square miles.

The peak flood flow expressed in cubic feet per second per square mile does not vary directly with drainage area for at least two reasons: (1) in any storm the average depth of rainfall varies inversely with the area covered; (2) the larger the area (other conditions being the same) the wider is the base of the unit hydrograph and, therefore, the lower the peak.

In Fig. 101 are plotted distribution-graph peaks showing how, for any flood, the peak discharge, expressed as cubic feet per second per square mile per inch of rainfall excess, varies with area. On all drainage basins having different topography, shape, slope, etc., the relationship will differ and new curves will have to be derived for each new set of conditions. Using the relationship shown in Fig. 101 for the Rouge River basin, we see that for an area of 100 square miles the peak runoff is 20 cfs per square mile per in. of rainfall excess. Therefore, there must be $5000 \div 20 \times 100$ or 2.5 in. of rainfall excess. After studying the storm distribution pattern we decide to reduce this figure to 2.3 in. for the larger basin. From Fig. 101 the peak of the distribution graph for an area of 200 square miles is found to be 18.5 cfs per square mile per in. of rainfall excess, giving a total flow of $18.5 \times 200 \times 2.3$, or 8500 cfs.

If curves similar to those shown in Fig. 101 are not readily obtainable, an approximation can be made by assuming that the peak flood

[25] N. R. Laden, T. L. Reilly, and J. S. Minnotte, "Synthetic Unit Hydrographs, Distribution-Graphs and Flood Routing in the Upper Ohio River Basin," *Trans. Am. Geophys. Union*, 1940, Part II, p. 649.

flow varies as the eight tenth power of the ratio of the drainage areas. This method indicates that the peak is 8700 cfs.

The accuracy of both of these methods of finding the peak flood flow at a given point from a record obtained during the same rain at another point on the stream depends principally upon the similarity of the physical characteristics of the areas above the two points. Also the greater the ratio is between these areas, the less reliable the results are.

MINIMUM FLOW

Except for streams that are fed by melting snows and those draining areas that contain a large amount of surface storage, low water flow is derived entirely from ground water. Horton has shown that the portion of the hydrograph that represents only ground-water flow is an exhaustion curve and may be expressed by an equation of the form

$$Q = Q_0 e^{-cd^n}, \tag{16}$$

in which Q is discharged in cubic feet per second at the end of d days after termination of surface runoff; Q_0 discharge when d equals zero; e Napierian base, 2.718; and c and n are constants.

In order to evaluate Q_0, c, and n for any drainage basin, a composite ground-water-depletion curve should be constructed from the recession graphs resulting from a number of storms. The various segments of recession curves are shifted with respect to the time axis until they appear to match, and then an average or composite curve is drawn through them as shown in Fig. 2. In order to evaluate the constants of equation 16, the location of the time scale must be arbitrarily selected. The time when $d = 0$ may be taken at or before the time of occurrence of the highest point on any of the recession curves that is deemed to be free of any surface runoff. Such a point is illustrated by c in Fig. 2. The zero of the time scale occurs 8 days before c. For any other location of the time scale, the equation of the curve below c may also be determined, but the values of the constants will be different. Exactly the same extension of the recession curve to lower discharges would be obtained, however, by any other choice of origin.

Written in logarithmic form, equation 16 becomes

$$\log Q = \log Q_0 - cd^n \log e \tag{17}$$

Equation 17 represents a straight line in which $\log Q$ and d^n are the variables. Figure 102 shows that equation 17 becomes a straight line

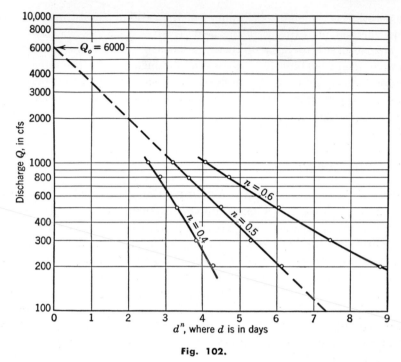

Fig. 102.

when $n = 0.5$. The value of Q_0 is the value of Q when $d = 0$ and is found to be 6000 in Fig. 102. The value of c, determined from the slope of the line, is 0.555. The equation for the line then becomes $Q = 6000e^{-0.555d^{0.5}}$.

By studying long-term records of rainfall in the region, the longest period likely to elapse between rains of sufficient magnitude to produce ground-water accretion may be determined. If some point on the recession curve is selected as representing the conditions at the beginning of such a period, the daily discharge throughout the period may be determined from the derived equation or from an extension of the straight line of Fig. 102.

YIELD

It is recalled that, in the determination of surface runoff, the method of procedure depended principally upon the size of the area drained. By way of contrast, the best procedure for determining yield depends not upon the size of basin but upon climate. For this purpose climate is classified as *arid, semiarid,* and *humid.* Streams draining *arid* basins carry only surface runoff and, therefore, are intermittent and flow only during and immediately following periods of intense rainfall. The water table, if there is one in the basin, is always below the bed of the stream. Basins whose climate is here classified as *semiarid* have a rainy season and a dry season. Nearly all the year's rainfall occurs in the rainy season, during which stream flow is continuous. During the dry season the stream is dry most of the time and carries water only intermittently after an occasional heavy storm. The prediction of runoff from semiarid basins is treated in Chapter 9. In *humid* regions, except for the smaller tributaries, the flow is continuous, and the water table is always above the bed of the stream.

Arid Basins

Inasmuch as the entire yield of arid basins is derived from surface runoff, it follows that in order to determine their yield the same procedure may be followed as has already been described for determining surface runoff from any basin. (See page 270.) There is, however, the distinction that in arid basins all infiltration may be included as a water loss, because none of the water that once infiltrates into the soil ever reaches the stream draining that basin, nor does ground-water storage affect this problem. In this case, however, the problem is made easier because the infiltration capacity is nearly constant throughout the year.

From the records of a number of intense storms and their hydrographs of surface runoff the average infiltration capacity of the basin can be determined. This average value is then applied to each intense storm and the resulting runoff is found.

Humid Basins

In humid regions such as the eastern part of the United States, except for streams that drain only small areas, the flow is continuous. The water table never drops below the bed of the stream. As a result, the yield of such a stream for any year or for any month is dependent upon the elevation of the water table at the beginning of the period. The change in ground-water storage, ΔS, now becomes important, whereas in arid regions it has no significance. In semiarid regions ground-water storage has only the effect of reducing the monthly yield during the early months of the rainy season and increasing it correspondingly during the later months. Ground-water storage has no effect upon the total seasonal or annual yield.

For humid basins the *average annual yield* usually can be satisfactorily determined from a comparatively short period of records. For instance, having available 10 yr of records of rainfall and runoff, the value of ΔS is small compared with the total yield. Also the average annual water loss as determined from 10 yr of records does not depart very much from the long-term average. Therefore, if the long-term mean annual rainfall and the corresponding average annual water loss are known, the average yield may be taken as the difference between the two. However, the determination of yield, month by month or even year by year, cannot be made with the same degree of accuracy, because of the increasing importance of ΔS as the time interval decreases, and because of the relatively greater influence of the various factors that affect evaporation opportunity. As an illustration, referring to *U. S. Geological Survey Water-Supply Paper* 846, page 57, we observe that the water losses on the Tittabawassee basin above Freeland, Michigan, for 1916 were 13.0 in., rainfall 28.0 in., and temperature 45° F. In 1914 the rainfall was 32.2 in., the temperature 45.6° F, but the water loss was 24.4 in. As a result, the yield in 1916 was 15 in. as compared with 7.8 in. in 1914, although the rainfall was 4.2 in. more in 1914. Also on the West River at Newfane, Vermont, in 1920 the precipitation was 36.9 in. and the water loss was 7.5 in., whereas in 1930 the rainfall was 38.7 in. and the water loss was 17.5 in., with only a small difference in temperature. Many other similar illustrations can be given which show a lack of correlation between water loss, rainfall, and temperature for short periods. (Also see Fig. 91.)

Because of the influence of soil, vegetative cover, land use, depth to water table, and other factors that often affect the water losses of adjacent basins in varying degrees, the average water losses cannot be reliably determined for a basin on which no stream-flow records are available.

Duration Curves. Estimating the yield of a stream upon which no records or only a short period of records are available can best be done by making use of records from adjacent basins. A most useful tool in such an analysis is the duration curve. Such a curve shows the per cent of time that any discharge was equaled or exceeded. The shape of the curve also gives a clear picture of the nature of the stream flow. A flat curve is derived from a river having few floods and a large ground-water discharge, whereas a steep curve indicates a flashy stream, subject to very low flows. These two types are illustrated by the curves for the Manistee and Tittabawassee rivers, respectively, shown in Fig. 104. For most purposes monthly flows are used, but if very little storage is available, daily discharges may be more appropriate. For some purposes, as for example estimating the power potential of a river, the ordinates of the curves are usually expressed in cubic feet per second, whereas for comparing the flow characteristics of two rivers it is more advantageous to use discharge per square mile.

An example of the derivation of a duration curve is given for the Flint River at Genesee, Michigan. Records of monthly discharge for the period from October 1931 through September 1952 (21 years) are available. The number of occurrences in each of the discharge categories shown in column 1 of Table 26 are recorded in column 2. The

TABLE 26

1 Discharge, cfs	2 Occur- rences	3 Accumulated Occurrences	4 Per Cent of Total
23– 49	10	252	100.0
50– 99	54	242	96.0
100–149	38	188	74.6
150–199	16	150	59.5
200–249	20	134	53.7
250–299	14	114	45.2
300–349	10	100	39.7
350–399	9	90	35.7
400–499	23	81	32.1
500–599	11	58	23.0
600–699	8	47	18.7
700–799	6	39	15.5
800–899	5	33	13.1
900–999	4	28	11.1
1000–1999	20	24	9.5
2000–2999	4	4	1.6
	252		

numbers of occurrences equal to or larger than the smallest value in each category are shown in column 3, and corresponding percentages of the total number of occurrences are shown in column 4. The duration curve resulting from these computations, curve 1 of Fig. 103, is obtained by plotting the percentages of column 4 versus the smallest discharges in each of the categories of column 1. Also shown in Fig. 103 is a duration curve for the same river during the period from October 1947 through September 1952. This period comprises the last 5 yr of the period for which curve 1 is derived. The difference between the two curves illustrates that a short period of records, 5 yr in this case, may give a very inaccurate indication of the long term yield of a stream.

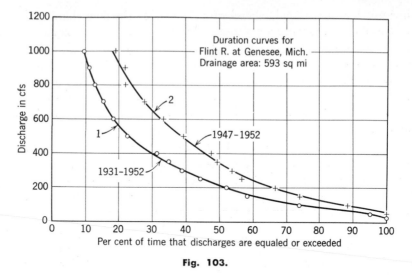

Fig. 103.

Use of Records on Adjacent Basins. Yield varies more or less regionally. As a result, if long-term records are available on one or more adjacent basins, those records may often be used advantageously. Two different conditions will be considered. In the first, no discharge records are available on the stream in question. In the second, records are available for a period of at least a few years that are also covered by records on the adjacent stream.

The solution of a problem of the first type is illustrated in Fig. 104, in which the duration-of-flow curve for the Sturgeon River in Michigan is estimated by comparison of the duration-of-flow curves for Deer Creek, Au Sable River, Tittabawassee River, and Manistee River. Of these streams, the Sturgeon River basin lies nearer to and is perhaps more similar to the Deer Creek basin on the west and to the Au Sable River basin on the southeast than it is to the other two. The Manistee is farther away to the southwest, and the Tittabawassee is still farther away to the southeast. Consequently, the estimated duration-of-flow curve for the Sturgeon River is drawn in between the duration curves for the Au Sable River and Deer Creek and is influenced only slightly by the curves for the Manistee and the Tittabawassee rivers.

This study was made for the City of Petoskey in 1927 at a time when no discharge records on the Sturgeon River were available. At that time the average yield of the Sturgeon River at Wolverine was estimated to be 202 cfs. In 1941, the U. S. Geological Survey established a gaging station at this same site and the actual average measured discharge for the 14 yr since that time has been 198 cfs. Such a high degree of accuracy should not ordinarily be expected, but, in general, this method is found to lead to more dependable results than are obtained from a theoretical determination of the probable water losses.

Figure 105 illustrates a method in which duration-of-flow curves can be used in estimating the yield of a stream for which short-term records are available and for which simultaneous and long-term records are available on at least one adjacent stream. Here it is assumed that there are records covering a period of 3 yr on stream B, and on stream A there are records covering a period of 30 yr, 3 yr of which are simultaneous with the records on B. Duration curves are then plotted for both streams for the 3 yr for which the records are simultaneous. Also the duration curve is plotted for stream A for the entire period covered by the records, which in this example is assumed to be 30 yr. Then, in order to obtain the 30-yr duration curve for stream B, the discharge values obtained from the 3-yr curves for B are multiplied by the ratio of the 30-yr yield to the 3-yr yield on A for a number of points on the curves. For instance, during 60 per cent of the 30 yr of records on A, the flow exceeds 0.96 cfs per square mile, whereas for the same percentage of time during the 3 yr of records it exceeds 1.10 cfs per square mile. For the same percentage of time the flow of stream B, during the 3 yr of records, exceeds 0.78 cfs per square mile. Therefore, for 60 per cent of the time the flow of stream B equals or exceeds

$$\frac{0.96}{1.10} \times 0.78 = 0.68 \text{ cfs per square mile}$$

The estimated yield of stream B for other percentages of time is obtained in the same manner.

If similar records are available for other adjacent basins, an estimated duration-of-flow curve should be derived from each. After plotting all such curves on the same sheet and after a careful comparison of the physical characteristics of each of these basins with those of stream B, we can draw in a final estimated curve.

If, for storage or other purposes, it is desired to obtain an estimated hydrograph of stream B, this estimate can be done in the following manner. Suppose that, at a certain time, the recorded flow of stream A was 0.84 cfs per square mile. From the 30-yr duration curve for stream A, it is found that this flow corresponds to 70 per cent of the time. For this same percentage of time, the 30-yr duration curve for stream B shows a flow of 0.55 cfs per square mile. The estimated flow

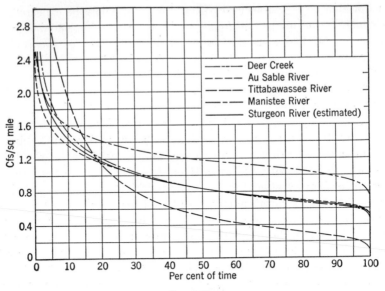

Fig. 104.

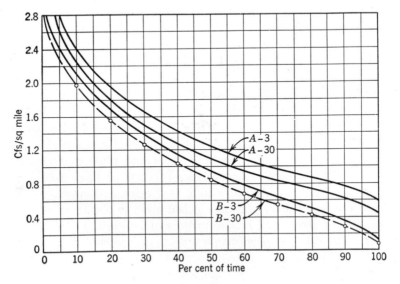

Fig. 105.

for each successive time interval is found in a similar manner. In this way, a continuous hydrograph, based upon either daily, weekly, or monthly average discharges, may be obtained for the entire period of records on the adjacent stream. However, the time interval used in deriving the hydrograph must be the same as was used in constructing the original duration curves.

Because the rainfall pattern for a long period is not the same on any two basins, it should not be expected that every minor variation in the hydrograph of any given stream can be accurately reproduced by this method. Nevertheless, the general behavior of the stream, the number of peaks of each different magnitude, and the number of periods of low flow should all be correctly shown. A hydrograph derived in this manner should be just as useful in making storage, water-supply, or power studies as though the fluctuations were chronologically represented perfectly. The value of the results is dependent only upon whether or not the various factors that affect the rainfall-runoff relation during the period of simultaneous records were normal. Therefore, the longer the period of overlapping records the more reliable will be the results.

Other Methods of Estimating Yield. From time to time various other procedures have been suggested for estimating yield. One of the earliest of these was proposed by Vermeule[26] in 1894. He was probably the first to recognize the importance of ground-water storage and to point out that there is a limit to the volume of this storage on any basin. This fact has also been discussed by Horton.[27] A number of articles describing this or related methods of predicting long-term yield are listed below.[28]

Storage and the Mass Diagram. When it is desired to use water at uniform or nearly uniform rates greater than the minimum discharge of a river, it is necessary to provide storage capacity in which to impound water during periods of high flow for use during periods

[26] C. C. Vermeule, *New Jersey Geological Survey*, vol. 3, p. 11.

[27] R. E. Horton, "Maximum Ground-Water Levels," *Trans. Am. Geophys. Union*, 1936, Part II, p. 344.

[28] F. F. Snyder, "A Conception of Surface Runoff," *Trans. Am. Geophys. Union*, 1939, Part IV, p. 725; R. K. Linsley, Jr., and W. C. Ackermann, "A Method of Predicting the Runoff from Rainfall," *Trans. A.S.C.E.*, 1942, vol. 107, p. 825; C. R. Hursh, M. D. Hoover, and P. W. Fletcher, "Studies in the Balanced Water-Economy of Experimental Drainage-Areas," *Trans. Am. Geophys. Union*, 1942, Part II, p. 509; C. K. Cooperrider, H. O. Cassidy, and C. H. Niederhof, "Forecasting Stream-Flow of the Salt River, Arizona," *Trans. Am. Geophys. Union*, October 1945, p. 275; F. Paget, "A New Forecasting Curve for the Kaweah," *Trans. Am. Geophys. Union*, June 1946, p. 389.

of low flow. The determination of the required storage capacity for various uniform use rates is a problem often encountered in hydrological investigations. It is recognized that many water uses are not uniform for all months of the year. However, the method described here for uniform use rates can be used with minor modifications for nonuniform use rates. In this discussion, evaporation from the reservoir surface, leakage through the dam, and inflow from the adjacent drainage area are neglected. These factors also can be included when the fundamentals of the mass diagram method are understood.

The *mass diagram* is a graphical representation of accumulated discharge versus time. The ordinates may be in acre feet, inches depth on the drainage basin (page 16), or any other unit of volume. Monthly discharges are usually used in deriving mass diagrams. A portion of a mass diagram is shown in Fig. 106. Because the difference in the ordinates at the ends of a small segment of such a curve is the volume discharged during the time given by the corresponding difference in the abscissas, the slope of the mass diagram at any point is equal to the rate of discharge at that time. In other words, the slopes of the mass diagram are numerically equal to the corresponding ordinates of the hydrograph. If, then, a mass diagram for a uniform use rate is plotted, it is a straight line such as *ae* in Fig. 106, which is drawn so that its slope is 100 cfs. Two other lines, parallel to *ae* and tangent to the mass diagram at points *b* and *c*, are also shown. During periods (*a* to *b*) and (*c* to *b'*), when the slope of the mass diagram is greater than that of the straight line *ae*, the river discharge

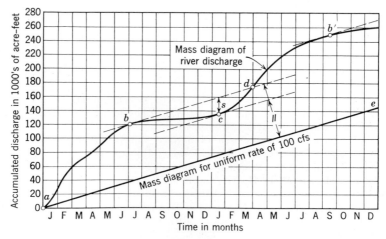

Fig. 106.

exceeds 100 cfs, whereas from b to c the flow is less than 100 cfs. If the reservoir is assumed to be full at a, then the line $abdb'$ becomes a mass diagram of outflow with a minimum outflow of 100 cfs. Inasmuch as any point on this line represents the total outflow up to that time, and the point on the mass diagram of inflow $abcdb'$ found on the same vertical line represents the total inflow up to that same time, the vertical distance between these two mass diagrams represents the amount the reservoir is drawn down at that time. Of course the greatest of these drafts is the size of reservoir needed during this period to provide a minimum flow of 100 cfs.

The mass diagram provides the following information regarding the condition of the reservoir:

1. From a to b the inflow rate exceeds the use rate and the reservoir is full and overflowing;

2. At b the inflow rate is equal to the use rate and the reservoir is full but not overflowing;

3. From b to c the use rate exceeds the inflow rate and the amount of drawdown is increasing;

4. At c the use rate is equal to the inflow rate and the drawdown (s) is a maximum.

5. From c to d the inflow rate exceeds the use rate and the drawdown is decreasing;

6. At d the reservoir is full; and

7. From d to b' conditions are the same as from a to b.

It follows then that the greatest vertical distance (s) between bd and bcd, which occurs at c, is the storage required to maintain a use rate of 100 cfs during the low flow period from b to c. The largest value, such as s for the entire period of record, is the minimum size of reservoir which would provide this uniform use rate.

9

Semiarid Regions

Francis G. Christian and Walter J. Parsons, Jr.

Although the same hydrologic laws apply in semiarid and in humid regions, the physical characteristics of the two areas are often so different that caution is needed in employing methods commonly accepted for one region, for the solution of problems arising in the other. The outstanding characteristic of hydrologic processes in semiarid regions is variability. Consequently, many of the simplifying assumptions and short cuts that are useful in humid regions may not be applicable to arid regions.

Variability in Time

Hydrologic processes in semiarid regions are variable with respect to time. Long-term cycles or secular swings in climate are often important. Consequently, probability studies or computation of long-term means are very likely to lead to erroneous conclusions, unless consideration is given to the position of the period of record in the cycle or swing. Likewise, the marked variation, in semiarid climates, among the seasons of the year may require segregation of data by seasons. A combination of hydrologic factors common in one season

---

This chapter has been contributed by Francis G. Christian, Supervising General Engineer, U. S. Army Engineer District, Sacramento, California, and Walter J. Parsons, Jr., Chief Hydrologist, U. S. Army Engineer District, Sacramento, California.

of the year may be virtually nonexistent during another season. Finally, a particular combination of factors may exist for only a few days in several years and may render hydrologic computations based on average values grossly erroneous. Another characteristic of semiarid regions is that nearly all precipitation occurs during the winter and spring.

Variability in Space

Hydrologic processes in semiarid regions often vary greatly among different parts of even a single river basin. A high elevation zone may be the only part of a river basin in which precipitation is received regularly or in which winter snow accumulates in deep snow packs. In such a basin, 90 per cent of the runoff may originate in 10 per cent of its drainage area. Therefore, runoff values expressed as discharge per square mile should be used with caution. Likewise, vegetative cover may vary radically across a basin. The variation from dense forests in a high elevation headwater area to barren desert along the lower courses renders average values of cover meaningless. Again, the slow rate of rock decay characteristic of semiarid regions tends to perpetuate geological differences among different parts of a basin, with resultant marked differences in infiltration capacities.

Probability and Duration Studies

In making probability or frequency studies of runoff in semiarid regions, an essential step is to determine the position of the available period of record in the long-term climatic cycle or swing. If the period of record lies entirely within a dry phase of the cycle, the results may differ substantially from those derived from another record within a wet phase of the cycle. Again, an analysis based on a period of record that is partially wet and partially dry may present a picture that is a meaningless average of two extremes or may contain a warp that is difficult to interpret. A possible solution is to develop the data as a broad band, with the data from any particular year or period lying along an intermediate line parallel to the center line of the band. An illustration is provided by a duration study of runoff rates on Kings River in California, shown in Fig. 107. The derivation and use of flow-duration or frequency curves is discussed on page 278.

In semiarid regions, because of marked variations in climate among different seasons of each year, segregation of data into seasonal fractions is often advantageous. For instance, it is usually best to divide a flood-peak series into two separate subseries, one containing all the

winter peaks caused primarily by rain, and the other containing all
the summer peaks caused primarily by snowmelt. Each series is then
analyzed separately and the final results combined, if necessary. In
some cases, even more segregation is desirable, such as dividing the
winter flood-peak series into an early winter fraction caused by rain
falling on dry, snow-free ground, a midwinter fraction caused by cold
rain falling on wet, partially snow-covered ground, and a late winter
fraction, caused by warm spring rains falling on an accumulated snow
pack. Each of these segregated fractions is usually more consistent
and easier to analyze. An illustration is a probability study of flood
peaks on Kings River in California, shown in Fig. 108.

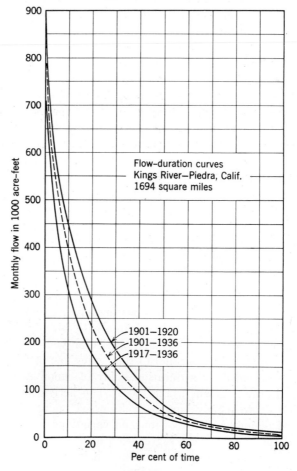

Fig. 107.

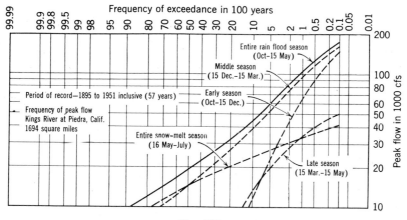

Fig. 108.

Precipitation Maps

In order to determine usable precipitation values in mountainous, semiarid regions, it is usually necessary to develop a detailed isohyetal map for the drainage area. Because of the complex precipitation pattern that occurs in such regions and the sparsity and generally nonrepresentative location of precipitation stations, the usual procedures of determining basin mean precipitation, either by the Thiessen method (see page 81) or from the arithmetic mean of all station values, are often impractical. Because most precipitation stations are located near habitations at low elevations or in sheltered valleys, they do not measure precipitation on the high ridges. However, reasonably accurate isohyetal maps can be constructed by utilizing types of hydrologic data not usually considered pertinent. Such diverse elements as snow-course data, seasonal storage-gage data, runoff records, forest cover maps, topographical maps, and evaporation data can be advantageously used.

The first step in developing an isohyetal map of a semiarid basin is to draw a normal seasonal precipitation map. Data for such a map are easier to develop than data for a short period, because the basic relationship between precipitation and·runoff becomes simplified when we deal with long-term normals. The basic formula is: Precipitation = runoff + evapo-transpiration losses ± the change in ground and channel storage. The simplified formula for a long period is: Precipitation = runoff + evapo-transpiration losses. Runoff for each unit of the basin can be determined from long-term stream-gaging records. Evapo-transpiration losses usually range from 15 in. per yr for barren rocky areas to 35 in. for heavily forested areas. These losses can be estimated with fair accuracy from forest cover maps, with check values from those few favored areas in which both precipitation and runoff are accurately known. Solution of the basic formula for each unit of a river basin gives the average precipitation over that unit and serves as a guide to the construction of isohyetal lines.

Another device is to construct average elevation-precipitation curves from precipitation data for stations at diverse elevations and then to apply these average curves to the topographical map. It is usually best to assign to each station an "effective elevation" based on the general elevation around each station, rather than to use the actual elevation. For instance, a station in a narrow, deep canyon usually receives a precipitation amount typical of the elevation of the surrounding plateau, rather than of the elevation at the bottom of the canyon. For best results, the topography around each station should be considered. On the lee side of a mountain range, the relationship between precipitation and distance from the main crest line may be more useful than the elevation-precipitation relationship. The annual precipitation may be estimated by adding to the snow-course data the probable losses from the snowpack and the rain which fell on bare ground. A forest cover map can also be used. For example, dense coniferous forest usually indicates an annual precipitation of more than 40 in., whereas sagebrush areas usually indicate less than 15 in. of precipitation, etc.

With the foregoing information, a normal seasonal isohyetal map is constructed by trial-and-error methods. Isohyetal lines are drawn through all known points and other points estimated by giving consideration to the topography and the degree of forest cover. These lines are adjusted successively until they produce the proper average precipitation for each runoff unit of the basin. It is usually remarkable how the various hydrologic elements interlock to define closely the normal isohyetal map and how even minor errors in basic data can be detected. Such a normal seasonal isohyetal map will be found to be a very useful tool for constructing detailed isohyetal maps for individual years or for particular storms.

Isopercental Maps

In regions where the precipitation is largely controlled by the topography, the pattern of individual storms, or of rainfall for short periods, is often quite similar to the normal seasonal precipitation pattern. That pattern can be used as a model for determining the precipitation distribution during short periods. This determination can be made most effectively by constructing an "isopercental map" which shows the relationship between the normal seasonal pattern and the individual storm pattern. An illustration is shown in Fig. 109. The first step is to compute the ratios of the particular storm precipitation to normal seasonal precipitation at all reporting stations. If the storm follows exactly the normal seasonal pattern, all the ratios are the same, and the most probable storm isohyetal map is simply a scaled-down version of the normal seasonal map. If the ratios vary consistently across the region, the storm isohyetal map is a warped version of the normal seasonal map. The amount of the warp is determined by drawing isopercental lines through the known points. The final storm isohyetal map can then be constructed by superimposing the isopercental map on the normal seasonal map. If the ratios vary erratically from station to station, and no rational isopercental pattern can be developed, it is probable that the storm does not follow the normal pattern, and the isopercental method is not applicable. By means of the isopercental method, a comparatively small number of stations can be used to develop a quite detailed isohyetal map. This forecasting device is particularly useful when speed is essential. It is often found that data reported by the first few stations closely define the basic storm pattern and subsequent reports only confirm the pattern.

A further use of the isopercental map is to obtain basin mean values of precipitation directly, without going through the step of drawing a complete isohyetal map. As an illustration, if inspection of the isopercental map for a particular storm indicates that the mean isopercental value over basin A is 7.8 per cent, the basin mean precipitation over basin A for this storm can be computed directly by taking 7.8 per cent of the normal seasonal basin mean for basin A. After the normal seasonal basin mean values have been determined by planimeter, the basin mean for a whole series of individual storms may be computed. This computation is very useful for rapid forecasting work.

An advantage of the isopercental method of estimating storm precipitation values from a limited number of station reports is that this method largely eliminates systematic errors caused by imperfect distribution of stations. This advantage is particularly important in storm-forecasting work, since reports from several key stations are often missing during major storms, because of damaged communication lines. The mean of the stations which do report may differ radically from the true basin mean. With the isopercental method, each station which does report provides an independent estimate of the true basin

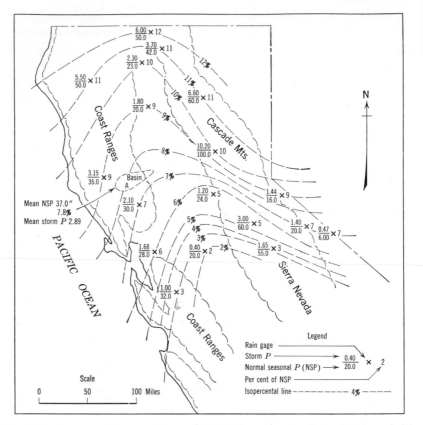

Fig. 109. Isopercental map, storm of 18–20 November in Central Valley, Calif.

mean, and additional reports progressively increase the accuracy of the estimate without introducing any systematic change.

Isochronal Maps

In analyzing storm precipitation by mass curves, it is essential to obtain accurate time data for all stations. Since many nonrecording stations fail to report the times of beginning and ending of precipitation and other critical time data, and since even recording stations may have serious errors in time, it is best to consolidate all available time data on an "isochronal map." Such a map shows, for a basin or area, the time contours of some key time element in a storm, such as beginning of precipitation.

An illustration is shown in Fig. 110. When such a map is prepared, the time that the selected event occurred at each station is first plotted on the map. An approximate set of time contours is then drawn through the known points with due consideration to the general weather synoptic map. Next, the individual station values are compared with the time contours to discover inconsistencies. The common reporting errors of 12 or 24 hr are easily detected by the method, and personal errors of observers are largely eliminated. Sometimes, re-examination of the original records of inconsistent stations uncovers errors of transcription. After all apparent errors have been eliminated, the time contours are successively readjusted until they represent the most probable time progression across the basin. Finally, derived time values are taken from the map for those stations which had missing time values or for basin units that did not contain stations. By this method, use is made of all available time data within the region, instead of relying solely on time data from the nearest station. In preparing an isochronal map it is best to cover an area several times larger than

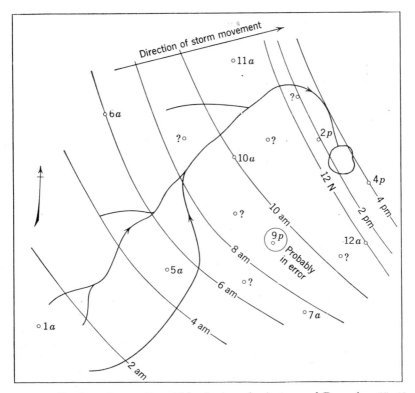

Fig. 110. Isochronal map, time of beginning of rainstorm of December 15, 19–.

the particular basin being studied. In this way the general trend of storm movement can be traced more readily.

Transposition of Storms

Because of the characteristic variability of precipitation in semiarid mountainous regions, direct transposition of either isohyetal patterns or depth-area values from one river basin to another may lead to quite unreasonable results. The observed storm isohyetal pattern over a river basin represents the unique effect of that basin's topography

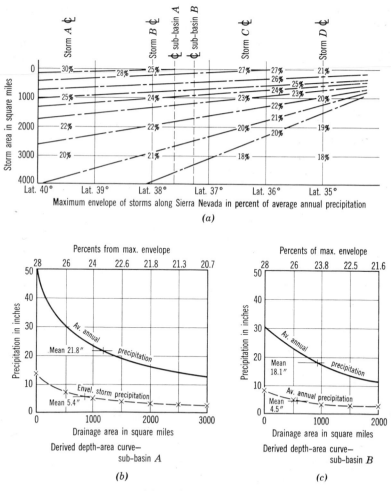

Fig. 111. Transposition of storms by isopercental method.

on the moving air masses and different patterns will inevitably result on different basins. Under such variable conditions the isopercental method of storm transposition can be used. In this method, only the isopercental pattern of the prototype storm is transposed to the other basin. New values of precipitation are computed from this isopercental pattern, and the average annual precipitation map of the new basin. In transposing isopercental patterns, the storm axis, in order to better fit the new basin, should be rotated with extreme caution, if at all. In regional studies, comparison of storms over different basins can be made by comparing percental-area values instead of depth-area values.

A more generalized method of comparing and transposing storms, which has been used along the eastern portion of the Sacramento-San Joaquin Basin in California, is illustrated in Fig. 111. This major river basin extends in a north-south direction from latitude 40° to latitude 35°. Figure 111a summarizes isopercental values from four maximum storms that are centered at 39° 30′, 38°, 36° 15′, and 35°. The diagonal parameter lines envelop maximum isopercental values in the several storms and provide a generalized pattern of storm potential throughout the entire region. From these generalized data, detailed depth-area data are derived for sub-basins A and B, located within the major basin at 37° 36′ and 37° 15′ respectively. Figures 111b and 111c show these derived data for sub-basins A and B respectively. On each of these diagrams, the upper curve represents depth-area data measured from the average annual precipitation map for that sub-basin. The lower curve on each diagram is derived from the upper curve by using the proper percental values from the upper envelope diagram. The resultant envelope depth-duration curves for each sub-basin are as severe as any storm observed in this region and can be used to develop design floods for that sub-basin.

Infiltration Analysis

The characteristic variation of hydrologic factors within a river basin in semiarid regions often renders the computation of overall average infiltration values for a river basin quite misleading and of little value. A low-level desert portion of a basin may have a large infiltration capacity, but it does not receive enough precipitation to utilize that capacity. The storm precipitation over a high level mountain area may fall as snow which cannot infiltrate until it melts, sometimes months later. It is therefore often necessary to divide a river basin, insofar as possible, into small homogeneous zones before attempting to derive infiltration values.

Infiltration values derived from even completely segregated areas should not be used for design-flood synthesis until these values have been correlated with a seasonal time factor. Infiltration values derived from a flood which occurs immediately after a characteristic summer drought may be very large and not applicable to a midwinter storm falling on thoroughly wet ground (see Fig. 41). In contrast, infiltration values from a midwinter storm are not applicable to an early winter storm when the ground is still dry to deep levels. It is therefore necessary to explore the seasonal variations in infiltration capacity and be sure that the selected infiltration value is applicable to a selected storm precipitation. A convenient method is to relate infiltration capacity at any time in the wet season to the accumulated infiltration from the beginning of the wet season to the given time. The infiltration value for each interval of a flood synthesis can then be taken from this relationship curve.

The presence of a snow blanket over all or a portion of a river basin inevitably changes the infiltration rates of a basin. When rainfall is small in proportion to the depth of the snow (less than 5 per cent of the water equivalent of the snow), the entire rainfall may be absorbed by the snow, and none is available for infiltration. If enough rain falls to saturate the snow and reach the ground, the percolating water may be so cold that it infiltrates at significantly lower rates than rain falling on bare ground. On the other hand, the obstructing effect of the snow on overland flow may hold water on the ground deeper and longer than normally occurs on bare ground, with a resultant increase in the total infiltration. The net effect of these various factors is difficult to determine and can only be approximated.

The most practical method of providing for all these variable infiltration factors in a computation of basin mean water excess for flood synthesis is to divide the river basin into several homogeneous zones on the basis of elevation (or another characteristic) and to compute water excesses for each zone from the estimated precipitation and infiltration values for that zone (see also pages 103–121). These water excesses are then combined to give a basin mean or total. In a synthesis of this kind it is often found that the water excesses from different zones are quite out of step with each other, so that the basin mean pattern at a given moment is markedly different from the pattern of any one zone or even of the storm. Low-elevation zones may be very dry at the beginning of the storm and not produce any water excess until late in the storm after the greatest rainfall rates have passed. Again, precipitation on high-elevation zones may be largely snow and may fall as rain only during the middle of a storm, so that infiltration starts and stops at times which differ considerably from the corresponding infiltration times at low elevations. At intermediate elevations, progressive melting away of snow to higher and higher elevations introduces other infiltration patterns. The summation of all these patterns is a complex pattern which would be almost impossible to compute as a basin mean in a single step.

Unit Hydrographs

In semiarid regions where hydrologic factors tend to be quite variable, application of the unit hydrograph technique is very difficult, since the underlying premise of that technique is the essential constancy of hydrologic factors over a river basin. However, effective use of this method can be made if the following substitutions and limitations are accepted.

First, it is often necessary to substitute a standard areal pattern of precipitation for uniform areal precipitation. As an illustration, a basin that consistently has twice as much precipitation over the headwater area as over the lower area should still produce a usable unit hydrograph.

Second, it is often necessary to substitute a standard time pattern of precipitation during each time period for constant precipitation. For example, a basin which consistently receives its storm precipitation in a series of diurnal waves in which, let us say, over 75 per cent of each day's precipitation occurs in the second and third quarter of the day, with 50 per cent of it in the second quarter, should still produce a usable 24-hr unit hydrograph. Under these circumstances, the peak value may be much larger than from a comparable humid basin with uniform precipitation.

Analysis of flood hydrographs of record often may indicate the existence of a family of unit hydrographs rather than a single unit hydrograph. However, such a family of unit hydrographs may be usable if the trend through the family can be related to a consistent change in one or more hydrologic factors. For instance, the progressive change in soil moisture during a winter wet season, from very dry in October (at the end of the summer dry season) to very wet in March (at the end of the wet season), may result in a progressive flattening of the unit hydrograph from very sharp in October to very broad in March. (See Fig. 112.) Each member of the family of unit hydrographs may be usable if it is limited to the proper phase of the annual cycle.

Again, the trend may be related to the position of the snow line.

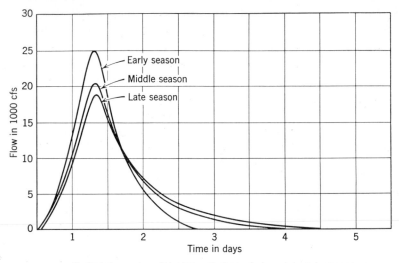

Typical change in unit hydrograph shape during winter rain season

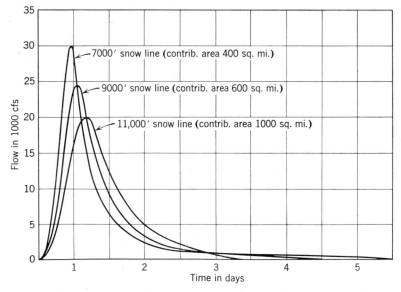

Typical change in unit hydrograph shape with change in snow line elevation

Fig. 112.

(See Fig. 112.) With a snow line at the 7000-ft elevation, the effective contributing area may be only 400 square miles, all in the lower part of the basin. With a snow line at 9000 ft, the effective area may be 600 square miles, with a resultant change in the unit hydrograph. Each member of the unit hydrograph family may be usable if it is limited to the proper elevation of the snow line. During a prolonged storm when the condition of the basin changes significantly during the course of the storm, it may be necessary to change from one unit hydrograph to another, as the storm progresses. Therefore it is seen that considerable ingenuity is necessary to make use of the unit hydrograph in semiarid regions. Frequently conditions are too complex to permit any reliable analysis by this technique.

Stream Gaging

Although a general discussion of stream gaging is presented in Chapter 12, the gaging of streams in a semiarid region requires consideration of many factors normally not important in humid regions.

First, the range of flows is often very great, from zero in the summer dry period to very high during major winter floods. It is therefore necessary to design stream-gaging facilities for an unusually wide range of stages. Because of the long interval between large floods, old high-water marks may have completely disappeared and an intensive search is necessary to determine the proper height of gage houses and cableways. Furthermore, the flow pattern during high floods may differ significantly from that during normal low flows, so that a measuring section selected on the basis of an observed flow pattern during low flows may be unusable during rare high floods. Since the interval between high floods is often impracticably long for direct observation, it is frequently necessary to supplement observation of flow conditions by hypothetical computations, prior to the building of gaging facilities.

Second, the prolonged dry or low-water periods that are characteristic of streams in semiarid regions permit vegetation to invade stream channels and to obstruct them to a variable extent before the next high-water period. As a result, ratings tend to be variable and dependent on the length of time that has elapsed since the last major flood. Regular maintenance cleaning of the control sections or even the provision of an artificial gravel blanket may be necessary to inhibit vegetative growth.

Third, flows in streams draining semiarid areas are usually of too short duration to develop a stable channel section, and occasional high flood flows may change the cross section radically. After a large flood, the control may shift for several years as the channel cross section slowly returns to one consistent with low flows. In extreme cases, an apparently stable channel that has been used for years may be entirely abandoned after a flood, and a new channel may be developed in a different location. During the change-over, the stage at the gage may bear no discernable relation to the flow.

Finally, high flows during rare floods may carry so much sediment that they behave as heavy sand-water or mud mixtures, rather than as normal water. Under these circumstances, flow conditions are radically different, and slope-area computations based on normal formulas and constants may give erroneous results. One source of error in such computations may be the use of low values of the roughness factor that are proper for moderate flows, instead of the extremely high values that probably occur with a sand-water mixture. Another error results from considering the entire cross-sectional area below the high-water profile as effective for flow. It is often probable that at the time of peak flow several feet at the bottom of the cross section may be temporarily occupied by a slow-moving mass of sand that is subsequently swept away before the cross section can be surveyed. Another error results from the extreme surges which often develop in a stream that is eroding and changing its cross section. Such surges may deposit debris far above the average water surface. A flood plane based on such debris may be erroneously high. In view of all the difficulties mentioned before, slope-area computations of peak flows on such streams should be used with great caution.

10

Snow

Walter T. Wilson

Of the approximately 30 in. of mean annual precipitation in the United States, about 4 in. occurs in the form of snow. The proportion of snow to rain increases with latitude and altitude, varying from almost zero at some of the southernmost stations, to nearly 100 per cent at high mountain stations in the North and West. This is particularly true in the Far West, where there is little summer precipitation.

The relatively small fraction of the total precipitation which occurs as snow has an importance that is out of proportion to its magnitude. Because of the low evaporation loss from snow and the delay in its melting, a large portion of it often remains on the ground for long periods. With a low rate of release by melting, nearly all of it enters the soil, whereas with a rapid rate of melt, it often runs off quickly, causing floods. As distinguished from rain, the accumulation of snow on the ground and on structures makes it important in connection with winter sports, agriculture, traffic, and the design and location of highways, railways, buildings, and power and telephone lines. The fact that the availability of water from snow depends on both its occurrence and its melting makes the study of snow more complicated

The author of this chapter is Walter T. Wilson, Hydrologist, U. S. Weather Bureau.

than that of rain. Much has been learned in recent years about the physical properties of snow[1] and of the processes involved in melting and the release of water. However, much of the practical knowledge applied to snow in the United States is empirical, largely because the application of physical laws is rendered difficult by the great variations in time and place of the quantity and properties of snow, and because of the several processes of heat transfer involved in the melting processes.

Definitions, Forms, and Formation

For practical purposes, snow may be regarded as any frozen form of precipitation, with the exception of hail, which is ordinarily a warm-weather phenomenon. This broad definition includes graupel, sleet, freezing rain, and deposits of frost and rime. Even rain falling on a snowpack and being held there, by freezing or capillary forces, may be included. The amount of snowfall is usually expressed in terms of its *water equivalent*, which is defined as the depth of water that would result from melting the snow.

New snow consists of relatively small flat ice crystals having familiar hexagonal shapes, though tiny needles and other forms frequently occur, too. These primary crystals form and grow on suitable condensation nuclei in the atmosphere, at temperatures below freezing. This process is not entirely understood, as it is complicated by the existence of supercooled water droplets at very low temperatures. Ordinarily, snowflakes comprise an aggregate of several of these primary crystals, which collide and adhere as they fall. Much of the rain in the United States consists of water drops which originated as snow particles, but melted while falling and grew by vapor exchange, collision, and other processes.

Areal Distribution and Frequency

Figure 113[2] shows the distribution of average annual snowfall throughout the United States. It may be observed from this map that the amount of snow increases northward from the Gulf of Mexico. It may be seen from the map that altitude is also an important factor, particularly in the West.

Within the large-scale climatic pattern of Fig. 113, variations in seasonal snow accumulation are related to the influence of topography,

[1] See publications of the Snow, Ice, and Permafrost Research Establishment, U. S. Army Corps of Engineers.

[2] U. S. Department of Agriculture, "Climate and Man," *Yearbook Agr.,* 1941, p. 227.

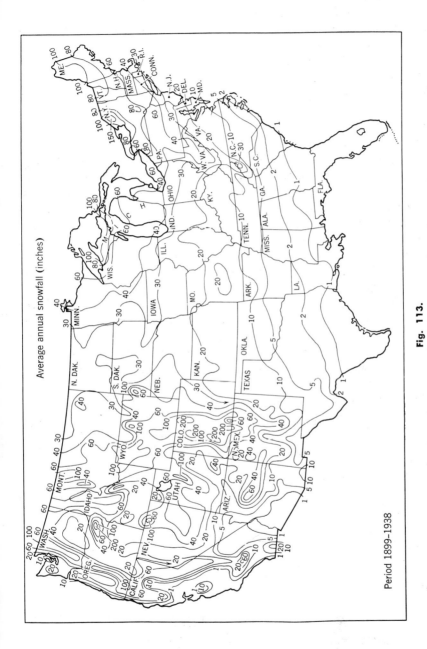

Average annual snowfall (inches)

Fig. 113.

Period 1899-1938

of which elevation is the predominant factor. Other topographic parameters are orientation, size of exposure sector, and steepness of slope.[3] Size of exposure sector distinguishes sheltered canyons from open prairies.

At any particular location, snow deposit may diminish with elevation, as indicated by the fact that wind-blown crests are relatively bare. However, deposits of snow may cling on the lee side of crests in the form of cornices. Windward slopes of small hills may frequently be swept clear of snow, whereas snow is deposited in the lee— much as with a snow fence. Snow accumulates in concavities even as small as plow furrows and is relatively shallow on projecting features of micro-relief. Individual trees and even small structures often have important effects, as everyone knows who has shoveled his driveway or sidewalk. Obstructions a few feet high commonly produce drifting to twenty times their height on the lee side and to as much as five times their height on the windward side. It is often difficult to determine whether observed variations result from one or more of the foregoing causes or from observational errors.[4] Observational errors include those of weighing and measuring during cold, windy weather and failure to get a satisfactory core with a snow tube. For example, with freezing weather and a snowpack containing wet snow in its lower strata, the cold tube may clog when it reaches the wet snow and chill the snow to freezing.

With respect to variability of seasonal snowpack,[5] in general, for regions where appreciable snowpack accumulates, the maximum recorded seasonal snowfall is about twice the mean annual. This two-to-one ratio corresponds to a frequency of about 1 yr in 50, although most periods of record are too short for accurate determination. For a frequency of once in 10 yr, the seasonal fall is about 60 per cent more than the mean annual.

The so-called lake effect is noteworthy;[6] in the Great Lakes region, stations on the lee shore of the lake receive more snow than stations farther back, or than those on the opposite shore. The air passing over these lakes in wintertime is heated from below by the relatively

[3] W. C. Spreen, "A Determination of the Effect of Topography upon Precipitation," *Trans. Am. Geophys. Union,* 1947, No. 2, pp. 285–290.

[4] W. T. Wilson, "Analysis of Winter Precipitation Observations in the Cooperative Snow Investigations," *Monthly Weather Rev.,* July 1954, pp. 183–199.

[5] R. D. Tarble and W. T. Wilson, "Estimated Frequencies and Extreme Values of Snow-pack Water Equivalent at Major Cities in U. S.," *Trans. Am. Geophys. Union,* vol. 33, pp. 871–880, 1952.

[6] B. L. Wiggin, "Great Snow of the Great Lakes," *Weatherwise,* December 1950, pp. 122–126.

warm water and becomes unstable. At the same time, these air masses pick up water vapor in passing over the lake. Snow flurries result when the air masses reach the far side and are forced to rise by the adjacent land mass.

Forest cover has an important influence on the accumulation and melting of snow.[7] A very dense cover may intercept a large part of the total fall, some of which may be blown into nearby clearings where the average accumulation usually exceeds that under the trees. The snow that reaches the ground under forest cover is protected from melting and evaporation by the forest canopy, which shades it and prevents the free circulation of air in contact with the snow. The net effect of forest cover is usually that the snow remains on the ground longer than in nearby open areas.

Seasonal Distribution and Extreme Occurrences

The seasonal distribution of snowpack is a function of the amount of fall and of the rate of melting. At stations having only a few falls per year, the maximum rate of fall and the maximum depth may occur with nearly equal likelihood anytime when the weather is sufficiently cold. At many mountain stations, snow has fallen every month of the year. At stations where great packs accumulate, the maximum depth usually occurs in January or February. The greatest water equivalent in the pack usually occurs in April, and ordinarily by late June almost all the snow has melted. Figure 114, from "Climate and Man," shows the average duration of snow cover of 1 in. or more depth in number of days per year.

Table 27 lists for selected first-order stations in the United States the mean seasonal snowfall, maximum seasonal snowfall, maximum fall occurring in 24 hr, the maximum recorded depth on the ground, and the average first date of 1 in. or more of snowfall. The period of record averages 50 to 60 yr for most of these stations. In a few instances, the figure given for seasonal maximum is for a calendar year instead of a single snow season.

At mountain stations, orographic falls of snow exceeding 5 ft in one day have occurred occasionally, but very few cities have experienced storms depositing snow at rates exceeding 1 in. per hr. Converted to water equivalent, this rate of rainfall is not very heavy. With moisture charge great enough for precipitation to occur at rates much higher than this, the air temperature has to exceed 32° F, and rain instead of snow occurs.

[7] H. G. Wilm, "The Influence of Forest Cover on Snow-melt," *Trans. Am. Geophys. Union*, No. 4, 1948, pp. 547–556.

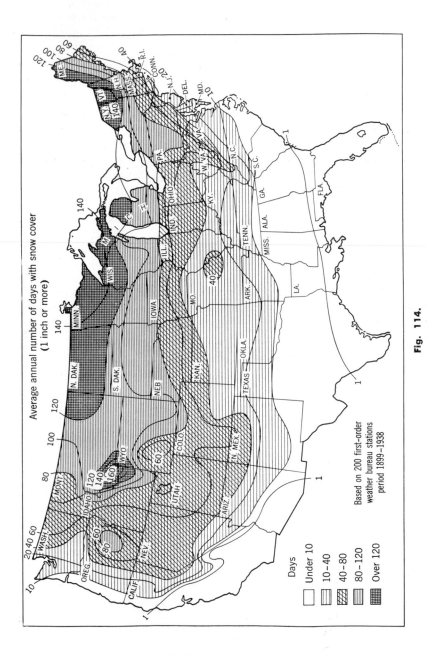

Average annual number of days with snow cover
(1 inch or more)

Based on 200 first-order
weather bureau stations
period 1899–1938

Days

Under 10
10–40
40–80
80–120
Over 120

Fig. 114.

TABLE 27

Station	Snowfall in Inches				Average 1st Date of 1 in. or More of Snowfall*
	Mean Seasonal	Max. Seasonal	Max. 24-hr	Max. Depth on Ground	
Albany, N. Y.	49.2	110.0	30.1	46.0	Dec. 2
Albuquerque, N. M.	7.3	23.4	6.8	6.8	Dec. 24
Alpena, Mich.	64.9	136.1	16.8	33.0	Nov. 17
Atlanta, Ga.	2.5	13.2	8.3	8.3	Jan. 17
Baker, Oreg.	40.7	71.6	16.7	18.6	Nov. 23
Bismarck, N. D.	34.3	88.3	13.5	22.4	Nov. 7
Boston, Mass.	42.8	89.2	16.5	23.0	Dec. 14
Charles City, Ia.	40.0	67.2	17.5	30.0	Nov. 26
Chicago, Ill.	33.0	64.1	14.9	24.7	Dec. 6
Cincinnati, Ohio	18.3	40.4	11.0	13.5	Dec. 16
Cleveland, Ohio	40.4	80.9	22.2	19.0	Nov. 28
Columbia, Mo.	20.0	46.2	12.8	13.0	Dec. 19
Dallas, Tex.	2.7	9.8	7.1	7.1	Jan. 11
Denver, Colo.	55.2	118.7	23.0	32.6	Oct. 27
Detroit, Mich	40.7	78.0	24.5	26.3	Dec. 1
Little Rock, Ark.	4.8	26.0	13.0	15.0	Jan. 15
Tucson, Ariz.	1.1	6.0	3.5	3.5	Jan. 10
Washington, D. C.	20.8	54.4	25.0	34.2	Dec. 22
Wichita, Kan.	14.2	39.7	12.3	12.0	Dec. 18
Yellowstone National Park, Wyo.	90.6	143.4	13.1	35.6	Oct. 12

* H. C. S. Thom, "Probabilities of One-inch Snowfall Thresholds for the U.S.," *Monthly Weather Rev.*, 1957, vol. 85, pp. 269–271.

Probably the greatest snowpack ever observed on the North American continent was measured March 30, 1946, at Loch Lomond snow course in British Columbia. It had an average water equivalent of 146 in. and a depth of 305 in.[8] The greatest depth of snow observed in the United States was at Tamarack, California, March 9, 1911— 454 in. The water equivalent was not measured. The average seasonal fall at Tamarack is 449 in., with an average depth on the ground March 15 of 144 in. During the winter of 1906–1907, 884 in. of snow fell at this station and in January 1911, 390 in. of snow fell.[9]

[8] R. C. Farrow, "Report of Committee on Snow, 1947–1948," *Trans. Am. Geophys. Union*, June 1949, pp. 444–451.

[9] Malcolm Sprague, "Monthly and Seasonal Distribution of Snowfall in California," *Monthly Weather Rev.*, No. 62, 1934, pp. 438–441.

On February 2, 1895, at Galveston, Texas, 15.4 in. fell and as much as 2 ft fell at places east of there, near the Gulf Coast.

Most snow falls at temperatures near 30° F. Although it is never "too cold to snow," very cold air has extremely little moisture charge and can support only low rates of precipitation. For example, in Arctic regions the annual snowfall measurements seldom exceed 10 in. water equivalent. On the other hand, snow has been known to fall through shallow layers of warm air having temperatures higher than 50° F at the ground surface.[10]

Where snowfall is so great and melting so little that the snow cover persists perennially, this old snowpack is called neve or firn and is very dense. Such deposits are usually small in the United States, except in Alaska, and confined to sheltered exposures at high elevations. A snowpack becomes an ice field when it is so dense that the voids or air pores are no longer connected. Glaciers may be distinguished from these perennial snow or ice fields by their plastic flow, usually of several feet per year. At the upper end of a glacier, the average excess of snow accumulation over melting approximately compensates for the glacier's downward movement. At the lower end or terminus of the glacier, the elevation is reduced enough for higher temperature, more melting, and possibly less accumulation of snow to occur. Thus a position of balance with the glacier's downward movement is maintained. Since about 1900, this balance has been at least temporarily upset by a small but definite upward trend of temperature in the United States which has resulted in a recession of most glaciers.

In the Sierras of central and southern California, and in Colorado, glaciers are usually found at elevations above 12,000 ft. Farther north, and especially near the Pacific Coast, where phenomenal falls of snow accumulate, glaciers are found at lower elevations. An example is Nisqually Glacier on Mt. Rainier, which extends down to less than 5000 ft elevation.

One type of glacier, entirely different from glaciers found in the high mountain valleys of the United States, is known as an ice cap, a prominent example of which covers most of Greenland. Fragments of these ice caps and glaciers break off from their lower edges at coast lines and become icebergs. Reference may be made to the chapter by Matthes in Meinzer's *Hydrology*[11] for a comprehensive discussion of glaciers.

10 J. P. McAuliffe, "Sleet and Snow at Unusually High Temperatures," *Monthly Weather Rev.*, No. 57, 1929, p. 460.

11 O. E. Meinzer, editor, "Physics of the Earth, IX," *Hydrology,* Chapter on Glaciers by F. E. Matthes.

Physical Properties of the Snowpack

Density. The specific gravity of freshly fallen snow varies over a wide range but the average is about 10 per cent, or, in other words, a 10-in. column of new snow contains about 1 in. of water. However, the longer the snow remains on the ground, the denser it becomes. This is a result of packing, alternate thawing and freezing, condensation, and the presence of absorbed rainfall and melt water. Specific gravities of 20 or 30 per cent are common, and values as high as 50 or 60 per cent occur occasionally.[12]

To translate seasonal fall into approximate water equivalent of accumulated snowpack,[13] empirical relationships may be applied. The proportion of total seasonal fall which contributes to the maximum pack for the season seldom exceeds 70 per cent at most stations. The remaining 30 per cent or more is comprised of falls occurring too late in the season and of losses from evaporation and melting prior to the time of maximum accumulation.

Structure. In the autumn, initial flurries of snow may fall on bare ground and melt. But eventually, because of cooling of the air and ground and additional falls of snow, a seasonal pack begins to accumulate in cold regions. In the intervals between successive falls of snow there may be slight melting at the upper surface of the snowpack. A crust may be formed by intermittent melting and freezing. Such crusts persist, under subsequent falls of snow, as identifying boundaries which mark in profile the top of each deposit of snow. These deposited layers have a tendency to follow the configuration of the underlying ground surface, as does the entire snowpack.

As the snowpack ages during the winter and spring season, the snow crystals undergo change. The flaky, feathery texture of the original hexagonal crystals gives way to a granular structure, due to circulation of water and water vapor and to intermittent melting and freezing. As this process continues, the snow grains merge and enlarge, until, after several months, they may assume the appearance of rock salt and are referred to as "corn" snow. This process is associated with settling and an increase in density of the snow.

Water Storage and Movement. When warm weather causes melting, or when rain occurs, water percolates to the lateral crusts or ice

[12] *Engineering Manual for Civil Works,* Part III, Chapt. 5, "Hydrologic and Hydraulic Analyses," War Department, Office of the Chief of Engineers, Washington, D. C.

[13] R. D. Tarble and W. T. Wilson, "Estimated Frequencies and Extreme Values of Snow-pack Water Equivalent at Major Cities in the U.S.," *Trans. Am. Geophys. Union,* vol. 33, pp. 871–880, 1952.

layers. Because of the relatively great density and intimate particle contacts along these crusts, water is conducted laterally within them.

Usually, after lateral movement of only a few feet on or through these crusts, gravity forces overcome the capillary forces, and the water breaks through the layer. This break-through may result from the building up of perched water tables melting through where relatively warm water accumulates, or from local variations in the permeability or structure of the snow. Because of the coarseness of its texture, most snow seldom supports capillary columns greater than 1 in.

Experiments with cores of snow to which cold water has been applied and allowed to drain show that seldom is the liquid water content of the snow more than 5 per cent of the total water equivalent. This percentage indicates the maximum capacity of a natural snow-pack for storing water in liquid form.[14] Values greater than this may be regarded as transient.

Recession curves of streamflow from melting snow on small water-sheds of thin soil mantle indicate very little storage and rapid rate of drainage. Laboratory and field experiments indicate as a rough average for deep mountain snowpacks that the lag due to percolation of melt water or rain water through the snowpack is about 1 hr, plus ½ hr for each foot depth of the snow. In many drainage areas of appreciable size, the lag due to percolation through the snowpack is so small compared to the lag in the soil and channels that its effect may be ignored and included in the aggregate average basin characteristics.[15]

Evaporation

The principles that govern evaporation from snow are the same as for evaporation from water and soil (see page 196). However, the vapor pressure at the snow surface is limited by a maximum snow temperature of 32° F, whereas water and soil temperatures may be much higher. Furthermore, the air over a snow surface is usually more stable than over water; thus the amount of turbulent mixing is reduced. If water evaporation formulas are applied to conditions that exist during snow cover, rates of less than 1 in. per month are

[14] R. W. Gerdel, "Physical Changes in Snow Cover Leading to Runoff, Especially Floods," *Proc.*, General Assembly, *Intern. Assoc. Sci. Hydrol.*, Oslo, 1948, vol. 2, pp. 42–54, 1949.

[15] W. G. Hoyt, "Some Characteristics of Winter and Non-winter Floods in the St. Lawrence River Drainage Basin," *Proc. Central Snow Conference,* E. Lansing, Mich., 1941, pp. 176–192.

usually obtained. Evaporation losses from a snowpack are balanced to some extent by condensation on the snow during periods of high humidity, when the vapor pressure in the air is greater than the saturated vapor pressure at the temperature of the snow surface.

Attempts to measure evaporation from snow as a residual in the hydrologic storage equation or by successive snow surveys during periods of no melting and no precipitation are inconclusive. Comparisons between accumulated snowpack and accumulated snow received in a precipitation gage protected from evaporation loss by an oil film are also inconclusive. These methods provide no way to interpret the effects of changing weather during the periods covered. Errors due to differences in exposure, to sampling, and in estimating large elements other than evaporation are so great as to obscure evaporation, which is usually a small residual.

In attempting to determine evaporation from a land surface by the use of turbulent exchange methods, Thornthwaite and Holzman (see Chapter 7) made their observations during a period which included a few days of snow cover. Their results showed that net evaporation exceeded condensation but still averaged less than 0.01 in. of water equivalent per day.

Pans have also been used to determine evaporation from snow. However, the pan itself influences the evaporation from the snow it contains. It has a tendency to trap heat and moisture, and the unnatural wetness of the confined snow probably leads to more evaporation than from snow in situ. Pan observations by Church,[16] Horton,[17] Croft,[18] Kehrlein,[19] and others, over many years and under a wide variety of conditions, indicate that evaporation from snow seldom exceeds 1 in. of water equivalent per month. Daily amounts are usually small enough to neglect among the large uncertainties of the more important hydrologic elements.

Sublimation is defined as direct loss of vapor from a solid, without the solid's passing through the usual intermediate liquid state. It is difficult and seldom necessary to distinguish between evaporation and sublimation from snow.

[16] J. E. Church, "Evaporation at High Altitudes and Latitudes," *Trans. Am. Geophys. Union*, 1934, Part II, pp. 326–351.

[17] R. E. Horton, "Water Losses in High Latitudes and at High Elevations," *Trans. Am. Geophys. Union*, Part II, 1934, pp. 351–379.

[18] A. R. Croft, "Evaporation from Snow," *Bull. Am. Meteorol. Soc.*, October 1944, vol. 25, pp. 334–337.

[19] Oliver Kehrlein, Eugene Serr, R. D. Tarble, and W. T. Wilson, "High Sierra Snow-ablation Observations," *Proc. Western Snow Conference*, April 1953, pp. 47–52.

The Melting Process

Snow melts as a result of the transfer of heat to the snow from the atmosphere, from warm rainfall, from the soil, and by radiation.

Because of the low conductivity of air, very little heat can be transmitted to the snow from still air. However, when air is in motion, the turbulent mixing process constantly replaces the air that is in contact with the snow with a new supply of warm, moist air. The atmospheric heat is transmitted to the snow by two processes: by the conduction of heat from the air to the snow and by condensation of atmospheric water vapor on the snow surface. The combined process may be expressed by the following simplified equation:

$$\text{Melt} = V[K_1(T_a - 32°) + K_2(p_a - 6.11)]$$

in which V is the wind velocity at a point above the snow, T_a is the air temperature above the snow in degrees Fahrenheit, and p_a is the vapor pressure above the snow in millibars. The term $(T_a - 32°)$ is the temperature gradient between the snow surface (temperature $32°$) and the air a short distance above the snow. The term $(p_a - 6.11)$ is the corresponding vapor pressure gradient, with 6.11 as the pressure of saturated vapor at $32°$ F. The constants K_1 and K_2 vary with the location and height of the instruments measuring V, T_a and p_a, the roughness of the surrounding terrain, and other factors. Attempts to use formulas of this kind have met with limited success.

The quantity of heat carried to the snow by a given amount of warm rain water may be computed if the temperature of the rain is known and if it is assumed that the rain is cooled to $32°$ F. The heat lost by each pound of rain water is $(T_r - 32)$ Btu, in which T_r is the temperature of the rain in degrees F. Because it requires 144 Btu to melt 1 lb of ice, each pound of rain water melts $(T_r - 32)/144$ lb of snow. It follows that any depth of rain, P, provides the depth of water from snow melt, D, shown by the following equation, in which D and P must be in the same units:

$$D = \frac{P(T_r - 32)}{144}$$

It has been indicated[20] that the temperature of the rain is usually about the same as the wet-bulb temperature.

Warm soil, because of its high density and specific heat, often

---

[20] W. T. Wilson, "An Outline of the Thermodynamics of Snow-Melt," *Trans. Am. Geophys. Union*, 1941, Part I, p. 182.

causes snow to melt as it falls. Matted vegetation between the soil and snow may provide a poor thermal contact and retard this process. An example of retardation is the rapid melting of snow falling on bare soil compared with the accumulation of snow on a nearby grassy surface. Once a snowpack becomes established and a relatively steady state exists, the conductivity of soil governs the rate of heat transfer. As a rough approximation, soil conducts heat about ten times as fast as snow.

The thermal conductivity of soil varies manyfold with normal changes in soil moisture content. Temperature gradients in the soil underlying a snowpack are seldom great. Computations based on average moisture content and average temperature gradients indicate rates of heat transfer and of melting snow that are consistent with observed minimum winter flow of streams, which do not continue their autumn recession, but often flow at a rate of about 0.01 in. average depth of water per day over the drainage area.

Heat is transmitted to snow both by long-wave terrestrial radiation and by short-wave radiation from the sun and sky. There is an exchange of heat by long-wave radiation between the snow and forest cover, atmospheric water vapor, and clouds. On cold, clear nights there is a net transfer of heat by long-wave radiation from the snow to interstellar space.

The amount of heat received from short-wave solar and diffuse sky radiation varies with the thickness and distribution of cloud cover, the angle of incidence with the sun, the amount of forest cover, and the reflectivity of the snow surface which commonly varies from 50 to 90 per cent. During an entire season, short-wave radiation is usually the principal cause of snow melt. However, during flood periods, when there is likely to be a dense cloud cover, this source is much less important.

Fortunately, air temperature as observed in a standard shelter is related to the factors which govern both the transmission of heat from the atmosphere and radiation from the sun. Air temperature is a common factor in the various methods of heat transfer, and, because of air circulation, a single measuring point represents a considerable area and time. For these reasons the degree-day method is commonly used as a practical means for estimating snow melt.

The degree-day method is based on the fact that air temperature at one or more index stations is the most important single meteorological characteristic influencing the rate of snow melt resulting from atmospheric heat and radiation. Snow melt is approximately proportional to the number of degree-days above a base temperature, which is usually taken as 32° F.[21] This relationship may be expressed by the equation

$$M = C(T_a - T_b)$$

where M is snow melt in inches of water per day, C is the degree-day factor, T_a is the air temperature, and T_b a temperature base, both in degrees Fahrenheit.

The air temperature is the average daily temperature (average of the maximum and minimum for the day) for the snow area. In mountainous areas, if the temperature records are obtained at an elevation not representative of the snow field, the temperature may be corrected[22,23] by assuming a standard lapse rate of 3° F per 1000 ft of elevation.

The degree-day factor varies from about 0.02 to 0.13 in. per degree-day. The smaller values are for areas sheltered by forest cover, whereas the larger ones are for unsheltered areas having a southerly exposure. For more average conditions representative of entire drainage basins, the factors usually are in the range from 0.04 to 0.10. A value of 0.05 has been found to give good results for storm periods in Michigan. The degree-day factor usually varies with time of year and is higher when the sun is higher and the days are longer.[24]

Forecasting Streamflow from Melting Snow

Seasonal Volume. In many drainage areas of the colder parts of the United States, a large portion of the annual precipitation occurs as snow and lies on the ground for several months, awaiting release by the melting temperatures of spring and summer. This lag of several months between the occurrence of precipitation and its resulting streamflow allows seasonal water-supply forecasts to be made. This is particularly important in the West, where many valleys have dry summers. These forecasts are often made at the beginning of each month, January through May, with increasing precision as the season advances and an increasing portion of the seasonal precipitation has been observed.

[21] North Pacific Division, Corps of Engineers, U. S. Army, "Snow Hydrology," 1956, pp. 244–245.

[22] *Ibid.*

[23] Ray K. Linsley, Jr., "A Simple Procedure for the Day-to-Day Forecasting of Runoff from Snow-melt," *Trans. Am. Geophys. Union,* 1943, Part III, pp. 62–67.

[24] L. L. Weiss and W. T. Wilson, "Snow-Melt Degree-Day Ratios Determined by Snow Laboratory Data," *Trans. Am. Geophys. Union,* August 1958, pp. 681–688.

One method of forecasting is based on snow surveys[25,26] that are frequently weighted according to elevation of the snow-survey station and the portion of basin area in each elevation zone. A curve of relationship between water equivalent of the snowpack and subsequent seasonal volume of runoff is determined from previous records. Having established such a relationship, early spring snow survey data serves as a basis for estimating the subsequent season's runoff.

Inasmuch as the seasonal runoff from basins having great packs of snow usually occurs during about the same length of period each season, the greater the volume of runoff, the higher the peak rate is likely to be. This fact enables fair forecasts of the magnitude of the seasonal peak flow to be made several months in advance, but reliable forecasts cannot be made until the effects of possible rain or unusual temperature can be assessed, nearer the time of the peak.

The United States Weather Bureau[27] uses precipitation data instead of snow surveys for making forecasts. This method has the advantage of a longer period of record on which to base the relationship and enables a better sampling of terrain parameters to be made. In this method, each station-month of record is weighted, both as to time of year and as to station characteristics. This computing is done by statistical methods, which integrate the many terrain factors without identifying the effects of each factor. Different weights for different stations express the combined effects of each station's elevation, orientation, exposure sector, etc. The monthly weights reflect the varying effectiveness of precipitation falling at different times of year. On the average, lower monthly weights are assigned the spring and autumn precipitation, which includes considerable rain, and higher monthly weights apply to winter precipitation, which is nearly all snow. The station records are subjected to double-mass analysis[28] to accommodate changes in station exposure and method of observation during the period of record of each station. A further operation, when the record shows a basin-storage carry-over from season to season, takes into account the precipitation of earlier years. The use

[25] R. A. Work, H. G. Wilm, and Morlan W. Nelson, "Use of Snow Surveys in Planning Regulation of Columbia River Floods," Western Snow Conference, Victoria, B. C., 1951.

[26] H. P. Boardman, "Snow Surveys for Forecasting Streamflow in Western Nevada," Univ. Nev. Agr. Expt. Sta., Bull No. 184, Reno, Nevada, 1949.

[27] R. K. Linsley, Jr., and M. A. Kohler, "Recent Developments in Water Supply Forecasting from Precipitation," Trans. Am. Geophys. Union, June 1949, pp. 427–436.

[28] C. F. Merriam, "A Comprehensive Study of the Rainfall of the Susquehanna Valley," Trans. Am. Geophys. Union, 1937, pp. 471–476.

of both snow survey and precipitation data results in better seasonal forecasts than does the use of either type of data alone.

Daily Rates of Streamflow from Melting Snow. When snow melt occurs rapidly over a short period of time, as is typical of the eastern portion of the United States, the resulting runoff has the same characteristics as that derived from rainfall, and the unit hydrograph (Chapter 8) may be used to predict runoff rates.

Where snow melt continues during the entire spring and early summer, as in the mountain basins of the western portion of the United States, the relationship between snow melt and runoff is often represented by a double-mass curve in which accumulated runoff is plotted against accumulated degree days.[29,30,31] A modification of this procedure has been described by Linsley.[32]

Phenomena of Frozen Soil

The heat conductivity of soil increases greatly with increased water content of the soil. Unless the soil moisture content is known, the computations to determine the conduction of heat may be very approximate. On the average, the annual temperature cycle in soil and rock is usually negligible at depths greater than 30 ft, and the diurnal cycle, as with snow, has negligible range at depths much greater than 1 ft. The lag in the annual temperature cycle increases with depth, and at depths of 15 to 20 ft it amounts to about 6 months, with the paradoxical result that the temperature at those depths is highest in winter and lowest in summer.

The mean annual temperature of the upper stratum of soil is about the same as that of the lowest layer of the air. From the depth of negligible annual temperature variation downward, the soil and rock increase in temperature an average of about 1° F per 80 ft, with gradients ranging from about half to twice this value. The outward flow of heat from the interior of the earth averages about 3 cal per sq cm per month.

In the extreme northern portion of central United States, the soil freezes nearly every winter to depths as great as 6 or 8 ft. The alternate expansion and contraction of the upper layer of soil, as

[29] North Pacific Division, Corps of Engineers, U. S. Army, "Snow Hydrology," 1956, p. 250.

[30] Stanley A. Miller, "Some Snow-Melt Runoff Characteristics," *Trans. Am. Geophys. Union,* October 1950, pp. 741–749.

[31] W. T. Wilson, "Some Factors Relating the Melting of Snow to Its Causes," *Proc. Central Snow Conference,* vol. 1, December 1941, pp. 33–41.

[32] Ray K. Linsley Jr., "A Simple Procedure for the Day-to-Day Forecasting of Runoff from Snow-Melt," *Trans. Am. Geophys. Union,* 1943, Part III, pp. 62–67.

the water in it freezes and thaws, produce action known as heaving, which poses serious problems with highways and other structures. When moist soil freezes, it expands because of the formation of ice, which has greater volume per unit mass than water in the liquid state. When the expanded soil thaws, instead of immediately settling back into its original shape and position, cavities are formed. Water enters these cavities, and the next freezing cycle causes additional expansion. Soils of moderate texture usually cause the most trouble. Clay is too impervious to permit much transmission of water in this process, and sand is usually too well drained. The problem becomes very complicated in areas where there is great variability of soil properties from place to place. The solution to this problem is usually provided by good drainage.

Permafrost is the condition that exists in regions where the soil is normally frozen to great depths and only a shallow surface layer thaws during the summer. In much of Canada, Alaska, and other extremely cold places permafrost is common. In general, permafrost requires a mean annual temperature a few degrees below freezing, and, in some places, depths of several hundred feet have been observed. Permafrost causes serious problems in construction work of nearly every kind. After a house built on permafrost is heated, the permafrost under the house thaws. The released water cannot percolate readily into the surrounding permafrost, which remains frozen. The house then literally floats in a basin of mud, with unequal settlement at various places and times. To avoid this situation, it is common practice to build structures in the Arctic on well-drained gravel "mats," or on piles which permit the circulation of air between the building and the soil. The heat from the building then does not thaw the underlying soil.[33,34,35]

Snow Loads on Structures

Any structure subjected to snow or freezing rain should be designed for a snow load of at least 10 lb per sq ft. Although it is unlikely that snow will accumulate on roofs to the depths it reaches on the ground, Table 27 and the information given earlier about frequencies may be a safe guide.

In addition to the static loads of snow resting on a roof or other surface, there is a severe type of loading which is analogous to what

[33] A. E. Benfield, "Earth Heat," *Sci. American*, December 1950, pp. 54–57.

[34] S. W. Muller, "Permafrost," Edwards Bros., Ann Arbor, Mich., 1947.

[35] H. B. Atkinson and C. E. Bey, "Some Factors Affecting Frost Penetration," *Trans. Am. Geophys. Union*, 1940, Part III, pp. 935–948.

is known as the projection condition of soil fill on culverts. An example of this loading is a brace or guy, enveloped in a snowpack, which supports not only the column of snow directly above it, but also a much greater load. As the snow settles, frictional forces develop between the column of snow directly above the guy, or other member, and the adjoining snow, which settles faster. Horizontal structural members or guys may thus be subjected to exceptionally heavy loads which may cause their failure.

11

Floods

Importance of Flood Studies

Floods in the United States cause extensive property damage, probably amounting to as much as $100,000,000 annually, in addition to a toll of human lives on which no monetary value can be placed. A full realization of the magnitude of the stakes involved in the solution of existing flood problems should impress those in charge of these studies with a deep sense of responsibility and obligation and should imbue them with a determination to spare no efforts to obtain the most reliable results possible. Nevertheless, except in the more important hydraulic structures, it is not uncommon for those in charge to devote an incredibly short time to the determination of the magnitude of the flood for which the structure should be designed. Far too frequently, all that is done is to apply a few convenient formulas, or perhaps to determine from the records what the maximum flood has been in the past and then add 25 or 30 per cent as a factor of safety. On the other hand, months are spent on structural design. This situation, perhaps, explains why dams, bridges, and culverts rarely fail because of structural defects; for it is a matter of record that a far greater number of such failures are the direct result of faulty determinations of the magnitude of the floods for which these structures should be designed.

The proper solution to this problem lies in making the best possible use of all available data. What are the data that are pertinent? In the first place there are, of course, the records of floods in the past, if any records exist; but just as important are the records pertaining to *the factors that affected and determined the magnitudes of those floods.* This latter type of data is too frequently ignored. It is difficult to understand why these additional data are not used more frequently for they are almost always available whenever flood records are available. Methods of using the data mentioned above are outlined in this chapter, following a general discussion of floods and of methods of estimating their magnitude and frequency.

Definition of Flood

A flood commonly is considered to be an unusually high stage of the river. It is often described as that stage at which the stream channel becomes filled and above which it overflows its banks. The valley then becomes "flooded." In *Webster's New International Dictionary,* a "flood" is defined as "a great flow of water; . . . especially, a body of water, rising, swelling, and overflowing land not usually thus covered; a deluge; a freshet; an inundation."

Inasmuch as the banks of a stream vary in height throughout its course, there is no definite stage above which a river can be said to be in flood and below which it is not in flood. Frequently, however, especially on the more important rivers, an arbitrary elevation has often been established, either by the U. S. Army Engineers or by others in authority, that is called "flood stage."

Causes of Floods

All floods are primarily due to surface runoff. Any drainage basin with soil so pervious that its infiltration capacity is never exceeded is rarely subject to floods. As an illustration, the Manistee River in Michigan, which is fed primarily by ground water, experiences no serious floods. (See Fig. 5.)

Floods may result from (1) an intense rainfall, (2) the melting of accumulated snow, or (3) the melting of snow combined with rain. In the southern states the melting of snow is seldom a factor in flood production, whereas in many parts of Canada it is the most common cause. In the latitude of southern New York and Michigan, floods result from all three of these causes. It is not uncommon in this latitude for the greatest floods on large drainage basins to result from an early warm spring rain falling on melting snow, whereas on small basins in the same area the largest floods may result from intense summer thunderstorms.

In any flood study the first problem is the determination of the factors that combine to produce floods on that particular basin. It may be found that some floods on the basin being studied result from each of the three causes mentioned above. If the problem involves the determination of the maximum flood to which the basin would ever be subjected, attention should be directed toward learning the cause or causes that produce the major floods. It may happen that the majority of the floods on this stream are caused by summer storms but that all major floods result from the melting of snows. If so, all summer floods may be disregarded and the investigation confined to floods produced by the melting of snow.

Furthermore, if it is found that all major floods are the result of rainfall, attention should next be directed toward determining the character and origin of these storms. As an illustration, Ruff,[1] in a study of the nature and origin of the storms that cause floods in Pennsylvania, examined the paths of the low-pressure areas for several days preceding a number of the largest floods that have occurred on all the principal streams and their tributaries in the state. As a result he found that winter floods occurring throughout the state were caused by storms that moved up the Ohio Valley in a northeasterly direction. Summer floods on streams west of the Appalachian Mountains were found to result from storms having the same origin and direction of travel. However, for all streams east of the Appalachians, the summer flood-producing rains came, in general, from the south. Such information is of great value, especially in comparing the magnitude and frequency of storms and floods in two or more nearby drainage basins.

Seasonal Distribution of Floods

In most regions floods occur more frequently in certain seasons of the year than in others. In *Water-Supply Paper* 771 the U. S. Geological Survey presents data on the principal floods that have been recorded on many of the more important streams in the United States. In order to show the seasonal occurrence of floods and the manner of seasonal variations throughout the country, ten typical streams whose records are listed in this publication have been selected and the percentages of the total number of recorded floods that have occurred during each month of the year have been computed. The results are shown in Fig. 115. Also shown for each stream are the area of basin, the number of floods, and the length of record.

[1] Charles F. Ruff, "Maximum Probable Floods on Pennsylvania Streams," *Proc. A.S.C.E.*, September 1940, vol. 66, No. 7.

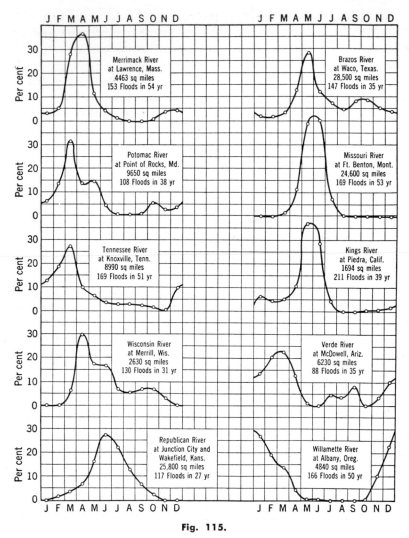

Fig. 115.

A study of this figure shows that in every basin there are a few months each year during which a major portion of the floods occur. For instance, in New England the Merrimack River is much more subject to floods during the months of March, April, and May than at other times, with the greatest number occurring in April. On the Potomac and on the Tennessee, the season advances slightly, with the greatest number occurring in March. On midwestern streams the season is delayed somewhat, reaching the peak in April, May, or

June. In the Far West, the flood period varies greatly. For instance, on the Kings River in California and on the Missouri River in Montana, most of the floods occur in May and June, whereas on the Willamette River in Oregon nearly all occur in the winter, with only a rare occurrence during the summer months from May to October inclusive.

Although usually the major floods occur during the period of greatest frequency, they perhaps do so only in conformance to the theory of probability. As a result, one of the greatest floods on a stream may occur when least expected. As an illustration, of 153 floods in 54 yr of records on the Merrimack River, only 6 occurred in November. Nevertheless one of those 6 was the second largest ever recorded on that stream.[2]

Is the Flood Hazard Increasing?

Nearly every year disastrous record-breaking floods occur on some streams in the United States and therefore there is a widespread belief among the general public that floods are increasing in magnitude and in frequency. A hasty survey might easily lead to such a conclusion. For instance, in over 100 yr of records at Sewickley, Pennsylvania, the maximum known discharge prior to 1936 was 413,000 cfs on March 15, 1907. On March 18, 1936, a peak flow of 574,000 cfs was recorded. On the Potomac River at Point of Rocks, Maryland, in nearly 90 yr of records the maximum flood prior to 1936 was 320,000 cfs on June 2, 1889. In March 1936, the discharge was 480,000 cfs. On the Connecticut River at Springfield, Massachusetts, in 140 yr of records, the greatest flood recorded was 281,000 cfs on March 19, 1936. The second highest flood in this period was 188,000 cfs on November 6, 1927. Many similar cases could be cited tending to show that the greatest floods have occurred in the most recent portion of the period of records.

Caution should be used, however, in coming to the conclusion that flood discharges are increasing in magnitude. It is well to remember that flood records are constantly growing longer. If 50 yr of discharge records are available on a given stream, and another 50 yr of records are added, the chances are even that the second 50-yr period will contain the record of a flood that is greater than any flood recorded during the first 50 yr. If we were to study the records of all the streams in the United States and find that for all streams, or even for a goodly majority of streams, the more recent half of those records

---

[2] A table showing records of 997 unusual flood peaks in the United States and foreign countries, with the dates of their occurrences, is given in Creager, Justin, and Hinds, *Engineering for Dams*, vol. I, John Wiley, 1945.

contained flood flows that are higher than any recorded in the earlier years, we would then have good evidence that the magnitude of floods is increasing. It is doubtful, however, that we would obtain this result.

Although it is questionable whether flood *discharges* are increasing on the majority of streams, it is only reasonable to believe that flood *stages* are increasing on most rivers, especially on those flowing through populous areas. All levees and flood walls that are built along rivers to protect adjacent property from overflow raise the stage upstream and, by reducing the volume of channel storage, tend to increase both stage and discharge at all points downstream. Every bridge and every dam built across a stream and every building or other structure built upon the banks or on the flood plain constitutes an encroachment upon the stream that tends to raise the stage of the water at all points upstream. In populous centers, where these encroachments are numerous, the summation of all the resultant rises oftentimes becomes surprisingly large.

The final answer to the question of whether or not flood *discharges* are increasing is directly dependent upon the answers to two other questions: (1) Are storms increasing in intensity? (2) Are the physical characteristics of the drainage basin changing, or have they been changed by man, so that for any given storm the rate of surface runoff has been increased? The answer to the first of these questions is most certainly in the negative. At least, if there are any climatic changes taking place that tend to affect the intensity of storms occurring in any given area, those changes are so slow that they go unobserved in the brief span of a century. Furthermore, the forces that govern our climate are so vast and widespread that any changes effected on the earth's surface by man have such a feeble influence thereon as to be utterly negligible.

The answer to the second of the foregoing questions is not so simple. That changes in land use do affect infiltration capacity and therefore the rate of surface runoff seems obvious. However, the nature and the magnitude of the effect of those changes are difficult to determine. The conversion of undrained forested areas into drained agricultural lands almost invariably increases flood flows, but the percentage of increase is far greater in small drainage basins than in large ones.

In basins that are rapidly being urbanized, flood flows are unquestionably being increased. Every new home that is built, with its pavements, driveways, and sidewalks, reduces the infiltration capacity of these residental areas nearly to zero. Storm sewers collect and convey this water to the stream channels, with a possible resulting increase in peak flows. A good example of this increase is provided by the Rouge River basin, which drains a Detroit suburban area of about 470 square miles. This area is growing so rapidly that if a flood study of the Rouge River were to be made today, based entirely upon past records of discharge and with no consideration of the effects of urbanization, the resulting estimates would probably be considerably in error.

The Design Flood

No structure of any importance, either in or adjacent to a river, should ever be planned or built without due consideration to the damage it may cause or the damage to which it may be subjected in time of flood. The destructive powers of a raging torrent are enough to fill the bravest heart with awe and respect. History reveals much evidence of the tremendous power for destruction that is possessed by a flood. The transportation of huge boulders and masses of concrete and the excavation of deep holes at the foot of dams attest to the need for careful design of any structure that is likely to be subjected to these tremendous forces.

To avoid destruction, dams must have sufficient spillway capacity and adequate protection against scour at the toe; bridges must have the needed waterway opening; flood walls and embankments must be high enough so that they will not be overtopped; reservoirs must have the required capacity; and so on. The maximum flood that any such structure can safely pass is called the *design flood.*

If a flood of a given magnitude occurs with an average frequency of once in 100 yr, there is a 1 per cent chance, or 1 chance in 100, that such a flood will occur during any one year; a flood whose magnitude is likely to be exceeded on an average of once every 25 yr is a 4 per cent-chance flood, etc. This method of designating flood frequency as suggested by Hazen[3] is to be preferred for the reason that the average person considers a flood having "a frequency of once in 100 yr" as carrying no present threat, but likely to occur only after a lapse of 100 yr. On the other hand, a "1 per cent-chance flood" at once conveys the impression that there is 1 chance in 100 that such a flood will occur within a year; furthermore, that it is just as likely to occur this year as any other year, and that is the exact impression that should prevail.

The first characteristic to be determined for any design flood is not its magnitude as perhaps might be expected but the chance or probability of its occurrence. In other words, should the structure be safe

[3] Allen Hazen, *Flood Flows*, John Wiley, 1930, p. 10. (Out of print.)

against the 2 per cent, or the 1 per cent, or the 0.1 per cent chance flood or against the maximum flood that may ever be anticipated? After this question has been answered, the problem is to determine the magnitude of the flood that may be expected to occur with that average frequency.

Contrary to common opinion there is little relationship between the frequency of the design flood and the normal life of the structure. If the structure has an anticipated life of 50 yr, it would plainly be folly to design it so that it would be safe only against floods that occur with an average frequency of once in 50 yr or less. If this were done, the chances would be even that it would be destroyed by flood before it had served its purpose through half of its normal life. Especially would this be folly if, as is often the case, by a slight additional cost it could have been made practically immune to such destruction.

How far one is justified in going in order to make a structure or flood-prevention system safe against damage or destruction by floods depends upon the following considerations:

1. *The extent to which human life would be endangered* by the occurrence of a flood of greater magnitude. It is impossible to place a monetary value upon human life. In the preparation of the plans for flood protection in the Miami Conservancy District, the engineers decided that the flood of 1913 was one of the great floods of centuries. Nevertheless, because of the great danger to human life in case of failure of the system, they designed protective works that would take care of a flood nearly 40 per cent greater than the flood of 1913. In a similar manner, any structure whose failure would seriously endanger human lives should be designed to pass safely the greatest flood that will probably ever occur at that point.

2. *The value of property that would be destroyed* as a result of floods of greater size. This consideration is purely economic. By determining the total losses that would result from greater floods during a long period of time, reduced to an annual basis, and by comparing this figure with the increased annual cost of the protective system that would be required to prevent those additional losses, we can determine the limiting size of flood against which it is profitable to protect.

3. *The inconvenience resulting from failure* of the structure due to greater floods. If, for instance, a bridge on a trunk-line highway should be destroyed because of insufficient waterway opening, all traffic might have to be detoured for a considerable distance over poor roads perhaps for several months until a new bridge is designed and built.

One other factor should be mentioned in connection with the design of any flood-control system: the sense of security against floods that will be provided by that system. Although this is another intangible value, it is, nevertheless, important. Some cities in protected basins use the security provided by their flood-protective system as an inducement to attract manufacturing enterprises to locate there. In general, property values within the areas protected are enhanced, often to a considerable extent.

If due consideration is given to these factors, the proper frequency of the design flood can be determined although, of course, good judgment must always play a major part in connection with the first and third items.

Factors Affecting Flood Flow

It has already been stated that floods are primarily due to surface runoff. Therefore, all factors that affect surface runoff also affect flood flow. These factors naturally fall into two classes, those that determine the intensity of the storms that are likely to visit any drainage basin and those physical characteristics of the basin which affect and determine the disposal of that rainfall.

The influence exerted by these factors upon surface runoff has been discussed in Chapter 3 and need not be expanded here. However, it would be well to review the effect of these factors in connection with the discussion that follows.

ESTIMATING MAGNITUDE AND FREQUENCY OF FLOODS

Although different procedures have been proposed for the determination of the size of flood that may be expected to occur on any stream with a given average frequency, all these methods may be grouped into three general classes:

1. Determination by means of empirical formulas.
2. Determination by statistical or probability methods.
3. Determination by the unit-hydrograph method.

The advantages and disadvantages of these methods will now be considered.

Empirical Formulas

Perhaps the earliest method proposed for the determination of the probable flood flow of a stream is the use of empirical formulas. These usually express the relation between flood flow and one or two of the most important variables. Seldom are definite specifications given for the frequency with which the computed flood flows might be expected to occur. Sometimes they are described as frequent or rare, terms that are comparative and, therefore, practically meaningless. When we consider that the magnitude of a flood of any given frequency depends upon fifteen or twenty variables, the futility of attempting to correlate that magnitude with only one or two of those factors and of obtaining dependable results at once becomes apparent. A quick and very rough approximation is all that should be expected. Nevertheless a few typical formulas of this type are presented here, although the student is urgently advised never to use them unless he has first investigated their origin, has become familiar with the data upon which they were based, knows the conditions under which they are intended to be used, knows the areas to which they are adapted, and understands the restrictions placed upon their use by their authors. Unless these precautions are taken, the blind use of any one of these formulas is likely to give results grossly in error—not by 20 or 30 per cent but by several hundred per cent and in some cases by a thousand per cent or more. In all these formulas Q is flood flow in cubic feet per second, and A is area of drainage basin in square miles.

One of the oldest and best known of these formulas, and one that has been used extensively for storm sewer design, is the so-called rational formula[4]

$$Q = 640KI_tA$$

where K is the percentage of the rainfall that becomes surface runoff, and I_t is the intensity of rainfall in inches per hour for the critical period, t.

The relationship expressed by this formula is at once apparent when one recalls that 1 in. of rain falling in 1 hr on 1 acre is equivalent to 3630 cu ft of water which, running off at a uniform rate in 1 hr, is equal to approximately 1 cfs. Perhaps, therefore, this formula should not be classed as an empirical formula as are the others that follow.

Although this formula has been called "rational," the results of hydrological research indicate that this term is misleading, except possibly for very small runoff areas of the type discussed on pages 231 to 247. Only for these small areas can the relation between rainfall intensity and runoff intensity that is implied by the formula become a reality. Even then it seems desirable to determine rate of runoff on the basis of sound principles, that is, as the difference between rainfall rate and infiltration capacity, rather than by the use of the coefficient K. For areas of 5 acres or more, it need only be recalled that

---

[4] Philip A. Morley Parker, *Control of Water,* D. Van Nostrand, pp. 277–282.

two storms of entirely different intensities but producing equal amounts of rainfall excess within the period of rise may produce the same rates of runoff (page 255) to know that there is no direct relation between rainfall rates and runoff rates. In other words this formula ignores the fact that for any watershed, runoff occurs in the form of a typical hydrograph as illustrated by Fig. 96.

Inasmuch as area is an important and also one of the most apparent factors affecting the magnitude of the flood flow of a stream, it is only natural that a great many formulas have been proposed in which the flood flow is made directly dependent upon the area of the basin. Formulas of this type take the form

$$Q = KA^n$$

where K is a coefficient depending upon the rainfall and runoff characteristics of the basin, and n is a constant whose value usually lies between 0.5 and 1.0.

Of this general type is the modified Myers formula,[5]

$$Q = 10,000p\sqrt{A}$$

in which p has a value of unity for the stream that has the greatest flood flow of that area. For any other stream, p is the fraction that the flood flow of that stream is of the maximum given above. For different streams the value of p varies from approximately 0.002 to 1.0.[6]

Although scores of other formulas have been proposed by various investigators for the quick determination of the flood flow of streams, the foregoing formulas are typical examples. When one considers the enormous range in the values of the coefficients and exponents in these formulas, a condition resulting directly from the fact that those terms must represent the combined effect of all the factors listed on page 31, the extreme difficulty encountered in making satisfactory and intelligent use of these formulas is apparent.

Statistical or Probability Methods

A very logical procedure to follow in the prediction of the occurrence of natural phenomena is to base that prediction upon the records of the past. Such a procedure possesses fundamental merits that cannot be denied. There can be no question that when this method is applied to the determination of the maximum flood expected on

[5] C. S. Jarvis and others, "Floods in the United States," *U. S. Geol. Survey Water-Supply Paper* 771.

[6] C. S. Jarvis, "Flood Flow Characteristics," *Trans. A.S.C.E.*, 1926, vol. 89, 994.

any stream with a given frequency, it yields correct results, *provided that there are sufficient records available upon which to base that determination and also provided that there have been no important changes in the regimen of the stream during or subsequent to the period of record.*

Especially prior to the development of the unit-hydrograph principle, statistical or probability methods were often used in making flood studies. On this subject the discussion that follows is by no means complete but is intended only to explain the general nature and limitations of the methods employed. These methods of estimating flood magnitudes and frequencies may be divided into two classes:

1. Estimating by the use of duration curves.
2. Estimating by the use of probability curves.

These two types of curves are closely related, as is shown presently.

Although a great many methods have been suggested for determining flood frequency by the use of duration or probability curves, only two of the simpler procedures is discussed. These methods can perhaps best be explained by use of an example. For this purpose the 54-yr record of floods on the Merrimack River at Lawrence, Massachusetts, as presented in *U. S. Geological Survey Water-Supply Paper 771*, has been selected.

Column 2, Table 28, shows the number of floods in this period during which the maximum 24-hr flow occurred between the limits shown in

TABLE 28

1 Flood Peak Limits, 1000 cfs	2 Number of Occurrences	3 Mass .Totals	4 Percentage of Total Occurrences
20.9–22.9	1	153	100
23.0–24.9	6	152	99.3
25.0–27.4	31	146	95.4
27.5–29.9	23	115	75.1
30.0–32.4	20	92	60.1
32.5–34.9	19	72	47.0
35.0–37.4	13	53	34.6
37.5–39.9	11	40	26.1
40.0–44.9	13	29	19.0
45.0–49.9	7	16	10.5
50.0–59.9	3	9	5.9
60.0–69.9	5	6	3.9
70.0–88.2	1	1	0.65

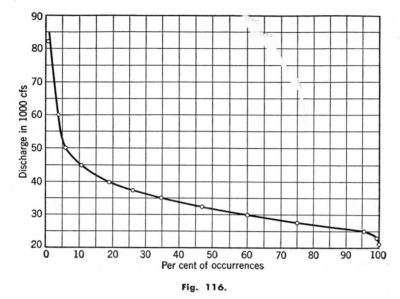

Fig. 116.

column 1. Column 3 gives a summation of these values starting with the maximum. In column 4 are shown the percentages of the total number of floods in which each of the lower values in column 1 is equaled or exceeded. For instance, 19 per cent of the 153 floods that occur in this 54-yr period equal or exceed 40,000 cfs. They all exceed 20,900 cfs, and so on. In Fig. 116 the percentages shown in column 4 are plotted against the corresponding lower values in column 1. In Fig. 117 these same data are plotted on logarithmic probability paper. The principal advantage in the latter method of plotting lies in the

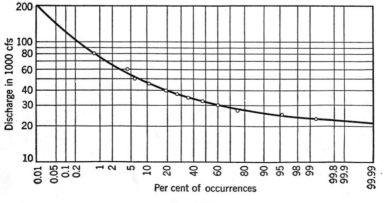

Fig. 117.

fact that especially throughout the lower percentages this curve is much flatter than the one shown in Fig. 116. It can therefore be extended more readily to cover the very low percentages.

It has been suggested by those who advocate the use of probability methods in making flood studies that curves such as these may be used in the following manner. Suppose that we wish to determine the maximum flood that may be expected to occur on the Merrimack River with a frequency of once in 1000 yr. We must not lose sight of the fact that both these curves show the percentages of the *total number* of floods that occur in any given period that equal or exceed the magnitudes as shown on the left. In the 54 yr of records there are 153 floods or 2.83 floods per year. Therefore, in 1000 yr there should be 2830 floods, and the greatest one expected in that period is of the magnitude shown at 100/2830 per cent or about 0.035 per cent of the time. In Fig. 117, we find that for this percentage the magnitude of flood is about 154,000 cfs. In Fig. 116 the scale is such that the corresponding value falls off the drawing, but the two curves should give the same result.

Many refinements of the foregoing methods, as well as a number of quite different procedures, have been suggested[7] for flood-frequency determinations by probability methods, but they all possess the same inherent defects. The discussion that follows applies equally to all these methods.

Limitations to Use of Probability Methods

In determining the value of any particular variable, the greater the number of samples upon which that determination is based the more accurate is the result. If, for instance, we wish to determine for a given stream the maximum flood that may be expected to occur with a frequency of once in 10 yr, and only 10 yr of records are available, the error in the result is likely to be great, because the answer is based upon only one sample. If the same determination were to be based upon 100 yr of records, the probable error would be greatly reduced, for we would now have 10 samples upon which to base our judgment

[7] Allen Hazen, *Flood Flows,* John Wiley, 1930. (Out of print.)

H. Alden Foster, "Duration Curves," *Trans. A.S.C.E.,* 1934, vol. 99, p. 1213.

J. J. Slade, Jr., "An Asymmetric Probability Function," *Proc. A.S.C.E.,* October 1934, p. 1007.

R. D. Goodrich, "Straight Line Plotting of Skew Frequency Data," *Trans. A.S.C.E.,* 1927, vol. 91, p. 1.

F. G. Switzer, "Probability of Flood Flows," *Proc. A.S.C.E.,* April 1927, p. 563.

L. Standish Hall, "The Probable Variations in Annual Runoff as Determined from a Study of California Streams," *Trans. A.S.C.E.,* 1921, vol. 84, p. 191.

instead of only one. Or again, if we had a 1000 yr of records or 100 samples, the probable error would then be so small as to be negligible. If, on the other hand, we wish to determine the maximum flood that is likely to occur with an average frequency of once in 100 yr and only 50 yr of records are available, the probable error is then very high, perhaps several hundred per cent or more, because not even one whole sample, or period of observation, is available upon which to base our judgment. It should be emphasized that the probable error depends upon the number of independent samples available and that no amount of juggling or manipulation of data can possibly reduce that error.

About ten independent samples should provide a satisfactory determination of the size of flood that may be expected to occur with any given frequency, although a greater number increase the accuracy. This means that the statistical or probability method may be used to determine the magnitude of floods that occur with a frequency of once a year, once every 2 yr, or even once every 5 yr, if 50 yr of records are available; but, for the determination of the greatest flood that may be expected once in 100 yr or once in 1000 yr with no more than 50 or 100 yr of records, these methods are entirely inadequate and likely to result in enormous errors.

Apparent justification for these conclusions is to be found in the results of some studies by Hazen[8] in the determination of the probable maximum floods to be expected on the Hudson River at Mechanic-ville, New York, and on the Arkansas River at Pueblo, Colorado. Prior to 1913 the maximum flood on the Hudson River for which there is any record occurred in 1869, during which the peak flow reached about 67,000 cfs. The records prior to 1888, however, were considered none too reliable, and therefore Hazen used only the records subsequent to that date. The greatest floods that occurred each year throughout the 23 yr of record from 1888 to 1912, arranged in the order of their magnitudes, were plotted on logarithmic probability paper. By extrapolating on this curve, he found that the 1 per cent-chance flood which is the maximum flood that can be expected to occur once in 100 yr, is 64,600 cfs. The maximum 1000-yr flood would be, by this same method, about 10 per cent greater. However, in 1913 a flood occurred at Mechanicville that reached a peak of 118,000 cfs.

In a similar manner throughout the 29 yr of record prior to 1921, the maximum flood on the Arkansas River at Pueblo, Colorado, was about 10,000 cfs. By the foregoing method, using only the records

[8] Allen Hazen, *Flood Flows*, John Wiley, 1930, p. 88. (Out of print.)

for this 29-yr period, Hazen estimated the maximum 100-yr flood to be about 11,650 cfs. In 1921 a flood occurred on this stream that was believed to exceed 100,000 cfs. This is many times greater than the maximum that would ever be expected on this stream as determined by the probability method. Nor are these two examples the only ones that could be cited of streams suddenly going on a rampage in a flood. The Republican River in Kansas, the Miami River in Ohio, and scores of others afford similar examples. This rather strange phenomenon, wherein an occasional flood occurs that is often many times greater than any previously recorded, may be explained as follows.

An especially great flood on any particular basin depends primarily upon: (1) the occurrence on that basin of a storm of high intensity or the sudden melting of a heavy accumulation of snow at a time when (2) the storage in lakes, swamps, ponds, depressions, and channels is filled and (3) the infiltration capacity of the basin is low.

It happens that the latter two conditions are very likely to occur simultaneously, and, as a result, it is safer to combine them as a single condition than to consider them as independent variables.

To simplify our problem, let us assume that the drainage basin under consideration is located in one of the southern states, where floods do not result from the melting of snows but only from intense rainfall. Suppose that a storm of a given intensity occurs on the basin with an average frequency of, for instance, once in 50 yr. Furthermore, assume that the surface storage is filled and the infiltration capacity at the minimum only 5 per cent of the time. As a result, only once in twenty times will a storm of the given intensity occur when these other conditions are favorable for the production of a maximum flood. Consequently, under these conditions the most intense storm that occurs with an average frequency of once in 50 yr produces the maximum flood only once in a thousand years. It is, therefore, not likely that these two conditions will occur simultaneously within a short period of records. If they do not, a record of 50 or even 100 yr will reveal no unusually high flood, but if they should happen to occur at the same time, a flood many times greater than anything that has ever before been recorded is likely to follow, with disastrous results.

In this country few streams have reliable discharge records covering a period of more than 50 yr. Therefore, if we wish to determine the magnitude of the greatest flood that is likely ever to occur on a given basin, as we would wish to do if the failure of the proposed structure would cause the loss of human life and the destruction of valuable property, it is clear that such a determination cannot be based upon the application of purely statistical methods to past records. It is easily conceivable that such a peak flood may either have been recorded in a 50-yr period or may exceed by 1000 per cent or more the maximum recorded in such a comparatively short time.

It is not possible to combine the records of a number of different streams in a manner similar to that followed in the station-year method of determining rainfall frequencies. This fact is evident when we consider the many factors which influence and determine the magnitude and frequency of occurrences of floods on different drainage basins. Because of the large number of these factors, it is manifestly improbable that any two basins would ever have the same flood-producing potentialities, without which their records cannot properly be combined.

Unit Hydrograph Method

The unit hydrograph provides the only known dependable method of determining the magnitude of floods that may be expected to occur with various frequencies on any given stream. The use of this method requires that there be available a period of continuous runoff and precipitation records on the basin for which the flood prediction is to be made. Enough records are needed to permit the determination of the manner in which the infiltration capacity varies throughout the year and also the plotting of a number of unit hydrographs (page 265) for the basin. Oftentimes from 2 to 5 yr of records provide these necessary data, whereas, in other instances, longer records are required. The accuracy of the results increases with the length of period covered, but only a few years of records provide a basis for a better flood estimate than can be made in any other way. If no records are available for the location where the study is to be made, less dependable results can be obtained by the use of records from other points on the same stream or from adjacent streams, by methods which will be described later.

The unit hydrograph method is limited to areas which are small enough so that areal rainfall patterns do not vary too markedly. Usually no difficulties are encountered for areas smaller than 3000 square miles. However, for areas of this size and larger it may be necessary to classify unit hydrographs into various categories related to the precipitation patterns. For very large basins, perhaps 10,000 square miles or more, it may be desirable to derive unit hydrographs for the principal tributaries and to determine the flood magnitude by routing the various components to the outlet of the basin. Also, a special method is required for determining the infiltration capacity of very large basins (page 117).

The following outline gives the steps used in the application of the unit-hydrograph principle to predict the magnitudes of floods of various frequencies. The Rouge River at Detroit, having an area of 193 square miles, is used as an example.

1. Plot the hydrographs for all stream rises of record.

2. Determine the average precipitation (page 81) and snow melt (page 312) during each stream rise, and plot on the same sheet with the corresponding hydrograph. For the determination of the snow melt, it is necessary to keep an account of the snow on the ground during the winter months preceding the stream rise. This account can be kept from Weather Bureau records by considering all precipitation that falls at average daily temperatures below 32° F (see page 314) as snow, and by accounting for any that is lost in subsequent days through melt, by methods described in Chapter 9.

3. Separate surface runoff (SRO) from ground-water flow for each stream rise (see pages 28 and 250), and determine the amount of SRO during each stream rise.

4. Determine the average infiltration capacity (f_a) during each stream rise by assuming that the precipitation excess (P_e) is equal to the SRO (see page 113), and plot the results with respect to time in the manner shown in Fig. 41.

5. Select the stream rises which are single peaked, and determine the distribution graphs (page 250). Comparison of the distribution graphs with a consideration of the rainfall durations discloses the critical rainfall period (see page 257). Distribution graph peaks and other runoff and rainfall characteristics for 27 unit hydrographs for the Rouge River at Detroit are shown in Table 24.

6. Determine the average peak value of the distribution graphs or, if needed, an average distribution graph (see Table 24, page 268, and pages 265 and 256).

7. From the infiltration capacity curve (Fig. 41) select portions of the year during which a single value of f_a can be considered as representative. Dividing the year into three or more periods may be more desirable. For the example shown in Fig. 41, only two periods are used. One period, designated as summer, includes the months of June through October. The second period, called "winter and spring," includes the remaining months. Based on Fig. 41, values of 1.50 and 0.50 in. per day are selected as typical values of f_a for the two periods.

8. The next step is the determination of rainfall-frequency curves for the selected periods of the year and for the desired duration, such as those shown in Fig. 32 and derived in Table 6. This determination may be made in the two ways described below.

(a) All rains (but no snowfalls) of record for the desired duration are combined with any simultaneous snow melt in the manner described under item 2 above. If no continuous rainfall records are available and daily totals must be used, the amounts should be increased by half of the largest rain occurring on either the day before or the day after the day of heaviest rain. This increase should be made for the reasons given on page 98. Frequency curves for each period should then be prepared in the manner described on page 86. Values may be used directly from these curves without adding any snow melt to spring or winter rains, because melting snow is included in the values.

(b) A second method which is less laborious but also somewhat less accurate consists of using all 24-hr rains in the manner described under (a) but without determining and adding any simultaneous snow melt to the rains. This procedure is used to derive the frequency curves of Fig. 32. In using the winter and spring rains derived in this manner for predicting runoff, it is now necessary to add the amount of snow melt which is likely to accompany the rainfall. For the Rouge River it is found that half of the important spring rains of record are accompanied by 0.50 in. or more of snow melt; therefore, this amount is added to all spring rains.

9. Prepare a curve relating point rainfall to average precipitation on areas of various sizes, as described in Chapter 4, page 99, and illustrated by Fig. 39.

10. Select a flood magnitude and determine the size of rainfall that would produce such a flood during each of the selected periods. For example, suppose a flood of 10,000 cfs is chosen for the Rouge River at Detroit. First, the probable ground-water discharge (400 cfs) is deducted, and the corresponding 24-hr winter or spring precipitation is found as follows, by the methods developed in Chapter 8:

$$\text{Peak rate of SRO} = \text{SRO} \times D_p \times A$$

where SRO is the surface runoff in inches, D_p is the average peak of the distribution graph in cubic feet per second per square mile per inch (18.5 from Table 24), and A is the area of the basin in square miles (193). Therefore,

$$9600 = \text{SRO} \times 18.5 \times 193$$

and

$$\text{SRO} = 2.69 \text{ in.}$$

Because the SRO is equal to the average precipitation (P_a) plus snow melt (SM) minus infiltration (F),

$$SRO = P_a + SM - F$$

$$2.69 = P_a + 0.5 - 0.5$$

and

$$P_a = 2.69$$

The magnitude of the summer rain which produces a flood of the same size may now be determined as follows:

$$SRO = P_a - F$$

$$2.69 = P - 1.5$$

and

$$P_a = 4.19 \text{ in.}$$

Before determining the frequencies of these rains they must be converted from average precipitation on 193 square miles to point. This conversion is made by referring to the upper curve of Fig. 39, from which the conversion factor is found to be 0.89. Then the corresponding values of point rainfall are 3.02 and 4.71 in., respectively.

11. The average return interval of each rain is then found from the frequency curve for that period of the year. In this example the return interval for a winter and spring rain of 3.02 and a summer rain of 4.71 in. is found from the curves of Fig. 32 to be 70 yr and 46 yr, respectively. Therefore, in a 1000-yr period a flood of 10,000 cfs or more occurs, on the average, 1000/70 or 14.3 times during the winter and spring and 1000/46 or 21.7 times during the summer, or a total of 36.0 times. Thus the average return interval of a flood of 10,000 cfs or more is 1000/36.0 or 27.8 yr. This value and others determined in the same manner are shown in Fig. 118.

The assumption that 0.50 in. of snow melt be added to all winter and spring rains gives results that are too high for the more frequent rains. Therefore, the lower portion of the curve is established by determining the probable magnitude of the 1-yr flood by means of statistical analysis, when we use methods described on page 329. This value, designated by an x in Fig. 118, is consistent with the points determined in the manner described previously. The statistical method satisfactory for determining the 1-yr flood, because 24 yr of records available.

Where no records are available at the point at which the flood ⌐e is to be made, discharge records obtained at nearby locations used. However, a very careful comparison of drainage basin

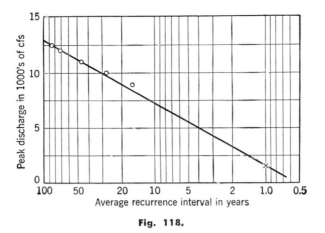

Fig. 118.

characteristics must be made to determine whether or not the values of f_a are comparable on the two basins. An approximate value of the distribution-graph peak may be obtained by plotting peaks against area in the manner illustrated in Figs. 98 and 101.

RELIEF FROM FLOOD HAZARD

Damages from floods may be avoided in three different ways.

1. By the construction of protective works.
2. Through the reduction of flood stage without appreciable change in the peak discharge.
3. Through the reduction of flood flows by storage, change in land use, or similar methods.

It should be noted that inasmuch as the first two of these methods do not reduce the rate of runoff, they afford protection only from flooding and do not prevent soil erosion. Which of these three methods or what combination of methods should be used for flood relief in any particular drainage basin or locality is a question that can be answered only after careful study and consideration of all the various possibilities. A method that is admirably adapted to provide the maximum possible relief and at the lowest cost in one situation may prove wholly inadequate and tremendously expensive in another.

In this field to a greater extent perhaps than in any other, there is an overwhelming tendency on the part of the public never to lock the barn until the horse has been stolen. It is doubtful if any adequate flood protection or flood reduction measures have ever been taken on any river until after a disastrous flood has been experienced. If prior to 1913 all the engineers in America had shouted from every house top in the Miami valley giving warning of the impending disaster that awaited that area, they would never have succeeded in arousing public sentiment to organize a Miami Conservancy District and construct the admirable flood-prevention system that was subsequently built— only a flood that took a toll of 360 lives and destroyed more than $100,000,000 worth of property could do that. This remark is not intended as the slightest reflection on the intelligence of the people living in that area. Human nature is the same everywhere. This complacency is seen in the many danger centers still existing throughout the country where the inhabitants are peacefully lulled by a sense of false security, blissfully ignorant of the terrible havoc that can and some day will be wrought by the innocent-looking stream that flows by their doors and that throughout the memory of the oldest inhabitant has always been comparatively docile and well behaved.

Flood Protection

Flood protection is provided mainly by means of levees and flood walls that are built along the banks and afford protection only locally to people and property within reach of the flood waters. Their purpose is to confine those waters within the natural stream channel. In so doing they actually increase the stage of the river at points upstream because of backwater and at points downstream because of the increased discharge resulting from the reduction in storage.

Although this method oftentimes provides satisfactory protection against the ordinary flood, it carries with it a serious danger. Because of the presence of a protecting levee or flood wall, the adjacent property owners acquire a new sense of security against floods and, as a result, build new homes at lower levels where before they did not dare to build. A levee protects only until it is overtopped; after that it is utterly useless. Consequently, when the exceptional flood comes along and overtops the levee, the resulting devastation and loss of life are likely to be far worse than if it had never been built.

Stage Reduction

Without affecting the rate of discharge, the flood hazard can oftentimes be greatly lessened by stage reduction. This may be accomplished in any instance by either or both of the following methods.

1. By straightening and deepening the river channel. Inasmuch as $Q = AV$, it follows that for any given Q, by increasing V, A is

correspondingly reduced, and hence the stage is reduced. The extent of the benefits that can be obtained in this manner depends upon the initial conditions of the channel. Even though it is extremely sinuous, as some of the reaches in the lower Mississippi, if the fall in the river is slight, the amount of stage reduction that can be accomplished by this method is usually quite limited. Furthermore, nature objects to man's interference when he attempts to show her how to improve the course of a mighty river, and, as a result, unless he paves the channel or at least the side slopes, he must expect an almost constant maintenance expense. If there is sufficient fall available, by paving the channel through populous areas the depth of water is reduced in almost the same proportion as the velocity is increased.

2. By providing a by-pass or additional flood channel past danger centers. Oftentimes large cities are located on rivers or on other bodies of water. It is here that because of encroachments by bridges, buildings, and filled-in areas, a bottleneck is created. Appreciable widening of the river channel is usually out of the question because of the cost. Not uncommonly, however, a flood channel can be constructed around the city at reasonable cost. The flood peaks on the Mississippi River at New Orleans and for a distance of more than a hundred miles upstream are materially reduced by the diversion of a portion of those flood waters into the Atchafalaya River, which thus becomes a by-pass channel direct to the Gulf.

Reduction in Peak Discharge

Peak discharges can be reduced by either (1) temporarily storing a portion of the surface runoff until after the crest of the flood has passed or (2) reducing the amount of surface runoff through a change in land use which increases the infiltration capacity. Either of these methods, if properly carried out, produces beneficial results at all downstream points.

Reduction by storage is accomplished in two ways, (1) by a large number of small, individual farm reservoirs located in the headwaters of the main stream or of its many tributaries, or by the use of terraces that detain the surface runoff long enough to permit it to infiltrate into the soil; and (2) by large reservoirs located in the valleys farther downstream.

Regardless of the size of the reservoir, however, there are two types of storage, controlled and uncontrolled. In controlled storage, gates in the impounding structure may regulate the outflow in any manner that is thought desirable. Only in unusual cases does such a reservoir have sufficient capacity to completely eliminate the peak of a major flood. As a result, the regulation of the outflow must be carefully planned.[9] The operators must estimate how much of the early portion of a flood may be safely impounded, taking into consideration the danger of having the reservoir filled before the peak of the flood has been reached. Where reservoirs exist on several tributaries, the additional problem of the timing of the release of the stored waters becomes a matter of very great importance. It may be possible to so release these waters that the peak flows would combine at a downstream point with disastrous results.

In uncontrolled storage, there is no regulation of the outflow capacity of the impounding dam. Such structures usually contain overflow spillways, and the only flood benefits obtained from them result from the modifying and delaying effects of the storage above the spillway crest.

The effectiveness of a large number of small reservoirs in the headwaters of a stream has never been demonstrated on any large scale. However, it has been given considerable publicity by its advocates who urge its use for soil-conservation purposes as well as for flood prevention. The value of such reservoirs in the prevention of floods is questionable because of the probability of their being either filled or partly filled at the time of a flood-producing rain.

On the other hand, terraces have been used, and if properly designed they are effective in flood reduction and as a soil-conservation measure. They follow the contour of the ground and have a base width of 5 or 6 ft and a usual height of 6 or 8 in. They are spaced close enough together to impound the surface runoff without overtopping. Actually they form small detention reservoirs which hold the water back long enough to give it time to infiltrate into the soil. This requires only a short time so that they are soon empty and ready for the next rain. They thus serve to reduce flood flow, prevent soil erosion, and increase ground-water supply.

Much has been written of the advantages arising from the multiple use of storage reservoirs. It is sometimes claimed that the same storage capacity can be utilized for flood control, storing the flood waters to be used later (1) as an aid to navigation by increasing the low water flow, (2) for the production of power, (3) for irrigation, or (4) for water supply and other purposes. Large storage reservoirs provide the most generally effective and satisfactory method of flood prevention in common use, but, unless a reservoir has a capacity far greater than is needed for storing the excess waters of a major flood, its value for other purposes is very limited if it is to be fully effective

[9] Robert M. Morris and Thomas L. Reilly, "Operation Experiences, Tygart Reservoir," *Trans. A.S.C.E.*, 1942, vol. 107, p. 1349.

for flood control. This necessarily follows from the fact that if a reservoir has only sufficient capacity to hold the waters from one major flood it must be emptied as quickly as possible after each flood in order to have its storage capacity available for the next flood that comes along. By always keeping sufficient storage capacity available for any probable flood, any additional storage can be utilized for other purposes. The reservoir capacity necessary to completely store the waters of any flood, reducing the outflow to some safe rate, can easily be found by means of a mass diagram. This capacity is given by the maximum ordinate between the mass curve of inflow and the mass curve of outflow. (See p. 283.)

Protective works such as levees and flood walls are always built at those places along the river that require protection. On the other hand, storage reservoirs are almost invariably located at some considerable distance upstream from the cities or areas that are to be protected. They must be located where the topography is suitable and cost is not excessive. Unless a topographical map of the basin is available, a survey is necessary to determine the existence of suitable reservoir sites on the main stream and on each of the several tributaries. The cost of development of each of the possible sites must be determined, and, after reducing this cost to an annual basis, it must be compared with the annual benefits that would accrue from its development. Only then can one determine which sites, if any, are economically feasible to develop.

Determination of Benefits from Flood Reduction

To determine the annual benefits that would result from any flood-control program[10] it is first necessary to establish a number of flood profiles throughout those reaches of the river, at least, where considerable damages occur. Also, a design-flood profile should be determined as well as the minimum profile at which there are appreciable damages. A careful field survey is then necessary to determine the amount of the damages that result from floods corresponding to the established profiles throughout the damage zone. These values can be plotted in the form of a curve, and for any intermediate stages desired the damages can be found.

Next, the frequency with which floods of each of these various magnitudes occur must be determined. With these data at hand, the manner in which they are used is illustrated.

Suppose that at the downstream end of the damage zone the range of the flood stage for which damages occur is 10 ft. Let us assume

[10] For a more complete discussion of this subject see Edgar E. Foster, "Evaluation of Flood Losses and Benefits," *Trans. A.S.C.E.*, 1942, vol. 107, pp. 871–924.

that the amount of damages has been determined throughout the entire length of the damage zone for profiles corresponding to flood stages at the lower end of 2, 4, 6, 8, and 10 ft, respectively. Also the number of times in 100 yr when each of these stages has been reached or exceeded has been determined. A table is then prepared as follows:

TABLE 29

Flood Stage, feet	Number of Times in 100 Years That Stage Is Exceeded	Number of Floods of This Stage but No Higher	Damages per Flood	Total Damages
10	1	1	$1,200,000	$1,200,000
8	2	1	800,000	800,000
6	5	3	500,000	1,500,000
4	9	4	250,000	1,000,000
2	20	11	100,000	1,100,000
		Total Damages per 100 yr		$5,600,000

If methods can be found whereby these flood stages can be reduced by 4 ft, a revised table similar to Table 29 is as follows:

TABLE 30

Flood Stage, feet	Number of Times in 100 Years That Stage Is Exceeded	Number of Floods of This Stage but No Higher	Damages per Flood	Total Damages
10	0	0	0	0
8	0	0	0	0
6	1	1	$500,000	$500,000
4	2	1	250,000	250,000
2	5	3	100,000	300,000
		Total Damages per 100 yr		$1,050,000

The annual benefits would therefore amount to $45,500. It should perhaps be explained that it would have been impossible to determine the amount of the damages occurring within any 2-ft interval and then consider this figure as being constant for all floods that reach or exceed this stage, because these damages vary for the different magnitudes of floods. For instance, a flood of a 10-ft stage uproots trees, carries away houses, and destroys bridges located at the lower levels, which would not be seriously damaged by a 2-ft or 4-ft stage of flood.

Flood Routing

It is assumed above, for purposes of illustration, that methods have been found whereby flood stages at the lower end of the danger zone can be reduced 4 ft. It remains to be explained how the *amount* of this reduction in stage can be computed. For this purpose it is necessary to learn the character of the contribution to the flood hydrograph at the lower station from each tributary area whose contribution to that hydrograph we propose to change. To do this we must first take the hydrograph of a recorded flood from the upper area and determine how and when that water reaches the lower stations, for this hydrograph changes as it moves downstream. Although the volume of water ordinarily remains almost constant, the base of the hydrograph broadens, the peak is reduced, and, of course, the time is delayed. Then, after determining to what extent this upper-station hydrograph can be reduced by storage or other means, we can route the revised graph down to the lower station and find how much the proposed upstream improvement affects flood peaks at the downstream station. The process whereby the hydrograph of a flood as it occurred at an upstream station is transferred to some point downstream is called flood routing through river channels.

Without this procedure, no intelligent planning of flood relief is possible. In fact, it can happen that a reservoir located on a certain tributary and constructed at considerable cost may actually prove detrimental by delaying the flood waters a sufficient time so that they arrive at the downstream damage point at the crest of the flood, instead of passing harmlessly by at an earlier period.

However, the flood hydrograph at any downstream station is affected and determined not only by changes in land use, by storage in small upstream reservoirs, and by channel storage, but also by storage in large downstream reservoirs. Before taking up the method of routing floods through river channels, the much simpler plan of routing through an uncontrolled reservoir will be considered. This latter procedure will be presented by means of a numerical example.

Flood Routing through Reservoirs

Figure 119, curve 1, represents two successive stream rises on the Monongahela River at Greensboro, Pennsylvania. It is assumed that a dam having a spillway length, L, of 600 ft, is to be built across this stream and that the relation between the discharge, Q, and the head, H, on the spillway is expressed by the equation

$$Q = 3.5LH^{3/2} \qquad (1)$$

This relationship is shown graphically as curve 1, Fig. 120. The relation between H and reservoir-surface area is shown by curve 2, Fig. 120. This curve permits the computation of the storage capacity, S, for various values of H by starting with zero storage when $H = 0$ and adding successive volumes for larger values of H. Since storage is a function of H, equation 1 might be written in terms of storage rather than H as follows:

$$Q = CS^n \tag{2}$$

The storage equation may now be written for some convenient time interval.

Let T = number of seconds in the time interval.
    I = average rate of inflow in cfs during interval.
    Q_1 = rate of discharge over the spillway in cfs at the beginning of a time interval.
    Q_2 = the corresponding rate at the end of a time interval.
    S_1 = storage above the spillway crest in cubic feet at the beginning of a time interval.
    S_2 = corresponding storage at the end of a time interval.

Then

$$S_1 + IT - \left(\frac{Q_1 + Q_2}{2}\right) T = S_2 \tag{3}$$

The unknowns in this equation for any time interval are S_2 and Q_2. These may be determined by simultaneous solution of equations 2 and 3. Because the values of S_2 and Q_2 thus determined are the values of S_1 and Q_1 respectively, for the next interval the procedure may be repeated for successive intervals until the entire hydrograph of outflow is determined. The foregoing equations can be solved only by successive approximations, which make the process very tedious.

The following graphical procedure greatly facilitates the solution.[11,12]

Equation 3 may be rewritten as follows:

$$\left(\frac{S_1}{T} - \frac{Q_1}{2}\right) + I = \left(\frac{S_2}{T} + \frac{Q_2}{2}\right) \tag{4}$$

[11] An outline of this graphical procedure was presented by L. G. Puls, "Flood Regulation of the Tennessee River," *House Document* 185.70, Congress 1st Session, 1928, pp. 43–55. The method was also derived independently at about the same time by E. R. Gustafson, of the U. S. Engineer Office, Duluth, Minn.

[12] Other graphical procedures for solving reservoir storage problems have been presented. See for example: R. D. Goodrich, "Rapid Calculation for Reservoir Discharge," *Civil Eng.*, February 1931, pp. 417–419; I. H. Steinberg, "A Method of Flood Routing," *Civil Eng.*, July 1938, pp. 476–477.

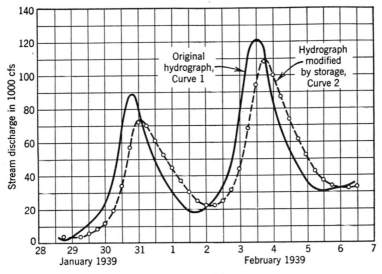

Fig. 119.

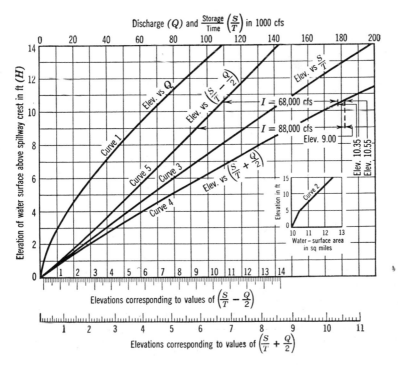

Fig. 120.

TABLE 31

1 Date 1939	2 I Average during Interval	3 Elevation at End of Interval	4 Q at End of Interval
Jan. 29	3,500	1.45	3,500
	2,800	1.40	3,500
	5,500	1.50	3,500
	10,000	1.90	5,500
Jan. 30	14,500	2.45	8,000
	19,000	3.15	11,500
	32,000	4.35	19,000
	55,000	6.40	34,000
Jan. 31	82,000	9.00	57,000
	88,000	10.55	72,000
	68,000	10.35	70,000
	53,000	9.50	61,500
Feb. 1	43,000	8.55	52,500
	36,000	7.70	45,000
	29,000	6.80	37,000
	21,000	5.85	30,000
Feb. 2	18,000	5.15	24,500
	19,000	4.80	22,000
	23,000	4.80	22,000
	29,000	5.15	24,500
Feb. 3	40,000	6.00	31,000
	60,000	7.60	44,000
	93,000	10.15	68,000
	118,000	12.60	94,000
Feb. 4	120,000	13.85	108,000
	93,000	13.15	100,000
	75,000	11.95	87,000
	61,500	10.70	73,500
Feb. 5	50,000	9.50	61,500
	41,000	8.45	52,000
	33,000	7.45	42,500
	30,500	6.75	37,000
Feb. 6	30,000	6.35	33,500
	31,500	6.20	32,500
	32,000	6.15	32,000
	34,000	6.25	33,000

In this example a time interval, T, of 6 hr was selected. Values of S/T were determined from curve 2, Fig. 120, for various elevations and plotted as curve 3, Fig. 120. Values of $Q/2$ were then added to and subtracted from the abscissas of curve 3 to obtain curves 4 and 5, respectively. For any time interval, equation 4 requires that the abscissa of curve 5, corresponding to the water-surface elevation at the beginning of an interval, plus I, be equal to the abscissa of curve 4 corresponding to the elevation of the water surface at the end of the interval. Values of I are obtained from column 2, Table 31. If it is assumed that the outflow is equal to the inflow during the first interval, then, since there is no change in storage throughout this period, the elevation at the beginning of the second interval is the one corresponding to a Q of 3500 cfs, or 1.45 ft. Beginning at this elevation on curve 5, Fig. 120, the value of I of 2800 cfs, is added graphically by measuring to the right, and the corresponding elevation at the end of the interval is determined from curve 4. This latter elevation is also the water-surface elevation at the beginning of the third interval thus permitting the process to be repeated. The steps involved in two intervals beginning at 6 A.M., January 31, are shown on Fig. 120. The elevation at 6 A.M. is shown in Table 31 to be 9.00 ft. The value of I, 88,000 cfs, is added to curve 5 at this elevation, and the elevation at the end of the interval, 12 noon, is found to be 10.55. The next I, 68,000 cfs, is added to curve 5 at this elevation, and by dropping down to curve 4 the elevation at 6 P.M. is 10.35.

This procedure may be simplified by projecting values of elevations taken from curves 4 and 5 on to horizontal scales as shown in Fig. 120. Then, a scale of discharge values may be cut to slide between these horizontal scales, thus permitting values of I to be added to values on the upper scale in order to get elevations at the end of intervals directly from the lower scale. Having determined the water-surface elevation at the end of each interval, we may read the corresponding discharge values from curve 1, Fig. 120. These values, shown in column 4, Table 31, are plotted as curve 2, Fig. 119. The modification of the hydrographs resulting from reservoir storage may be determined by a comparison of this curve with the original hydrograph (curve 1).

Flood Routing through River Channels

The method of flood routing described in the previous pages provides a means for the determination of the modified flood hydrograph that enters a river from a flood-control reservoir. Because flood-protection reservoirs are likely to be located many miles upstream from the cities in which most of the flood damage occurs, it is necessary to route the flood hydrographs to these downstream localities. The problem is similar to routing through a reservoir, in that the stream channel itself is an elongated reservoir, and the solution is again effected by successive applications of the storage equation in conjunction with the relationship between storage and discharge. However, a number of difficulties arise in river routing that make the problem more complex. In an extensive study of this problem, Thomas[13] states: "In a large river with many tributaries, the movement of a flood wave is a phenomenon of such utter complexity as to defy complete and exact analysis by human beings." In this same paper Thomas suggests a graphical "trial-and-error" solution which satisfies the fundamental equations of wave movement. This method, presented in more detail in a later paper,[14] is the only one of the several proposed by various writers that may be termed an exact method, all others being properly called approximate methods. Owing to the laboriousness of the exact method, or because inaccuracies in basic data do not justify its use, most routing has been done by the approximate methods.

A complete description of the routing procedure by any one of the approximate methods is not given here, because any particular method usually applies only to a limited number of rivers. Generally it is necessary to select or devise a procedure to meet the needs of any particular situation. A brief résumé of some of the published material on the subject is given, followed by a general discussion of the methods used.

In 1939 an article was published[15] giving a rather complete description of methods used on the Tennessee River. The operations presented in this article apply to situations in which complete and accurate information concerning storage capacity of the river is available. In 1942 the authors presented a method[16] that was devised for the case in which no storage data were available. Another method that is used extensively by the U. S. Engineers Corps has been described

[13] Harold A. Thomas, "The Hydraulics of Flood Movements in Rivers," *Eng. Bull.*, Carnegie Institute of Technology, Pittsburgh, Pa., 1937.

[14] H. A. Thomas, "Graphical Integration of the Flood-Wave Equations," *Trans. Am. Geophys. Union,* 1940, pp. 596–602.

[15] Edward J. Rutter, Quintin B. Graves, and Franklin F. Snyder, "Flood Routing," *Trans. A.S.C.E.*, 1939, pp. 275–313.

[16] C. O. Wisler and E. F. Brater, "A Direct Method of Flood Routing," *Trans. A.S.C.E.*, 1942, pp. 1519–1562.

by a number of writers.[17,18,19,20] This method has been called the
"coefficient method,"[19,21] or the Muskingum method,[20] and its development has been credited to[20] T. S. Burns, F. B. Harkness, and
G. T. McCarthy.

Four difficulties encountered in river routing that do not appear in
reservoir routing will now be discussed.

1. Determination of Storage. The storage capacity of the river
at various stages must be known to provide the relationship between
discharge and storage (equation 2, page 346). Accurate topographical data of the type used to determine reservoir capacity are frequently
not available for long river reaches. The storage may be determined
by two other methods. If hydrographs of a flood are available at
the lower and upper ends of the reach, the method used by the authors[16]
may be employed. In this method, the fact that the lower portion
of the recession side of the hydrograph represents outflow from storage
is utilized. This idea has also been presented by Horton.[22] A second
method requires, in addition to the hydrographs at the upper and lower
ends of the reach, a hydrograph of inflow from the intervening area,
that is, the drainage area contributing flow to the river between the
upper and lower ends of the reach. With this information available,
all quantities in the storage equation (equation 3, page 346) except
$S_2 - S_1$ become known, and increments or decrements of storage may
be determined for all intervals throughout the flood period. If some
assumption is made as to the value of storage at the beginning of the
flood, the increments may be added cumulatively to determine actual
values of storage.

2. Inflow from the Intervening Area. Usually in reservoirs, the
increase in drainage area between the upper and lower ends is so small

17 Gerald T. McCarthy, U. S. Engineer Office, Providence, R. I., "The Unit
Hydrograph and Flood Routing." A paper presented at the conference of the
North Atlantic Division, U. S. Engineer Department at New London, Conn.,
June 24, 1938; revised, March 21, 1939.

18 W. B. Langbein, "Channel-Storage and Unit Hydrograph Studies," *Trans.
Am. Geophys. Union*, 1940, pp. 620–627.

19 B. R. Bilcrest and L. E. Marsh, "Channel-Storage and Discharge Relations in
the Lower Ohio River Valley," *Trans. Am. Geophys. Union*, 1941, pp. 637–649.

20 C. O. Clark, U. S. Engr. Office, Winchester, Va., "Storage and the Unit
Hydrograph," *Trans. A.S.C.E.*, 1945, pp. 1419–1488.

21 N. R. Laden, T. L. Reilly, and J. S. Minnotte, "Synthetic Unit-Hydrographs,
Distribution Graphs and Flood Routing in the Upper Ohio River Basin," *Trans.
Am. Geophys. Union*, 1940, pp. 649–659.

22 R. E. Horton, "Natural Stream Channel Storage," *Trans. Am. Geophys.
Union*, 1936, pp. 406–415 and 1937, pp. 440–456.

that the inflow from this area may be neglected. For river reaches, however, this area may be of considerable magnitude, and the inflow from it cannot be neglected. If hydrographs for a flood at the upper and lower ends of the reach are available, and if the relation between discharge and storage is determined, the inflow from the intervening area can be found by successive applications of the storage equation.[23] The storage equation would be written with inflow at the upper station, Q, and inflow from the intervening area, I, as separate terms, as follows:

$$S_1 + \left(\frac{Q_1 + Q_2}{2}\right) T + \left(\frac{I_1 + I_2}{2}\right) T - \left(\frac{O_1 + O_2}{2}\right) T = S_2 \quad (5)$$

Values of Q and O being known, and with values of S determined from the storage-discharge relation, values of I are the only unknowns.

If either the upper or lower hydrograph or the storage is unknown, the inflow from the intervening area must be estimated from rainfall, utilizing an assumed distribution graph to synthesize the hydrograph. This procedure is likely to give uncertain results unless hydrographs from a very similar watershed are available as a guide in estimating the shape of the distribution graph.   A number of writers have discussed this problem.[24,25,26]

3. Storage-Discharge Relationship. In very large reservoirs, the water surface is nearly level at all times, so that a change in storage must be accompanied by a corresponding change in water-surface elevation at all points in the reservoir. Therefore, since the rate of outflow, O, is directly related to water-surface elevation, it may also be directly related to the storage as shown by equation 2, page 346. In a long river reach, however, the storage begins to increase as soon as the flood wave arrives at the upper end of the reach. It continues to increase until the wave front reaches the lower station, which may be hours later.   During all this period of increasing storage the outflow, O, may have been constant. It follows, therefore, that O is not directly related to storage. The authors, assuming that the storage in any reach is related to the average of water-surface elevation at the two ends and therefore to the average of the discharges at the two ends, have plotted storage against $(Q + O)$ with satisfactory results.[27]

[23] Footnote 16, page 350.

[24] Footnote 20, page 351.

[25] Footnote 21, page 351.

[26] Franklin F. Snyder, "Synthetic Unit-Graphs," *Trans. Am. Geophys. Union*, 1938, p. 447.

[27] Footnote 16, page 350.

A somewhat similar procedure is used in the Muskingum method. In this method, storage is related to the weighted average of the total inflow $(Q + I)$ and O as follows: $S = K(xI_t + (1 - x)O)$, where $I_t = (Q + I)$. The value of x is selected to give as nearly as possible the same storage-discharge relation during rising and falling river stages. When $x = 0$, the relation applies to reservoir storage (compare with equation 2, page 346). The authors' method[27] described above also provides for a variable value of x, because I was not used in their plotting. Consequently, the weight given to I_t depends upon the relative magnitudes of Q and I. If, for example, I is approximately equal to Q, S would, in effect, be plotted against $\left(\dfrac{I_t}{2} + O\right)$, which would correspond to using $x = \frac{1}{3}$ in the Muskingum formula. When I is zero, the weighting would correspond to $x = 0.5$. In the Tennessee River work[28] previously mentioned, a graphical method is used to accomplish this same purpose.

4. Variable Stage-Discharge Relations. Unlike outflow from a reservoir, discharge at a river-gaging station may vary with the slope of the energy gradient as well as with the stage. At such stations the relation between gage height and discharge are somewhat different for rising and falling stages (see Chapter 12, page 384). It follows that a relation between channel storage and discharge would also depend to some extent upon whether the discharge is increasing or decreasing. Several methods of correcting for such effects have been described.[29,30] Each of these is developed for a particular situation and is not sufficiently general to warrant a detailed description here.

[28] Footnote 15, page 350.
[29] Footnote 15, page 350.
[30] Footnote 16, page 350.

12

Stream-Flow Records

If the exact relationships between rainfall, evaporation, transpiration, infiltration, and runoff were fully understood, there would be little need for the establishment of gaging stations and the collection of discharge records. Inasmuch as long-term rainfall records are available almost everywhere, the necessary stream-flow data could then be computed more quickly and at less expense than they can be collected in the field. However, these relationships are not and perhaps never will be sufficiently well understood to enable the engineer to make a satisfactory determination of the yield of any stream without having actual discharge records covering a more or less extended period. Regardless of the advances that will unquestionably be made in this science, it is doubtful if discharge records will ever cease to play an important role in the solution of all problems involving a knowledge of stream flow.

A brief treatment of the technique involved in obtaining stream-flow records is given here. Special problems encountered on semiarid basins have been discussed in Chapter 9. For a more complete discussion the reader is referred to the various treatises on the subject.[1]

---

[1] Grover and Harrington, *Stream Flow,* John Wiley, 1943. (Out of print.)

W. A. Liddel, *Stream Gaging,* McGraw-Hill, 1927.

D. M. Corbett and others, "Stream-Gaging Procedure," *U. S. Geol. Survey Water-Supply Paper* 888.

Methods of Obtaining Discharge Records

The principal types of installations used to obtain continuous records of stream discharge are classified as follows:

1. Weir stations.
2. Control meter stations.
3. Power plants.
4. Velocity area stations.

No one of these methods is the best suited to all conditions, but one is always to be preferred to the others. It is the engineer's duty to study carefully each situation and determine the best procedure.

Weir Stations

Weirs are overflow structures for which there is a mathematical relationship between head, or height of water above the crest, and the discharge. A record of head may, therefore, be translated into a record of discharge. Weirs are often installed on small streams for the purpose of measuring discharge. Large installations are seldom made because the cost is prohibitive. However, spillways of dams are often used as weirs to measure the discharge of large streams. There are two types of weirs, sharp-crested and broad-crested. Sharp-crested weirs are characterized by a knife-edge overflow section from which the jet springs free. Broad-crested weirs include all other types of cross sections, such as flat-topped weirs and ogee spillway sections. Either type requires that the elevation of the tail water be low enough to avoid backwater at the crest. ·

Sharp-crested weirs, when built in accordance with standard practice, have the advantage of not requiring the establishment of a rating curve from field measurements. V-notch weirs are used to measure small discharges. A 90° V-notch is suitable for accurate determination of flows as low as 0.01 cfs. Some of the formulas derived for these and other types of weirs are found in standard books on hydraulics. Rectangular sharp-crested weirs are used for larger flows. Sharp-crested weirs are not adaptable to streams carrying loads of silt and debris. Such material collects in the stilling pool above the weir, thus raising the velocity of approach higher than under calibration conditions. Floating debris is likely to injure the crest of the weirs or to become lodged on the sharp crest where it affects the weir reading.

Broad-crested weirs may also be precalibrated, but for accurate results they are usually calibrated in the field. When such weirs have a horizontal crest they follow the general law that

$$Q = CLH^{3/2} \tag{1}$$

where Q is the discharge in cubic feet per second, L is the length of the crest in feet, H is the head in feet, and C is an empirical coefficient that must be determined from discharge measurements. King[2] gives a large number of values of C for various types of broad-crested weirs. In order to provide a greater sensitivity to low discharges, broad-crested weirs having a parabolic notch have been utilized with good results. One such type developed by the U. S. Geological Survey is called the Columbus Deep Notch. It has the additional advantage of permitting the passage of most floating material and of being only slightly sensitive to changes in velocity of approach such as result from sedimentation.

Control Meters

A control meter is a structure built in the channel of a stream, by which critical depth is produced by raising the bottom of the channel, decreasing the width, or both. The throat of the section is usually made rectangular or trapezoidal in cross section. Such a device permits the application of the well-known relationships between discharge, minimum energy, and critical depth[3] for determining the discharge. The floor of the throat is made level, whereas the floor of the expanding outlet is given a sufficiently steep slope to cause the water to leave the throat at supercritical velocities and thus insure the presence of critical depth at some point in the throat. The expanding side walls of the outlet have the same effect as the steep bottom slope. A properly designed control meter is characterized by the presence of a hydraulic jump. The jump is below the constriction when the original depth in the channel is greater than critical depth and above the control when the original depth is less than critical.

It is not possible to measure critical depth directly, since its exact position in the throat varies with the discharge and is not easily found even for a particular discharge. The discharge is determined by measuring the head at a point above the throat and applying the relationship between discharge and specific energy at critical depth. For a rectangular throat, this relationship is $Q = 3.087bH^{3/2}$, in which b is the width of the throat and H is the specific energy at critical depth as shown in Fig. 121.[3] An application of Bernoulli's equation between

[2] H. W. King, *Handbook of Hydraulics,* McGraw-Hill, 1954, page 5–1.

[3] H. W. King, *Handbook of Hydraulics,* McGraw-Hill, 1954, page 8–7.

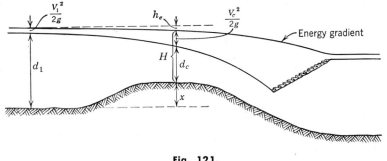

Fig. 121.

point 1 where the gage is placed and the throat, and solved for H, results in the following relationship

$$H = d_1 - x + \frac{V_1^2}{2g} - h_e \qquad (2)$$

in which only the two minor quantities V_1 and h_e are unknown. V_1 may be found by trial, thus leaving only the energy loss unknown. Studies made by the U. S. Bureau of Reclamation[4] indicate that, when all surfaces are connected by tangent curves, the energy loss is so low that it may be neglected. A meter with one angular change in direction at the beginning of a constriction is found to have a coefficient of discharge of 0.95.[5] The length of the throat must be kept as short as possible to avoid energy losses and at the same time long enough to insure that the critical depth will fall within the throat. A throat length of about three times critical depth has been found to give good results.

The chief advantage of the control meter over the weir is its ability to measure discharge in debris- and silt-laden streams.[6] Since the flow immediately above the control is accelerated rather than retarded as it is in the stilling pool of a weir, silt and debris tend to be swept through the control. Its rugged construction permits the passage of logs and debris that would seriously damage a sharp-crested weir. This type of control is especially suited to intermittent streams on which there is little opportunity to find a natural control. The capac-

[4] Julian Hinds, discussion of "The Improved Venturi Flume," *Trans. A.S.C.E.*, 1926, vol. 86, p. 859.

[5] Dr. F. V. A. E. Engel, "The Venturi Flume," *Engineer*, August 3 and 10, 1934.

[6] H. G. Wilm, J. S. Cotton, and H. C. Storey, "Measurement of Debris-Laden Stream Flow with Critical-Depth Flumes," *Trans. A.S.C.E.*, 1938, vol. 103, p. 1237.

ity may be made as large as desired by simply making the throat wider. The lower limit for accurate discharge measurements increases with the capacity of the meter. A typical ratio of maximum to minimum discharge is 125 to 1. Since it is usually necessary to measure discharges below the lower limit of large meters, a second smaller control meter or a weir is often set in parallel with the large one.

Power Plant Records

At most modern power plants, operating records are kept that provide an excellent basis for the determination of the mean daily discharge past those plants. On many streams the head is so fully developed for power purposes that no suitable places are left for velocity-area stations because of backwater. In addition, many other streams are located where the climate is rigorous, and it is impossible to get discharge records without ice interference. Where such interference occurs good records are both difficult to obtain and expensive.

The total flow that passes a power plant is equal to the sum of the flow (1) through the turbines, (2) over the spillway, (3) through the various gates, sluices, fish ladders, etc., and (4) through, underneath, and around the dam, powerhouse, and embankments.

The hydraulic turbine is an excellent water meter. The discharge capacity at various gate openings of most modern turbines has been accurately determined. If it is unknown, it can be found by means of tests. If it is a low-head plant and the turbines are set in an open wheel pit, the discharge for the various gate openings can be measured by current meters in the head race, by the salt-solution method, or possibly by means of a weir in the tail race. If it is a high-head plant and the water is conducted to the turbines through a closed penstock or pipe line, it may be more convenient to measure the discharge by the salt-velocity method, the Gibson method, or possibly by means of a Pitot tube. After a turbine has once been rated for the various gate openings, its rating is affected only slightly by years of service.

The coefficients (equation 1) of discharge for nearly all types of spillways as they are built at the present time have been quite accurately determined.[7] For other types, the coefficient can be determined by current meter measurements made at a time when all turbines, gates, sluices, etc., are closed. Almost all modern power plants keep a complete log of head-water and tail-water elevations. If the elevations of the crest of the dam and of the zero of the head-water gage are

[7] Robert E. Horton, "Weir Experiments, Coefficients and Formulas," *U. S. Geol. Survey Water-Supply Paper* 200, Government Printing Office, Washington, D. C. H. W. King, *Handbook of Hydraulics*, McGraw-Hill, fourth ed., 1954.

known, the head over the spillway is found, and, with the length of spillway known, the discharge is computed.

A similar procedure is followed for finding the discharge through the various gates, sluices, etc. If they are of such construction that the proper coefficients cannot be found in engineering literature, they can be calibrated by the use of current meters or by other means. Horton[8] has provided a good method for determining the proper coefficients to be used for partially open Tainter gates.

The leakage past the dam may be determined by closing the turbines and other openings for a short time during low water, with the head drawn down enough to prevent overflow during the test, and then measuring with a current meter the total flow downstream from the plant. The quantity is sometimes so small that it may be neglected.

By adding these quantities the total daily discharges are determined. With regard to accuracy, the results obtained by this method are the very opposite in character to those obtained at weir stations. In this instance, during periods of low flow nearly all the water passes through the turbines and that flow should be accurately determined. In rigorous climates the winter flows are usually low and therefore difficult to determine accurately at either weir or velocity-area stations. Again during flood periods the peak discharges can ordinarily be determined more accurately from power-plant records than by either of the other methods.

Velocity-Area Stations

At velocity-area stations discharge measurements are made by dividing the stream cross section into a number of parts for each of which the area, velocity, and discharge are determined separately. By adding these partial discharges, we obtain the total for the stream. After a sufficient number of such measurements have been made, they are plotted against their corresponding gage heights to produce a station-rating curve or a discharge curve as it is called. Such a curve is shown in Fig. 122. After having been established, gage readings that have been taken at regular intervals, such as daily or oftener, may be applied to the curve and the corresponding discharges thereby determined.

Every velocity-area station has three essential features: (1) a control, (2) a gage, and (3) a metering section. The characteristics and relative locations of these component parts may vary considerably at different stations.

[8] Robert E. Horton, "Discharge Coefficients for Tainter Gates," *Eng. News-Record,* January 24, 1934.

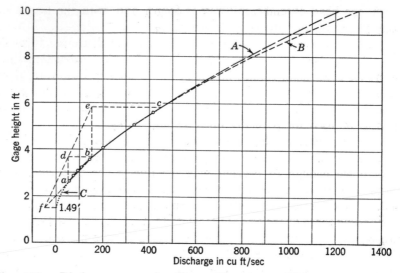

Fig. 122. Discharge curve for Huron River near Whitmore Lake, Mich. Extended by: A, $A\sqrt{D}$ method; B, Logarithmic method; C, Running method.

The *control* is a cross section or reach of river channel that determines the relationship between stage and discharge at that section and for some distance upstream. The *gage* is an instrument that is installed upstream from but within the range of influence of the control for the purpose of determining the fluctuations in stage with respect to time. The *metering section* is the cross section of the stream where the discharge is measured.

Inasmuch as the discharge measured at the metering section is plotted against stage measured at the gage, it follows that there should be no appreciable inflow to or outflow from the stream between these two points. Beyond that, there is no restriction as to their relative locations. In other words, although the gage must be located as noted previously with respect to the control, the metering section may be either upstream or downstream from either the gage or the control, as long as the quantity of water passing it per second is substantially the same as that passing the gage.

The Control. The control may well be considered the most important of the three component parts of the station. Upon its permanence very largely depend both the cost and value of the discharge records obtained. In establishing a station the control should, therefore, receive first consideration; the gage should never be installed until after the location of the control has been determined.

In Fig. 123 are shown the longitudinal profiles of the bed of a stream and the water surface for a given reach. $ABCDEF$ represents the profile of the water surface during a low stage of the stream. At this stage the section at C serves as a control for the reach extending up to B, and the section at E is the control for the reach from D to E. The reaches AB, CD, and EF act as their own controls throughout their respective lengths at this low stage. A reasonable amount of erosion or sedimentation at any point throughout these reaches does not appreciably affect the elevation of water surface for any considerable distance upstream. Nor does any similar change occurring anywhere between B and C or between D and E measurably affect the water surface anywhere upstream. On the other hand, any change occurring either at C or at E produces a corresponding effect upon the water surface throughout the reach BC or DE, respectively, during the low stages of the river. However, when the water surface rises approximately to the stage represented by the profile $A'E'F'$, the section at E becomes the control for the entire length of channel from A to E. For this stage or for higher stages, any ordinary changes in the cross section of the channel, even though they occur at C or between A and B, have but slight effect upon the elevation of water surface although a similar change at E produces a marked effect throughout the entire reach from A to E. Thus many sections of the channel which act as controls during low stages of the river become completely drowned out in the high stages and have almost no effect on the water surface at points upstream.

Except in places where a rock outcrop creates either a waterfall or a rapids with considerable drop, a longitudinal river profile is a practical necessity in determining the location of the various controls in any given length of stream channel. The best control is the one that is the most nearly permanent and that functions as a control throughout all stages of the river.

No control is absolutely permanent. The continuous flow of water combined with the effects of temperature changes causes even the hardest granites to slowly disintegrate. Nevertheless, a control that is

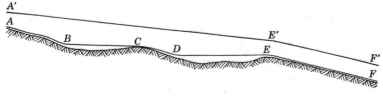

Fig. 123.

formed by an outcropping of good, hard, resistant rock may be considered permanent at least for several decades. Most other controls are subject to a slow and gradual change through long periods or to a more rapid change during floods. After a gaging station has been established and sufficient discharge measurements have been made to determine the relationship between stage and discharge, it becomes the engineer's duty and responsibility to make additional discharge measurements at various stages from time to time to learn just how rapidly or how slowly the control is changing. Such measurements should especially be made soon after the occurrence of major floods, for the most marked changes ordinarily occur then. A control should never be assumed permanent until it has been proved so by a number of measurements made after the passage of such floods.

In some locations, especially on small streams, artificial controls are installed. The use of control meters and weirs has already been discussed. When properly installed, such devices require no special calibration. More generally, however, an artificial control is a low overflow dam or lined section of stream bed built for the purpose of stabilizing the stage-discharge relationship. The low dam type serves the additional purpose of providing sufficient depth for a current meter in shallow streams. An artificial control should have adequate cutoff walls and an apron on the downstream side as protection against erosion. The shape of the cross section should be designed to facilitate the passage of floating debris and bed material, whereas the curvature of the crest should be designed to provide the desired sensitivity at low discharges. The U. S. Geological Survey has developed a number of standard types of low dam controls.[9]

The Gage and Its Location. All gages may be classified as either recording or nonrecording. Recording gages draw a continuous graph of the fluctuations in stage. Nonrecording gages require an observer who reads the gage and records the readings at regular time intervals.

Regardless of the type of gage employed, it should be located so as to conform to the following specifications:

1. It must be upstream from, but within the range of influence of, the control.

2. Its support should be rigid and immovable so that the elevation of the datum is unlikely to change.

3. It should be as sensitive as possible; in other words, it should be located where the greatest range of fluctuations in stage occurs. In Fig. 123 the proper location is at or near D.

    [9] Grover and Harrington, *Stream Flow,* John Wiley, 1943. (Out of print.)

4. It should be in a protected spot so that destruction by ice or other floating debris is improbable.

5. It should be easily accessible.

6. If the gage is nonrecording and on a northern stream, it should be located at a point in the stream where the velocity of the water is great enough to prevent ice formation. Oftentimes a good location is on the side of a bridge pier near the downstream end. At this point the water usually flows smoothly, does not freeze or pile up on the gage, and the danger of destruction and probability of change in datum is slight.

7. The gage should never be located upstream from the junction with another stream near enough to be affected by backwater from that stream. Nor should it ever be located within the influence of backwater from a hydroelectric plant. At neither of these locations is the relation between stage and discharge constant.

Recording Gages. Automatic recording gages have so many advantages over the nonrecording type that they are being used more and more. Their principal advantages are:

1. The personal equation is almost entirely eliminated. In disagreeable weather or at times when the observer of a nonrecording gage is busy with other matters, there is a strong temptation not to read the gage for considerable periods at a time and then to interpolate the missing values. Authenticity of records may therefore be questionable at times.

2. A nonrecording gage is usually read by the observer once or twice a day. Especially on the smaller streams, large fluctuations may occur between readings, and as a result the hydrograph obtained by plotting the discharges from the daily gage readings does not present a true picture of the actual behavior of the stream. This matter becomes doubly important when one or more power plants are located upstream from the gage and also when diversions for irrigation, municipal, or industrial uses are made at upstream points which change the natural flow of the stream.

In Fig. 124 is shown a continuous-recording river gage. In this instrument the cylinder is driven by the clock at a constant speed represented on the record sheet by scales varying from 1.2 in. per day to 864 in. per day. The pen carriage, actuated by a float as the water surface in the well rises and falls, travels back and forth. The rate of travel varies from 0.2 in. to 10 in. for each foot of fluctuation in stage. To permit the recording of unlimited fluctuations in gage height, the

record sheet, winds the clock at regular intervals, and sees to it that the gage operation is continuous.

When these gages are installed in isolated places with no attendant present, there is always the danger of a break in the continuity of the records because of the clock stopping or because of some other instrumental failure. The longer the period of operation without attention the more delicate is the mechanism and therefore the greater is the probability of breakdown. Gages operating no longer than a week or 10 days are relatively sturdy in construction and free from failures. Even when such gages stop, the interruption is for such a short period that the missing records can be interpolated quite satisfactorily. On the other hand, it is almost impossible to interpolate records that are missing for a period of a month or longer. The value of discharge records increases tremendously with their continuity. Frequent interruptions render them of little value for many purposes.

In the long-distance transmitting type of gage, the transmitter is installed at the point on the stream where the records are to be obtained. By means of an electric line, such as a telephone circuit, the gage heights are automatically transmitted to any distant point, where receiving instruments are installed. The receivers are usually of the continuous-recording type, although they may also be of the indicating type in which the gage height is only indicated on a dial and is not recorded. Although this type of gage is expensive to install, especially where the records are to be obtained at a remote point and a long transmission line must be built, it has several great advantages over other types of gages. The receiver may be installed in a power plant or office where someone is always present to observe a break in operation and to dispatch a repair man to find and correct the trouble, thereby insuring continuity of records. No additional employee in the field or long trip from the office or power plant is necessary to change the record sheet at regular intervals. Radio-operated remote-recording systems are also available. They have the advantage of not requiring a wire between the gage-height transmitter and the recorder.

All recording gages that are not in power plants or in pumping stations should be housed in permanent shelters preferably of concrete and located on the stream bank. The floor of the gage house should be above the extreme high-water level. The float well should be excavated to a depth below the extreme low-water stage, so that the float can rise and fall freely with the fluctuations of the stream. A pipe having a diameter of about 4 in. should connect the float well with the deepest portion of the stream. A bank of earth or other material around the gage house may prevent freezing in the winter. Otherwise an electric light in the well or some other device must be employed for this purpose.

Nonrecording Gages. Nonrecording gages are of four general types: (1) staff, (2) weight, (3) float, and (4) hook.

Staff gages are either vertical or inclined and are usually located at or near the water's edge to be easily readable and readily accessible to the observer. The zero of the gage should be below the stage of extreme low water to prevent the occurrence of negative readings. If the stream is subject to large fluctuations in stage, and the banks slope gently to the water's edge, either two or more sections of vertical staff or an inclined staff may be used. If the vertical staff is adopted, special care should be taken to insure that the several sections are so installed that the gage readings on all sections refer to exactly the same datum. If an inclined staff is used, it should be securely anchored to concrete piers that extend well below the frost line to prevent a change in datum through frost action.

Vertical-staff gages may be either metal or wood, although the former are much to be preferred. Alternate subjection of wood-staff gages to air and water causes rapid deterioration, and painted graduations soon peel off. Enameled metal staffs have a much longer life, can be obtained in various lengths of section, and can be graduated to tenths, half tenths, and hundredths of feet if desired. Inclined staffs, on the other hand, are usually made of wood. The graduations are put on after the gage has been installed, and the space depends upon the slope at which the gage is set.

Weight gages are so designed that a weight, attached to the end of a tape, chain, or wire, can be lowered to the water surface and the gage is read to determine the elevation of the water with respect to some fixed datum. A gage of this type is illustrated in Fig. 127. In this instrument the weight, W, is lowered by means of a narrow metal tape, T, which has a low coefficient of expansion and is graduated in feet only. The tape is wound on the reel, R, and passes

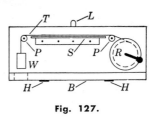

Fig. 127.

over the pulleys, P, and the scale, S, which is 1 ft long and is graduated in tenths and hundredths of feet. When the reel is released and the weight is lowered to the water surface, only one foot mark can be over the scale. The gage reading is represented by that foot mark plus the tenth and hundredth appearing on the scale directly beneath the foot mark. Only the back and base of the gage box are shown in the figure. The remainder of the box, with hinges at H, has been removed.

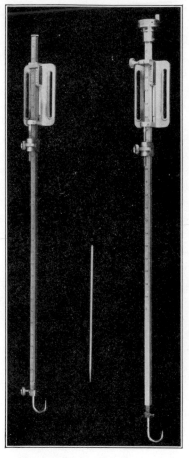

Fig. 128. Hook gages. Also straight point that can be substituted for hook. Courtesy W. and L. E. Gurley.

A float gage consists of a float and a counterweight connected by a tape, wire cable, or chain that passes over a pulley located near the upper end of a vertically graduated scale board. The gage reading is indicated on the scale by an index marker on the tape, cable, or chain. To prevent its being carried away by the current, the float must be enclosed in a stilling well which consists of a vertical box usually made of timber or concrete and having holes in the sides or bottom to permit the water to stand at the same level inside and outside. The principal use of such gages is at power plants and at pumping stations.

Hook gages, examples of which are shown in Fig. 128, are the most accurate of all types of gages. A hook gage is usually installed in a stilling well in order to provide a calm water surface. The hook, which is attached to the lower end of a vertical rod, is lowered until the point is beneath the water surface where it is clamped in position. By means of a slow-motion screw it is then raised until the point causes a slight rise to appear on the water surface. By means of a vernier the stage can be read to a thousandth of a foot. Because the accuracy attained is not justified in view of the difficulty in making the readings, this type of gage is seldom used in stream-gaging work, except at some weir stations where slight fluctuations in stage cause appreciable variations in discharge.

Gage Datum. Regardless of the type of gage that is used, it is of utmost importance that the elevation of its zero be determined with respect to at least two permanent bench marks in the near vicinity. After a gage has once been installed, its datum should if possible be kept unchanged.

The maintenance of a permanent datum is of such fundamental importance that the elevation of the zero of the gage should be checked annually, and the gage should be reset whenever any change is found to have occurred. Unless this precaution is taken, long periods of records are likely to have doubtful value because of a change in the elevation of the gage. Inasmuch as the time when this change occurred is unknown, corrections are impossible. With an annual check, however, this difficulty is greatly reduced.

Measurement of Velocity

For the determination of the velocity of a stream a great many different kinds of instruments have been developed. These instruments fall into three general classes depending upon the principles on which they operate: (1) floats, (2) pressure instruments, and (3) current meters.

Floats, inasmuch as they move with the same velocity as the adjacent water, provide a direct means of measuring that velocity. There are three kinds of floats: surface, subsurface, and rod. For surface floats almost anything that floats may be used, such as apples, oranges, bottles partly filled with water, cakes of ice, driftwood, pieces of paper, and so on. The surface velocity is found by timing the travel of these floats at various points across the stream through measured distances that usually range between 100 ft and 500 ft. The mean velocity in the vertical is taken as the product of the observed surface velocity and a coefficient. This coefficient should be determined experimentally (see page 378). Rod floats are usually of wood, about 2 inches square, and of a length slightly greater than the depth of the water. They should be well coated with waterproof paint or varnish to prevent them from becoming waterlogged and should be so weighted at their lower end that they float vertically and almost submerged. Subsurface floats are no longer used. The use of all kinds of floats should be restricted to straight stretches of river channel having a practically uniform cross section throughout. Because natural river channels seldom if ever fulfill this requirement, floats are not extensively used in stream-gaging work.

From time to time various instruments have been devised for the purpose of measuring the velocity at a point in the stream based upon the principle of converting the kinetic energy of the water into pressure energy and then measuring the pressure head. The Pitot tube, which is the most noteworthy of these instruments, can be used successfully in pipes and in experimental channels but is not adapted for use in natural rivers. Another instrument of this type utilizes a flat plate, the pressure on whose face is transmitted through a hollow tube and indicated on a dial. Numerous other devices employing this principle have been developed, but none has proved satisfactory for measuring velocities in natural streams.

At nearly all velocity-area stations the velocities are determined by current meters in which a wheel is made to rotate about its axis by the force of the current. The speed of rotation depends upon the velocity of the water. Inasmuch as this relationship is affected by many factors such as bearing friction and the shape and surface condition of the moving parts, it is necessary to rate each meter even though it may appear to be an exact replica of another rated meter. The rating should be checked after severe usage, when it has been accidentally damaged, and about once a year under ordinary usage.

Rating of Current Meter

The usual method of rating a current meter is to draw it through still water and observe the time of travel and number of revolutions made as the meter travels a given distance. The number of revolutions per second and the corresponding velocity in feet per second are then computed. When these quantities are plotted one against the other on ordinary cross-section paper, a straight line is usually found to fit the points closely enough for all practical purposes. Ordinarily, however, there is a change in the slope of this line at some certain velocity that seems to vary for different meters, so that two equations for this relationship must be derived, one for the higher velocities and the other for the lower. These equations are then solved for different velocities and a rating table is made up.

Among the current meter-rating stations in the United States are those at the Bureau of Standards, Washington, D. C.; University of Michigan, Ann Arbor, Michigan; Cornell University, Ithaca, New York; and Rensselaer Polytechnic Institute, Troy, New York. At all these stations the meter is suspended from a car, driven by a motor at uniform speed, that is running on a track over a tank or channel filled with water. Time, distance, and number of revolutions are automatically recorded on a revolving drum.

It has been found that for any given velocity of the car a meter supported by a rod revolves faster than if it were supported by a cable. Hence, when a meter is being rated it should be supported in the same manner in which it will be used in making measurements. If sometimes it will be supported by rod and at other times by cable, it should then be rated both ways.

Types of Current Meters

All current meters may be divided into two general classes, differential and direct-acting, depending entirely upon the type of wheel employed. In the differential meter, of which the Price (Fig. 129) is an example, the wheel consists of a series of cups that rotate on a vertical axis. It is observed that half of the cups are convex and half are concave to the current. The difference in pressure produces the rotation. In the direct-acting meter, such as shown in Fig. 130, the wheel, which resembles a propeller, carries a number of vanes on a horizontal axis whose direction coincides with the direction of flow. The force of the current acts directly and uniformly on all the vanes and tends to cause rotation.

Current meters may also be classified in accordance with the manner in which the observer determines the number of revolutions that the wheel makes during the period of observation. Under this method of

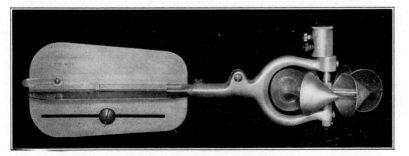

Fig. 129. Price current meter. Courtesy W. and L. E. Gurley.

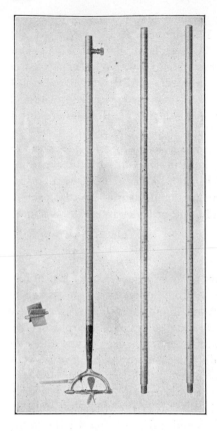

Fig. 130. Direct-acting meter. Courtesy Leupold & Stevens Instruments.

classification, the different types are (1) mechanical, (2) acoustic, and (3) electric.

The mechanical meter, through a worm gear on the shaft of the meter wheel, operates a set of gears that indicates the number of revolutions the meter wheel has made during the observation. A cord or light wire-cable connection enables the operator to throw the gears in and out of mesh at the beginning and end of each observation. On account of trouble from floating debris and the inconvenience of taking the meter out of the water for each reading, this meter has never gained extensive use.

The acoustic meter and also the electric meter are so designed that a signal is produced at each revolution or at every second, fifth, tenth, or other number of revolutions. In the acoustic meter the signal is conveyed directly to the ear of the observer through a hollow tube. As these meters must be held in position by the observer, their use is restricted to shallow streams. In the electric meter a telephone circuit energized by a battery carries the signal to a telephone receiver at the ear of the observer. Because of its general adaptability to the wide variety of conditions encountered in natural rivers, this type of meter is almost universally used.

In making an observation with either an acoustic or an electric meter, the meter is submerged to the desired depth, whereupon the observer with the aid of a stop watch determines the time required for a certain number of revolutions. As the velocity at any given point in a river is not usually constant but is subject to pulsations, a sufficient number of signals should be timed so that the true mean velocity at that point is closely approximated. For this purpose the time of observation is usually about 50 or 60 sec. After we know the time required for a given number of revolutions, we determine the velocity from the rating table (see page 370).

The vulnerable parts of current meters are the cups or vanes and the bearings. After every measurement the meter should be dismantled and carefully dried, and the bearings should not only be dried but oiled, using only high-grade watch oil. One of the advantages of differential meters is that they have vertical shafts and therefore operate on point bearings with a minimum amount of friction. To protect the bearings from injury, they should be released from contact when not in use. The spinning time of every meter should be known. Just before starting the gaging, the meter should be given the spinning test in still air to make certain the bearings are properly adjusted. The operation of the meter wheel should be watched constantly. If it appears to be sluggish, repeat the spinning test. Cup meters are slowed down when algae become wound around the axis near the bearings either above or below the wheel. When algae or other foreign matter is found in the bearings upon the completion of the gaging, all measurements that were made after the bearings were last inspected or tested should be repeated. In operating the meter near bridge piers or rocks, great care should be taken to prevent injury to the meter wheel. If the cups or propeller are dented, bent, or chipped in any way, its rotating speed for any velocity of water has most likely been changed, and the meter should be rerated before being used again. When the contact signals are received irregularly, the observer should determine the cause; such irregularity may result from pulsations in the currents, from missing contacts, or from breaks in the electric circuit.

Stop watches also are delicate instruments and should be checked frequently to determine whether or not they properly record the time.

Methods of Making Current Meter Measurements

Current meter measurements may be made (1) from bridges, (2) from cableways, (3) from boats, and (4) by wading. Bridges provide the most convenient method, when they are available and when the cross section and velocity of the stream at the bridge are favorable to accurate measurement. However, the best cross section is rarely found at a bridge. If there are piers in the river, they usually create turbulence and scour. Often old cofferdams and piling are left from the construction of the bridge, and these impair the value of the section for current meter work. There is then the question of whether or not the convenience provided by the bridge more than offsets the inaccuracy resulting from its use.

Cableways are frequently used by the U. S. Geological Survey. Although rather expensive to install, they have the advantage that they can be built at sites that are the most favorable for gaging. From the cableway a car is suspended by means of which the observer propels himself from point to point across the stream. The cable, which is usually ⅝ in. to ¾ in. stranded steel wire, may be suspended between trees or between specially constructed and well-anchored supports.

Sometimes discharge measurements can be made advantageously from a boat, especially if the velocity of the stream does not exceed 3 or 4 ft per sec. For higher velocities and for rough water it becomes difficult to hold the boat steady enough to permit accurate measurements. For large, wide rivers the boat must be anchored and its position determined by means of sextant or by triangulation. For narrower streams it can be held in position by a cable stretched across the river, and tagged with the stationing usually at 10-ft intervals. The meter should be suspended from a boom projecting several feet from the boat, so that the measured velocities are unaffected by the presence of the boat.

Measurements by wading are restricted to streams that are relatively shallow and of moderate velocity. A tagged measuring line or tape must be stretched across the river near the water's surface. The meter must be held far enough away from the observer that his presence does not affect the velocities being measured.

Measurement of Area

In making discharge measurements with current meters the biggest errors usually result from measurements of area rather than of velocity. For this reason the seemingly simple operation of measuring

empirically and is equal to $K \times ef$.
sec θ and also values of K as deterr...

TABL...

θ	sec θ	K
4	1.0024	0.0006
6	1.0055	.0016
8	1.0098	.0032
10	1.0154	.0050
12	1.0223	.0072
14	1.0306	.0098
16	1.0403	.0128
18	1.0515	.0164
20	1.0642	.0204

In making measurements

1. Measure the distanc...
2. Lower the weight u...
measure af.
3. Find ae from ab se...
4. Subtract ae from ...
Subtract the result fro...
5. To make a veloci...
the stream, the meter...
a distance equal to ...
from the bottom of ...
6. To make a me...
is lowered until the...
equal to ae plus tv...

As an illustrati...
$af = 29.7$ ft, and...

If the distan...
meter wheel...
the stream ...
tenths of tl...

the depth of the stream receives considerable attention. When the velocities are low (less than about 4 ft per sec), no serious difficulties are encountered; but, when the velocities are around 5 or 6 ft per sec or more, and when the river is deep, accurate measurements are not easily made.

Occasionally the stream bed is nearly permanent and is subject to neither erosion nor sedimentation. In this instance a standard cross section should be taken in time of low water. With a level and rod, elevations of the river bed are obtained at the intervals necessary to define its contour properly. This cross section is plotted, and the depths below zero gage height are indicated at all points at which velocity measurements are made. The depths existing at the time of any measurement are then found by adding these values to the gage height. When such standard cross sections are used they should be checked at frequent intervals to make certain of their permanence.

If the stream bed at the metering section shifts too much to permit the use of a standard cross section, it is necessary to determine the depth by sounding at each measuring point every time a gaging is made. For this sounding there are two general methods of procedure, depending somewhat upon the depth, velocity, and equipment at hand.

With ordinary velocities, the depths are easily measured. However, when the velocities are high, a heavy lead weight suspended from a small but strong wire cable can be swung upstream and dropped so that it reaches the bed upstream from the metering section. By pulling up the cable until it becomes taut the weight can be lifted just enough to allow it to slide along the bed until it reaches the measuring section. Then with the cable as near a vertical line as possible it is gripped or marked at some reference point, as, for instance, the corner of the bridge rail, if the measurement is being made from a bridge. The weight is then lifted until the bottom just grazes the water surface. The depth is found by measuring the amount the cable has been raised. Such soundings are made successively at all points at which velocity measurements are to be made later. Frequent gage readings should be taken to determine whether or not the stage is changing. If the regular gage is not near at hand, a temporary gage or reference mark should be established. If the stage does change, the proper corrections must be made to the measured depths when the velocity readings are taken. In this manner the depths are found at all the stations before any velocities are measured.

In the other method, and this is perhaps the more common procedure, the meter, weight, and cable are first used for sounding the depth and then for measuring the velocity at that same station before moving

up to the next station. When
in swift, deep water, especia
cableway, corrections have
vertical depth of stream a
depth below the surface.

In the Annual Report of
F. C. Shenehon describes
placements in deep, swi
assumed by the soundin
stream, is supported ent
that if the weight is slo
from the length of cab
difference between the
depth bc, assuming t
are functions of the a
ence between the l

$(0.2 \times 10.55) - 0.50 = 1.6$ ft. Also if a velocity measurement is to
be made at two tenths of the depth below the surface, the meter should
be let down a distance of $18.7 + 0.2 \times 11.0 = 20.9$ ft below a.
The values in Table 32 are given to the fourth decimal place mainly
for purposes of interpolating, and depths should be recorded to the
nearest tenth of a foot only. Corbett[10] warns that this method is based
upon the following assumptions:

1. That the weight and wire are such that the weight will go to the bottom
despite the force of the current.
2. That the sounding is made with the weight at the bottom but entirely
supported by the wire.
3. That the horizontal pressure on the weight, when in the sounding position, is neglected.
4. That the table of coefficients is applicable for any wire or sounding
weight provided the wire or weight is designed so as to present as little
resistance as possible to the current.

Warning is also given that the method yields correct results only
when the direction of the current is approximately normal to the
metering section. If it deviates by more than 10 degrees, an additional
correction should be made to the vertical angle. In such instances,
however, the results are perhaps of questionable accuracy because of
the probable difference in depth at f from that at c.

Mean Velocity in Vertical

At any point in the cross section of a stream the velocity varies
from the surface down to the bottom. If velocities are plotted as
abscissas and depths as ordinates, the resulting vertical velocity curve
normally resembles a parabola with its horizontal axis located at
about 20 or 25 per cent of the depth below the surface. The exact
shape of the curve varies greatly, however, for different depths of
stream and for different velocities. For any given mean velocity, the
deeper the stream the less is the maximum velocity and the more
nearly is the velocity uniform throughout.

The more commonly used methods of determining the mean velocity
in the vertical with a current meter are the following:

1. Vertical velocity curve.
2. Two-point method.
3. Six-tenths depth method.
4. Two-tenths depth method.

[10] Don M. Corbett, "Stream Gaging Procedure," U. S. Geol. Survey Water-
Supply Paper 888, Government Printing Office, Washington, D. C.

5. Three-point method.
6. Surface method.
7. Integration.

In the vertical velocity-curve method, measurements are made at regular intervals from a point just beneath the surface down to the bottom of the stream. For each curve the velocity should be measured at no less than six points and preferably at ten or twelve. The points are plotted on cross-section paper. The curves are drawn in and extended up to the water surface and down to the bottom of the stream. The area within each curve is then planimetered and divided by the total depth to find the mean velocity. At least one vertical velocity measurement should be made at every station at a high stage of the river, another at a medium stage, and another at a low stage. The results of these measurements are used to determine the coefficients that must be applied to the results obtained by each of the short-cut methods of measurement. For each of these methods for which coefficients are found to be needed, a curve can be obtained by plotting the coefficients, as determined by the measurements, against gage height. By extending this curve to higher stages, we can find the coefficient for any gage height.

In the two-point method an observation is made with the meter at two tenths of the depth and again at eight tenths of the depth below the surface. The average of these two results is taken as the mean velocity in the vertical. Seldom is a coefficient necessary in this method, if the channel is straight, uniform, and unobstructed for some distance upstream from the section. This method is the most widely used and perhaps most generally satisfactory of all. It cannot be used, however, at points where the depth is less than five times the distance from the bottom of the meter weight to the center of the meter wheel, because the meter wheel cannot be submerged to eight tenths of the depth.

In the six-tenths method a single observation is made at six tenths of the depth below the surface, and the result is taken as the mean velocity in the vertical, except where the vertical velocity measurements indicate the need of a corrective coefficient. Although this method usually gives fairly accurate results, it is not as dependable as the two-point method and is not often used, except where the two-point method cannot be used because of insufficient depth or because of interference by grass, weeds, or rocks at eight tenths of the depth.

Before the 0.2-depth method can be used at a station, it is necessary to make a number of discharge measurements at various stages, using either the vertical velocity-curve method or the two-point method. For each such measurement a hypothetical discharge is computed by considering the mean velocity in each vertical as the velocity that was found at two tenths of the depth. Each of these hypothetical discharges is then plotted against the corresponding values of the true measured discharge. The results are usually found to produce a straight, or nearly straight, line passing through the origin.

One of the advantages of the two-tenths method is that at two tenths of the depth the velocity is either the maximum or very nearly the maximum. Therefore in that vicinity the velocity curve is practically vertical, and the velocity varies only slightly with considerable variations in depth. For this reason it is not so important that the meter be placed at exactly the proper depth as in a six-tenths measurement. Also this relationship is more nearly constant than the relation between the surface velocity and the true mean velocity. This method possesses considerable merit.

The three-point method is a combination of the two-point and the six-tenths methods. Observations are made at two tenths, six tenths, and eight tenths of the depth, and the mean of the three is taken as the mean velocity in the vertical. Sometimes the mean of the velocities obtained at the two-tenths and eight-tenths depths is averaged with the velocity at six-tenths depth. This procedure does not seem to be logical, for it is admitted that the six-tenths method does not give as accurate results as the two-point method; it follows, therefore, that the average of these two methods is not as accurate as the two-point method. It may be advantageous, however, to use the three-point method in gaging deep streams and give equal weight to all three measurements.

Surface measurements are sometimes made in which the meter is submerged either a constant depth below the surface for measurements made at all stages, or the meter is submerged a certain percentage of the total depth. Whichever method is used, a coefficient must be applied to each surface velocity to get the mean velocity in the vertical. These coefficients are obtained from vertical velocity measurements by dividing the mean velocity in each vertical by the velocity obtained from the curve at the depth at which the surface measurement is made. By plotting these coefficients against gage height and, if necessary, by extending the curves to higher stages, the proper coefficients can be found for any gaging.

In the integration method, the meter is lowered from the surface to the bottom and returned to the surface at a constant rate at each vertical, and the revolutions are counted and timed for each observation. Because (1) it is difficult to raise and lower the meter at a uniform speed, (2) the observations are affected by the vertical movement of the meter, and (3) the lowest velocities occurring near the stream bed are not included in the integration, this method is not often used nor is it to be recommended.

Characteristics of a Good Metering Section

Regardless of the method employed, the accuracy of current meter measurements depends in a large measure upon the characteristics of the metering section. If those characteristics are ideal or even favorable, an amateur at this work should obtain satisfactory results without much difficulty. On the other hand, if these conditions are adverse, it may tax the ingenuity of the most skillful and experienced hydrographer to make a satisfactory discharge measurement. The conditions that favor good results are as follows:

1. The section should be straight and uniform for a distance upstream equal at least to five times the width of the stream and for a distance downstream equal to twice the width of stream.
2. The bed of the stream should be smooth. It should be free from vegetal growth, boulders, or other obstructions. Bridge piers are particularly objectionable.
3. The bed and banks of the stream should be firm and stable.
4. The current should be normal to the metering section.
5. Velocities should be greater than 1 ft per sec and less than 4 ft per sec.
6. There should be no large overflow section at flood stage.
7. The section should be accessible.

Spacing of Verticals

The number of sections into which the stream should be subdivided depends largely upon the character of the cross section. If the channel is straight, smooth, and uniform for some distance above and below the metering section so that the velocity variations are uniform, perhaps no more than ten sections are necessary, except for very wide streams. Normally, however, there should be more. At two adjacent verticals, neither the depth nor the velocity should differ excessively, since the method of computing the discharge is only approximate. The mean velocity in the section is really not the same as the average of the velocities in the verticals at the ends of the section. If the two depths were the same, the velocities could differ, or, if the two velocities were the same, the depths could differ without causing an error. But, for example, if one depth is 1 ft, the mean velocity is 1 ft per sec, the other depth is 5 ft, and the corresponding velocity is 5 ft per sec, the mean velocity for the section is not 3 ft per sec, because the same weight should not be given to the velocity occurring at the 1-ft depth as to that at the 5-ft depth. If the velocity varies as a straight line between these two verticals, true mean velocity occurs at the center of gravity of the section. At the vertical through that point the mean velocity is 3.44 ft per sec instead of 3 ft per sec, an error of about 15 per cent. If an intermediate vertical is taken where the depth is 3 ft, and the mean velocity is 3 ft per sec, this error would be reduced to about 4 per cent. Errors of this kind are nearly always cumulative for the reason that almost invariably the higher velocity occurs at the same vertical with the greater depth. Because of this effect, the computed discharge is too low.

Effect of Swaying of Meter

Especially if the meter is suspended on a cable from a point that is some distance above the water surface there is a tendency for it to be carried not only downstream but also back and forth across the current. All meters are affected by such motion, although in a different manner; differential meters are speeded up by the full amount of the movement, whereas direct-acting meters are retarded to a certain extent. This lateral motion can be prevented, if the stream is not too wide, by means of a light stay line fastened to the meter cable near the water surface and held taut from each bank. Even when a meter is supported on a rod, swift water often causes a short but rapid vibration that affects the velocity observations. The proper solution of difficulties of this sort can usually be best determined by the observer in the field, as the problem varies considerably with the conditions attending each case.

Effect of Angle of Current

The discharge of a stream is the product of the area of cross section and the velocity component normal to that section. Seldom is the direction of the current normal to the cross section, especially at bridges. A meter suspended from a cable swings into line with the current, and therefore any velocity so measured should be multiplied by the cosine of the deflection angle in order to get the velocity component normal to the cross section. Where this angle is no more than 8 degrees the correction is less than 1 per cent and may ordinarily be ignored. For great angles, however, it should be measured and correction made. If no protractor is at hand, the angle can be measured by holding the notebook parallel with the metering section and, with a ruler or straightedge lined up with the direction of the current, drawing a line whose angle with the normal is later measured with a protractor.

Effect of Turbulence

On page 370 it has been explained that in the usual rating of current meters, the meter is drawn at known velocities through still water. The effect is the same as though the meter were held still and the water moved past it—*but with streamline motion.* All meters are affected in one way or another by turbulence. Differential meters overregister in turbulent water by an amount that depends upon the degree of turbulence. Direct-acting meters underregister. An investigation by Yarnell and Nagler[11] indicates that for both kinds of meters the percentage of error increases quite rapidly with the degree of turbulence and is roughly the same for each type. Their tests, however, were all conducted with the meter suspended on a rod, and it is known that a meter behaves differently for different types of support. By far the greater number of the gagings of natural streams are made with meters suspended on cables rather than on rods.

Groat[12] found that differential meters overregister from three to six times as much as direct-acting meters underregister. In view of the difference in the results obtained in these two investigations, it seems that further study should be given to this subject. From the information available at present, it appears that for streams that are only slightly turbulent a measurement made by either type of meter should give satisfactory results. In gaging very turbulent streams, however, if a high degree of accuracy is desired, neither type of meter used alone should be trusted. Either duplicate gagings should be made using both types of meters simultaneously, taking perhaps the average of the results obtained by the two as being correct, or some other method of measurement should be used.

Measurements under Ice Cover

When a stream freezes over, the wetted perimeter is increased by the width of the stream. The hydraulic radius and, therefore, the velocity and discharge are correspondingly reduced for any given stage. Because of the friction with the ice cover, the velocity of the

[11] David L. Yarnell and Floyd A. Nagler, "Effect of Turbulence on the Registration of Current Meters," *Trans. A.S.C.E.*, 1931, vol. 95, pp. 766–860.

[12] B. F. Groat, "Characteristics of Cup and Screw Current Meters," *Trans. A.S.C.E.*, 1913, vol. 76, pp. 819–870.

water near the ice is retarded and the location of the thread of maximum velocity is lowered. Despite this redistribution of velocities
in the vertical, however, it has been found that the average of the
measurements made at two tenths and at eight tenths of the depth
gives the mean in the vertical accurately enough for practical purposes.
The technique of gaging is changed slightly, however.

Holes are cut in the ice preparatory to making measurements at
the same points in the cross section as those used during open-water
conditions. The total depth of the water is then measured. The
distance from the water surface to the bottom of the ice is measured
at each hole and deducted from the total depth. Both these measurements are recorded in the notes. Two tenths and eight tenths of the
difference are computed, and to these values is added the distance
from the water surface to the bottom of the ice. After placing the
center of the wheel on the water surface, these distances are measured
off on the cable, the meter is lowered, and the observations made.
Where the depth under the ice is less than five times the distance
from the bottom of the weight to the center of the meter wheel, a
single measurement should be made at mid-depth below the ice cover,
and a coefficient of about 0.85 should be applied to this result to obtain
the mean velocity in the vertical. A number of vertical velocity
curves should always be derived to check whatever short-cut method
is used.

Effect of Rising or Falling Stage upon the Discharge Curve

During a rising stage of river the velocity and discharge are greater
than they are for the same stage when the discharge is constant.
Likewise, during a falling stage the discharge is less for any given
gage height than it is when the flow is steady. Therefore, when
plotted, the results of discharge measurements made during rising or
falling stages do not fall on the true discharge curve but fall to the
right or left thereof, respectively. The amount of departure from
the true curve does not depend upon the total rise or fall during the
measurement but only upon the rate at which that change occurred.
It is, therefore, important that whenever discharge measurements are
made for the purpose of determining or of checking the discharge
curve, the gage height and time should be recorded at the beginning
and at the end of the gaging in order that the rate of change may be
computed. Figure 132 shows the discharge curve for the Ohio River
at Wheeling, West Virginia. On this curve are also shown the results
of measurements made during the flood of March 1905 and the rates
of rise and fall expressed in feet per hour.

The engineers of the U. S. Geological Survey have developed several methods of correcting discharge measurements and gage heights obtained during changing stages. Most of these methods depend upon the relationship between discharge and slope. The simplest method of making these corrections is to derive curves of relation between percentage of correction in discharge and rate of change in stage. The results are expressed in any convenient units such as feet per hour or feet per day. Such curves can be obtained after a number of discharge measurements have been made during both rising and falling stages and also at constant stage. A smooth discharge curve is then drawn in, passing through or near those points that were obtained at constant stage, to the left of those points obtained at a rising stage, and to the right of those for which the stage was falling. Then for each measurement during a changing stage the percentage is computed by which the discharge obtained from the curve has to be changed to make it agree with the measured discharge for the same gage height. These percentages are plotted against the respective rates of change in stage as shown in Fig. 132. A relationship is found during a rising stage different from that of a falling stage. Usually this relation is expressed as a straight line or a very flat curve.

With such a set of curves available for any gaging station, one can determine the rate of rise and fall during periods of sudden change,

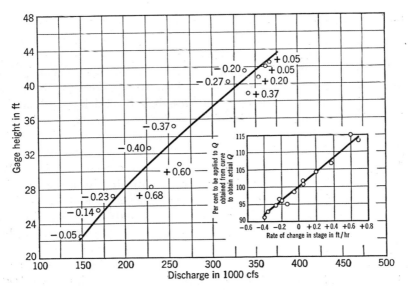

Fig. 132.

read off the percentages of correction, and apply these corrections to the discharge obtained from the rating table.

The Effect of Ice on the Stage-Discharge Relation

Three different kinds of ice occur in natural rivers: surface ice, anchor ice, and slush ice or frazil. Everyone is familiar with surface ice or sheet ice that forms on the surface of still or slowly moving water when its temperature falls below 32° F. Anchor ice in the form of long, slender needles freezes on the surface of rocks in the beds of rivers and on steel bars, beams, and other similar objects beneath the water surface. It forms usually at night and only in very cold weather. If even for only a few minutes during the day the rays of the sun strike objects on which anchor ice has formed, the temperature of those objects is raised enough to cause the ice to release its grip and rise to the surface. Frazil or slush ice occurs in the form of scales or flakes and gives the water a muddy appearance when it occurs in quantity. It usually forms at rapids, on clear nights when the air temperature is well below zero. At such times enough cold air becomes mixed with the water to reduce its temperature the small fraction of a degree below freezing that is required for the formation of ice. When this frazil ice comes in contact with steel, rocks, or the under side of surface ice, it is likely to catch hold and collect there, forming large masses. This ice is often very troublesome at power plants and at other intakes, since it collects on the trash racks and completely chokes off the water supply.

Ice affects the stage-discharge relation in three different ways.

1. Anchor ice may form on the control. If the control consists of rocks extending across the stream and anchor ice forms thereon, the gage height may be raised by approximately the thickness of the ice formation. Inasmuch as this thickness does not usually exceed a few inches and the ice leaves with the first sunshine, the errors in the discharge records resulting from this cause are not usually serious. Furthermore, if the station is equipped with a recording gage, the occurrence of anchor ice at the control is indicated by a gradual rise in the hydrograph during the extremely cold period and followed by a sudden drop when the ice goes out. If we eliminate this rise, the corrected gage readings can then be applied to the open-water discharge curve.

2. Ice jams may form below the control, backing the water up, drowning out the control, and completely destroying the stage-discharge relation during their existence. These jams may result

from floating cakes of surface ice wedging between bridge piers or other constricted sections or at the upstream margin of unbroken ice cover. They may also result from frazil ice being carried under surface ice where it catches on the under side and collects in the form of huge masses, almost completely choking the channel and forcing the water to flow over the top of the surface ice.

3. Surface ice may form at the control, entirely changing the relation between gage height and discharge. The magnitude of this change varies, however, throughout the period that the control remains frozen over. It appears to be roughly proportional to the cumulative below-freezing air-temperature deficiency beginning with the initial ice formation.

Obtaining Discharge Records with Control Frozen Over

Perhaps the best procedure for obtaining discharge records at stations where the control freezes over is as follows: (1) Make discharge measurements at the regular metering section at frequent intervals— the necessary frequency is learned only from experience (2) Determine from the open-water-rating curve or table the gage height at which the measured discharge occurs during open water, and find the amount of backwater by deducting this gage height from the gage height existing at the time of the measurement (3) Plot these amounts of backwater as gage-height corrections with the time scale as abscissas (4) Now compute the cumulative temperature deficiency below freezing, starting with the date of the initial freezing over, and plot these values to the same time scale and on the same drawing with the gage-height corrections (5) Draw a gage-height-correction graph through the points obtained from the discharge measurements and as nearly as possible parallel to the mass-temperature-deficiency curve (6) From the recorded gage heights subtract the corrections, day by day, as obtained from this correction graph and apply these corrected readings to the open-water-rating curve or table, to obtain the daily discharges.

As long as the control section remains free from ice and no ice jams form downstream to drown out the control, the open-water stage-discharge relationship is not appreciably affected by the formation of ice anywhere upstream from the control; under those conditions the only effect on the gage is the result of the increased friction with the ice cover between the gage section and the control, and this friction is usually negligible. As soon as the control section freezes over, however, the foregoing statement no longer holds true, for then the constricted section at the control is entirely changed, and as a result the stage-discharge relation at the gage may be radically altered.

Obtaining Records on Stream with Shifting Control

Only in exceptional cases is it definitely known at the time a gaging station is established that the control is going to be really permanent; nearly always the determination of the degree of permanency should claim first attention. At first, discharge measurements should be made at as many different stages as possible, but after a lapse of some time they should be repeated in order to determine whether the stage-discharge relation has remained constant in the interim. Especially should measurements be repeated after periods of high water, for it is usually during such times that the most pronounced changes in the control occur.

After a number of measurements have been made at different stages, the discharge curve should be drawn. The location of each of the observed points with respect to the curve should then be studied in detail to determine whether or not the stage-discharge relationship has been changing. These points should be studied in chronological order and consideration given to the effect of either the constancy or the rate of change of the stage at the time each measurement was made. If a measurement made during a rising stage falls on or to the left of the curve, or a point obtained during a falling stage plots on or to the right of the curve, or a point obtained during a constant stage plots on either side, then either such measurements are in error, the curve is wrongly drawn in the first place, or the control has changed. Even though no evidence is found of such a change after several years of records, vigilance should be relaxed only by degrees. Instances have been known in which a control showed no signs of change for a period of five years and then changed quite radically in a short time.

If the control is found to be changing, the next step is to find the rapidity with which it changes, because the best method of obtaining records under such conditions depends upon that rate. When such changes occur slowly or only at infrequent intervals during time of flood, the simplest method of getting daily-discharge records is to apply the daily gage heights to the prevailing discharge curve until the discharge measurements indicate sufficient change in the stage-discharge relation to require a new curve. Enough measurements are then made to properly define the new location of the discharge curve that is then used until gagings indicate another change in the control. The gaging station on Fall Creek at Ithaca, New York, is one of this type. On an average of about once each year the control changes enough to require a new rating curve.

At many stations, especially on streams in the plains of the Middle West, the control is almost constantly changing. The Stout method of obtaining daily-discharge records is perhaps the most commonly used in such cases. Its use is illustrated by an example.

Table 33, column 2, shows for a given month the recorded daily gage heights. In column 3 are the results of the discharge measure-

TABLE 33

Date (1)	Recorded Gage Height (2)	Discharge (3)	Gage-Height Correction (4)	Corrected Gage Height (5)	Q (6)
June 1	7.62	9470	−0.03	7.59	9470
2	7.58		− .09	7.49	9240
3	7.50		− .16	7.34	8920
4	7.36		− .21	7.15	8520
5	7.11		− .25	6.86	7930
6	6.80		− .29	6.51	7250
7	6.45		− .32	6.13	6530
8	6.04	5760	− .34	5.70	5760
9	5.40		− .33	5.07	4780
10	4.75		− .31	4.44	3800
11	4.21	3110	− .28	3.93	3110
12	3.77		− .20	3.57	2650
13	3.48		− .09	3.39	2440
14	3.66		+ .15	3.81	2950
15	3.97		+ .33	4.30	3590
16	4.39	4290	+ .39	4.78	4290
17	5.01		+ .34	5.35	5180
18	4.83		+ .21	5.04	4690
19	4.52		+ .14	4.66	4110
20	4.07		+ .09	4.16	3400
21	3.65	2810	+ .06	3.71	2810
22	3.34		+ .05	3.39	2440
23	3.12		+ .04	3.16	2170
24	2.93		+ .03	2.96	1960
25	2.77		+ .04	2.81	1800
26	2.63		+ .05	2.68	1670
27	2.51		+ .06	2.57	1560
28	2.60	1660	+ .07	2.67	1660
29	2.66		+ .09	2.75	1740
30	2.62		+ .12	2.74	1730

ments that were made during this period. Figure 133 shows the discharge curve as determined from these measurements. The exact manner in which this curve is drawn is not of vital importance. In column 4 are shown in bold-faced type the corrections that must be applied to the gage readings taken at the time of the discharge measurements, in order that the discharge values as obtained from the curve may be the same as the measured discharges. These values are plotted in Fig. 133, and the gage-height correction curve is drawn through these points. For the intervening days between measurements the gage-height corrections shown in column 4 are obtained from this gage-height correction curve. These corrections applied to the recorded gage heights shown in column 2 give the corrected gage heights in column 5, which are then applied to the discharge curve shown in Fig. 133 to obtain the daily discharges shown in column 6.

Discharge measurements are taken during subsequent months at intervals whose necessary frequency at each different gaging station can be determined only by experience. The same discharge curve as shown in the figure can be used for subsequent periods, as long as the measured discharges continue to fall on both sides of the curve. If, however, it becomes apparent that another curve fits the points better than the original curve, such a curve should be drawn in and used.

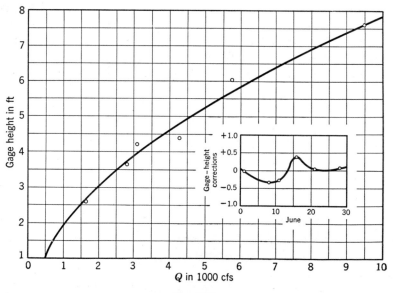

Fig. 133.

Plotting and Extending the Stage-Discharge Curve

After a number of discharge measurements have been made at a station, the results should be plotted on ordinary cross-section paper as shown in Fig. 122. It is customary to plot discharges as abscissas and gage heights as ordinates. Ordinarily difficulty is encountered in drawing in a complete and satisfactory discharge curve with the first set of measurements for several reasons. In all probability most of the gagings are made within a rather limited range at or somewhere near the average stage of the river. The curve usually has its greatest curvature in the low stages where there may be no measurements. It is necessary, therefore, to extend the curve downward for the low stages and upward for the flood stages.

By breaking the discharge measurements into their two component parts and plotting the mean velocity and area curves therefrom on the same drawing and to the same gage-height scale as that of the discharge curve, it is often possible to discover errors in the measurements. In order that this may be done, however, it is essential that the water surface at the metering section and at the gage fluctuate in similar amounts and also that the cross section at the metering section be almost permanent. If these conditions prevail, the mean velocity curve normally is found to be concave upward, and the area curve is concave downward. If there is ponded water at the section at the stage of zero discharge, the mean velocity curve reverses and is concave downward in the low stages. The data from which the area curve is drawn can be determined accurately by means of level and rod for all stages. It is then a matter of extending the velocity curve only. According to the Manning formula the velocity in the stream is

$$V = \frac{1.486}{n} r^{2/3} s^{1/2} \tag{3}$$

Oftentimes $s^{1/2}/n$ becomes almost constant for the higher stages after all the rapids have become drowned out, and this formula may then be written

$$V = Kr^{2/3}$$

With the cross section and area known for all stages, the hydraulic radius can also be found for all stages. By taking various values of V from the known portion of the mean velocity curve and the corresponding values of r, values of K can be computed for the range in stage for which the mean velocity curve is known. By plotting these values of K against gage height, we obtain a curve that should

approach a vertical line as an asymptote in the higher stages. By
extending this line, we should obtain values of K quite accurately,
which when combined with their respective values of $r^{2/3}$ and A give
values of discharge that may be used for extending the discharge curve
for all higher stages.

Stevens Method of Extension. Stevens[13] has devised a procedure
that is commonly known as the $A\sqrt{D}$ method, which is a variation
of the one described previously. For streams that are relatively wide
and shallow, the mean depth, D (which is found by dividing the cross-
sectional area, A, by the width of stream measured at the water surface),
does not differ greatly from the hydraulic radius, r, which is A divided
by the wetted perimeter. Therefore by substituting D for r, we may
write the Chezy formula for flow in open channels in the form, $Q = C\sqrt{s} \times A\sqrt{D}$. When, in the higher stages, $C\sqrt{s}$ becomes constant,
values of Q plotted against $A\sqrt{D}$ form a straight line. Both A and D
are functions of gage height and values of $A\sqrt{D}$ may be obtained for
all stages of the river and plotted against gage height as shown in
Fig. 134. By plotting the measured discharges against the corresponding values of $A\sqrt{D}$ as obtained from this curve, we may obtain a
straight line provided that $C\sqrt{s}$ is a constant for this range of stage.

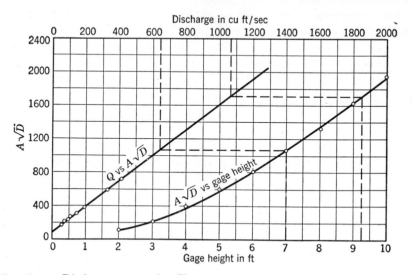

Fig. 134. Discharge curve for Huron River near Whitmore Lake, Mich.
Extended by the $A\sqrt{D}$ method.

[13] J. C. Stevens, "A Method of Estimating Stream Discharge from a Limited
Number of Gagings," *Eng. News*, July 18, 1907.

Even if it is not a straight line for the entire range, it will probably be a flat curve approaching a straight line in the higher stages. By extending this curve upward the discharge can be found for the value of $A\sqrt{D}$ corresponding to any desired gage height, as illustrated in Fig. 134. It may be found sometimes that instead of using $\frac{1}{2}$ as the exponent of D, some other value such as $\frac{2}{3}$ may produce better results.

Logarithmic Method of Extension. If the cross section of a stream at the site of the gage is, or even approximates, a uniform section to which can be roughly fitted either a segment of a circle, or of a parabola, or a rectangle or trapezoid, then the logarithmic method can be used advantageously. The relation between discharge and gage height can be expressed by the equation

$$Q = C(G - a)^n \tag{4}$$

in which Q is the discharge in cubic feet per second, G is the gage height in feet, a is the gage height corresponding to zero discharge, and C and n are constants for any station. Equation 4 may be written in the logarithmic form,

$$\log Q = n \log (G - a) + \log C \tag{5}$$

which is the equation of a straight line whose slope is expressed by n and whose intercept on the discharge axis is equal to $\log C$.

Ordinarily the gage height corresponding to zero discharge is unknown and must be determined, for if $\log Q$ is plotted against $\log G$ for any value of a other than zero, a curve is obtained that possesses no advantage in extension over that obtained by ordinary plotting. There are two methods of determining the value of a without making a field investigation.

The simpler and more direct of these two was first suggested by the late Dr. T. R. Running, Professor of Mathematics at the University of Michigan, and is illustrated in Fig. 122. In the application of this method three values of discharge are selected from the known portion of the curve, one value near the upper end of the segment, another near the lower end, with the intermediate value so chosen that the three form a geometric series. In Fig. 122 these values are represented by a, b, and c, having values respectively of 50, 150, and 450. Through a and b vertical lines are drawn, and through b and c horizontal lines are drawn intersecting the verticals at d and e. Through d and e a line is drawn that intersects a line through a and b at f, the latter point being at the elevation of the gage height corresponding to zero discharge. This method is based upon the assumption that the lower portion of the discharge curve including the points a, b, and c

is a parabola. In most cases the curve approaches a parabola near enough to give reasonably accurate results.

The gage height of zero discharge may also be determined by trying various values of a, until values of log Q plotted against values of log $(G - a)$ form a straight line. Instead of plotting logarithms of the values on coordinate paper, it is more convenient to plot actual values on logarithmically ruled paper. Although the actual measured values of Q and gage height may be used in this plotting, better results are usually obtained by selecting a number of points from the measured range of the discharge curve that seem to represent the average trend of these values. A series of such values taken in this manner from the discharge curve shown in Fig. 122 are plotted for a

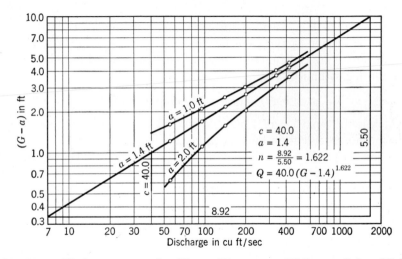

Fig. 135. Discharge curve for Huron River near Whitmore Lake, Mich. Extended by the logarithmic method.

number of assumed values of a in Fig. 135. It is seen that for a equal to 1 ft the curve is concave upward, whereas for a equal to 2 ft it is concave downward, thus indicating that the value of a lies between one and two. In the example shown, a value of 1.4 results in a straight line which can be extended to higher stages. From this line values of Q may be read directly, or the values of C and n, the constants in equations 4 and 5, may be determined and the higher values of Q obtained algebraically. C is the value of Q at the point on the straight line where $(G - a)$ is equal to one, and n is the tangent of the angle that the line makes with the $(G - a)$ axis.

Slope Stations

Occasionally it is necessary to establish a gaging station in a location that is affected by backwater. Examples are locations above dams where flow is controlled by various gates, or above the confluence of two rivers. Under such conditions the slope of the energy gradient no longer remains nearly constant, but it may differ greatly even for the same stage. Thus it is no longer possible to obtain a single stage-discharge relationship, but the third variable, slope, must be considered.

The slope is obtained by using two gages some distance apart. If the gages are placed at the same datum, a measure of the fall in the energy gradient may be obtained by adding the corresponding $V^2/2g$ to each gage reading and then subtracting one energy gradient elevation from the other. Often the two values of $V^2/2g$ are so nearly alike that the fall becomes equal to the difference in the two gage readings.

Several techniques employed by the U. S. Geological Survey for utilizing records from slope-gaging stations are described in *U. S. Geological Survey Water-Supply Paper* 888. An example of one of these procedures, the "constant fall" method, is given here. In columns 1, 2, and 3, Table 34, are shown a number of values of measured discharge, Q_m, fall, and gage height. Values of Q_m are plotted against gage height, usually for the upper gage as before, but with each point

TABLE 34

1 Qm, cfs	2 Fall, ft	3 Gage Height, ft	4 Q_c, cfs	5 $\dfrac{Q_m}{Q_c}$
20,300	1.07	8.60	19,300	1.050
18,500	0.96	8.65	19,400	0.953
23,500	1.06	9.35	22,900	1.025
16,500	0.51	9.40	23,100	0.714
20,000	0.60	9.90	25,400	0.787
25,000	0.78	10.70	29,000	0.862
32,500	0.78	12.30	36,800	0.883
35,800	0.78	13.05	40,900	0.875
36,500	0.81	13.10	41,000	0.890
54,500	0.94	16.15	57,000	0.955
57,000	0.99	16.55	59,300	0.961
69,000	1.00	18.25	69,200	0.997
75,000	1.02	19.20	76,000	0.987
78,500	1.02	19.20	76,000	1.035

the value of fall is noted as shown in Fig. 136. It may be seen that
these points are well scattered. However, some order may be noted
among those points having similar values of fall. Therefore, some
particular value of fall is arbitrarily selected for which to draw a
discharge curve. This value is called a "constant fall" discharge curve
and is illustrated by curve 1, Fig. 136, which is drawn for a fall of
1 ft. It is noted that points having a fall greater than 1 ft are to the
right of the curve whereas those having a fall less than 1 ft are to

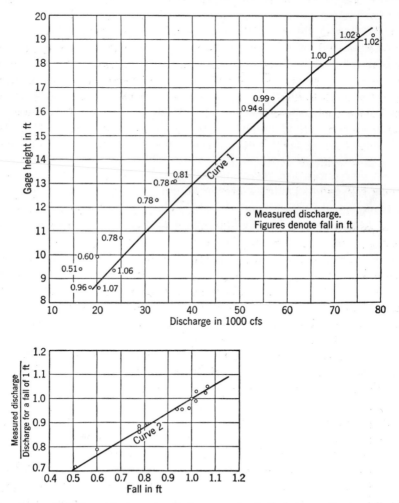

Fig. 136. Relation of stage to discharge and of discharge ratio to fall for
Tennessee River at Chattanooga, Tenn. Data were taken from Plate 9,
U. S. Geological Survey Water-Supply Paper 888.

the left. For any gage height the corresponding discharge measured from the "constant fall" curve is called the "constant fall discharge" and is designated as Q_c. The next step is to determine Q_c from the curve for the gage height corresponding to each plotted point. These values are shown in Table 34, column 4.

Values of Q_m/Q_c are then computed (column 5) and plotted against corresponding values of fall as shown by curve 2, Fig. 136. Usually it is desirable to check on the adequacy of curves 1 and 2 before proceeding to use them for determining discharge. This check is accomplished by converting each value of Q_m to Q_c by dividing it by the value of Q_m/Q_c taken from curve 2. When plotted, these values of Q should fall on or near the "constant fall" curve. If they do not appear satisfactory, a second curve should be drawn and the process repeated. These curves are used to convert recorded values of gage height and fall to discharge in the following manner. The value of Q_c for the recorded gage height is read from curve 1. For the corresponding measured fall, the value of Q_m/Q_c is read from curve 2. The product of Q_c and Q_m/Q_c is the discharge corresponding to that pair of gage readings.

The Measurement of Peak Flood Flows

The determination of the maximum discharge occurring during flood periods often introduces special difficulties even on streams where gaging stations are already established.

There are many reasons why few current meter measurements are made at or near the time of peak flow. Often the U. S. Geological Survey and the various engineering organizations that normally do such work are otherwise occupied at the time and sometimes it is impossible for them to make measurements at all the locations on the various flooding streams within the relatively short duration of the flood. Transportation difficulties may make it impossible to reach the various metering sections, and sometimes it is impossible to operate a current meter during flood periods because of floating debris or bridge washouts.

If the maximum gage height is determined at an established gaging station, a good estimate of the discharge may be obtained by extending the rating curve to this gage height. Various methods of extending such curves were described on pages 391–393. If there is no gaging station, the discharge may be obtained at a constriction[14] in a river by applying the basic energy equations along with estimated energy losses in

---

[14] C. E. Kindsvater, R. W. Carter, and H. J. Tracy, "Computation of Peak Discharge at Contractions," U. S. Geol. Survey Circular 284, 1953.

a manner similar to the one described on page 356. Good approximations of discharge over embankments, over low dams, and through culverts can be made on the basis of experimental work on similar structures. At falls it is often possible to apply critical-depth formulas to obtain the discharge. It is always necessary to know at least one water-surface elevation. In the absence of a gage, water-surface elevations must be obtained from high-water marks. In the event that such marks do not exist near the location in which they would be used, it may be possible to utilize one some distance upstream or downstream by developing the water-surface profiles to the desired point. This procedure may also be used to tie old high-water marks in with newly established gaging stations.

The "slope-area method" is often used to estimate peak discharges where no gaging station exists. This method is based on an open-channel formula for determining the velocity of flow that in combination with the measured areas gives the discharge. The first step in applying this method is to select a reach of river having a relatively uniform channel and clearly defined high-water marks. The length of the reach, the difference in elevations of the high-water marks at the ends of the reach, and the cross-sectional area at each end are measured. The average hydraulic radius is determined from the areas. If an assumed value of kinetic energy is added to the elevation of the water surface at each end of the reach, the difference between these values, divided by the length of the reach, gives the average slope of the energy gradient. A value of roughness coefficient is then determined and the velocity and discharge computed by means of an open-channel formula such as the Manning formula. It is recommended that a number of careful measurements of s, r, and v be made for this reach of river at different discharges to permit the determination of values of n in the Manning formula. These values may then be plotted against water-surface elevations. An extension of this curve to the elevation during the flood may be expected to give a reasonably accurate value of the coefficient. This answer is only a first trial, since it is necessary to check the values of kinetic energy previously assumed.

Index